Beyond Varieties of Capitalism

Conflict, Contradictions, and Complementarities in the European Economy

Edited by

BOB HANCKÉ, MARTIN RHODES,
AND MARK THATCHER

OXFORD
UNIVERSITY PRESS

OXFORD

UNIVERSITY PRESS

Great Clarendon Street, Oxford ox2 6DP

Oxford University Press is a department of the University of Oxford.
It furthers the University's objective of excellence in research, scholarship,
and education by publishing worldwide in

Oxford New York

Auckland Cape Town Dar es Salaam Hong Kong Karachi
Kuala Lumpur Madrid Melbourne Mexico City Nairobi
New Delhi Shanghai Taipei Toronto

With offices in

Argentina Austria Brazil Chile Czech Republic France Greece
Guatemala Hungary Italy Japan Poland Portugal Singapore
South Korea Switzerland Thailand Turkey Ukraine Vietnam

Oxford is a registered trade mark of Oxford University Press
in the UK and in certain other countries

Published in the United States
by Oxford University Press Inc., New York

British Library Cataloguing in Publication Data

Data available

Library of Congress Cataloging in Publication Data

Beyond varieties of capitalism: conflict, contradictions, and complementarities in the
European economy/edited by Bob Hancké, Martin Rhodes, and Mark Thatcher.
p. cm.
Includes bibliographical references and index.
ISBN 978-0-19-920648-3 (alk. paper)
1. Europe—Economic policy. 2. Capitalism—Europe. I. Hancké, Bob. II. Rhodes,
Martin, 1956 Feb. 23– III. Thatcher, Mark.
HC240. B455 2007
330.94—dc22   2007003060

Typeset by SPI Publisher Services, Pondicherry, India
Printed in Great Britain
on acid-free paper by
CPI Antony Rowe, Chippenham, Wiltshire

ISBN 978-0-19-920648-3 (Hbk.)
ISBN 978-0-19-954701-2 (Pbk.) 1005592870

1 3 5 7 9 10 8 6 4 2

Preface

The idea for this book dates back to 2002 when Martin Rhodes, then a professor at the European University Institute (EUI) in Florence, and Mark Thatcher, an EUI Jean Monnet Fellow, first discussed a project to critically examine the new 'varieties of capitalism' (VoC) volume edited by Peter Hall and David Soskice. A year or so later, a similar conversation with Bob Hancké, by then also a Jean Monnet Fellow, brought the idea to fruition. A workshop was organized at the EUI for July 2004 with the aim of confronting the VoC approach with the contemporary challenges facing Europe: EMU, eastward enlargement, the completion of the Single Market, and pressures everywhere on welfare states and labour markets.

Everyone we invited to that first workshop enthusiastically accepted: some were contributors to the initial VoC volume; some were in the wider VoC orbit; still others were quite critical of the approach. Many of the papers presented were still at the outline stage and the discussions ranged widely. We were therefore pleasantly surprised by the high quality of the revised versions presented at a second meeting at the LSE the following summer and by the degree to which they heralded a coherent volume. The London discussions also proved fruitful to the editors in refining the introduction. The process concluded with a session at the Conference of Europeanists in Chicago in March 2006, where a number of the chapters were presented and critically appraised by Sabina Avdagic and other commentators. Along the way, all of us learned a great deal from one another. As a result, this volume expands the boundaries of VoC in ways that many of us had not foreseen, revealing important extensions to the approach and its considerable hidden strengths.

Many colleagues who are not in this volume made significant contributions. Bruno Amable, Rachel Epstein, and Bruce Kogut gave challenging presentations at the first workshop that sharpened our thinking in developing the study and preparing the meeting that followed. Abby Innes and Laszlo Bruszt made critical comments on the introduction on several occasions. We also owe our thanks to Maureen Lechleitner at the EUI and Jen Hammarberg at the LSE for their organizational inputs. Sotiria Theodoropoulou, Marco Simoni, and Manuel Palazuelos-Martinez helped set up the workshop at the LSE. Stephen Coulter did an excellent job in copy-editing and pulling the volume together. A deeply felt word of thanks also goes to our graduate students at the LSE and the EUI whose many questions and criticisms significantly influenced the introduction. Finally, we thank the Anglo-German Foundation, the EUI, and the LSE for their generous financial and organizational support.

Our most important debt is also the most visible. This book would not exist without Peter Hall and David Soskice's initial statement of the problem and theory of VoC and their more recent encouragement and insights. They deserve our respect and admiration for their inspiration and their willingness to re-examine their own theory.

BH, MR, MT

Contents

PART I. VARIETIES OF CAPITALISM: TAKING STOCK

PART II. MACRO-ADJUSTMENT AND VARIETIES OF CAPITALISM

PART III. THE SINGLE MARKET, REGULATION, AND FIRMS

List of Figures

List of Tables

List of Contributors

Alexander Börsch works as Manager of International Pension Research in the asset management industry. He holds master degrees in political science and in economics from the University of Munich as well as a Ph.D. in political science from the European University Institute. He is the author of *Global Pressure, National System: How German Corporate Governance is Changing* (Cornell University Press 2007). Other publications include contributions to the *Journal of European Public Policy, German Politics* and *New Political Economy.*

Magnus Feldmann is a Ph.D. candidate in Political Economy and Government at Harvard University. His research focuses on comparative and international political economy and post-socialist transition, and his articles have appeared in *Comparative Political Studies, The World Economy, Government and Opposition,* and various edited volumes.

Michel Goyer is assistant professor in the Industrial Relations and Organizational Behavior unit, Warwick Business School, University of Warwick. He holds a PhD in Political Science from MIT. He has published in the areas of comparative corporate governance with a focus on France and Germany, institutional theory and diversity in advanced capitalist economies, and on labour relations in France.

Peter A. Hall is Krupp Foundation Professor of European Studies at Harvard University. His publications include *Varieties of Capitalism* (with David Soskice, Oxford University Press 2001), *Changing France* (with Pepper Culpepper and Bruno Palier, Palgrave 2006), *The Political Power of Economic Ideas* (Princeton University Press 1989), and *Governing the Economy* (Polity Press 1986).

Bob Hancké is a Reader in European Political Economy at the LSE. He studied industrial sociology in Brussels and political economy at MIT. His previous appointments include the Wissenschaftszentrum Berlin, and the J. F. Kennedy School at Harvard University. He published *Large Firms and Institutional Change* (Oxford University Press 2002).

Anke Hassel teaches public policy at the Hertie School of Governance. She studied Political Science, Economics and Law in Bonn and at the London School of Economics and Political Science (LSE). Previous appointments include the Max Planck Institute for the Study of Societies, the German Federal Ministry of Economics and Labour, and the International University Bremen. She published *Wage Setting, Social Pacts and the Euro: A New Role for the State* (Amsterdam University Press 2007).

Lawrence King is Reader in Sociology at Faculty of Political and Social Sciences, University of Cambridge. His previous appointment was at Yale University. He studied political and economic sociology at U.C.L.A. He has published extensively on the transition to capitalism in Eastern Europe and the Former Soviet Union.

Andrea Monika Herrmann is a research fellow at the Max-Planck-Institut für Gesellschaftsforschung (Cologne). She holds a PhD from the European University Institute (Florence), and an MSc from the LSE (London). Her work includes publications on industrial relations and methodology, and a book in preparation on *Alternative Pathways to Firm Competitiveness*.

Torben Iversen is Harold Hitchings Burbank Professor of Political Economy at Harvard University. He is the author of *Capitalism, Democracy, and Welfare* (Cambridge University Press 2005), *Contested Economic Institutions* (Cambridge University Press 1999) and many articles on comparative political economy, the welfare state, and electoral politics.

Óscar Molina is a lecturer in the Centre d'Estudis Sociològics sobre la Vida Quotidiana i el Treball (QUIT), Department of Sociology, Faculty of Political Sciences and Sociology, Autonomous University of Barcelona. He studied economics in Barcelona and obtained his PhD at the European University Institute, Florence. His research focuses on institutional change in the political economies of Southern Europe, patterns of corporatist intermediation and regulatory change in industrial relations.

Vlad Mykhnenko is a Research Fellow at the Centre for Public Policy for Regions, University of Glasgow. He studied international relations in Kyiv and international relations and European studies at the Central European University, Budapest. Recently he received his PhD on the political economy of post-communism from Darwin College, Cambridge University.

Martin Rhodes is Professor of Comparative Political Economy at the Graduate School of International Studies, University of Denver, Colorado. Until 2006 he was a professor in the Department of Political and Social Sciences at the European University in Florence, Italy. He writes on comparative welfare states and labour markets as well as on European Union social and economic policy.

David Soskice teaches political economy at Duke University and the London School of Economics. After teaching macroeconomics from 1967 to 1990 at University College, Oxford, he directed a research programme on varieties of capitalism at the Wissenschaftszentrum Berlin until 2001. He now works on the co-evolution of capitalist and political systems, as well as the political economy of macroeconomics.

Mark Thatcher is a Reader in Public Administration and Public Policy, Department of Government, London School of Economics and Political Science. He has also been a visiting professor at Sciences Po Paris and Fellow, European University Institute, Florence. His recent publications include *International and Economic Institutions* (OUP 2007), 'Regulatory agencies in France: A comparative perspective', *Journal of European Public Policy* 14(7) (2007), and 'Varieties of capitalism in an internationalized world', *Comparative Political Studies*, 37(7) (2004). His research interests include comparative public policy and political economy, regulation of network industries, independent regulatory agencies, and delegation to non-majoritarian institutions.

Part I

Varieties of Capitalism: Taking Stock

1

Introduction: Beyond Varieties
of Capitalism

Bob Hancké, Martin Rhodes, and Mark Thatcher

1.1. INTRODUCTION

The European political economy is facing a host of entirely new challenges, arising from both external forces and internal conflicts and contradictions. These include a novel macroeconomic regime under Economic and Monetary Union (EMU), supranational regulation under the Single Market of economies traditionally dominated by national governments and national champions, the accession to the European Union (EU) of Central and Eastern European nations still struggling with the transition to democratic market capitalism, the impact of globalization (the internationalization of production and finance), and a series of destabilizing domestic, demographic, and economic pressures.

How should we understand these developments and their effects? Recent advances in political economy and the 'varieties of capitalism' (henceforth VoC), school of analysis in particular, have given us new tools for analysing and comparing national political economies. The notions of 'complementarities' and 'system coordination' define the core of the VoC approach. Institutional subsystems (which govern capital, labour, and product markets) shape the evolution of political economies and often mutually reinforce each other. The presence of several 'correctly calibrated' subsystems increases the performance of the system as a whole, while producing specific adjustment paths in response to pressures for change.

But broad economic shifts and shocks may have important consequences for each of these subsystems and for the broader institutional framework that supports them. Thus, in their orthodox interpretations, EMU imposes pressures for adjustment on labour markets, the Single Market Programme frees up product and financial markets, Eastern European enlargement raises questions about the viability of different development models within one economic zone, and high-unemployment levels and pension systems crises demand a rethinking of welfare state priorities. All may disrupt the existing equilibria of national subsystems, generating conflict and contradiction within and between them.

This collection of essays confronts the VoC framework with these shocks and explores its capacity to build research agendas and answer questions related to them. Our aim, in this introduction and in the chapters that follow, is to pay particular attention to four areas in which the VoC approach has proven most vulnerable to criticism. First, through an analysis of the role of political and distributive struggles in generating change and adjustment; this theme runs through all chapters in the volume, but receives particular attention by Hall, Iversen, and Soskice. Second, by reconsidering the nature and function of complementarities in shaping and constraining institutional change, a topic on which Hancké and Herrmann, Thatcher, Goyer, and Börsch all focus. Third, by extending the VoC approach to a broader range of political economies than traditionally receives attention, from Southern Europe (Molina and Rhodes) to Central and Eastern Europe and Russia (Feldmann, Mykhnenko, and King). And fourth, by restoring the role of the state in VoC analysis, not just where that role is most overt (Molina and Rhodes, Mykhnenko, and King) but as an important factor in the construction everywhere of what Hall (this volume) refers to as 'institutional ecologies'.

We undertake our analysis in this introduction in four steps. In Section 1.2, *A 'Critique Raisonneé'*, we briefly confront the core VoC arguments with its critics and argue for the importance of retaining the key VoC notions of functional coherence, coordination, and complementarity while also bringing power, politics, and conflict onto centre stage. In Section 1.3, *Interests, Coalitions, and Institutional Frameworks*, we take on several critiques of the VoC approach: that it is static and unable to accommodate conflict, that it ignores the role of the state, and that it is reductionist in focusing on two 'ideal-type' economies (LMEs and CMEs). We respond to those claims by thinking seriously about the role of interests, classes, and coalitions, by 'bringing the state back in', and by extending the typology to mixed-market economies and emerging market economies (MMEs and EMEs), although the latter we view less as a separate 'variety' of capitalism as such than a cluster of countries in transition with only partially formed institutional ecologies. In Section 1.4, *Exogenous Shocks and Domestic Change*, we build on the previous sections and the contributions to this volume and show how different forms of coordination and complementarities condition institutional adjustment in contemporary Europe. Section 1.5 concludes.

1.2. 'VARIETIES OF CAPITALISM'— *A CRITIQUE RAISONNEÉ*

Recent contributions from the VoC school (e.g. Hall and Soskice 2001*a*; Amable 2003) have reinvigorated a long analytical tradition that dates back at least to the work of Alexander Gerschenkron (1962) and Andrew Shonfield (1969) and include more recent landmark publications such as Zysman (1983) and Gourevitch (1986). Like its predecessors, VoC is concerned with the macro-characteristics of national political economies. But one of its most important contributions has been to give micro-foundations to a more general theory of cross-national capitalist organization and adjustment. By placing the firm at the centre of the analysis, and adopting a 'relational view' of its role as an exploiter of the core competencies and capabilities in its environment, VoC demonstrates the links between the competitiveness of the firm and the 'institutional comparative advantage' of national economies.

The architecture of 'comparative advantage' is portrayed in terms of key institutional complementarities—between labour relations and corporate governance, labour relations and the national training system, and corporate governance and inter-firm relations. These relationships determine the degree to which a political economy is, or is not, 'coordinated'. The 'coordinated market economy' (CME) is characterized by non-market relations, collaboration, credible commitments, and the 'deliberative calculation' of firms. The essence of its 'liberal market economy' (LME) antithesis is one of arm's length, competitive relations, formal contracting, and supply-and-demand price signalling (Hall and Soskice 2001*b*; Hall and Gingerich 2004). VoC argues that institutional complementarities deliver different kinds of firm behaviour and investment patterns. In LMEs, fluid labour markets fit well with easy access to stock market capital, producing 'radical-innovator' firms in sectors ranging from biotechnology, semiconductors, software, and advertising to corporate finance. In CMEs, long-term employment strategies, rule-bound behaviour, and the durable ties between firms and banks that underpin patient capital provision predispose firms to 'incremental innovation' in capital goods industries, machine tools, and equipment of all kinds. While the logic of LME dynamics is centred on mobile 'switchable assets' whose value can be realized when diverted to multiple purposes, CME logic derives from 'specific or co-specific assets' whose value depends on the active cooperation of others (Hall and Soskice 2001*b*; Hall and Gingerich 2004).

If the centrality of the firm is one key innovation, contrary to the claims of many of its critics VoC also has a strong understanding of both domestic change in political economies and the impact of exogenous pressures. VoC attributes the persistence of capitalist diversity to 'positive feedbacks', whereby the different logics of LMEs and CMEs create different incentives for economic actors, generating in turn a differential politics of adjustment. As Hall and Gingerich (2004: 32) characterize this process, 'in the face of an exogenous shock threatening returns to existing activities, holders of mobile assets will be tempted to "exit" those activities to seek higher returns elsewhere, while holders of specific assets have higher incentives to exercise "voice" in defence of existing activities'. In LMEs, holders of mobile assets (workers with general skills, investors in fluid capital markets) will seek to make markets still more fluid and accept further deregulatory policies. In CMEs, holders of specific assets (workers with industry-specific skills and investors in co-specific assets) will more often oppose greater market competition and form status quo supporting cross-class coalitions (Hall and Gingerich 2004: 28–9).

This logic of adjustment and diversity is reinforced rather than undermined by globalization (Hall and Soskice 2001*b*; Gourevitch and Hawes 2002). Globalization will often reinforce comparative institutional advantage, for foreign direct investment (FDI) will flow to locations rich in either specific or co-specific assets, depending on investors' sector or firm-specific requirements. CMEs and LMEs will be located at different points in international production chains, again reflecting their respective institutional advantages: high value-added, high skill-dependent, high-productivity production will tend to remain in the core CMEs; lower value-added, lower-skill, price-oriented production will relocate to lower-cost jurisdictions. But the globalization of finance may prove to be more problematic (though not necessarily destructive) for CMEs. International capital flows could disrupt long-standing relations and cross-shareholdings between banks and firms, and bring the notion of 'shareholder value' and demands for higher rates of return into formerly closed and collaborative environments.

While Hall and Soskice (2001*b*: 61–2) imagine that this 'could engender shifts in strategy all the way down to production regimes', this is considered unlikely: rational owners and stakeholders in CMEs will not demand a wholesale adoption of Anglo-American management practices if it would endanger their comparative institutional advantage. Although an economic shock may trigger changes to existing institutions and practices, and may even entail a period of conflict and suboptimal outcomes, a new equilibrium will be induced by the incentives for renewed coordination imparted by existing deliberative institutions (Hall and Soskice 2001*b*: 63–5). Change, therefore, is most likely to be path-dependent, and significant path-shifting or equilibrium-breaking behaviour on the part of actors—producing a fully fledged shift from a CME to an LME, for example—is very unlikely to occur due to the 'general efficiencies' for distinctive political economies created by 'complementarities'. As Hall and Gingerich (2004: 27) put it, 'rates of

economic growth should be higher in nations where levels of market coordination or levels of strategic coordination are high across spheres of the
political economy but lower in nations where neither type of coordination
is well developed or market and strategic coordination are combined'. There
is no 'one best way', as in arguments for neoliberal convergence, but 'two', on
which middle-spectrum countries (with muddled institutional architectures)
may 'divergently converge'.

A salvo of criticism provoked by the Hall–Soskice approach to VoC theory
has raised many points of contention:

- that it is too static and focused on permanency and path-dependence,
  missing important dynamic elements of economic change (Crouch and
  Farrell 2004; Crouch 2005*a*; Hancké and Goyer 2005; Streeck and Thelen
  2005; Jackson and Deeg 2006);
- that it is functionalist (Howell 2003; Allen 2004; Boyer 2005*a*);
- that it ignores the endogenous sources of national system transformation
  and 'within-system' diversity (Coates 2005; Boyer 2005*b*; Crouch 2005*a*;
  Panitch and Gindin 2005);
- that it has a propensity to 'institutional determinism' in its mechanistic
  conception of institutional complementarities and neglect of underlying
  power structures, including social class (Thelen 2003; Crouch and Farrell
  2004; Coates 2005; Pontusson 2005; Jackson and Deeg 2006);
- that it has a truncated conception of the firm as an 'institution-taker'
  rather than an autonomous, creative, or disruptive actor and neglects
  variation among firms within national models (Allen 2003; Crouch and
  Farrell 2004; Crouch 2005*a*; Martin 2005);
- that it divides the world into reified notions of LME and CME archetypes
  and lacks the tools for moving beyond this bifurcation (Schmidt 2002,
  2003; Watson 2003; Hay 2005; Pontusson 2005; Boyer 2005*b*);
- that VoC theory is not built deductively, to create Weberian 'ideal-types'
  that could be used for the construction of hypotheses, but rather creates
  'types' by reading back empirical information from the countries it seeks
  to make its paradigm cases—the USA and Germany (Crouch 2005*a*);
- that it has a manufacturing bias and cannot deal with the presence of
  sizeable service sectors in CMEs (Blyth 2003);
- that it treats nation-states as 'hermetically sealed' and neglects the linkages between them and the forces of convergence and globalization
  (Crouch and Farrell 2004; Martin 2005; Panitch and Gindin 2005; Pontusson 2005);

- that it is 'apolitical', equilibrium-biased and downplays conflict (Howell 2003; Watson 2003; Kinderman 2005; Pontusson 2005);
- that it is 'sex-blind' and has problems understanding class inequalities among women and class differences in the nature and patterns of gender inequality (Estévez-Abe 2005; McCall and Orloff 2005*a*);
- and that it neglects the role of the state (Schmidt 2002, 2003; Regini 2003; Watson 2003).

However, many critics caricature rather than fully explore the VoC approach. Regardless of its formulation by Hall and Soskice (2001*b*: 1–3, 68) as an agenda for future research rather than 'settled wisdom', there is a general tendency for critics to treat it as if it were a 'unified theory of everything', attribute to it claims that it has never made, and consequently to fall wide of the mark in their attacks (see, e.g., the rebuttal to several critics in Hall and Soskice 2003). Even from the brief synopsis above, it is clear that, far from being static, VoC has a strong, non-deterministic understanding of change, given its appreciation that the institutions that underpin coordination are subject to constant renegotiation. The accusation that it is reductive and limited to LME and CME 'paradigm types' is belied by the attention paid (e.g. by Hall and Gingerich 2004) to economies—characterized as 'mixed-market economies', or MMEs—that fall outside this analytical dichotomy, even if that seam of analysis has yet to be fully exploited. The notion that the firm in VoC lacks the power to innovate in its environment is quite inconsistent with the complexity of its interactions with labour, finance, and other economic agents, as explored in multiple studies inspired by the VoC approach. The claim that the nation-state in VoC is 'hermetically sealed' is unsustainable, given its focus on the nature and dynamics of comparative institutional advantage.

More acute and clearly focused criticisms (such as that concerned with 'sex-blindness') have already produced new and highly productive realms of scientific enquiry (on gender see, e.g., Estévez-Abe 2005; Iversen, Rosenbluth, and Soskice 2005; Soskice 2005), and these suggest that the potential richness of VoC has still to be exploited—the principal motive, in fact, behind the conception of this volume. This is true of its relevance for understanding the conflict generated by political–economic change, its utility for analysing economies beyond the LME–CME archetypes, and its insights into the inter-sectoral dynamics and tensions generated by the rise of the post-industrial economy and labour market 'dualism'. The key ambition of this book is to mine the rich VoC seam as much as possible in our attempt to understand contemporary European developments. Yet we also want to build on its foundations in ways that make it less vulnerable to charges of determinism, functionalism, and over-concern with institutional equilibria. We seek to reveal its capacity for accommodating and understanding the centrality of conflict (class-based and otherwise) in political economies and; the reconfiguration of long-standing coalitions; the consequent challenges these coalitional shifts may pose to complementarities and coordination; and the centrality and changing role of the state in all political economies—LMEs, CMEs, MMEs, and others.

We therefore focus in this book on four key dimensions that are ripe for development and exploration—conflict and coalitions, complementarities and institutional change, the nature of 'mixed market' (and other) political economies, and the role of the state—and answer the more serious criticisms made of VoC.

1.2.1. Conflict and Coalitions

First, regarding *conflict*, questions arise for VoC from numerous directions. Two important challenges that strike at the core of what are presumed to be deeply engrained preferences and structural characteristics in CMEs are first, the apparent willingness of employers in certain key countries to break with long-established commitments to coordination, and second, the potentially disruptive consequences for system stability of company internationalization. According to VoC, one would expect CME businesses to hesitate in liberalizing their main factor markets. But while this was true of the 1980s (Wood 2001), today businesses are pushing a competitive, 'deregulatory' agenda in both labour and financial markets. In Germany, these changes appear to complicate coordination on both the employer and union sides and threaten the long-term stability of the system (Thelen and van Wijnbergen 2003; Kinderman 2005).

Several of these developments are related to internationalization. VoC argues that globalization will confirm rather than subvert the comparative institutional advantage of nations. Competition and the spread of global production networks will reward difference and drive divergence. Evidence suggests that production networks do extend globally in this fashion. But a subversion of institutional structures and relations in *home* locations may also result. A range of studies (Berger et al. 1999; 2001; Berger 2000; Lane 2003; Herrigel and Wittke 2005) demonstrates, for example, that national manufacturers who create diversified cross-border, producer–supplier linkages (spanning Western and Central and Eastern Europe) often use them to change institutional incentive structures, both inside and outside the firm, in their own economies.

Some critics suggest that VoC is unable to accommodate the kind of conflict and change associated with these developments (Regini 2003; Watson 2003). For Howell (2003:122), this is because it renders 'invisible the exercise of class power that underlies coordination and equilibrium in the political economy'; for Allen (2003) and Crouch (2005a), it is because VoC tends to interpret the strategic preferences of firms, mistakenly, as endogenous—or complementary—to their environments. Whilst business obviously can be competitive while its location is not or becomes decreasingly so, thus creating a source of incongruity and pressures for eventual change from disruptive firms (Siebert 2003), it is not clear that Howell, Allen, and Crouch are correct in claiming that VoC is unable to accommodate this relatively uncontroversial fact. Their argument does raise a number of questions, however, about the role of class power and the notion of 'complementarities' in VoC theory. We return to these issues below.

Conflict often leads to, or stems from, a reconfiguration of coalitions and alliances. This process may include new alliances with external actors, as economies become more open to foreign capital, including multinationals and pension funds (Rhodes and van Apeldoorn 1998). Hall and Soskice (2001*b*: 64) argue that actors in LMEs will react to globalization by calling for more deregulation, while cross-class coalitions in CMEs will defend strategic inter-action and coordination. But there is evidence that a new politics of coali-tions in CMEs may be disrupting rather than strengthening existing alliances. Deeg (2005*b*) argues that a domestic coalition for reforming the German financial system has allied with external investors to achieve its goals. Höpner (2001) argues that conflicts over shareholder value in Germany have shifted long-standing coalitions between shareholders, management, and employees. Berndt (2000) portrays an alliance of German small- and medium-sized firms in favour of breaking industrial relations bargains favoured by larger firms. Kinderman (2005) examines the coalition of firms within the large German business associations that is opposing the wage bargaining status quo.

One way to innovate in VoC theory to accommodate such developments is to specify more clearly the circumstances in which firms will exercise 'exit', 'voice', or 'loyalty' and the extent to which exit and voice will imperil or be shaped by existing systems of coordination and complementarities. Another is to identify conditions under which firms will behave *creatively* in ways that challenge the prevailing institutional environment and begin to transform it (Hancké and Goyer 2005: 5). Explaining such developments requires a more dynamic conception of firm interests according to sector or market circumstances than VoC has traditionally provided and leads us to look at how complementarities affect institutional change.

1.2.2. Complementarities and Institutional Change

Can a literature that has largely focused on system coherence and com-plementarities accommodate contradiction and disjunction? The notion of complementarity has been central to VoC, and its continued relevance is strongly advocated by its main proponents (e.g. Hall 2005: 376). Building on Aoki (1994) and North (1990), Hall and Soskice (2001*b*: 17–18) argue that 'nations with a particular type of coordination in one sphere of the economy should tend to develop complementary practices in other spheres as well' (2000*a*: 18). This notion of institutional reinforcement explains VoC's arguments for path-dependent change in line with certain system logics. Crouch and Farrell (2004: 8–9) counter that a focus on the 'coherent logics of ordering' prevents an understanding of 'incongruencies, incoherence, and within-system diversities'. In one of the most thoughtful recent critiques, Streeck and Thelen (2005) contrast VoC's overemphasis on system stability with other approaches (including their own) that are more open to the dynamics of institutional innovation and punctuated equilibria.

This debate indicates a divide in the literature between the complementarity-based VoC form of analysis and a looser, power/interest-based perspective. Deeg (2005*d*) refers to these, respectively, as the 'equilibrium-functionalist' and 'historical-political' approaches. But such methodological distinctions may be less important than at first glance. The commonalities rather than contrasts are highlighted if we place Hall's notion (this volume) of institutions as flexible, subject to defection and always demanding a renewal of support alongside Streeck and Thelen's conception (2005: 12ff.) of institutions as a 'regime (...) continuously created and recreated by a great number of actors with divergent interests, varying normative commitments, different powers, and limited cognition'. The critical difference seems to be the role for rational calculation in the Hall–Soskice view of strategic interaction versus the importance of agency and open-ended (though power-driven) outcomes in the analysis by Streeck and Thelen (Deeg 2005*d*).

In this volume, we wish to retain the notion of complementarities as used in VoC but chart a path between its more functionalist interpretations and the dangers of a more open-ended, unstructured voluntarism. The direction of that path is signalled by recent analyses of European political economies that reveal several competing interpretations of the relationship between complementarities and change, whether generated endogenously, by external pressures, or by a combination of the two.

The first interpretation is that *change can occur in a given institutional architecture without changing the nature of core complementarities*. This is because actors will seek institutional and functional equivalents to pre-existing forms of coordination. Such action, we argue, reveals strategic calculation as well as power-driven agency—suggesting there is little analytical merit in trying to divorce the two. Thus, Goyer (2002; this volume) argues from his study of French and German corporate governance that complementarities coexist with change and evolution: while in theory there are multiple responses available to firms when confronted with external stimuli or shocks, in reality the range of responses available is limited by their institutional context. Thatcher (this volume) suggests that while formal sectoral institutions in MMEs such as France or CMEs such as Germany may begin to emulate their LME counterparts, informal networks, opportunity structures, and actor (including government) strategies remain distinct. Vitols (2004) argues that the German financial system remains bank-based, despite a shift towards a US-style regulatory framework: continuity is driven by 'complementarities and continuities in household savings and investment behaviour and in patterns of company sector demand for finance'. Hassel and Rehder (2001) and Hassel (this volume) argue that while the function of German wage bargaining has changed to accommodate the emerging cost competition-driven model of wage regulation, its strongly organized and centralized form remains stable. Actors still face incentives to preserve the existing system of coordination.

A second interpretation is that *change may be limited to one sub-sector of the economy, which may be significantly transformed, without spilling over, or snow-balling into others*. We argue in this book that compartmentalized change can occur without threatening coordination as such, as CMEs open up, for example, to 'alien' forms of organization such as growing service sectors. As Hall and Hassel (both in this volume) argue, an increasing degree of dualism in labour market organization indicates a loosening of coordination in some spheres of the economy, while strategic coordination remains important in others and for many firms. Höpner (2006) argues that certain institutional features of a political economy may turn out to be redundant rather than complementary and that their decline or demise may have little or no impact on the coordination of the production regime as such. Support for this thesis also comes from Deeg (2005a, 2005b) whose analysis of German finance suggests that subsystems are less closely linked than often assumed. Jackson, Höpner, and Kurdelbusch (2005) make the same argument regarding the relationship between patient capital provision and employee involvement in German firms. Though complementary to one another, they argue that the relationship is neither rigid nor causal—preventing change or implying coevolution—and that the linkages between them are subject to constant renegotiation.

A third interpretation argues, by contrast, that under certain circumstances *spillovers, snow-balling and contagion can occur, spreading change from one subsystem to another, precisely* because *complementarities in the purer CMEs are so tightly coupled*. Vitols (2004) notes that path-shifting change *could* occur in German finance, altering the centrality of banks, in the event of an increase in income inequality and a further pensions reform encouraging more private retirement savings. Höpner (2001: 35) argues that competitive impulses are spreading beyond German corporate governance, as in the causal link between the increasing adoption by firms of shareholder value principles and their demands for more market-driven industrial relations. Contesting the stable equilibrium analysis of German ownership (e.g. Kogut and Walker 2001), Höpner (2001; Höpner and Krempel 2003) argues that complementarities between different fields of corporate governance are also unwinding the ties that bind the country's large companies together, threatening strategic coordination. In a more recent contribution, Höpner (2006) makes the interesting observation that non-liberal economies have two important properties—coordination *and* organization (the latter is defined as the web of institutionally sanctioned collective interests surrounding the firm)—and that market liberalization may differentially affect the two. While spillovers and contagion might undermine coordination, organization (as he argues for the German case) may remain strong.

But will coordination erode to the point of collapse, auguring a transition in Germany towards a capital market-based system? Or will firms retain the critical aspects of coordination that have served them well in the past? Although there is much speculation regarding the former (e.g. Hackethal, Schmidt, and Tyrell 2005), most evidence points to the latter. Thus, Peter Hall (this volume; also Callaghan 2004) argues that countries in Europe have indeed altered their institutions in the face of domestic challenges and changing international conditions, but those changes have been strongly conditioned by past institutions and underlying complementaries have been maintained.

1.2.3. The Nature of Mixed (and Emerging) Market Economies

A further set of questions concerning the nature, function, and future of complementarities are raised by developments in what Hall and Gingerich (2004) portray as 'mid-spectrum', mixed-market political economies, or MMEs. Although they focus on the purer CMEs and LMEs, Hall and Soskice (2001*b*: 35–6) claim that VoC can also be useful for understanding political economies beyond these ideal-types and that each economy displays capacities for coordination that condition how its firms and governments behave. This begs the question, though, of how pertinent the core concept of complementarities is for analysing such countries and how one should understand their dynamics of change.

The evidence (Molina and Rhodes, this volume) shows that 'mid-spectrum' MMEs (and what we refer to as EMEs in Central and Eastern Europe) mix market regulation with some elements of coordinated regulation as well as state-compensating coordination, sustaining subsystems that are far from 'correctly calibrated' over time. But does the absence of CME- or LME-type complementaries, and the lower degree of 'general efficiency' they generate, compel actors in these economies to create them, and move in a CME or an LME direction? Will they remain in their suboptimal institutional locations because strong actors—including state actors—wish to retain their stakes in the status quo (Bebchuk and Roe 2004; Pontusson 2005)? Will they derive only diminishing returns from the absence of ideal-type complementarities in their systems unless they can achieve some kind of systemic recalibration? Hall and Gingerich (2004) argue that this will indeed be the case: that 'hybrid' systems—such as those of southern Europe and the emerging market economies of Central and Eastern Europe—will *ceteris paribus* underperform 'purer' types.

But others (Boyer 2005*a*, 2005*b*; Crouch 2005*a*) have warned against what they call the 'functional assumptions' underpinning this form of reasoning, pointing to the operation of complementarities across policy domains with different rationales and the potentially positive effects of hybridization when national architectures are heterogeneous and loose. Höpner (2005: 383) also suggests that, even if the broad institutional contexts lack coherence because of conflicting governance modes, certain institutions, or clusters of institutions within them may still be complementary in a functional, mutually reinforcing sense. An example might be the 'northern galaxy' of large firms and the localized industrial districts found in Italy. If we accept institutional heterogeneity as a valid—and logically possible—source of institutional complementarities, then it may also be possible, in theory, for mixed economies to find their own forms of coordination in line with the needs of their respective production systems. Nevertheless, as evidence from analyses of MMEs and EMEs in this volume and elsewhere reveals (e.g. European Commission 2003; Radosevic 2005; Jones and Rhodes 2006), the core Hall–Gingerich insight that economies with mixed or poorly calibrated modes of coordination will be outperformed by more coherent systems remains a valuable one. As Amable (2003) argues in his analysis of social systems of innovation and production, this relates in particular to their poor capacity for developing 'technological intensity'—the consequence precisely of institutional 'a-complementarities'.

1.2.4. The Role of the State

Given its concern with the micro-foundations of the political economy and specific focus on the firm, macro-*political* as opposed to macroeconomic structures have not played a prominent role in the Hall–Soskice approach to

VoC. This has led critics to either stress the role that the state (still) plays in coordinating and shaping the political economies of many countries or to develop alternative typologies in which the state is a major determining variable.

Differentiating himself from the basic Hall–Soskice approach, Whitley (2005) argues that the state plays a critical role in determining the characteristics of the business system and how employers behave associationally. He also argues that where the state adopts an active role in economic development (the 'developmental state') by directly intervening in certain sectors of the economy, the result is a greater diversity in employment policies, bargaining procedures, corporate governance, systems of skills formation, etc., between firms of different size within the same sector. Other authors go further, identifying separate models of capitalism in which the state plays a predominant organizing role. Schmidt (2002) creates her own typology of capitalist models, separating 'state capitalism' (France) from 'managed' and 'market capitalisms' (Germany and Britain, respectively). Amable (2003) introduces a grouping of countries in his analysis of the diversity of modern capitalism in which the state plays a determining role—the European-integration/public social system of innovation and production (SSIP)—alongside three other European SSIPs (market-based, meso-corporatist, and social-democratic) and goes on to propose five international models of capitalism: market-based, social-democratic, Asian, continental European, and south European. Boyer (2005*b*) favours a similar categorization.

In the following, we share the VoC focus on coordination as the distinguishing feature of comparative political economies and suggest that the state can be accommodated within the basic VoC framework. This is because we view the state as one element among others of coordination and one that is present everywhere—in different forms, with different functions, and to varying degrees. There is too little analytical value-added to be derived from adding a separate variety of capitalism defined exclusively by the role of the state—especially given the transformation and diminution of that role wherever it may have been strong in the past. An approach that focuses on state mediation, control, and direction derived from the empirical case of pre-1990s France (Schmidt 2002) also fails to illuminate the still central though quite different role of the state played, for example, in the southern European economies which we refer to below (see also Molina and Rhodes, this volume) as predominantly 'compensatory'. The basic (and uncontroversial) insight that the state is important across a diverse range of political economies also inspires Amable's search for even more capitalist varieties, based on a wide range of indicators and characteristics, including not just the state and public intervention but science, technology, labour markets, competition, finance, and more. But the dangers in this approach (cf. Crouch 2005*a*) are that analytical power and parsimony are sacrificed in favour of a greater capacity for detailed description; and that in an effort to account for the entirety of national political economies, the quantity of variables proliferates but the number of core insights is reduced.

1.3. INTERESTS, COALITIONS, AND INSTITUTIONAL FRAMEWORKS

The questions raised by the preceding discussion can only be resolved by empirical analysis; however, that discussion does help us appreciate the ways in which the concept of complementarities can be nuanced and rendered less rigid than it is often thought to be, thereby enriching the VoC approach. It can also lead us via further theoretical development to a more complete understanding of the dynamics of change in different kinds of political economies. We believe, as stated earlier, that achieving that goal demands paying closer attention to class, coalitions, and the role of the state than is the case in either conventional VoC analysis or in most of the literature that has criticized it for its alleged functionalism.

Streeck (2005*a*: 583–4) has argued strongly that what are often regarded as institutional complementarities in political economies today were born from class and industrial conflict in the past and the solutions that were found to them 'in the interstices of functionally interdependent institutions built with distributed power and in pursuit of particularistic sectoral interests'. We are broadly sympathetic with that claim, and its core insight helps inform our discussion of networks and class- and sector-based coalitions below. There we make institutions the dependent rather than the independent variable, as they frequently are in much recent analysis. Specifically, we focus on the ways in which networks and class coalitions evolve (and potentially also *devolve*) around 'friction points' in relations between institutional subsystems. By raising the profiles of networks, class coalitions, and the state in the VoC framework, we argue that many of the problems and weaknesses frequently attributed to it can be resolved without detracting from the power and parsimony of its core insights.

1.3.1. Business Interests and Networks

Many of the contributions in this volume suggest an understanding of coordination and complementarities that builds on a set of prerequisites associated with networks of actors with broadly similar interests. Hall and Soskice (2001*b*) repeatedly refer to different modes of coordination in these terms, but give less attention to the ways in which such networks emerge. However, at least since Olson (1965) we have been aware that a confluence of interests is an insufficient condition for collective action to ensue. But while Olson locates the capacity for collective action in the distribution of sanctions and rewards, we emphasize the historical emergence and reproduction of networks. We make three broad points: that different modes of economic governance reflect a politically constructed institutional matrix, built in large part on elite networks; that these elite networks sought to control the strategic levers of the economy and state at politically opportune moments; and that the mechanisms that reproduce network structures provide for different levels of coordinating capacity.

As for the character of the institutional matrices, in LMEs, strong networks do not emerge easily because their competition regimes preclude trusts and 'collusion'. In the UK, moreover, business networks have in any case been fractured by historical divisions between banking and industrial capital. By contrast, the origins of post-war German 'organized' capitalism can be found in the networks that tied many large firms and banks together in powerful industrial-financial groups before the Second World War (Hilferding 1910; Gerschenkron 1962; Herrigel 1996). Even after the break-up of large cartels by the Allies, it took little time for these groups to be reconstituted (Berghahn 1996). In France, modernizing elites constructed such business networks after the Second World War (Kuisel 1981). The founding of new, and the revamping of old, elite schools (*Grandes Écoles*), and the central role of the Treasury in allocating industrial credit, produced a state-centred system (Zysman 1983). Italy's pyramidal ownership structures and conglomerates with strong horizontal ties, spanning firms and banks, allowed pre- and post-war elites to create collaborative, defensive, and closed business networks. As for Central and Eastern Europe, King (this volume) argues that the roots of contemporary CEE economies lie in their pre-1989 class structure, in which party bureaucrats wielded power and technocrats managed production. Depending on which of these sectors gained the upper hand prior to the 1990s transition, the emerging form of economic governance reflected these relative positions of power: liberal capitalist in the case of the technocrats; oligarchic in the case of the party bureaucrats.

Different modes of economic governance, in both the 'old' and 'new' capitalist states of Europe, thus reflect a matrix that is frequently politically constructed. The French state-centred elite system, German cartels, and Communist technocrats differ in many respects; but all share networks as the basis for their country's prevailing mode of business governance. The post-war French and the state-socialist networks, moreover, have their roots not in the economy but in the state apparatus (even if the boundaries between state and economy are highly permeable), whereas the German cartels were orchestrated by leading industrialists. This matrix socializes economic elites and provides a central building block for the rest of the political economy, since the broad orientations developed by these leading groups also influence the choices that other actors can make.

Second, elite networks achieved their centrality because they sought to control the strategic levers of the economy and state at politically opportune moments: the post-war governments led by De Gaulle in France did just that; the reconstruction of the post-war German economy along 'ordo-liberal' lines provided the ideological framework for the social market economy; the large public sector under IRI in Italy merged and modernized a scattered small- and medium-sized industrial sector; and the political and economic chaos of the post-communist transition was exploited by some networks better than others. The role and function of the state is important in all three instances and contributes to both the structural coherence of economic governance and the potential for functional complementarities. In the German case, it provides a strong legal framework for intensive interaction between the core elements of the corporate governance system—finance, firms, and labour; in France (and other Mediterranean economies), state intervention has both impeded autonomous interest intermediation and articulation and compensated for the consequent weakness of economic coordination; in the Communist countries, the suppression of freely coordinating actors has given way since the early 1990s to quite different forms of market governance, depending on the pre-capitalist balance of power between bureaucrats and technocrats.

Third, the mechanisms that reproduce network structures provide for quite different levels of coordinating capacity. For networks to become and remain building blocks for coordination, they require both *external* reproduction (the recruitment of new members into the network) and *internal* reproduction (the development of sanctioning mechanisms that secure compliance). The *Grandes Écoles* in France, family-based, holding-type ownership patterns in Italy, the importance of industry associations built on technical knowledge in Germany, and party membership in the former Soviet block countries have all performed such functions. Internal reproduction mechanisms run from simple reputation games in France (see Hancké and Soskice 1996; Hancké 2001), via binding sanctions for club members in Germany (Soskice 1999; Wood 2001), to family-dominated, firm–finance linkages in Italy, to political promotion in the former Communist countries. But whether functional compatibility and complementarity result will depend on the extent to which markets and their actors are *freely coordinated* (high in Germany's bank–firm–labour complex, medium in France's state-business system, and low—at least outside the industrial districts—in highly politicized Italy), rather than coerced and suppressed (as in the command economies of the former Soviet bloc).

Business networks are therefore to be found at the basis of coordination via three mechanisms: the institutional architecture of business, a set of short-term and long-term reproduction mechanisms, and a political opportunity for the groups that make up the networks to secure influence over the economy and, if necessary, the state. If they are all present, we claim, together they will help create a form of institutional coordination that will be structurally coherent and functionally complementary; if they are absent or only partially present, then core complementarities are unlikely to develop and an economy may even take an LME-type path. The radical and deep collapse of national state-economy links in Central and Eastern Europe provides a case in point, for their instant immersion into the international economy (captured in the metaphor 'rebuilding the ship at sea') made it very difficult for non-liberal capitalist elites to capture their commanding heights (Innes 2005). Slovenia (see Feldmann, this volume) is the exception where the political opportunity was clear, its elite sufficiently cohesive and nationalistic and the possible trajectories open. It was, therefore, able to convert its pre-1989 institutions into a CME-type framework.

If networks are at the basis of business coordination, what does this imply for the construction of broader institutional frameworks? One answer to this question, which is implicit in the VoC framework, is that institutions reflect the needs of business. This conception has, correctly in our view, come under criticism for its unnecessarily functionalist assumptions: capital may indeed be crucial in capitalist economies, but, paraphrasing Marx, it does not choose the conditions under which it operates. We therefore introduce the two other central actors in capitalist economies that influence these conditions: labour (and its relationship with capital) and the state.

1.3.2. Labour, Capital, and Cross-Class Coalitions

Labour constrains business in two ways: directly, because business needs workers and their skills to produce goods and services, and indirectly, via the constraints of collective organization. National 'settlements' between capital and labour reflect their relative positions of power. While VoC analysis typically focuses on companies rather than labour, we argue—in VoC-compatible fashion—that these settlements result from a confluence of equilibrium strategies on both sides (see also Iversen 2005; Iversen and Soskice 2006a).

Regarding labour, if skills are predominantly industry- or firm-specific, it will prefer CME-type institutions and policies. As Iversen (this volume) argues, employees in CME countries who have a high proportion of specific skills will also prefer a higher level of social insurance (and hence redistributive spending) than employees in LME nations where the proportion of general skills is higher. But when skill profiles are more general, as they predominantly are in LMEs, the choices are more complex. Employees in the primary segments of the labour market (lawyers, consultants, investment bankers, etc.) are likely to prefer liberal market institutions and individual rather than collective action. The rest may then be forced to fall in line and develop strategies that increase their survival in highly competitive labour markets. As for capital, two equilibrium strategies are available, VoC tells us, since the nature of skills is tightly linked to other labour market institutions. Specific skills, plant- and firm-level workers' participation, and coordinated wage bargaining all help safeguard the high value-added product market strategies of large CME firms, while general skills, unilateral management, and decentralized wage-setting allow for quite different company strategies in LMEs. Cross-class coalitions in CMEs can be understood as the point where the strategies of labour and capital meet: both have strong preferences for thick, inclusive, and well-institutionalized frameworks. Because both benefit, they will therefore fight for their survival. In LMEs, the interests of both employers and highly skilled employees tend to converge on a less well-regulated institutional framework.

Introducing class into the standard VoC framework allows us to explore several points of criticism levelled against it. One is that institutional frameworks are not simply reflections of the strategic needs of firms, or the functional needs of 'systems', but express underlying cross-class coalitions, which in turn reflect the relative power—and agency—of important sections of capital and labour. Note, though, that while rendering the VoC framework and arguments more dynamic and realistic, this emphasis on class dynamics does not alter their basic logic. However, there are clear analytical gains from introducing the notion of a cross-class settlement—not least because it offers a more dynamic view of the emergence of institutional frameworks than many find in VoC and allows for a finer grained analysis of institutional change.

Equally important, an emphasis on cross-class coalitions allows us to respond to criticisms of VoC's alleged conception of the firm as an 'institution-taker' rather than an autonomous, creative, or disruptive actor (cf. Allen 2003; Crouch and Farrell 2004; Crouch 2005a). As suggested above, coordination is not constructed by the business class *as a whole*, but by its dominant sections, primarily those that are found in the large firms in CMEs and in the labour markets surrounding the leading sectors in LMEs—and often only after protracted struggles for control of the class agenda. Few doubt, for example, that

CME-type institutions are in the best interests of large firms in CMEs, which may derive significant complementarity-like benefits from the institutional relationships that underpin the cross-class coalition (Hassel, this volume). But it is considerably less evident that they are also in the interests of small firms in CME, for whom collectively bargained labour costs, and other concessions related to the cross-class settlement, may simply be prohibitively high, or become so as the dynamics of economic growth shift from manufacturing to services (Rhodes 2005).

Cross-class coalitions and their institutional settlements therefore face a perennial problem. Since the rules and institutions that reflect the settlement may not be in the interest of all, and may even be against the interests of important sections of the class, cross-class coalitions are fundamentally unstable. Large and small firms in an economy, for example, do not necessarily have the same interests, nor do firms that produce primarily for export as compared with those based in domestic markets. The interests of large firms in the exposed manufacturing sector will diverge substantially from those of small firms in the sheltered sector, and as employment in the latter expands, the potential for disruption of the cross-class settlement will increase (Gourevitch 1986; Rogowski 1989; Frieden 1991; Franzese 2002). Similarly, workers in small companies do not necessarily share the priorities of workers in large firms, and—arguably a more contentious statement—according to some economists, unskilled workers may find themselves kept in low-paid employment (or worse, unemployment) by what they call a 'wage cartel', led by large firms and their workers and trade unions (Lindbeck and Snower 1989). If underlying interests within classes in a political economy can be as diverse as this, the cross-class coalitions at the basis of coordination in CMEs (and possibly other non-LMEs) appear to be highly fragile arrangements which require permanent reaffirmation. However, if they are intrinsically unstable, why do we not witness more defections from the system as a whole?

One important part of the answer to this question is obviously related to intra-class politics, and the codification of institutional arrangements in favour of the winners who lay down the rules for others—an example of the ways in which institutions can develop complementary forms of intensive interaction from a cross-class settlement of conflict. Swenson's analysis (1989) of labour politics in Sweden and Germany showed how in interwar Sweden the export sector and the metalworkers union forged a coalition against the interests of firms and their workers in the sheltered sector to impose a centralized wage bargaining system. More generally, the post-war settlements in most of Europe primarily reflected the interests of the fast-growing modern sector—business and workers in large, mass-producing firms (Piore and Sabel 1984). And even today, collective bargaining systems frequently use large firms, with standardized job classifications and wage scales, as their main point of reference. Yet these struggles were not settled by power alone: side-payments made the settlement acceptable to those whose interests were inadequately reflected.

On the workers' side, institutionalized subservience has come with an important benefit: in most (non-LME) European economies, wages for workers outside the core sectors of the economy are negotiated in the shadow of the modern large firm-led sector, and their wages are usually set following the prevailing rules in large industrial firms. Wages for these workers thus acquired a level of protection, predictability, and standardization that they would not have had otherwise. Even small firms gain from the arrangement, since they are allowed to exploit the benefits of coordination (such as well-developed skill provision and technology transfer systems, standardized wage grids, and social peace) without incurring all the costs. In most countries, small firms have choices with regard to the menu offered by the institutional framework: workers' representation thresholds exclude the vast majority of small firms, negotiated wages set a maximum for them (while frequently providing a de facto minimum for large firms), employment protection may differ between large and small firms, and escape clauses for small firms have either been in existence for a while or were recently introduced in the more 'rigid' systems such as Germany.

Throughout this analysis of the nature of class coalitions runs a question that has been addressed to VoC since its inception. How can we differentiate between (*a*) an institutionalized compromise that worked well in the past (irrespective of why it existed in the first place) and which persists because of the potential and actuality of strategic, functional complementarity and (*b*) an institutional arrangement that was consciously designed, in part as a result of strategic interactions between socio-economic actors, and whose complementarities stem from distributive settlements whose *raison d'être* may erode and decline (Streeck 2005*b*)? This issue goes to the heart of the debates on the neoinstitutionalist approach to political economy: in the first case, actors have internalized the constraints of the institutional framework (and the framework becomes to a large extent constitutive of those very actors), while the second case leaves more room for contingencies. The difference between the two is clear in how they account for change: if institutions are indeed constitutive of actors, then actors permanently reproduce the institutional framework, and change can therefore only occur when it is exogenous and sudden. In the other view, change in the institutional framework can occur in several ways: shifts in the existing cross-class coalitions, in the intra-class politics underlying coordination (e.g. when public sector trade unions dominate), or in the sociological conditions underlying the reproduction of business networks. In such cases, as Hall and Thelen (2005) have argued, the likely result is a shift in the mode of coordination. While VoC's critics maintain that the approach is imprisoned in the first perspective, we see no reason for that assumption if the agency of cross- and inter-class settlements are given their full and rightful place in VoC analysis.

Recapitulating our argument thus far, the causal chain that we have developed has the following three steps: (*a*) business networks are translated, to varying degrees, into modes of coordination; (*b*) the dominant sections of labour and capital enter a cross-class coalition, coercing and bribing others to follow; (*c*) this cross-class coalition then sets mutually agreed rules that strengthen the internal reproduction of the network and, by extension, the mode of coordination and its specific national manifestations. But only in certain circumstances—when markets and their actors are freely coordinated—do synergistic or strategic forms of complementarity emerge.

1.3.3. The State

This brings us to the third neglected issue regarding the nature and origins of coordination in VoC: the state. The dual equilibrium strategies and stable class coalitions examined above are obviously ideal-types, closely resembling LMEs and CMEs. However, most empirical instances will differ in one way or another. For example, business coordination may be underdeveloped, and/or labour representation may be far from unitary and based on ideological divisions. Under those conditions, strategic interaction may only occur sporadically, and infrequently produces stable institutional arrangements (Molina and Rhodes, this volume). As suggested by Hall and Gingerich (2004), in 'mid-spectrum' economies, CME-type strategic complementarities, positive spillovers, and public goods provision are inhibited by power asymmetries, organizational fragmentation, and class conflict, as (for the same reasons) are the complementarities that derive from the less visible market discipline found in LMEs. Yet instead of facing permanent and destructive economic dysfunctionality, in economies that exhibit such patterns—e.g. France, Italy, or Spain—stability appears to prevail as well (as too does strong economic performance), and often the state provides that element of stability (if not fully fledged coordination) by compensating for weaknesses elsewhere in the political economy.

The main problem with the state in VoC analysis is that it is too often regarded as a reflection of the existing mode of coordination with no autonomous role to play. In its simplest form, the assumption seems to be that where the state attempts to push through reforms that contradict the basic interests of a well-organized business class—even if that implied substantial deregulation (see Wood 2001 on Germany)—the outcome would be the status quo, barely modified. Conversely, where business had a clear interest in deregulation, but was too weak to pursue this, as in the UK (and perhaps in a different way in France), government policies were simply aligned with the interests of business. The Thatcher and Reagan reforms were, in this view, nothing more than the state waging class war by proxy. Government policies will only work if they are *incentive compatible*, that is if they reflect the underlying mode of competitive or cooperative business coordination (Rhodes 2000; Wood 2001). In other words, politics follows economics: the nature of the state reflects the interests of business.

In many nations, however, the state is considerably more activist (Evans and Rueschemeyer 1985). In countries as diverse as France, Japan, Italy, and Korea, the state played a crucial role in defining, supporting, or organizing the post-war growth model. In later arrivals on the capitalist scene, the state's role has been both more (e.g. in Latin America and Southern Europe) and less (as in Central Europe) than the simple LME–CME dichotomy suggests. The transition to capitalism involved a dramatic *expansion* of the state's activities in the economy in the former, and a forced *reduction* in the latter, sometimes against the immediate interests of a nascent business class at the time (Innes 2005). The diversity in state–economy relations that persists until today suggests that there is a benefit in establishing the state and the mode of business coordination as analytically independent properties of any given model of capitalism.

1.3.4. A Revised Typology of Capitalist Varieties

Let us begin with the two basic forms that relations between the state and the (supply side of the) economy can take in advanced capitalism: either the state has close direct influence over the economy (e.g. as the owner of industries and/or main provider of industrial credit) or the state is primarily a regulator operating at arm's length. Post-war France and to some extent post-war Italy, as well as some Central European economies fall into the first category, while the UK, Sweden, and Germany fall into the second. Class-based interest organization, in turn, can run from being highly structured to being highly fragmented. In most countries, the levels of business and labour organization tend to mirror one another in this respect. In the first (highly structured) category, individual companies and industry associations or industrial groups balance their respective strategies and are able to strike bargains with organized labour. In the second (fragmented) category, collective interest definition above the company level is more or less absent, either

State–Economy Relations

	Close	Arm's-length
	Étatisme	*LMEs*
	France pre-1990s	UK, Baltics
	Compensating state	*CMEs*
	Italy, Spain some EMEs	Germany Slovenia

(Vertical axis label: **Fragmented — Organized** / **Interest Organization**)

Figure 1.1. State-economy relations, interest organization, and modes of coordination

among firms or between their representatives and (similarly fractured) trade union organizations. Dichotomizing these two continuums into a matrix (Figure 1.1) leads to the following four ideal-types of coordination.

We want to stress that we are hereby creating logical categories for analysis, to which particular countries will broadly (though never precisely) conform, rather than constructing a typology by 'reading back' from empirical examples which we consider paradigmatic—a charge that has been levelled (though wrongly, we believe) at the original Hall–Soskice formulation of the LME–CME ideal-types (Crouch 2005a). Note also that we do not identify EMEs as a separate variety of capitalism of equivalent analytical status to the rest: we simply wish to indicate by this term their transitional character and that their respective mixes of modes of coordination (market and non-market) are embryonic in some cases, more developed in others, but in all cases still in a process of institutional construction.

The first 'type' or mode of coordination, *étatisme*, has traditionally been associated with post-war France, where the state controlled the strategic levers of the economy through outright ownership of many companies and control of industrial credit (Hall 1986: 204). Partly as a result of the state's dominance and partly due to the deep interpenetration of the state and the economic elites, business organization in France has been weak. In privately owned companies, management and owners have typically relied on themselves for providing the resources they needed, refusing to allow external agents, including associations, to play a role in that process. Similarly, unions have been weakened by ideological fragmentation and their weak roots in the workplace (outside the public sector), while they lack effective vertical links between confederal, sectoral, and firm levels. Since both business and unions were weakly organized, and the state predominant in economic governance, the capitalist model was built on the state (Levy 2000). Strategic complementarities, to the extent that they have existed at all, could be found in state–business linkages in the large-firm sector, based in the credit-allocation system, and predominantly in traditional manufacturing and public utilities (see Börsch and Thatcher, both in this volume). State-protected markets and business in high-technology sectors have, by contrast, been highly dysfunctional, delivering poor results and high-profile policy failures (Rhodes 1985). In industrial relations, atomized business finds a parallel in the weak and ideologically divided labour movement. The result is less a class compromise or coalition than a permanently contested truce that frequently breaks down into conflict.

A different constellation can be found where the state is important as an actor in industrial policy, but where business is also relatively well-organized, more as a result of the type of ownership structures than associational capacity. Italy exemplifies this type (Molina and Rhodes, this volume), although Rhodes and van Apeldoorn (1997) embed it in a broader Mediterranean family. There the state organized a large state-controlled business sector that has provided key basic industrial inputs and compensated for the absence of autonomous arrangements for capital and labour. The 'compensating' role includes state-funded wage-compensation schemes during industrial restructuring and a social transfer-oriented welfare state. Business and labour tend to be better organized, and wage bargaining more coordinated than in France. But the scope for synergistic, VoC-type complementarities is limited. Interest organizations are strong enough to make demands on the state but insufficiently cohesive to provide it with dependable bargaining partners. Attempts to build more effective coordination also run up against prisoners' dilemma-type collective action problems, including anticollective behaviour on the part of firms (and employees); an acquiescence in 'inefficient inertia', due to the sunk costs confronting agents for change; and the capacity of firms to offset the lack of complementarities by seeking competitive advantage by other means (Bebchuk and Roe 2004). In Italy, the latter have included frequent competitive devaluations, government subsidies, cheap immobile factors of production, and evasion of taxation and labour laws. Only in the northern industrial districts do local functional equivalents of coordination appear to operate.

The third type of state–business relations, and form of coordination, is the one we usually associate with LMEs in VoC. The state sets detailed legal frameworks, leaving business to operate within them, and guards the integrity of market operations by closely monitoring ownership arrangements and market concentration. In part resulting from its history and ownership structures business is weakly organized, and the regulatory frameworks set by the state reinforce this by precluding most forms of deep cooperation. The labour movement, in turn, is decentralized and poorly coordinated, contributing to a conflict-ridden form of industrial relations and strong, endemic weaknesses in employer–employee relations—until submitted, that is, to the market discipline of a Thatcher–Reagan type re-regulation of employment law and labour markets. In LMEs, the political strategies of business are primarily oriented towards influencing the regulatory framework, and considerably less towards finding a compromise with labour (Wood 2001). Some CEE emerging market economies (e.g. the Baltics) have also rapidly moved towards this model. Nonetheless, continual debates take place over the appropriate boundary between the state and the economy. In the principal European LME, the UK, it is only since the 1990s, and the Thatcherite solution to the decades-long contestation of the state–market divide, that liberal market synergies have operated freely (Rhodes 2000).

The fourth and final type of coordination is conventionally associated with the north-west European economies (CMEs in VoC), of which Germany is the prime example. The state plays a small direct role in the economy (but organizes a large and robust welfare state) and offers broad frameworks for companies to operate within. Business is highly organized and relies on strong industry and employer associations for the provision of collective goods. The high level of economic regulation is less the result of state intervention, but rather follows from voluntary agreements by associations (including labour unions) to set limits on the behaviour of individual companies. In this model, state policies only appear to have an effect if they are carried out or sanctioned by these associations. Here too, as in the LME model, the coherence of economic governance is reinforced by functional complementarities. Yet if the class settlement between capital and labour in the LMEs has been fully settled in favour of the former, in the CMEs, as discussed above and in Hall, Hassel, and Soskice (this volume), the class settlement, based on a much more equal balance of power, is now subject to significant strains.

This typology allows us to explore several dimensions of the state's role in contemporary capitalism and to correct its absence in VoC. In the original iteration of VoC theory (Hall and Soskice 2001*b*), the underdevelopment of the state as a factor in economic organization was largely the consequence of the heuristic focus on two types of capitalism in which the state played a relatively distant role. But there is nothing in the approach as such that prevents a fuller accommodation of the state as an actor—architectural or otherwise (see the discussions in Streeck 2005*b*; Hall 2005). We wish to stress that the state plays an important role everywhere, but in different ways. In some forms of capitalism, the state is a central actor in the sense that it provides both a framework for business activities and a means for pursuing them. In other forms of capitalism, as we have discussed, the state is less a promoter of economic activity than a compensator for coordination deficits and provider of political consensus and legitimacy. In still others, the state allows markets to operate within a broad set of regulatory frameworks and refrains from direct interference.

'Bringing the state back in' thus provides us with a typology in which LMEs, CMEs, MMEs, and some EMEs can be accommodated. We believe that this approach is superior to attempts to produce a third model or variety of capitalism alongside 'market' and 'managed' types (Schmidt 2002), in which the state is architectonic (because it is, but to different degrees in all systems), and to other approaches (e.g. Amable 2003; Boyer 2005*b*) which multiply the number of capitalisms in line with a large number of variables or characteristics. While the former conflates a distinctive mode of coordination with a different model of capitalism, the latter accommodates greater empirical complexity, but excessively dilutes the analytical strength of the VoC approach. The typology above also allows us to think about the institutional substructures of these systems, especially the capacity for coalition building and collective goods provision, given contrasting organizational characteristics of capital and labour, different modes of state involvement, distinctive forms of coordination, and the extent and importance of positive complementarities. Section 1.4, where we address some of these points, investigates the ways in which modes of coordination in European economies condition, and are altered or disrupted by responses to contemporary exogenous shocks.

1.4. EXOGENOUS SHOCKS AND DOMESTIC CHANGE IN VARIETIES OF EUROPEAN CAPITALISM

A central question for VoC is its ability to deal with change. Our cases provide a wealth of evidence on this, as over the past two decades European political economies have faced a series of dramatic shocks. These include increasing competition in a liberalized trading order, the massively increased volume and speed of capital flows, and Europe's own responses to the collapse of the Golden Age (the end of Bretton Woods, the oil price hikes, and stagflation of the 1970s and 1980s) in the form of shifts associated with the Single European Market and EMU. After 1989, the Central and Eastern European countries underwent a radical transition from state socialism to capitalism in which economic growth collapsed, and business and welfare systems were forced to adjust. With their lower labour costs and tax rates, they may now pose a challenge themselves to the higher-cost, highly-regulated jurisdictions to their west. These shocks are 'exogenous' in that they are not fully under the control of domestic policymakers who, at most, can influence them by acting collectively, notably through the EU.

How have different countries responded? One argument, popular with economic liberals, is that 'continental' Western economies have failed to adjust, maintaining 'rigid' labour markets, 'excessive' state ownership and regulation, and 'bloated' government spending; in contrast, LMEs, such as Britain and Eastern European nations, have moved swiftly to become more competitive. Our view, by contrast, is closer to the basic VoC insight that distinctive forms of economies—those close to the LME and CME ideal-types—derive their competitiveness from distinctive sources of comparative institutional advantage and will respond to exogenous shocks in quite different, but perhaps equally effective ways (Iversen, this volume). Those economies that diverge from these types and contain mixes of coordinating modes of varying degrees of coherence will struggle to recalibrate their systems (Molina and Rhodes, this volume). Past forms of coordination between labour, the state, and firms, based on pre-existing coalitions and institutionally shaped interests, will condition national responses to exogenous shocks. But we depart from a functionalist reading of VoC in a critical respect in arguing that not all institutional arrangements that underpinned successful cross-class coalitions and were positive for competitiveness in the past will continue to succeed under altered economic circumstances.

Drawing on the contributions to this volume, we compare four different types of nation in Europe: countries that lie closest to the CME type, such as Germany and Switzerland; MMEs such as France, Italy, and Spain in which the state has played a more active role, as promoter, regulator, or compensator in processes of change; Central and Eastern European nations (which we refer to as EMEs) that have rapidly evolved from state-socialist to capitalist economies; and Britain as Europe's most fully developed LME.

The British LME had already liberalized labour markets, retrenched the welfare state, and altered macroeconomic policy in response to the crises of the 1970s and 1980s (Rhodes 2000), and more recent exogenous shocks would seem to have had little impact on coordination in an economy that removed most vestiges of cross-class institutional compromise under Thatcherism. This is not to say that these shocks have no economic effects: there are repercussions, especially in the rapid redeployment of employees across sectors and the creative destruction and rebuilding, in particular of the services sector, that has accommodated so many former industrial workers as well as immigrant labour. Many of Europe's CMEs weathered the storms of thirty years ago with less dramatic consequences. But more recent international shocks seem to threaten the very essence of the cross-class settlements on which these economies have long been based. A host of challenges are regularly cited: high wages, strong employment protection rights, and coordinated national bargaining systems appear threatened by the loss of national control over interest rates and exchange rates, rising cross-national capital mobility, and increasing product-market competition. The social insurance foundations of their generous welfare states are undermined by heightened labour-cost competition, while the state's revenue base is threatened by tax competition. Exogenous forces also pose serious challenges for MMEs such as France, Italy, or Spain. In particular, fiscal constraints, international competition, and the monetary inflexibility associated with EMU and EU regulations all threaten the size of the state, the extensive protection it has typically offered workers and national suppliers and its capacity to compensate for the traditional coordination deficits of these systems.

Both CME- and MME-type nations have responded to these challenges by introducing sweeping reforms over the last decade or so. Take welfare and labour policies. Faced with EMU, greater international competition, and greater sectoral differentiation in productivity gains, national wage bargaining in Germany has been supplemented since the early 1990s by firm-level bargaining that can utilize opt-outs from national-level agreements. Today no fewer than one-third of private sector companies have plant-level accords that allow terms which differ from national collective bargains (Hassel, this volume). German companies have responded by becoming evermore concentrated in high value-added sectors (Hancké and Herrmann; Hall, both in this volume). At the same time, with the creation of badly paid jobs that are not covered by collective agreements and have little security, a dual labour market has emerged: by September 2003, 6.7 million workers were employed in such jobs in Germany, which had the third highest proportion of low-paid workers in the EU after the UK and Ireland (Hassel, this volume). Low wages have been partially offset by increases in government spending on transfer payments. MMEs too have attempted to undertake major reforms that have altered the role of the state and the benefits it traditionally provides to large groups of citizens. Thus for instance, France, Spain, and Italy have liberalized employment rules, and effectively moved to dual labour markets, divided between those workers enjoying permanent contracts protected against dismissal and others working under other forms of arrangement (e.g. temporary or part-time work).

Similar patterns of rapid change can be found in the regulation of markets and firms. Surprisingly, perhaps, Germany and France often supported EU regulation that ended national monopolies in strategic markets such as telecommunications or energy. Domestically, they radically transformed regulatory institutions by privatizing public utilities, allowing competition and creating new independent regulatory authorities (Schmidt 1996, 2002; Thatcher 2004*a*, 2005). Some CMEs, such as Switzerland, but also Germany and MMEs, such as France, have also greatly encouraged stock market development and shareholding, though both remain underdeveloped in Italy and to a lesser extent Spain (Börsch, this volume; Lane 2005; Deeg 2005*b*). In corporate governance, faced with the need to attract foreign investment, France and Germany have both introduced major reforms, notably greater transparency that protects minority shareholders in Germany and an extensive adoption of shareholder value strategies in France (Goyer, this volume; Hancké and Goyer 2005; Deeg 2005*a*).

CMEs and MMEs differ from each other and from LMEs in the extent to which networks, varieties of coordination and complementary institutions have facilitated, obstructed, or otherwise shaped these changes and how cross-class coalitions have been sustained or fragmented. Four examples of coordination mechanisms that shape change can be given here: the structure of business and union associations, informal networks that link public policymakers and suppliers, intra-firm relations, and collective bargaining over training, skills, and wages. Even the transition to capitalism of the countries of Eastern Europe has been shaped by the nature of pre-existing networks.

As discussed in Section 1.2, the nature of class settlements has produced quite different sets of relationships between capital and labour, both inside and outside the firm. When firm-level capital–labour arrangements are weak, management can restructure and switch product market strategies rapidly. In LMEs, this involves relatively low risks for managers; but in MMEs, it is either pursued with limited transparency, or remains contested, as workers may seek to respond, either at firm or company level or by pressuring the state to claw back management autonomy. In contrast, in CMEs, managers have less autonomy than in LMEs and MMEs due to strong mechanisms for workers representation such as works councils that restrict their ability to hire and fire in pursuit of short-term profitability. But in return, as a result of long-standing mutual commitments, employers can offer higher levels of transparency to and enjoy higher levels of cooperation with employees. Both France and Germany, for example, have sought foreign investment, but they have done so in different ways and with different results (Goyer, this volume). Germany has increased transparency, which is attractive to foreign investors; yet because of the pre-existing consultation laws that granted works councils deep information rights, this transparency did not lead to the exposure of sensitive information that management wished to hide from employees. At the same time, these institutions, in combination with stable stakeholder-type finance, limited the inflow of 'impatient capital' and a major restructuring of corporations. As a result, Germany disproportionately attracted patient overseas investors such as US pension funds. In contrast, French firms have enjoyed higher degrees of management autonomy and have restructured and diversified conglomerates to attract mobile foreign capital that demands short-term returns, notably US mutual funds. The transparency measures that were introduced were considerably weaker than in Germany, as management in large companies feared that offering unions and employees more information would in turn limit their power and autonomy.

Inherited coordination mechanisms based on cross-class coalitions, notably between strongly organized labour and employers, also affect national responses to EMU, increased international competition, and liberalized European markets. A central choice for firms is whether to follow a high-value, high-quality product strategy or a low-price, low-cost strategy. The former requires a highly skilled and cooperative workforce, whereas the latter depends on management autonomy to reduce costs. In CMEs such as Germany and Switzerland, powerful coordination mechanisms have allowed cross-class cooperation and associated complementarities to persist, although cooperation has begun to devolve to the firm from industry level in large exporting companies (Hancké and Herrmann; Börsch, both this volume). Firms in export sectors have built on the traditional model of high skills and high wages by using inherited coordinating arrangements and complementarities that link bargaining over wages, conditions, and employment with high levels of training and specialization in skills, in order to specialize further in high-value sectors.

One of the consequences of the latter strategy is that higher productivity gains and greater skills specialization will be labour-saving, compounding the problems of rising long-term unemployment in CMEs such as Germany, and in MMEs with large, highly competitive manufacturing sectors such as France and Italy. As Soskice (this volume) suggests, the combination of strong vocational training (and hence specific skills), an associated risk-aversion to loss of jobs and income, and proportional representation (PR) has led to profound problems in Germany and possibly elsewhere. Governments in the proportional electoral systems that typically characterize CMEs are facing strong demands to maintain the protection of unemployed workers through high transfer payments—ultimately contributing to higher labour costs and adding to, rather than alleviating, the CME service-sector trilemma (Iversen 2005: ch. 6 and this volume). In contrast, in the UK, 'deregulated' labour markets and the absence of labour as a countervailing force make a lower-cost, lower-price strategy, underpinning service-sector expansion more realistic than in the high-value, high-skill approach of the CMEs that continues to serve their manufacturing companies well.

High-value, high-skill strategies in LMEs are concentrated instead in high-tech companies, advertising, corporate finance, and consulting, while service-sector development (both high- and low-value added) in the CMEs is more restricted. Moreover, the majoritarian political system discourages a redistributive coalition between the middle and working classes to pay for high social spending, while the high level of general skills reduces the fear of income loss from unemployment and hence demands for such spending (Iversen, this volume). As Hall convincingly argues in his chapter in this volume, these factors figure prominently among those that have shaped the distinctive ways in which Germany, Britain, Sweden, and France have dealt with wage, work, and total factor productivity challenges over the past several decades. Economic strategies (and government policies) remain differentiated, and in some respects increasingly so, thus supporting the core VoC insight that LMEs and CMEs will evolve in different directions, depending on their respective strengths in mobile versus specific and co-specific assets.

In his chapter, Soskice takes this logic to its conclusion by modelling the interactions between production regime, electoral system, and macroeconomic policymaking. Macroeconomic policy in LMEs, he argues, is less restrictive than in CMEs because of two critical factors which differ. One is a strong, single-party government with a clear majority and fiscal policies that force them to internalize the costs of expansion; the other is the absence of strong trade unions. In such a configuration, central banks need not fear adopting a highly responsive and often less conservative monetary policy, since there are no actors in the LME political economy who would exploit a monetary expansion. In CMEs, in contrast, strong trade unions and an electoral system based on PR can produce an endemic inflationary bias which strong conservative independent central banks have to curtail. In both LMEs and CMEs, inflation is low today, but both arrived there with very different underlying institutional architectures and with very different effects on economic growth and unemployment.

Nevertheless, as Hassel (this volume) argues, LMEs and CMEs are beginning to share one very important development—an increasingly segmented labour market and rising income inequality, due in the latter case to opt-outs and concessions in the wage bargaining system (see Thelen and Kume 2006 for a comparative perspective on this issue). These developments are driven in part by the threat and reality of large manufacturing company relocation to lower-cost jurisdictions in Central and Eastern Europe, and the declining countervailing power of labour. In this context, the strategic complementarities that have long-characterized the German system are intact, and perhaps even deepening. But they are devolving on an ever-smaller core of the economy in employment terms if not in terms of contribution to GDP.

These developments have important implications for the cross-class settlement, which has become more fragile, and for the sectoral interests that underpin it, which have become more diverse. The small firm/large firm, sheltered sector/exposed sector divisions that have always been important (and destabilizing) in MMEs such as Italy and Spain are now becoming an increasingly important feature of the CMEs such as Germany as well. While this does not necessarily mean the demise of CME-type institutional complementarities, it does mean that the nature of the coordinated economy has become more contested and its reaffirmation and renegotiation less amenable to consensus-based solutions as 'insider–outsider' divisions grow (Hall, this volume; Rueda 2005). It also means, as Hassel effectively shows, that there is no necessary complementary link between a CME production system and (more equal) distributive outcomes.

The structure of private interests is important for the policy options that can be implemented by the state, especially when the role of the state is pervasive. Thus, while in MMEs the state is much more directly involved in leading responses to exogenous forces for change than in CMEs (cf. Levy 2005), its actions are conditioned by its ability to coordinate decisions with interests such as business and labour. When those other actors have been fragmented and weakened, governments have been able to introduce liberal market reforms. But responses requiring coordination have been much more difficult. In contrast, when other interests have been stronger, the opposite pattern has been seen. Thus, for instance, in employment policy, Spain has been able to go further than Italy in following an LME-type policy of competing via a low cost, flexible labour force, but has found it difficult to engage in coordinated, active labour market policies (ALMPs) because employers and unions are too fragmented (Molina and Rhodes, this volume). In contrast, faced with more cohesive unions, Italian governments have been obliged to move forwards via concertation, resulting in a slower process of labour market liberalization than in Spain and larger-scale state funding for retrenchment.

Our discussion in Section 1.3 claimed that the role of the state vis-à-vis business coordination is important, though to varying degrees, in the different forms of capitalism that we identify. As our 2×2 matrix demonstrated, that role will differ in terms of the relationship between strategic and arm's-length state intervention, and atomized or organized business and labour interests. These distinctions and their evolution over time, in the transition from conventional public control and ownership through to the regulation of privatized companies, are illustrated in this volume (see Thatcher) by the transformation of Europe's public utilities. An arm's-length state and atomized business and labour organizations, as in the UK, produce weak networks and facilitate market competition. Thus, having introduced competition and privatization much earlier than elsewhere in the EU, the UK saw EU liberalization as an opportunity to export its own market model.

But marketization elsewhere has been heavily conditioned by existing state–business relations. When links between policymakers and national suppliers are traditionally strong, as in France, they can aid a state-led form of privatization and re-regulation. Thus, while French policymakers may have used EU competition regulations to justify domestic reforms desired for non-EU reasons, long-established state–business networks allowed a retention of domestic market control, the building of international champions and an exploitation of expansion opportunities in other liberalized EU markets. But when business organization (in this case horizontal supplier networks) is stronger, and the role of the state is less central, as in Germany, industry-led strategies have resulted. There, privatization and liberalization have been governed by networks linking industry associations, government, and suppliers that have limited the independence in practice of new regulatory agencies (Coen and Héritier 2005).

The transition countries of Central and Eastern Europe provide fascinating laboratory cases of how the state and business interact to create different forms of economic coordination. These countries have all witnessed extensive institutional and political rupture over the last decade or so from which two broadly different types of coordination have emerged—one more market-oriented and LME-like, the other a form of MME, but one in which a powerful though atomized business class dominates and the state is weak. If the old nomenclature is defeated, and patchwork forms of economic control can be established through an alliance between an organized, technocrat-led state and a mixture of foreign and domestic firms, then 'liberal dependent' systems, with open economic relations and high levels of FDI result, as in the Czech Republic, Hungary, and Poland (King, this volume). Trade unions are weak, but the state provides a range of public goods (pensions and other social transfers) for the economy and has modest steering capacity. In contrast, if the nomenclature retains power, as in Russia, Ukraine, or Romania, it uses its offices to acquire private property, giving rise to 'patrimonial' systems in which economic control (coordination would be much too strong a term) is exercised by the nomenclature and domestic producers through patron–client ownership networks. Foreign direct ownership is weak, and the state is also weak and unable to provide adequate public goods.

Complementarities and coordination as understood in VoC theory cannot be said to exist in these countries (whereas 'a-complementarities' abound). As Mykhnenko shows in his chapter on Poland and Ukraine, these economies are currently characterized by rather unstable and largely incoherent mixes of labour market institutions, financial intermediation, and corporate governance. Their evolutionary trajectories are as yet unclear, even if the former bears some resemblance to a Mediterranean MME, and the latter to a continental CME, though with neither its coherence of governance nor its productive interplay of complementarities. But some clearer and more coherent forms of incipient coordination have emerged in other, smaller transition economies. These have taken on a CME-type character in Slovenia but are closer to the LME archetype in the Baltic states, as revealed in their contrasting institutional characteristics, including levels of unionization, the presence or not of works councils and the relative strength of business organizations (see Feldmann, this volume). Each had different institutional legacies: while Slovenia had proto-coordinating institutions such as works councils and horizontal ties between companies, Estonia was highly embedded in the USSR's central planning structure. They also made different policy choices in transition based on different views towards national autonomy. Slovenia, with its stronger sense of national destiny, sold its enterprises to managers and workers, introduced legally supported chambers of commerce and used flexible monetary policy. But Estonia privatized state-owned enterprises (SOEs) to overseas buyers and introduced a non-accommodating monetary policy.

Thus, overall, and in the face of strong exogenous pressures, major institutional reforms have been undertaken in all of Europe's capitalist varieties. But change is particularly arduous in the CMEs and MMEs: it involves visible (re)distributive decisions which question the cross-class settlements that underpin coordination mechanisms, and requires the assent of powerful actors with key positions in those arrangements.

1.5. CONCLUSIONS

There is little doubt that VoC has revolutionized the study of contemporary political economy. Core VoC concepts, such as comparative institutional advantage and complementarities, the (soft) rationalist method that underpinned it, the attention to institutions as building blocks for coordination, and the CME–LME typology that resulted, have become the stock in trade of political economists everywhere, either used approvingly for building research agendas or critically as a foil for developing alternative approaches. The extraordinary range of critiques and debates of the VoC framework is perhaps the best indication of its impact on the field. Even though we have argued that many of those criticisms are unwarranted, many others raise important issues of analysis and logic in VoC, and have led us in this introduction to reconsider some of its basic tenets.

As we have tried to show, an extended VoC framework offers several ways of addressing these critiques. Three avenues of research in particular appear to be promising to us and have underpinned our argument above. The first is to consider the origins of different forms of coordination and different models of capitalism. The political–economic laboratory opened up in Central Europe and a brief comparison of some core European countries suggested that elite networks played a critical role in determining the type of coordination that emerged. The second introduced a more dynamic interpretation of VoC by examining the cross-class coalitions that underpin the different modes of coordination. Finally, we explored the nature of the state and suggested that its relative absence in the original iterations of VoC theory was more related to its heuristic emphasis on CMEs and LMEs and less to intrinsic deficiencies in the framework. We then tied these insights to the broad empirical themes of this volume and showed how they helped us shed new light on the process of political–economic adjustment in Europe.

Our general verdict is that VoC provides a remarkably flexible framework for analysis which, in both its more and less orthodox versions, allows for the development of a highly innovative research agenda. Drawing on both the chapters in this volume and on broader debates, we have demonstrated that VoC can accommodate relatively easily the most important critiques levelled against it. The framework can be extended to incorporate cases that fall outside the standard CME–LME typology without losing the analytical sharpness that came with the original Hall–Soskice formulation. Focusing on cross-class coalitions allows us to explore how coordination is sustained but also how it can be threatened, demonstrating that models of capitalism are not simply class compromises, as Amable (2003) argues, but are as much the products of struggles within as between classes. And the state clearly matters, but in different ways in different models of capitalism. LMEs and CMEs share an arm's-length state–economy relationship, while in other types of capitalism the state is either a central coordinating mechanism (as in France) or compensates for weaknesses in the organization of capital and labour (as in Italy).

As a result of these conceptual extensions, a dynamic picture of capitalism emerges which can take account of change and the political–economic dynamics underpinning change, while keeping us aware of the continuities in the frameworks and in the strategies of the central actors in the different models. The interaction between the role of the state, shifting cross-class coalitions, and the ability of the latter to dominate political–economic agendas may be especially fruitful in analysing changes in modes of coordination. For as long as large manufacturing firms in the export sectors (and their workers) dominate these class agendas—a function of their high degree of collective organization and interest definition—national economies are likely to continue to follow existing patterns. However, when new cross-class coalitions emerge, perhaps furthered or instrumentalized by the state, and if these coalitions come to dominate domestic agendas, modes of coordination may shift.

If we place the analyses in this volume alongside others found in a burgeoning literature that the VoC framework has inspired, we can begin to grasp its power. In recent years, the framework has been usefully extended to include such diverse areas as gender politics (McCall and Orloff 2005b), emerging models of capitalism in Central Europe (King, Feldmann, and Mykhnenko, in this volume; Bohle and Greskovits 2004; Innes 2005), links between macroeconomic frameworks and microeconomic adjustment (Hancké and Rhodes 2005; Carlin and Soskice 2006; Soskice; Hancké and Herrmann, both in this volume), electoral politics (Iversen and Soskice 2006b), and the political economy of liberalization and privatization in OECD countries (Thatcher 2004b). A very rich harvest indeed, and one which has significantly enriched our understanding of the world. If only ten years ago, we thought that we probably knew less than ten years earlier,[1] we can now say with certainty that we currently know more, and that VoC helped us get there.

Ultimately, however, an analytical framework such as VoC is only as good as its ability to make sense of what is going on in the world around us. And that world is changing quickly. We have tried to show that VoC is a useful tool to make sense of many of these changes, but others may disagree. We can therefore only emphasize the closing words of Hall and Soskice in their introduction to VoC (2001b: 68). They claimed, and the essays in this collection along with many others prove, that their volume was not an end point but a start—an invitation to a 'fruitful interchange among scholars interested in many kinds of issues in economics, industrial relations, social policymaking, political science, business, and the law'. This book, we hope, will become part of that ongoing discussion.

NOTE

1. The words in the text are John Zysman's, who echoed and inverted the phrase of Bob Dylan's 'My Back Pages'—'but I was so much older then, I'm younger than that now'—at one of the founding conferences of the project that led to VoC.

2

The Evolution of Varieties of Capitalism in Europe

Peter A. Hall

We live in an era when processes of globalization and liberalization are inspiring changes in the political economy extensive enough to lead some analysts to question whether it still makes sense to speak of distinctive types of capitalism. Some argue that CMEs are converging on liberal models (Lane 2004; Thatcher 2005). Others believe that most political economies are becoming 'hybrids' (Jackson 2005). As economic performance deteriorates in economies that once did well, while former laggards advance, some question whether there is still more than one route to economic success. Is the magnitude of challenge and change today rendering a 'varieties-of-capitalism' (VoC) approach to comparative political economy obsolete?

If one fixates on the changes currently taking place in Europe, an affirmative answer to this question may seem appropriate. Institutional change is altering contemporary VoC. Measured against a static conception of how national institutions once differed, changes in regulatory regimes and institutional practices may seem to be rendering all political economies similar. From this observation, it is but a short step to the conclusion that national political economies diverge only marginally from some 'best practice' to which all are destined to converge and thus there is little value in construing political economies as distinctive VoC.

This chapter advances a different view. It argues that cross-national divergence in institutional practices and patterns of economic activity of the sort emphasized by VoC approaches persists over time, and that those approaches are important for understanding change in the political economy because they direct our attention to the ways in which the institutional structures of the political economy condition it. I argue that the institutional structures constitutive of distinctive VoC have influential effects, not only on the actions of firms and governments, but on the response of political economies to socio-economic challenges. While never fully determining that response, these structures and the strategies they engender at the firm level tend to push political economies along distinctive adjustment paths. This perspective generates a dynamic conception of VoC that sees them, not as a set of institutional differences fixed over time, but as bundles of institutionalized practices that evolve along distinctive trajectories. Seen from this angle, institutional change of the magnitude that attracts attention today is not an uncommon occurrence or a sign that VoC are dissolving, but a continuous feature of VoC.

This perspective has implications for the formulations of Hall and Soskice (2001) that associate distinctive VoC with underlying modes of coordination. On the one hand, it explains why basic patterns of coordination in the economy often persist through periods of institutional change. As institutions that support the efforts of firms to manage some of their endeavours through strategic or market coordination shift, firms often find alternative sources of institutional support for such coordination, and the advantages they derive from distinctive modes of coordination give them incentives to do so. Institutional change can relax the tightness of coordination or shift its equilibria without eliminating strategic or market coordination altogether. In some cases, such loosening is instrumental for conserving capacities for strategic coordination in various spheres of the political economy.

On the other hand, this analysis extends the perspective elaborated in Hall and Soskice (2001). Into an analysis focused largely on national economic performance, it incorporates greater concern for the distributive effects of institutions and political problems associated with them. I observe that the institutional reforms undertaken by governments are often inspired by distributive conflict, and, building on the point that social policy is a crucial adjunct to coordination, I integrate an appreciation for variation across welfare states into a VoC analysis. Second, by comparing institutional change in several countries over time, I attempt to identify the circumstances under which institutional change that radically alters the modes of coordination used by firms is adopted. Third, into an analysis focused largely on the institutions of the domestic economy, I integrate international institutions in order to explore some ways in which the effectiveness of domestic institutions can be affected by how they interact with international institutions. Although this extension does not contradict the argument of Hall and Soskice (2001) that there is more than one path to economic success, it helps explain some of the variations in economic performance displayed over time by distinctive VoC.

My starting point is the premise that, if we are to appreciate the import of institutional change in Europe today, we have to put contemporary developments into historical perspective. Accordingly, this essay considers institutional developments in the wake of successive waves of socio-economic challenges. To structure the analysis, I consider the response to challenges occurring in three periods: from the late 1940s to early 1960s, from the late 1960s to the early 1980s, and in the 1990s and early 2000s.[1] I focus on Britain, France, Germany, and Sweden, chosen because their political economies display much of the institutional variation relevant to contemporary typologies of capitalism.

I begin by proposing a stylized conception of what the institutions of the political economy do that integrates the formulations of Hall and Soskice (2001) with standard understandings of the welfare state. This formulation identifies three types of problems with which firms and governments must cope. Using it, I identify the challenges facing these four nations at each of the three periods and chart the principal changes to policy regimes and institutional practices taken in response to them. Without attempting a full explanation, I try to show how these responses are conditioned by existing institutional structures and cumulate into a set of adjustment trajectories with characteristic economic effects.

For some of the issues, this analysis is suggestive rather than dispositive. My principal goal is to put the institutional changes occurring today into historical perspective. This reveals that institutional change in the political economy is not a new phenomenon and VoC are best seen, not as a set of stable institutional models, but as a set of institutionally conditioned adjustment trajectories displaying continuous processes of adaptation. Indeed, some of the features most associated with contemporary models of capitalism appeared in the 1970s rather than the 1950s. However, similar socio-economic challenges rarely called forth identical national responses. Over six decades, the challenges have not swept away important cross-national national differences in the organization of economic activity.

2.1. THE CORE PROBLEMATIC

The starting point for my inquiry is Eichengreen's pioneering analysis (1996) of post-war growth. He locates its roots in the confluence of international institutions that allowed an expansion of trade to feed aggregate demand and domestic institutions that restrained wages enough to allow investment to grow in tandem with that demand. These institutions resolved time inconsistency problems that might have prevented nations from realizing such high levels of investment and growth.

The regulation-school economists advance an analogous argument, suggesting that Fordist production regimes were underpinned by collective bargaining institutions and Keynesian economic regimes that sustained adequate levels of domestic demand and apportioned productivity gains between wages and profits (Boyer 1990). In each case, the precondition for prosperity was an industrial economy that could increase productivity by moving labour out of agriculture into industry (Crafts and Toniolo 1996).

From Eichengreen's analysis, I take the insight that the effectiveness of the institutions of a domestic political economy depends on the international institutions with which they are paired. From the regulation school, I take the point that their effectiveness depends as well on their fit with production regimes. Both perspectives imply that the institutions of the political economy play two types of roles. They perform a coordinating role aimed at the contracting and time inconsistency problems that stand in the way of gains from exchange, and they resolve distributional conflict about who is to receive the fruits of economic growth. Their tasks are political as well as economic.

To sharpen this perspective, I suggest that the institutions of the political economy address three types of problems. The first is the problem of ensuring that wages increase at rates moderate enough to allow profits enabling firms to raise adequate levels of investment, yet high enough to sustain levels of demand consistent with growth. The associated distributive issue is how to allocate economic returns between capital and labour with a minimum of industrial conflict. I call this the wage problem.

The second problem is one of securing levels of employment high enough to ensure national prosperity, while providing levels of compensation to those without work high enough to secure social peace.[2] There is a loose trade-off here because payments to those not employed affect the terms on which they will seek work. The problem has a high political profile because it bears on the distribution of work and social benefits. It also turns on the resolution of the first problem because employment varies with levels of real wages and aggregate demand.[3] I call this the work problem.

I term the third issue the problem of securing total factor productivity. Eichengreen (1996) treats economic growth primarily as a matter of ensuring adequate amounts of capital investment. As the Harrod–Domar models tell us, growth also requires adequate inputs of qualified labour. However, economic growth is not simply a matter of securing capital and labour. It also depends on the efficiency with which they are deployed. In many models that is treated as a simple function of the level of technology. But there is mounting evidence that institutions also affect the efficiency with which labour and capital are deployed.[4] The problem is to specify just how the institutions of the political economy affect that efficiency.

Hall and Soskice (2001) provide terms for addressing this issue. Building on relational theories of the firm, they argue that the efficiency with which labour and capital are utilized depends on how well firms coordinate with other actors to secure skills, technology, finance, and the engagement of their employees. They identify two ways of coordinating such endeavours, based on market competition and strategic interaction. The implication is that firms utilize resources more efficiently where market competition is sharper or where high-equilibrium outcomes can be reached via strategic coordination.[5] The institutions of the political economy affect these outcomes by modulating the intensity of market competition and providing support crucial for strategic coordination. In short, by conditioning the ways in which firms coordinate their endeavours, national institutions enhance or erode the total factor productivity of the economy. The problem of total factor productivity entails developing sets of national institutions that provide appropriate levels of support for market or strategic coordination at the firm level.

Of course, this is a stylized portrait. Firms and policymakers in post-war Europe faced many other dilemmas. But there is value in focusing on the problems of wages, work, and total factor productivity. Few issues are more consequential for national well-being, and all have loomed large on the political agendas of post-war Europe.[6]

2.2. THE POST-WAR DEVELOPMENT OF VARIETIES OF CAPITALISM

In the fifteen years after 1945, each of the European nations developed distinctive solutions to these three problems. Those were built on institutional legacies with roots in the timing and character of industrialization, but the prospect of intense international competition following a war that was destructive in institutional as well as physical terms inspired a wave of institution building. It is beyond the scope of this chapter to describe how these institutional regimes were constructed.[7] Governments and the political parties that led them played crucial roles, as did producer groups pressing for certain types of arrangements. Firms also contributed to institutional reconstruction, as they reconfigured production regimes to meet the challenges of post-war competition and sought new avenues of access to technology, skills, and finance.

Although I emphasize the import of post-war institutions for the three problems associated with economic prosperity, it is important to note that they were built by coalitions of actors with diverse interests.[8] Many were designed to achieve a certain distribution of resources rather than simply to improve economic performance. Ruggie (1982) captures this dimension of the process when he notes that the institutions of post-war Europe embodied specific visions of social purpose. One implication is that the stability of those institutions would rest, not only on their coordinating capacities, but on the continuing viability of those visions.[9]

My principal objective in this section is to show that Britain, France, Germany, and Sweden developed institutions that addressed the wage, work, and productivity problems in distinctive ways. The institutional architects of post-war Europe built VoC as well as engines for growth.

2.2.1. Britain

The institutional solutions that the British adopted to address their post-war economic problems were those of the classic LME described by Hall and Soskice (2001), heavily reliant on competitive market relationships underpinned by formal legal contracting. The wage problem was addressed by measures to regularize collective bargaining between trade unions and employers. However, the British tradition of craft unionism meant that, even when bargains were struck at the sectoral level, firms often had to negotiate several such bargains because more than one union was represented in their workforce, and shop stewards remained powerful in many parts of the economy. As a result, Britain never secured the high levels of wage coordination that Eichengreen associates with post-war European growth. Levels of industrial conflict were relatively high, and rates of investment and growth correspondingly low (see Tables 2.1 and 2.5). At periodic intervals, British governments intervened to secure an incomes policy or to seek industrial relations reform, but the wage question was never fully resolved. It remained high on the political agenda throughout the post-war years (Howell 2005).

The efforts of post-war British governments to address the employment problem turned on two sets of initiatives. One was the construction of a 'liberal' welfare regime, built, as Beveridge recommended, on benefits administered by the state but minimalist in the low replacement rates it provided.[10] Broadly speaking, the motivating idea was to provide work for all, but only minimal support for those who did not work. That regime had important effects on the character of post-war economic development in Britain. It pushed a large portion of the labour force into employment, put little pressure on firms to increase wages, and provided workers with few incentives to develop industry-specific skills (Finegold and Soskice 1988).

The second dimension of the British approach to the work problem was an emphasis on activist macroeconomic policy, based on the principles of John Maynard Keynes. Keynes suggested that governments could secure full employment by responding to recessions with deficit spending to expand

Table 2.1. Comparative economic performance by period

Years	Economic growth			Real wages			Total factor productivity		
	1950–74	1975–85	1986–2004	1950–74	1975–85	1986–2004	1950–74	1975–85	1986–2004
Britain	2.8	1.7	2.7	3.1	0.9	1.9	1.7	1.5	1.4
France	5.0	2.0	2.3	4.7	2.1	1.2	3.1	1.6	1.0
Germany	5.8	1.9	1.9	4.5	1.2	1.7	2.0	1.0	1.3
Sweden	3.7	1.6	2.1	3.4	0.5	2.0	2.0	0.4	1.5

Source: The Conference Board and Groningen Growth and Development Center, Total Economy Database. Germany is West Germany until 1990. Figures are annual average percentage increases for the years indicated in the second row of the table.

consumer demand. Although influential across Europe, his ideas were embraced with most enthusiasm in his own country. Although they were constrained by a tenuous balance-of-payments, successive British governments operated an activist fiscal policy (Hansen 1968; Hall 1989).

The approach of British firms to the problem of total factor productivity was influenced by the institutional inheritance of early industrialization (Kurth 1979). Large firms obtained finance, skills, and technology via the types of competitive market relationships prominent in LMEs. In many cases, they secured finance through short-term bank credits and securities on terms that were sensitive to a firm's current profitability. Although a few sectors sponsored apprenticeship programmes, over the course of the 1950s, companies became increasingly reliant on the general skills provided by a formal educational system. The absence of serious legal limitations on lay-offs discouraged workers from investing in specific skills. Firms secured technology through licensing arrangements or the acquisition of companies with appropriate technology. Firm organization itself was highly hierarchical (Lane 1989).

These features of the institutional environment influenced the productivity strategies of British firms. Some retained long-standing reputations for high-quality production (HQP) based on highly skilled labour. But an industrial relations system prone to conflict limited the cooperation many firms could secure from their employees, and the abundance of general, relative to specific, skills encouraged firms to rely on high volumes of production and low labour costs for competitive advantage (Rubery 1994). Many British firms found it difficult to move up the value chain to compete in HQP niches.[11] As a result, rates of productivity growth lagged those on the continent (see Table 2.1).

2.2.2. Germany

Although their economy was in ruins after the war, the firms and policymakers of West Germany could draw on an institutional inheritance from late industrialization that included strong industry unions, well-developed employers associations, collaborative institutions for skill formation, and a Bismarckian welfare regime. These were soon adapted to the purposes of economic reconstruction. Post-war Germany built a CME that provided firms with substantial institutional support for strategic collaboration (Hall and Soskice 2001) and experienced an 'economic miracle' that saw the size of its economy quadruple over thirty years.

The institutional support Germany developed for strategic coordination is well displayed in the institutions it developed to address the wage problem.

In 1952, the government legislated a controversial system of co-determination that gave workers a powerful voice on the supervisory boards of many large firms and strong works councils. Facing a labour movement powerfully organized at the sectoral level, German employers began to collaborate in sectoral wage negotiations, usually guided by a leading settlement in the metalworking sector and moderated by threats from an independent central bank to retaliate against inflationary increases (Thelen 1991; Hall 1994). Bolstered by a plentiful labour supply and strong desires to rebuild the economy, this system kept wage increases in line with productivity gains throughout the 1950s and 1960s. Over time, however, it also put slow but steady upwards pressure on wages that encouraged firms to invest in high value-added forms of production. In many respects, the German system for wage coordination exemplifies the engine for growth that Eichengreen describes.

Its corollary was a particular approach to the work problem. Faced with the challenge of finding work for ten million refugees from the east, the new Bundesrepublik rebuilt an economy that produced full employment by the early 1960s.[12] However, it did so by focusing investment on an industrial core whose production regimes relied heavily on a male labour force equipped with high levels of industry-specific skills generated by intensive training schemes run collaboratively by employers associations and the trade unions. Pension and unemployment schemes supplying increasingly generous benefits pegged to wages provided young men with the incentives to secure the sector-specific skills that would ensure them high wages (Mares 2004). The result was a system well equipped to channel men into industrial occupations but less good at providing jobs to women or those without specific skills. Built on a male breadwinner model, the system of social benefits assumed that most women would prefer to work at home rather than in paid employment. As a result, once the industrial economy had been reconstructed, further expansion of the labour force was discouraged, and the proportion of the population in employment grew more slowly than in many nations (see Table 2.2). German institutions also encouraged firms to take particular approaches to the total factor productivity problem. Despite the efforts of the Allies to eliminate cartels, Germany's banks soon assumed key roles in industry, as sources of long-term finance and the representatives of investors (Zysman 1983). Powerful employers associations helped German firms form close relationships with other firms to operate vocational training schemes or to secure technology through collaborative ventures. While British firms acquired finance, technology, and skills on competitive markets, German companies relied more heavily on collaborative relationships with other firms rooted in the reputations they built up in dense inter-corporate networks (Streeck 1992).

Table 2.2. Average rates of growth of gross domestic product and employment

	Growth of GDP				Growth in employment			
	UK	France	Germany	Sweden	UK	France	Germany	Sweden
1951–64	2.9	5.0	7.2	3.9	—	—	—	—
1965–74	2.6	4.9	3.9	3.5	0.17	0.92	0.06	0.78
1975–84	1.5	2.1	1.9	1.6	−0.29	0.13	−0.06	0.72
1985–94	2.6	2.2	2.3	1.3	0.65	0.21	0.03	−0.59
1995–2004	2.9	2.3	1.5	2.9	0.99	1.02	0.04	0.70

Source: The Conference Board and Groningen Growth and Development Center, Total Economy Database. Figures are average annual percentage increase for the period.

Regulatory regimes that privileged stakeholders (including creditors, managers, collaborators, and workers) over shareholders reinforced this type of strategic coordination (Casper 2001). Powerful works councils and the two-board supervisory system privileged consensus decision-making. Because these institutions made it difficult for firms to lay-off workers, many began to base their competitive strategies more heavily on quality rather than cost considerations. Rather than move aggressively into new lines of business, many firms found it easier to cultivate a skilled workforce and use it to make continuous improvements to existing product lines and production processes. As a result, by the end of the 1960s, West Germany had the largest industrial economy in Europe. More than half of its workforce was employed in the industrial sector, well compensated, and highly skilled.

2.2.3. Sweden

Neutral during the Second World War, Sweden was well placed to benefit when it ended. During the 1950s, the nation developed a distinctive approach to wage, work, and productivity problems known as the 'Rehn–Meidner' model after its two most prominent exponents. That model was built on three institutional pillars. The first was a system of 'solidaristic' wage-bargaining at peak level between a centralized union movement and employers confederation designed to tie wage agreements to average increases in national productivity.[13] The effect was to narrow wage differentials and force less efficient companies to close down or become more productive. Its second pillar was a set of macroeconomic policies that used restrictive fiscal policy to encourage firms to rationalize, and an accommodating monetary policy to provide low-cost capital for doing so, as well as taxes on uninvested profits to assure workers that wage moderation would be rewarded. The third pillar was a set of active labour market policies designed to facilitate the movement of workers out of less productive firms into more productive ones, by upgrading their skills and supporting the job search (Martin 1979).

These institutions offered a solution to the wage problem that conforms closely to Eichengreen's conception of how such institutions should work. In exchange for wage moderation, workers were given assurances that capital would be invested in productive endeavours. The work problem was addressed by active labour market policies designed to improve the skills of the work-force and find jobs for the unemployed. In keeping with the emphasis on moving people into work, the duration of unemployment benefits was lim-ited to six months. In order to encourage workers to acquire skills, however, benefit rates were tied to previous wages, as were retirement benefits from 1960.

These institutions encouraged firms to take approaches to the problem of total factor productivity characteristic of a CME. Steady wage pressure forced firms to seek continuous improvements to products and production processes, and it encouraged them to cultivate the high-skill levels that make such innovation feasible. Social benefits tied to wages encouraged workers to invest in such skills. Extensive cross-shareholdings that protected companies from hostile takeovers allowed them to privilege investment over profitability, and strong employers associations promoted the close ties among firms that facilitate collaborative research and development.

2.2.4. France

At the end of the war, the leaders of France were eager to declare a military victory but anxious about the prospect of economic defeat in a more open world economy. A third of the nation's labour force was still employed in agri-culture, and many of its firms were too small to compete on the world stage. Accordingly, French officials decided to break with the past and modernize the economy from above, seeking support wherever they could among the fractious parties of the Fourth Republic.

Industrial relations were regularized by laws that gave unions legal standing and mandated collective bargaining at the sectoral level, but officials hesitated to strengthen a labour movement dominated by a communist union. Thus, the state assumed a leading role in wage coordination. It set a minimum wage to which the wages of 40 per cent of employees were ultimately linked and assumed the statutory authority to impose wage agreements negotiated with some unions on entire sectors. By the 1960s, almost 80 per cent of employees were covered by such agreements.

The French approach to the work problem had several dimensions. A programme of aggressive agricultural modernization pushed labour into the industrial sector. But support for those who could not find work increased only gradually. Old-age pensions were introduced after the war, but unemployment insurance remained a patchwork quilt of benefits administered by trade unions and employers associations, tied closely to employment status, and financed from social charges on employers and employees. Although the government funded day care facilities, many women remained outside the workforce. Like Germany, France retained a 'continental' welfare state (Esping-Andersen 1990).

The approach French officials took to the problem of total factor productivity was more aggressive. In 1947, they established a system of indicative economic planning bolstered by tripartite 'modernization commissions' that chanelled funds into priority sectors with the support of a financial system dominated by state-owned banks. By the 1960s, the government was heavily subsidizing firms designated 'national champions' (Zysman 1977, 1983; Hall 1986). Para-public institutions were set up to promote research and development (Ziegler 1997). As a result, large French firms modernized quickly, but depended heavily on the state for access to finance, technology, and skills. A cohesive set of social networks revolving around the *grandes écoles* and *grands corps* linked senior executive closely to civil servants (Suleiman 1979). Among large firms in post-war France, there was a good deal of strategic coordination orchestrated by the state. Relations inside the firm, however, were slower to change. Companies responded to a fractious labour movement by clinging to rigid job classifications and steep managerial hierarchies that allowed firms to operate mass production successfully but limited the autonomy of workers and the scope for incremental innovation in production processes (Crozier 1968; Maurice, Sellier, and Silvestre 1986). There was a sharp division between middle managers drawn from the ranks of the firm itself and senior managers, who were often parachuted in from the outside world of public affairs.

2.2.5. Comparative Perspectives on Institution-Building

During the 1950s and 1960s, Britain, France, Germany, and Sweden developed institutional solutions to wage, work, and productivity problems successful enough to allow these countries to grow more rapidly than they ever had before. Although Eichengreen stresses the institutions these nations had in common, there were striking differences in the institutions each developed to address similar economic problems. By 1965, Western Europe had distinctive and familiar VoC.

Some of those differences are well described by the distinctions Hall and Soskice (2001) draw between LMEs and CMEs. In Britain, firms secured access to outside finance, skills, and technology primarily via competitive markets. Although wage bargaining was often collective, it was not strategically coordinated across the economy. By contrast, strategic coordination was more prominent on the continent. However, there was substantial variation in how it was achieved. In France, the state played a central role in the coordination of industrial relations, corporate governance, and technological development. In Germany, employers associations and trade unions coordinated wage-setting and vocational training at the sectoral level, while wage-setting was coordinated at the peak level in Sweden where the state also bore more responsibility for vocational training. Influential banks and networks in both nations built on cross-shareholding played major roles in the allocation of capital, and many firms acquired technology through collaboration with other firms.

It is important to note that national differences extended all the way down to corporate strategies and production regimes. Firm strategies and national institutions tend to adjust to one another over time. By making some types of strategies easier and others more difficult to pursue, the macro institutions of the political economy tend to push firms in distinctive directions.[14] Systems of wage coordination that raised wage floors in Sweden and Germany, for instance, pushed their firms towards diversified quality production (DQP) (Streeck 1991). Limited institutional support for the development of industry-specific skills encouraged many firms in France and Britain to focus on Fordist modes of production.

As this suggests, there was no 'big bang' here. These VoC were constructed via incremental processes, marked by experimentation by firms and governments, the layering of institutions on top of one another, and gradual mutual adjustment of strategies to institutions (Thelen 2004; Streeck and Thelen 2005). Some of the features later associated with distinctive welfare states and national patterns of economic activity developed only gradually. In 1960, for instance, the European country with the highest proportion of the adult population in employment was Germany, and the one with the lowest proportion of women in employment was Sweden (Crouch 1999: 58).

2.3. THE RESPONSE TO CHALLENGES IN THE LATE 1960s AND 1970s

How do VoC respond to economic challenges? Do powerful economic shocks erase the institutional differences between them? As I have noted, many scholars are asking those questions today. One way to answer them is to examine the response of political economies to previous challenges. For that purpose, the late 1960s and 1970s provide a natural experiment, since that was an era when the European political economies came under serious strain.

This period is revealing about the sources of the challenges that put political economies under pressure. Some analysts treat such challenges as exogenous shocks arising, for instance, from developments in the international economy (cf. Frieden and Rogoswki 1996). However, the history of this period suggests that some of the most profound challenges facing political economies are endogenous by-products of existing institutions or the patterns of economic development they promote. By the end of the 1960s, three kinds of developments were putting serious pressure on the institutions of the European political economies. They were rooted in (*a*) an important change in international regimes, (*b*) structural developments in the economy, and (*c*) unintended effects flowing from the operation of existing institutions.

Eichengreen's observation (1996) that the effectiveness of domestic institutions depends on the character of international regimes was confirmed by the collapse of the Bretton Woods exchange-rate regime in 1970. Its exchange-rate anchor had limited wage demands and inflationary pressures in the European economies. It allowed some countries, such as Germany, to maintain undervalued exchange rates to foster export-led growth and others, such as France, to devalue in an orderly way when distributive conflict that domestic institutions could not resolve spilled over into inflation, thereby offsetting the impact of wage increases on the nation's international competitiveness. In such ways, the Bretton Woods regime provided crucial support for the domestic institutions regulating distributive conflict. The move to a regime of floating rates in 1971 made such conflict more difficult to contain, thereby increasing the likelihood that it would spill over into inflation.[15]

Structural economic developments intensified distributive pressure. By the end of the 1960s, the movement of West European labour out of agriculture into industry was largely at an end. As a result, productivity began to increase more slowly (Blanchard and Wolfers 2000).[16] This meant that the 'productivity increment' available for distribution among capital, labour, and the state began to decline, thereby intensifying the challenges facing the institutions developed to regulate conflict about the distribution of this increment, such as those in the arena of collective bargaining.

The patterns of economic development to which the institutions of the European political economy contributed also began to undermine them. As I have noted, most of the European countries developed collective bargaining institutions that sustained relatively powerful trade unions. By the middle of the 1960s, these nations had also secured high levels of employment that strengthened the trade unions further. As a result, the unions were able to increase the share of value-added going to labour relative to the share going to capital, ultimately cutting into the profits that inspired investment (Armstrong, Glyn, and Harrison 1991). Prosperity also began to shift cultural values in ways that brought more women into the labour force and improved national productive capacity but intensified the problem of finding employment for a larger labour force (Inglehart 1990).

By the end of the 1960s, these developments were resulting in stagflation, the pernicious combination of rising rates of inflation and unemployment. Inflation rose as distributive conflict in the industrial arena increased and gave rise to inflationary wage settlements, unrestrained by an exchange-rate anchor (see Table 2.5). Unemployment increased as more people sought work in a context where profits had been eroded enough to depress investment. That erosion was linked both to more assertive trade unions and to the difficulties of apportioning a lower productivity increment among profits, wages, and the social wage administered by the state. However, these problems were greatly intensified by rapid increases in the price of oil in 1973–4 and 1979–80 that drove rates of inflation up and rates of growth down. The wage, work, and productivity problems of Britain, France, Sweden, and Germany intensified. How did their institutions shift in response to these challenges?

2.3.1. Britain

The British political economy was ill-suited to cope with increasing rates of inflation in the late 1960s and the intense distributive conflict behind them because it had never developed institutions for effective wage coordination. As a result, rates of inflation rose steadily to peak briefly at 23 per cent in the spring of 1975 even though unemployment was also rising. Not surprisingly, much of the British response focused on efforts to improve wage coordination. In theory at least, this might have been a period in which Britain developed more effective institutions for strategic wage coordination of the sort visible in CMEs on the continent. Successive governments took steps in this direction, beginning with the ill-fated In Place of Strife proposals of the late 1960s and culminating in the Social Contract negotiated between the unions and 1974–9 Labour government (Crouch 1977).

The failure of these efforts is an indication of how difficult it is to transform an LME into a CME (see Wood 2001).[17] The structure of the British labour movement was a major impediment. Although the Social Contract brought down rates of inflation, by narrowing wage differentials it fuelled pressures in the fissiparous union movement for their restoration that ultimately precipitated a wave of industrial conflict during the 1979 'winter of discontent'. The weakness of British employers associations made the task more difficult. They had little to offer the government in the way of support. In the end, these efforts to control inflation by regulating wages from Westminster strained the reservoir of legitimacy of the British state, and the 1970s saw a political reaction against state-led efforts to intervene in the economy.

The beneficiary of that reaction was Margaret Thatcher who came to power in 1979 on a platform that promised to roll back state intervention in the economy. Under her leadership, a series of Conservative governments responded to the economic crisis by sharpening the intensity of competition in Britain's LME. They broke the power of the unions, moved away from Keynesian demand management, deregulated markets, privatized the national enterprises, and shifted Britain's social policy regimes so as to force the able-bodied even more aggressively into employment (Riddell 1991). After experiments with more forceful state intervention in the late 1960s and 1970s, Britain ultimately responded to the challenges of the period by reinforcing the institutions of its LME.

2.3.2. France

The response of France to the socio-economic challenges of the 1970s was, by contrast, transformational. As in Britain, the initial inclinaton of French governments was to treat the economic downturn of the 1970s as a temporary recession, rather than a structural change, and to address it with traditional policy instruments. A series of governments under President Valéry Giscard d'Estaing increased state aid to industry and expanded social programmes for those without employment (Berger 1985). The Socialist government elected in 1981 under President François Mitterrand initially deepened the dirigiste response, raising the minimum wage to reflate the economy and increasing subsidies to industry on the premise that public investment could be used to replace private investment, which had been stagnant since 1974.

If these measures had been successful, the French model might not have changed, but they failed to restore rates of growth or investment, and growing public sector deficits put downwards pressure on the franc, forcing Mitterrand to choose, in the spring of 1983, between his dirigiste strategy and his commitment to the European monetary system, established in 1979 to stabilize exchange rates in Europe. Disillusioned with the fruits of his strategy, Mitterrand abandoned it in favour of an effort to revive the French economy by promoting more open European markets, a goal that was to be enshrined in the Single Europe Act 1986.

The question of the day was how to alter the institutions and regulatory regimes of the French political economy so as to ensure it prospered on those markets. About this, there was a lively debate. Some argued for the value of moving towards the CME model exemplified by Germany (Albert 1980; Maurice, Sellier, and Silvestre 1996). Its egalitarianism and success in high value-added sectors were attractive to many in France. But the effectiveness of the German model rested on the presence of powerful employers associations and trade unions. Not only would those have been difficult to create in France, where the labour movement was deeply divided, but some politicians had qualms about trying to strengthen a labour movement that had been a thorn in the side of many governments and in which a communist trade union was prominent. As a result, the efforts of the government to give the unions a greater role in firm-level bargaining, with the Auroux laws of 1982, and to promote regional cooperation between business and labour were desultory at best (Howell 1992; Culpepper 2003).

Beginning in 1983, a series of governments opted for regulatory changes that would put firms under more intense competitive pressure and enhance the extent to which they depended on markets to coordinate their endeavours. Two factors made this a viable strategy. One was the special role of the state in the economy. Up to this point, strategic coordination had been a prominent feature of the French economy, but much of that coordination had been orchestrated by the state. Therefore, the government could shift the ways in which firms coordinated their endeavours by reducing its own coordinating role. The other relevant factor was the industrial weakness of the union movement. Although a potent force in politics, the French trade unions were poorly organized in the industrial arena and weakened by the unemployment of the 1980s. As a consequence, they could offer little resistance to the shifts in firm strategy that more intense market competition dictated Goyer (2006*a*).

Although policy moved in fits and starts, seen from afar, the French governments of the 1980s pursued what might be described as a new kind of modernization strategy. During the 1950s and 1960s, the French state had modernized the economy from above through active state intervention (Hall 1986). In the 1980s, by contrast, the state put pressure on firms from below— enforcing modernization by exposing them to increasingly intense market competition. Policymakers sold off the state's holdings in banking and industry and encouraged companies to seek finance on international markets. They expanded the Paris Stock Exchange, welcomed foreign investors, and fostered a competitive market for corporate control. Many markets were deregulated, industrial subsidies reduced, and French firms were forced to compete in a new 'single European market' initially under a high exchange rate that put them at a competitive disadvantage. Although the state retained the right to fix minimum wages and to impose wage agreements across sectors, it used these powers sparingly to encourage firm-level bargaining instead (Lallement 2006).

The result was a revolution in corporate practices. Renault laid off half its workforce in the space of five years (Hancké 2002). By the end of the 1990s, almost 40 per cent of the shares in the leading French firms of the CAC40 were in the hands of foreign investors. Although close ties between corporate executives, often forged during an elite education, continue to give French companies capacities to coordinate with each other that their British counterparts do not always enjoy, markets have assumed a more important role in the coordination of firm endeavours. In important respects, France moved towards the practices of an LME.

Where it continued to diverge from those practices, however, was in its approach to the work problem. In contrast to the British governments of the 1980s that reduced employment protection and tightened eligibility for social benefits, the French governments of the 1980s initially responded to the unemployment of the 1970s and 1980s by expanding early retirement programmes, so as to reduce the numbers seeking work. The effect was to hold down the size of the workforce, even though women were entering it in increasing numbers. The proportion of men over 50 years of age in the workforce declined from 51 per cent in 1975 to 36 per cent by 1990. French social benefits became increasingly generous, and governments that had once lavished subsidies on industry now spent equivalent sums to subsidize training schemes and the social charges of employers who took on young or unemployed workers. By 1986, the French state was spending 4 per cent of gross domestic product (GDP) on such schemes.

From the perspective of conventional liberal theory, which expects more intense market competition to be accompanied by meager social benefits, the result is a remarkable dualism. In response to a more open European economy, France made its markets more competitive and increased its levels of social protection at the same time. By 1990, its social spending almost reached Swedish levels (see Figure 2.1). Moreover, the posture of the state had undergone a quiet reversal. In 1960, the French state provided minimal social benefits but lavished subsidies on protected industrial firms. By 1990, it had given up on industrial protection in favour of social protection.

2.3.3. Sweden

Like its neighbours, the Swedish political economy was also buffeted by the economic waves of the late 1960s and 1970s. In the wake of intense distributive

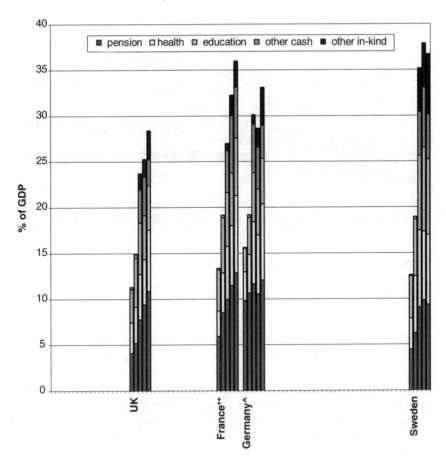

Figure 2.1. Gross size and composition of welfare states (FY 1960, 1970, 1980, 1990, and 2001)

Source: OECD and Irwin Garfinkel, Lee Rainwater, and Timothy Smeeding. 2007. *The American Welfare State: Laggard or Leader?* New York: Russell Sage Foundation, chapter 4.

** 1960 education estimated by 1975 data; 1970 education estimated by 1975 data.

^ Data for 1960–90 are from Western Germany; data for 2001 are from the unified Federal Republic of Germany.

conflict, important modifications were made to its institutions addressing the work and wage problems.

In Sweden, the work problem became an important concern in the second half of the 1960s, as growing numbers of women began to seek paid employment. In a CME that relies heavily on highly skilled labour, female employment poses a special problem because women are more likely than men to take time out from work for childrearing. As a result, they have fewer incentives to

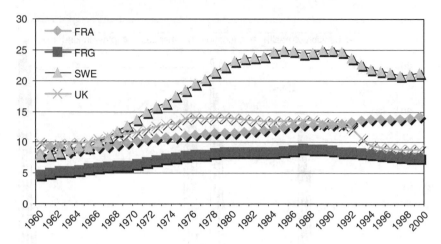

Figure 2.2. Government employment as a percentage of working age population 1960–2000

Source: Huber and Stephens data-set, Luxembourg Income Studies, compiled by Thomas Cusack.

acquire skills that might be used for shorter periods or become outdated when they are not in work, and firms that depend on a committed labour force are less likely to invest in providing women with those skills (Estévez-Abe et al. 2001). After considerable debate, the Swedish government responded to this problem by increasing the number of jobs in the public sector and expanding a public day care system that made it easier for women to work. The number of employees in the Swedish public sector doubled between 1965 and 1980, and 500,000 of the 700,000 new jobs went to women, who served as providers of public health care, day care, education, and medical services (see Figure 2.2). By 1980, 72 per cent of adult Swedish women were working, compared to 55 per cent of British women (Benner and Vad 2000).

This is when the Swedish welfare state acquired the distinctive character so often associated with it today, namely as one that provides exceptionally high levels of public services based on high levels of female employment (Esping-Andersen 1990). There is nothing primordial about this type of welfare state. As late as 1970, social spending in Sweden was actually lower than it was in France and Germany (see Figure 2.2).

However, this shift in the approach to the work problem put further strain on the institutions Sweden had developed for resolving the wage problem. As employment in the public sector grew, the Swedish union confederation saw an increasing proportion of its members drawn from the non-traded sector, where concerns about maintaining internationally competitive wage levels were not as intense as they were among workers and employers in the traded sectors of the economy. Partly as a result, wage levels began to increase (and wage differentials began to decrease) to the point that firms in the large traded sector began to worry about whether they could maintain their competitiveness.

These pressures were exacerbated by the boom and bust years of the 1970s that generated unexpected profits in the first half of the decade for which unions sought recompense in the second half, just as a global recession hit the economy. The government's response to recession worsened the problem. By increasing industrial subsidies and relaxing fiscal policy in the hope of reflating the economy, the government violated the dictates of the Rehn–Meidner model that called for austere fiscal policy in order to discipline wage bargainers. As wage rates increased faster than the rate of productivity in the second half of the 1970s, unit labour costs soared and many smaller firms were forced out of business.[18] The government responded by intervening more actively in wage negotiations, offering tax incentives in exchange for wage moderation and ultimately legislating an incomes policy. When these measures failed, it devalued the exchange rate to offset the impact of wage increases on the traded sector. More active government intervention in wage bargaining was a feature of the response of most European nations to the strains on wage regulation in this period.

Although the devaluation of 1982 stabilized Swedish wages, the long-standing system of peak-level wage bargaining collapsed under the weight of these pressures. Some of those pressures were endogenous to the system itself. By narrowing wage differentials, successive solidaristic wage settlements undermined the incentives on which employers relied to recruit and motivate skilled labour, notably in the traded sector. Seeking greater flexibility in the face of foreign competition, the engineering employers federation withdrew from centralized bargaining in 1983 to strike a separate deal with the metalworkers union (Pontusson and Swenson 1996). Over the next decade a series of efforts were made to find a new mode of wage coordination, issuing ultimately in sectoral-level bargaining loosely coordinated across sectors.

These developments took a toll on Swedish companies, which responded in two broad ways. Some intensified mass production with a view to reducing the share of labour in total costs. Others, such as Volvo, took advantage of skilled labour to develop more flexible production regimes, focusing on high value-added products and high levels of quality control (Pontusson 1997: 66). On the whole, however, the approach of Swedish firms to productivity issues did not change dramatically during the period.

2.3.4. Germany

In Germany, an industrial relations system that successfully tied wages to productivity between 1950 and 1972 worked badly during the 1970s when rates of profit rose and fell unexpectedly. As levels of industrial conflict rose, unit labour costs increased by 56 per cent between 1972 and 1975. Tensions grew between an independent Bundesbank, quick to retaliate against inflationary wage settlements with restrictive monetary policy, and governments that took a more Keynesian approach to economic management in the late 1960s. But the German system for wage coordination survived these shocks—a measure of its robustness—and delivered wage increases moderate enough to restrain inflation throughout the 1980s (Hall 1994; Streeck 1994).

As the German work problem in the 1960s became one of labour scarcity, firms responded by importing foreign labour. Between 1959 and 1971, over two million 'guest workers' had entered the country. During the 1970s, however, unemployment rose to 4 per cent, and employment began to shift out of industry into services.[19] The government reacted with more activist macro-economic management and restrictions on immigration. However, the most notable feature of the German response to the work problem was an effort to hold down the size of the workforce. A liberal definition of disability allowed older workers to move onto generous benefits, and those who had been unemployed for a year could claim full pension benefits at age 60, thereby making it feasible for firms to push workers into retirement at age 59. In 1972, legislation raised pension benefits for the low-paid and mandated early retirement at age 63. By 1985, the proportion of German men between the ages of 55 and 64 in paid employment had fallen to 60 per cent from 80 per cent in 1970. Concerned about the fiscal consequences, the Kohl government took the replacement rate for unemployment insurance down five points to 63 per cent of previous wages and the social assistance rate down two points to 56 per cent in 1983–4. However, these measures did not substantially alter a strategy designed to limit the size of the labour force.[20]

During the 1970s, German firms also faced challenges to the practices they had used to ensure high levels of total factor productivity. During the 1960s, they had benefited from an undervalued exchange rate that lowered the price of German goods relative to foreign ones. Partly as a result, Germany became the world's second-largest industrial exporter, and its exports rose from 8 per cent to 24 per cent of GDP between 1950 and 1974. With the collapse of the Bretton Woods regime, however, a low exchange rate could not be sustained without importing inflation, and, as the exchange rate rose, German firms came under more intense competitive pressure. Because of the power of works councils and unions, firms could not readily respond by reducing wages. Instead, they focused on increasing the productivity of labour.

There were two components to the strategies many firms used to increase productivity. One was to use labour more flexibly. To secure union support for such efforts, companies traded reductions in working hours for more flexible work arrangements. In 1985, the large metalworking union, IG Metall, agreed to such arrangements in return for a reduction in the workweek from 40 to 38.5 hours. The union hoped that, if working hours were shorter, more employees would be hired. The second notable element of firm strategy turned on higher levels of investment designed to make each worker more productive, in effect substituting capital for labour. Between 1970 and 1985, the capital intensity of German industry rose dramatically, and the proportion of adult men in employment fell from 93 to 82 per cent.

By and large, these responses were successful. Germany weathered the crises of the 1970s with the institutions of its political economy intact. Rather than abandon DQP, German firms fine-tuned it, and the industrial relations system managed the trade-off between inflation and unemployment well. Relative to that of its neighbours, Germany's economic performance in the 1980s was good. However, the approach to the work problem adopted in this era capped the size of the labour force and reduced working hours. In the short term, the results satisfied many. Those who had work were well paid, and those who did not enjoyed generous social benefits. But this approach was to haunt the German political economy in later years.

2.3.5. The Adjustment Process in Comparative Perspective

The response of these countries to the socio-economic challenges of the late 1960s and 1970s is informative about the processes whereby political economies adjust to socio-economic challenges. Several features are striking.

As the institutions regulating distributive conflict began to founder, all of these countries saw higher levels of state intervention. Governments intervened to stabilize wage bargaining systems under strain. The French state could have been expected to quell the general strike of 1968, but even British governments, whose stance is customarily less interventionist, imposed statutory incomes policies on unions and employers. The Swedish government began to play a more active role in wage negotiations, and even Germany experimented with tripartite wage talks. In the wake of the oil price shocks, every government increased subsidies to industries.

In each case, however, there were two phases to the government's response. During the 1970s, governments reacted to new challenges with familiar formulae. All initially responded to rising unemployment with a Keynesian stimulus, of the sort often used in Britain and France but taken up with new enthusiasm in Germany and Sweden. Instead of provoking cutbacks in spending, the sharp downturn in economic growth inspired new social programmes designed to cushion the populace against the effects of recession. As a proportion of GDP, social spending was to grow faster across Europe during the 1970s than ever before or since, partly because of new programmes and partly because the denominator grew more slowly (see Figure 2.2). Many of the social benefits being cut in the 1990s are ones established during the 1970s. These developments confirm that governments see through a glass darkly. Many responded as if the slowdown in growth that began in 1974 was a temporary recession rather than the climacteric it proved to be. Few saw that the taxes used to pay for new social programmes would bite deeply into the share of value-added that might otherwise be used for investment.

The second phase of policymaking was a reaction to the first, born of rising disillusionment with the fruits of heightened government intervention. To one extent or another, the governments of the early 1980s moved towards more restrictive fiscal and monetary policies and a supply-side view of employment that led to cuts in industrial subsidies in favour of manpower policies. The turning points were 1979 in Britain, 1982 in Germany, 1983 in France, and 1985 in Sweden. The Single Europe Act 1986 of ratified a 'move to the market' that was a reaction against the poor economic performance of the 1970s and the activist state intervention associated with it (Hall 1986).

Although their role is often unacknowledged, firms were also important agents of adjustment in this period. German and Swedish firms replied to wage pressure by reorganizing production to secure more value-added per unit of labour, negotiating more flexible wage and work arrangements with trade unions. To do so, Swedish employers dismantled the system of centralized wage bargaining in which they had participated for decades. Even in France, given a green light by the state, large firms took the initiative to reorganize financial relations and supplier networks (Hancké 2002; Culpepper 2006).

The response to the crises of the 1970s suggests that VoC are often resilient in the face of socio-economic challenges. In three of these four cases, firms turned to modes of coordination they had long used to adjust to the challenge, and governments did not radically alter the institutional framework of the political economy. In Britain, market competition was intensified. In Germany and Sweden, strategic coordination remained central to the operation of the economy. Only in France were the ways in which firms coordinate their endeavours radically altered, as coordination under the aegis of the state gave way to modes of allocating resources in which market competition played a more prominent role.

How might these continuities be explained? To some extent, governments remained committed to economic modalities with which their nations had long been familiar. Thatcher broke with a Keynesian style of policymaking that had become mildly more interventionist, but only to embrace market principles that had long been an important part of British economic ideology (Wood 2001). Kohl's flirtation with a Wende in 1982 was half-hearted at best and quickly abandoned when found to conflict with the principles of a social market economy. The limiting case here is France, where successive governments dismantled many of the pillars of dirigisme, albeit without forsaking all of its rhetoric. However, the move away from strategic coordination in France can be explained, at least in part, by the fact that the French state was responsible for much of that coordination. In reaction to the 1970s, there was a retreat from state intervention across Europe, and in France, when the state retreated, strategic coordination was bound to decline. French policymakers flirted with the idea of trying to move towards strategic coordination built on the German model, only to find that the legacy of dirigisme was a set of producer groups too weakly organized to support it (Albert 1980; Levy 1999).

The stance taken by producer groups also explains some of the resilience of VoC in this period. Firms were reluctant to endorse institutional reforms that threatened the viability of corporate strategies in which they had made major investments. Tempted though they were by policies that might have weakened the trade unions, many large German firms were reluctant to dismantle the institutions that allowed them to coordinate with other firms and operate production regimes requiring close cooperation from the workforce (Wood 2001). Swedish employers withdrew from centralized bargaining arrangements when those no longer served their purposes, but they soon embraced new forms of strategic wage coordination.

In such contexts, power relations between capital and labour matter. French firms were willing to embrace a more competitive market for corporate governance, partly because the French trade unions were too weak to prevent them from pursuing the profit-oriented strategies required to prosper in such an environment (Goyer 2006). During the early 1980s, German firms hesitated to dismantle wage coordination, fearing the consequences of decentralized bargaining with powerful unions. Only when those unions were weakened further by membership losses and high unemployment during the 1990s did firms begin to defect in significant numbers from cooperative bargaining arrangements (Thelen and Winjbergen 2003). The Thatcher government is the exception that defines the limits to this rule. It took on the trade unions and dramatically reduced their power. However, Thatcher did so from a position of considerable strength. Facing a divided opposition, she was electorally secure, and the British trade union movement was not only divided but weakened by high levels of unemployment.

2.4. THE RESPONSE TO THE CHALLENGES
OF THE 1990s AND 2000s

Over the past decade, Europe has faced another set of socio-economic challenges substantial enough to threaten VoC. Many see their origins in 'globalization' construed as an exogenous shock. However, the precise nature of the challenge should be specified. The imports of cheap foreign goods with which it is often associated do not pose a dramatic challenge to countries long used to operating open economies. Two other dimensions of globalization pose greater problems.

One arises from the expansion of markets in emerging economies, including Russia, China, Brazil, and India, as well as Eastern Europe where the collapse of communism in 1989 opened up neighbouring markets.[21] Although the volume of European imports from the emerging economies is small relative to intra-European trade, their emergence has shifted the opportunity structure facing European firms. These economies offer growing markets that large firms cannot ignore, lest they lose economies of scale to foreign competitors, and some are attractive sites for high-volume production of goods made with moderately skilled labour. As a result, investment that might have gone into domestic production has shifted to emerging markets, and domestic operations using low-skilled labour have been closed in favour of foreign ones (Wood 1994). These developments have intensified the work problem, putting pressures on the European political economies to raise skill levels and create jobs in high value-added manufacturing or the service sector.

The second challenge posed by globalization stems from the internationalization of finance. Although foreign investment has been rising for decades, it has recently increased exponentially. As a result, international investors are now an important source of finance for most large firms, and the largest European banks have reduced their commitments to domestic firms in order to secure global market share.[22] These developments have unsettled the relationship with domestic funders that gave many European firms access to finance on terms that allowed them to concentrate on long-term growth rather than current profitability (Hall and Soskice 2001). Foreign investors are pressing firms to secure higher returns and governments to render markets for corporate governance more open and transparent.

Alongside the issues of globalization that capture headlines, however, the European economies confront another set of challenges endogenous to institutional development in Europe itself. As they have in the past, those challenges stem from changes in international regimes, structural changes, and the unintended effects of institutional development.

With the Maastricht Treaty of 1992 and the maturing of the '1992 initiative' embodied in the Single Europe Act 1986, Western Europe shifted its trade and monetary regimes. The advent of a single market forced all major firms to reorganize to meet more intense European competition. The result was an intense process of 'creative destruction' that created new jobs and eliminated many others (Schumpeter 1949). Europe suddenly faced a new work problem, as nations struggled to find positions for workers displaced by processes of economic reorganization.

Equally important has been a shift in the power and posture of the European Union. Over the past twenty years, the powers of its Commission, Court, and Council have increased, and a Union once inspired by the ideal of political integration has become an agency dedicated to market liberalization. As a result, its member-states now face a supranational agency that puts continuous pressure on them to deregulate protected markets, eliminate industrial subsidies, and promote free flows of capital. Across its member-states, the European Union imparts a liberal bias to initiatives for institutional reform (Scharpf 1995).

In 1992, twelve of the member-states also agreed to create an EMU managed by a central bank independent of political control.[23] The EMU, and the stringent requirements for entry into it, restricted the macroeconomic instruments available to national governments for responding to economic shocks. Devaluation was no longer an option for offsetting the impact of wage increases on national competitiveness. The scope for responding to a downturn in demand with a fiscal stimulus was restricted, and member governments lost control over monetary policy altogether.[24] As a result, the member-states have had to address adjustment issues on the supply side, through manpower policies or structural reforms to markets for capital, goods, and labour.

Structural changes intensify some of the dilemmas. A continuing shift in the locus of demand towards services means that virtually all job creation has to be in the service sector, and low birth rates are putting pressure on Europe to secure high levels of employment, because a smaller workforce will now have to support a larger proportion of the population in retirement (Iversen and Wren 1998; Scharpf 2000; Pierson 2001).[25]

The confluence of these developments has magnified the European work problem. Just when the corporate sector was shedding labour to reorganize, first for the single market and then for emerging markets, demand was shifting towards services. Not only must jobs be found for displaced workers, but jobs in services have to be found for workers equipped with industrial skills. Of course, early retirement is the logical option for many, but demographic pressures now militate against the extension of early retirement. Moreover, just as they faced this work problem, the members of EMU lost their macroeconomic instruments for coping with it and have had to depend on structural policies. If the 1970s was dominated by a wage problem, the principal challenge facing Europe in the 1990s has been a work problem.

How have Britain, France, Germany, and Sweden responded to these challenges? I will compare their responses with an emphasis on the distinctive features of national adjustment trajectories.

2.4.1. Britain

The new single market proved congenial to British firms because they were accustomed to coordinating their endeavours through competitive markets rather than strategic forms of interaction. The liberalizing initiatives of the European Commission simply sharpened the types of market coordination on which most British firms depended for comparative advantage, and many found the new market propitious terrain for expansion. Between 1990 and 1994, Britain's share of European trade increased accordingly. In the wake of Thatcher's initiatives, British firms were able to reorganize relatively easily. By the 1990s, barely a third of them had any employees represented by a union, and most could alter wages and work processes relatively freely. That flexibility was reflected in a widening of pay differentials more substantial than those in most continental countries.

The institutions of an LME also made it relatively easy for Britain to move resources out of industry into services. A skill-setting system that privileged general skills enhanced labour mobility, and British governments were able to raise levels of general skills by increasing formal schooling. The British welfare state was also well suited to the creation of jobs in services. Levels of employment protection were low and part-time employment encouraged. Minimalist social policy regimes provided few incentives for people to linger on the unemployment rolls. The 'New Deal' of the 1997 Labour government strengthened the relevant incentives by making receipt of social benefits contingent on an active work search or participation in training schemes (Rhodes 2000).

Britain declined to enter EMU and adopted a floating exchange-rate regime. Where trade unions are powerful, such regimes can be a disadvantage, as Britain found during the 1970s. But Thatcher had dramatically reduced the

Table 2.3. Employment in services as a percentage of total employment

	1963	1973	1983	1993	2003
Britain	48	54	63	69	75
France	40	48	57	66	72
Germany	40	45	53	57	65
Sweden	46	56	65	71	75

Source: OECD.

power of the British labour movement. Between 1979 and 1992, union membership fell from 50 to 30 per cent of the workforce, and the proportion of firms in employers associations declined from 25 to 13 per cent (Rhodes 2000: 50). As a result, wage pressures remained moderate. Moreover, British governments retained macroeconomic tools denied its continental counterparts and used them to maintain domestic demand at high levels.[26] They used judicious depreciations to offset the effects of domestic inflation on competitiveness. As his European neighbours were cutting back spending, a Labour Chancellor of the Exchequer embarked on a spending spree on public services.

Not surprisingly, rates of growth of employment and national product have been higher in Britain than in France or Germany over the past fifteen years (see Table 2.2). The move to service-sector employment has also been more extensive (see Table 2.3). The weaknesses continue to be those that have long afflicted Britain's LME. Because many firms compete by holding down labour costs rather than by investing in new technology or highly skilled labour, many Britons work at wages lower than in the other three countries examined here.

The shift in international regimes of the 1990s did not induce radical institutional change in the British political economy. Its institutions were already well suited to the competitive environment of the single market, and the City of London was well placed to profit from the internationalization of finance. The reforms made to education and social policy over the past decade reinforced the market coordination and general skills regime already characteristic of the economy, and efforts to improve corporate governance in the wake of the Cadbury commission were consonant with a highly fluid capital market.

2.4.2. Germany

By contrast, the shifts in international regimes of the 1990s posed severe challenges to the German political economy. Germany coped well with the economic turbulence of the 1970s, when the principal problem was to secure wage moderation, because it had robust institutions for strategic wage coordination. However, those institutions made rapid industrial reorganization more difficult to achieve. In order to reorganize production regimes or shift resources across endeavours, German firms had to engage in intensive negotiations with powerful works councils and trade unions reluctant to agree lay-offs, larger wage differentials, or more onerous working conditions. As a result, the process of economic reorganization in Germany was inevitably more protracted than elsewhere.

Moreover, these challenges coincided with German reunification, greatly exacerbating the work problem (Streeck 1997). Because few east German firms were equipped to compete in open markets, east German workers swelled the ranks of the unemployed, and efforts to cushion that adjustment increased the fiscal pressure on the German government. Since 1990, 4 per cent of GDP a year has been spent on social transfers to the east, and taxes were increased substantially to fund them. The pace of job loss was accelerated by a 'solidarity pact' in 1991 that specified wages in the east should match those in the western Länder. Although rates of unemployment in the west were a hefty 7 per cent by 2000, they hovered around 20 per cent in the east.

Membership in EMU has also eroded, rather than enhanced, the effectiveness of adjustment in Germany. In some respects, the institutions of Germany's CME operate less well under EMU than they did when German institutions controlled monetary and fiscal policy. Given the structure of its taxation system, the non-wage costs of German firms are high. To meet competition from the single market and the east, those firms have had to hold down wages. Strategic wage coordination allowed them to do so. The effect has been to restore the competitiveness of German industry, as rising export levels indicate. But the slow growth of wages has depressed domestic demand, and the macroeconomic environment has not been propitious for growth. The CMEs can generally control inflation effectively. However, because nominal interest rates set by the European central bank respond to continentwide rates of inflation, they have often left German firms facing real interest rates higher than those in other member-states, where wage bargaining is less coordinated and inflation higher. German fiscal policy has also been constrained by the accompanying Growth and Stability pact that proscribes deficits above 3 per cent of GDP. As a result, although German exports reached record levels in the early 2000s, its domestic economy stagnated. German firms reorganized themselves to become more competitive, but the economy has been unable to create jobs for the workers they shed.

As Soskice (this volume) observes, CMEs have special trouble coping with high levels of unemployment or low levels of demand because they deploy a labour force equipped with industry-specific skills. In the face of unemployment, workers with specific skills find new jobs at comparable wage rates more difficult to secure than do workers equipped with general skills. Accordingly, they respond to rising levels of unemployment by increasing their level of savings more than workers in LMEs. That magnifies the effect of unemployment on domestic demand. The solution lies in reflationary fiscal or monetary policy, but monetary union deprived Germany of this option.

The commitment of the European Commission to market liberalization has also posed challenges to German institutions. In many spheres, German firms depend on forms of strategic coordination that more intense competition would undercut. As a result, German politicians have often resisted such initiatives (Callaghan 2004). However, as German firms reorganized to meet the competitive challenges of a more open global economy, there have been significant changes to established practices that are often read, with some justification, as a liberalization of the German economy. Examined closely, however, they can also be seen as a loosening of some aspects of strategic coordination, that preserves residual capacities for such coordination, should they subsequently be needed.

Developments in the realm of wage coordination are a prominent example. Many smaller firms have defected from sectoral agreements in order to seek concessions from the unions at the firm level (Schröder and Silvia 2005). As a result, wage rates are less uniform and local deviations from sectoral agreements more common. Wage rates in the east are now 62 per cent lower on average than in the west. Facing unionists willing to make concessions because unemployment is high and large firms unwilling to tolerate the industrial conflict necessary to enforce sectoral wage moderation, many firms have preferred to negotiate locally (Thelen and Wijnbergen 2003).

These developments represent a substantial loosening of wage coordination. But they can also be seen as a sign of the flexibility with which the wage-setting system can respond to competitive exigencies. Many of the capacities for strategic coordination embodied in the system remain intact and could be called upon should labour-market conditions tighten. Employers associations have adjusted to defections by devising new forms of membership (Hassel and Williamson 2004). Wages and working conditions continue to be bargained with works councils and unions. Sixty per cent of the German workforce is still covered by a collective bargain, compared to 20 per cent in Britain, and industry and labour continue to operate collaborative training schemes conferring high levels of industry-specific skills.

Parallel developments in the financial sector are open to a similar interpretation. The large German banks have reduced their commitments to domestic industry in order to retain the scale to compete on more open global markets. Legislation mandating more transparent balance sheets and protection for minority shareholders has encouraged firms to reorganize under the rubric of securing 'shareholder value'. But most firms still fund investment from retained earnings and bank finance, and the government has resisted measures that would enforce shareholder value by promoting hostile takeovers (Callaghan 2004). Although cross-shareholdings have shifted, enough exist to protect many firms from takeovers (cf. Beyer and Höpner 2004).

To address a severe fiscal crisis and move the unemployed into work, the Schröder government trimmed social benefits and required training or a job search in return for them. But the structure of the German welfare state has not been seriously altered. Benefits continue to be funded by social charges and early retirement programmes still assist firms seeking to reduce their labour force (Streeck and Trampusch 2006).

The principal institutional transformation in the German political economy has been the development of a dual labour market, based on the promotion of part-time 'mini jobs' now occupied by more than four million workers on whom social charges are not levied. At 20 per cent of jobs, part-time employment in Germany is now almost at British levels and employment protection in this secondary labour market is low. The key issue is whether this development will gradually enforce similar changes in the core labour market, now dominated by skilled industrial labour, but Japan's capacity to operate dual labour markets suggests that it need not do so.

Broadly speaking, coordination in some spheres of the German political economy has been loosened in response to the challenges of the 1990s but strategic coordination remains prominent in the endeavours of many firms. After a painful decade, German firms have reorganized themselves effectively. Unit labour costs are again competitive (see Table 2.4). Female labour force participation has increased from 61 per cent in 1991 to 66 per cent in 2005, and service-sector jobs are being created at a pace in line with the European average (see Table 2.3).[27] But the work problem remains unresolved. Five million unemployed drag down German rates of growth and

Table 2.4. Real unit labour costs (1995 = 100)

	1963	1973	1983	1993	2003
Britain	104	104	101	103	101
France	108	105	112	102	99
Germany	104	108	106	102	99
Sweden	117	111	112	105	107

Source: OECD.

put intense fiscal pressure on the government (Streeck 2006). A political economy that performed well in the industrial era has been unable to create jobs fast enough to absorb the large eastern labour force it inherited with reunification.

To some extent, these problems are an artefact of the German model itself, which has remained competitive by substituting capital for labour in a core industrial sector that remains the largest in Europe. That strategy delivered high incomes and substantial amounts of leisure time to a core labour force but created employment only slowly. Called upon to create jobs more rapidly, Germany has turned towards a secondary labour market that is generating jobs on terms that threaten the egalitarian values long associated with its economic model. The result is political disillusionment and widespread insecurity, as those in the core economy face cuts in benefits to which they have become accustomed, while stagnating levels of demand impede the creation of jobs.

2.4.3. France

French governments were enthusiastic sponsors of the single market and EMU, in the belief that the latter would offer monetary policies more accommodating than those of the German Bundesbank to which France had been in thrall during the 1980s. When these hopes were disappointed, the French found themselves in a relatively austere macroeconomic environment with stubbornly high levels of unemployment. The government reacted with a two-pronged strategy that extended the approach to such problems developed during the 1980s.

One dimension of government strategy was to promote the role of markets in the allocation of resources. In 1993, the government resumed the privatization of public enterprises (on hold since 1988) and allowed sales of the core shareholdings assembled to protect newly privatized companies. France saw a wave of mergers and acquisitions, as many French conglomerates reorganized around more focused sets of operations. The amount of equity raised by French corporations increased by 38 per cent during the 1990s, and foreigners owned almost 40 per cent of the shares of the leading 40 French corporations by 2003 (Culpepper 2006). In the sphere of industrial relations, a series of government initiatives encouraged bargaining at the firm, rather than the sector, level between employers and a weakened set of trade unions, whose membership, at 5 per cent of the labour force, fell to the lowest level in Europe. The effect of these steps was to improve the efficiency of French business, whose unit labour costs fell during the 1990s.

The second dimension of French policy was orthogonal to the first. Successive governments increased public spending to create subsidized jobs, notably for the young or unemployed, and to provide social benefits as a cushion against the unemployment generated when French firms rationalized. When an effort to create jobs by reducing the workweek to 35 hours had little effect on unemployment, these subsidy programmes were expanded. The Jospin government created new positions in the public sector and made few cuts to the generous benefits available to those in the most privileged positions of France's welfare state. As a consequence, public spending rose faster in France than elsewhere in Europe, reaching Nordic levels at 51 per cent of GDP in 2004.

If France moved towards market modes of coordination by intensifying competition, the character of its social policies continued to distinguish France from classic LMEs, such as those of Britain or the USA, where low social benefits are used to push workers into jobs. However, the nation moved faster than Germany to reform its continental welfare state. In both countries, a social policy regime that funds benefits from social charges on labour has discouraged the creation of low-wage jobs (Scharpf 2000). However, French governments began earlier to shift costs to general taxation, increasing the CSG (*contribution social générale*), introduced in 1990 as a temporary 1.1 per cent surtax on income, to 7.5 per cent of income by 1998. They have also used a national minimum income, the RMI (*revenu minimum individuel*) like an earned-income tax credit to encourage the unemployed to take low-paying jobs. Like Germany, therefore, France has begun to encourage the development of a dual labour market. Many employees in the public service and some segments of the private sector enjoy high levels of employment protection and generous retirement benefits (Smith 2004). By easing restrictions on part-time and temporary employment over the course of the 1990s and early 2000s, the government has begun to create a sizeable secondary labour market where employees work without substantial benefits or job security.

These measures dramatically improved the performance of French business (see Table 2.4). By 2000, the average French worker was as productive as his American counterpart, and rates of growth in France have remained close to the EU average over the last decade (Blanchard 2004). But, at 12 per cent in 2006, French unemployment has remained persistently high, and political discontent is palpable (Hall 2005). In May 2005, French voters rejected the constitution of the European Union, which many saw as the agent of liberalization, and, in May 2006, massive demonstrations forced the government to withdraw a plan to introduce short-term labour contracts for those under the age of 26.

2.4.4. Sweden

Swedish institutions proved effective enough to secure high levels of employ-ment and growth during the 1980s, and the country did not enter the EU until 1995, thereby putting off some of the challenges facing its neighbours. But Sweden experienced a crisis of its own at the beginning of the 1990s. Sparked by the deregulation of credit markets in 1985, an asset boom fuelled wage pressures that a bargaining system, still reeling from the collapse of centralized negotiation, could not contain. In the years immediately after 1990, inflation rose to 10 per cent, Sweden experienced negative rates of growth for three successive years, and the public-sector deficit ballooned to 17 per cent of GDP.

Some of Sweden's capacities for strategic coordination had clearly failed. The question was whether they could be revived and, if so, in what form. In the medium term, concerted action by the government and producer groups eventually re-established a stable system for wage coordination. Although reaching agreement proved difficult, by 1997, the government and producer groups had negotiated new arrangements that provided for more formal mediation and a government-sponsored council to provide wage guidance for bargains generally struck at the sectoral level (Elvander 2003). Around these bargains, however, there was to be more scope for firm-level agreements on wages and working conditions, which Swedish firms have used to reorganize production in the face of international competition. That system has proved durable.

In the short term, the exchange-rate regime proved crucial to Sweden's capacity to recover from this disastrous episode of distributive conflict. Taking advantage of a floating exchange rate, in 1992, the government initiated a devaluation that ultimately reached 32 per cent, and the trade unions accepted most of the reduction in real wages it implied, partly because the crisis had taken the rate of unemployment to 8 per cent. By 2000, Sweden's competi-tiveness had been restored enough to generate a trade surplus of 2 per cent of GDP. The case provides an example of how a flexible exchange-rate regime can be used to address the problems that result when the institutions normally charged with resolving distributive issues fail.

Less obvious but equally consequential were reforms made during the 1990s in the sphere of corporate governance. As the share of investment financed from abroad increased around the world, Swedish firms became concerned about securing access to it. Accordingly, they pressed the government to lift existing restrictions on the foreign purchase of shares, and, in order to attract investors, many of the family groups that long dominated the stock exchange began relinquishing their preferred shares, which had put minority investors at a disadvantage. Partly as a result, the Stockholm stock market grew 24-fold during the 1990s and, by 2001, 43 per cent of its equity was foreign-owned by 2001, compared to 8 per cent in 1990 (Reiter 2003: 113).

Based on cross-shareholdings revolving around several large family-owned firms, strategic coordination in corporate governance had long been high in Sweden. The effect of these measures was to reduce the level of strategic coordination and expose firms to more market pressures. These moves went substantially further than analogous reform efforts in Germany. Why were they practicable in its CME?

Part of the answer may lie, as in the cases of France and Germany, in the character of labour markets. The organization of industrial relations conditions the feasibility of reforms in corporate governance (Hall and Gingerich 2004). German firms have been hesitant to expose themselves to intense competition in the market for corporate governance because the commitment of powerful works councils and trade unions to employment protection make it difficult for them to respond to the demands of aggressive shareholders. Although trade unions are equally powerful in Sweden, they are much less committed to employment protection, by virtue of the arrangements developed under the Rehn–Meidner model. Those promote labour mobility, offering high unemployment benefits in the short term (with replacement rates reaching 90 per cent of previous wages for 180 days) and substantial assistance in the job search in lieu of employment protection. The system encourages investment in the industry-specific skills on which Swedish firms depend, not by protecting jobs, but by offering assurances that another job will soon be found and few wages foregone in the search (Estévez-Abe et al. 2001). Swedish firms could embrace a more competitive market for corporate governance because labour market arrangements made it relatively easy for them for them to shed labour if they had to meet heightened demands for profitability.

Moreover, the Swedish reforms did not go as far as those in France. Despite the waning dominance of its old family firms, Swedish equity markets are still characterized by many cross-shareholdings that protect companies, such as Sandvik and Skanska, from hostile takeovers. Closed-end investment funds that often perform such functions have substantial holdings on the Stockholm Stock Exchange (Högfeldt 2004). Sweden moved from a bank-based system of corporate finance towards an equity-based system that draws heavily on foreign investment without exposing its firms to all the pressures characteristic of an LME (cf. Henrekson and Jakobsson 2003).

In tandem with these developments in the sphere of corporate governance, Swedish governments took steps to enhance the mobility of labour. Spending on active labour market policy was intensified, rising from 3 per cent of GDP in 1990 to 5 per cent by 1995, the highest level in Europe, and employment

Table 2.5. Days lost in industrial conflict

Years	1953–61	1962–6	1967–71	1972–6	1977–81	1982–7
Britain	28	23	60	976	112	88
France	41	32	350	34	23	13
Germany	7	3	8	3	8	9

Source: *Employment Gazette* (various issues); Armstrong et al. (1991). Average number of days per year occupied in industrial conflict per 100 workers in industry and transport.

in the public sector was increased to absorb those who had difficulty finding work. However, the government also reduced the marginal tax rate for many individuals and its own revenue by about 3 per cent of GDP, agreed to fund social services operated by private organizations, and made reforms to sick pay that reduced absenteeism rates (Benner and Vad 2000; Steinmo 2000).

These institutional innovations have worked well. For almost a decade, Sweden has again secured rates of growth well above the EU average and rates of unemployment well below it. Its institutions for wage-setting have been rendered more flexible but remain coordinated enough to deliver real wage increases commensurate with increases in productivity, and its approach to the work problem, based on active labour market policy and public employment, remains intact. Using its capacity to mount autonomous fiscal and monetary policies, the government has smoothed periodic fluctuations in demand. It may not be coincidence that the two economies among our cases that have performed best over the past decade—one liberal and one coordinated—are those that remained outside EMU.

2.5. CONCLUSION: ASSESSING INSTITUTIONAL TRAJECTORIES

I have argued that, over the course of the post-war years, the nations of Western Europe developed distinctive sets of institutions for managing the wage, work, and productivity problems confronting them. Extending from institutions for firm-level coordination to features of the welfare state, these institutions were constitutive of distinctive VoC, and I have traced the ways in which those institutions changed, as firms and governments encountered successive waves of socio-economic challenges. What lessons does this survey contain for those interested in the fate of VoC today?

It provides grounds for scepticism about claims that the magnitude of the challenges facing Europe today are rendering VoC approaches to comparative capitalism obsolete. The socio-economic challenges that preoccupy

Evolution of Varieties of Capitalism in Europe

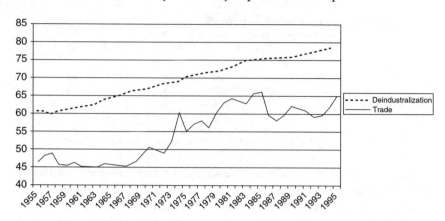

Figure 2.3. Trends in deindustrialization and trade in the OECD, 1955–95

Source: OECD, National Accounts, Part II; Iversen (2005). Trade is sum of exports and imports as a percentage of GDP. Deindustrialization is 100 minus the sum of employment in agriculture and industry as a percentage of the working age population.

these political economies today are far from the first they have faced, and many of the developments considered corrosive of VoC are not new (see Figure 2.3). Measured by the exports of the average West European nation, trade grew by almost 9 per cent a year from 1950 to 1970. As early as the 1960s, firms were preoccupied by technological change, and policymakers by foreign investment. Employment also began to shift sharply from industry to the service sector in the 1960s (Servan-Schreiber 1969; Bell 1974; Iversen and Cusack 2000). There is little basis for seeing ours as a uniquely convulsive era.

Moreover, institutional change is not new. Each of these political economies experienced continuous institutional change throughout the post-war period. Firms and governments frequently revised their strategies to meet emerging conditions, and some of the features most associated with distinctive models of the political economy, such as the use the Nordic nations make of public employment, are relatively recent developments. From this vantage point, it is not surprising to find institutional change in Europe today. Those who see it as a sign that VoC will soon cease to exist misunderstand the character of those varieties.

I have tried to show that VoC are constituted, not by static sets of institutions, but by distinctive trajectories that are institutionally conditioned, as new practices are developed to cope with the problems generated by past practice and integrated into a network of interacting institutions, some of which remain stable as others change. As a result, while configured somewhat differently than in the past, the political economies examined here continue to display divergences in institutionalized practices as pronounced as those at most moments since the war. In large measure, that divergence extends to the modes of coordination that Hall and Soskice (2001) associate with different VoC.

Over time, competitive markets have become an even more important feature of coordination in Britain's LME. Market relations have also become more important to the coordination of some types of firm endeavours in Germany and Sweden. Their large firms are now more likely to seek capital on competitive international markets. Sweden has scaled back employment protection to create a more fluid labour market, and Germany has adopted regulations that allow for the growth of a low-wage, part-time labour market in which wages are not collectively bargained. Coordination of wages at the sectoral level in Germany has become looser, as small firms defect from sectoral agreements to reach firm-level accords with unions and works councils (Thelen and Kume 1999; Schröder and Silvia 2006).

However, to emphasize these developments is to neglect the many respects in which strategic coordination is still important in Sweden and Germany. Sectoral wage agreements, while looser than they once were, are still key features of these political economies. At the firm level, wages and working conditions in Germany are more often bargained with works councils than set arbitrarily. Cross-firm collaboration remains an important element of technology transfer, and of vocational training in Germany. The industrial sectors of Germany and Sweden continue to operate production regimes that rely on highly paid workers equipped with industry-specific skills, while British firms make greater use of general skills and low-wage labour. Although foreign investors now supply a greater proportion of investment everywhere, German firms continue to draw more heavily on long-term bank-based finance than British firms, and hostile takeovers are much less frequent in Germany and Sweden than in Britain.

Some argue that the introduction of more competitive market relations into various spheres of these economies is the thin end of a wedge that will drive them inexorably away from coordinated capitalism (Höpner and Jackson 2001). Hall and Soskice (2001) provide some grounds for thinking this when they observe that strategic coordination in one sphere of the economy often enhances its value elsewhere. However, recent developments suggest that efforts to render some markets more competitive need not erode strategic coordination elsewhere in the political economy. Among those examined here, the move by Sweden towards more competitive markets in corporate governance is one striking case, and the dual labour market developing in Germany another.[28] It is important to acknowledge that some forms of market competition are compatible with strategic coordination of other endeavours.[29]

The analytic challenge, deserving of more research in the coming years, is to establish which kinds of moves towards more intense market competition erode existing capacities for strategic coordination and which are compatible with them. That issue has been obscured by the tendency of the literature to describe institutional reform in Europe as part of a monolithic process of 'liberalization' sweeping over the continent. That captures an important feature of the political *Zeitgeist*: liberal reform is popular in international circles and that popularity lends political impetus to measures adopted across Europe, including increases in part-time employment, temporary labour contracts, benefit cuts that push people into work, and measures to render balance sheets more transparent or to protect minority investors.

With respect to impact, however, the concept of 'liberalization' is misleading. Measures that are all described as 'liberal' can have different economic or institutional effects (Hall and Thelen 2005).[30] Some are corrosive of strategic coordination elsewhere in the economy, while others enhance it. Balance sheets can be rendered more transparent without much impact on how firms raise finance, but measures to encourage hostile takeovers have dramatic effects on firm strategies. Similar developments can also have impacts that vary across institutional settings. In Britain, devolving wage bargaining to the firm in Britain usually means setting wages by demand and supply in local labour markets, while similar moves in Germany usually mean that wages are negotiated with trade unions or works councils at the firm level. We need to disaggregate the concept of 'liberalization', lest we overstate its impact. Despite important common trends, the political economies of Europe are not converging rapidly on a common liberal model.

However, those political economies are changing. I have suggested that VoC follow institutionally-conditioned adjustment trajectories and, in keeping with that account, we can see important moments of divergence in those trajectories. The most dramatic occurred in the case of France, where strategic coordination in the spheres of corporate governance and labour relations recedes, in the decades after 1985, to give way to forms of coordination in which market competition plays a more prominent role. Although the French state has not lost all of its capacities, it has relinquished important elements of the coordinating role it once played in the economy.

Another occurred in the 1970s, when Sweden and Germany responded differently to the prospect of rising unemployment. The Swedish government expanded public employment to provide a reservoir of jobs for those with general skills, thereby bringing large numbers of women into the labour force. At roughly the same time, the German government reacted with early retirement and disability schemes designed to reduce the numbers seeking employment. Although both routes proved compatible with the operation of a CME, over the long term, these were fateful decisions. Facing demographic pressures that foretold fiscal crisis, Germany was subsequently to find it difficult to increase the share of the population in employment. As the result of the accumulated effects of such choices, there have been important divergences in the institutional trajectories of CMEs.

2.5.1. Institutions and Economic Performance

This analysis helps explain why some types of political economies perform better in some eras than others. It provides an account of the impact of institutions on economic performance that highlights three types of effects. As others have noted, institutions mediate the response to (partly) exogenous shocks (cf. Blanchard and Wolfers 2000). Two prominent shocks in this era provide examples—the stagflation of the 1970s and shift of employment to services. Faced with stagflation, the CMEs of Sweden and Germany secured better levels of performance, largely because their institutions for wage coordination contained the effects of inflation more effectively. Their institutions were well configured for coping with inflation. Because they set high wage floors and privileged specific skills, however, their institutions were less suited to creating jobs in the service sector. Swedish governments responded better by expanding public employment based on general skills, while Germany did not. By contrast, Britain and France suffered more economic losses in the inflation of the 1970s, but created jobs faster in the service sector, partly because their economies were already geared toward general skills. Of the two, Britain was more successful, arguably because its low minimum wages and social charges encouraged firms to create service-sector jobs (Scharpf 2000; cf. Iversen 2005).

However, institutions do not simply mediate the response to economic shocks. Over time, they contribute to the challenges an economy faces. European inflation was generated, in the late 1960s and 1970s, partly by institutions that gave trade unions a powerful role in wage bargaining; and national variations in rates of inflation corresponded to differences in the institutions coordinating wage bargaining (Crouch and Pizzorno 1978; Hall and Franzese 1998; Iversen 1999). The slow growth of employment in Germany during the 1980s and 1990s had roots in an institutional model developed to secure increases in productivity via continuous innovation by highly paid skilled labour whose social benefits were funded from charges on employment. High labour costs encouraged firms to increase labour saving investment rather than take on new employees (Manow and Seils 2000). In Britain, institutional support ·for low-wage employment expanded the labour force but discouraged firms from moving into high value-added lines of production, thereby limiting the growth of national income. In each case, the institutional solutions devised by firms and governments to address the problems of one era conditioned the shape of the challenges they were to face in later periods.

I have also argued that changes in international regimes affect economic performance by virtue of how they interact with the institutions of domestic political economies. The move to floating rates in the 1970s eroded the effectiveness with which European systems for wage coordination operated (Eichengreen 1996; Iversen 1999). By reducing the scope for national reflation and focusing cross-national competition on unit labour costs, the subsequent move to EMU hit CMEs with high non-wage costs and highly skilled labour relatively hard, as firms held down wages to compete and highly paid workers increased their savings to guard against unemployment (Soskice, this volume). In short, institutions that deliver high levels of performance under one set of international regimes or in the face of some socio-economic challenges may not do so under others.

2.5.2. Explaining Institutional Trajectories

The image of political economies presented here sees them as institutional ecologies built up gradually over time. How can the shape and direction of those trajectories be explained? That is a question to which answers are only beginning to emerge (see Streeck and Yamamura 2001; Thelen 2004). However, these cases suggest some observations.

Given the impact of regulatory regimes on the political economy, the partisan complexion of government is likely to play a role in the construction of the political economy. Political parties use ideologies to build reputations, and differences in the ideologies of social democratic, Christian democratic, and liberal parties are salient to the political economy (Esping-Andersen 1990; Iversen and Wren 1998; Huber and Stephens 2001). Social democratic parties tend to have a high tolerance for public spending and an interest in expanding employment (Bradley and Stephens 2007). Christian democratic parties have been less inclined to move women into the labour force. Divergence in the paths taken by Sweden and Germany during the 1970s and 1980s may be attributable partly to the influence of social democracy in Sweden.[31] The neoliberal initiatives in Britain during the 1980s owe something to the ideology embraced by its Conservative Party.

However, the initiatives taken by parties vary over time and space more than an emphasis on partisan ideology usually allows, and the evolving character of the political economy can influence the positions parties take on issues of institutional reform. We need analyses of the construction of the political economy that incorporate a role for partisan competition but allow the accumulated institutions of the political economy to influence partisan positions. The first step is to acknowledge that the behaviour of governing parties also depends on the coalitions they can organize among the electorate. The next step is to identify how institutions influence that process of coalition formation. Iversen and Soskice (2006) move in this direction when they note that the latter depends on the structure of the electoral system (see also Swank 2002). Existing policy regimes can also influence the interests of potential coalition partners. Pierson (2004) notes that actors acquire vested interests in policy regimes by virtue of their network externalities. Iversen (2005) suggests that skill systems and related production regimes generate variations in the electoral support available for different types of social policy regimes. By virtue of the divisions of interest they create between economic insiders and outsiders, the institutions of the political economy also influence the types of coalitions that social democratic parties can assemble (Rueda 2005, 2006). Each of these perspectives suggests that, as the institutional structure of a political economy develops, it conditions the terms of partisan competition in ways that tend to create distinctive institutional trajectories. We need further research into the ways in which the platforms and fortunes of parties vary over time with the institutional development of the political economy (Kitschelt and Rehm 2004).

In the same vein, Swenson (2002) points to the ways in which the character of institutions conditions the demands emanating from producer groups for reform. Following Goyer (2005, 2006), I have argued that French employers were supportive of the liberalization of French markets for corporate governance, partly because the character of industrial relations in France posed few impediments to corporate reorganization. In Britain, the Blair governments made few moves to restore the power of the trade unions, partly because employers had developed production regimes congruent with the market reforms initiated by the preceding Thatcher governments. Here, as elsewhere, social democracy adapted itself to the institutional configuration of the political economy.

Of course, such processes are far from mechanical. Governing parties respond to the electorate as well as producer groups. They often face conflicting factions within each, and all governments have minds of their own. Their measures are frequently inspired by distributional concerns rather than economic optimality (Hall and Thelen 2005). Over the long term, however, political feedback effects from the structure of the political economy sustain distinctive VoC.

2.5.3. The Prospects for Europe

As Mark Twain might have said, rumours of the death of CMEs are greatly exaggerated. In some countries, such as Sweden, they are performing reasonably well. Even in Germany, where the headlines stress high levels of unemployment, reorganization in the corporate sector has been profound, as in France. Many of Germany's firms are highly profitable, and its exports have reached record levels. Although intensified by the challenges of reunification, its adjustment process has been protracted but highly effective in some respects. I read the loosening of sectoral coordination as an adjustment that preserves many of the strategic capacities inherent in German institutions. It is not surprising that wage coordination should operate differently when unemployment, rather than inflation, is the main economic problem. However, it is undeniable that France and Germany are suffering from high levels of unemployment that depress their rates of growth. Their institutions have been better at improving productivity than at creating jobs, and that fact is creating political, as well as economic, dilemmas.

Eichengreen (1996) notes that the institutions of the macroeconomy resolve coordination problems, but I have stressed that they also regulate distributive conflict. When they failed to do so during the 1970s, the result was inflation (Goldthorpe 1978). Today, however, the conflict is about the distribution of work, and the approaches nations are taking to the problem are creating distinctive political dynamics. Building on institutions developed in the 1960s and 1970s, Sweden is promoting labour mobility and secure public sector employment oriented to general skills.[32] The effect has been to lower the institutional divisions between economic insiders and outsiders, making it more feasible for the Swedish social democrats to build cohesive political coalitions.

By contrast, France and Germany are building dual labour markets that create a growing number of temporary or part-time positions at relatively low wages alongside those in the industrial or public sectors that offer higher levels of wages and job security. In each economy, more than four million people now hold such jobs. From the perspective of job creation, the strategy has merit, and it may not seriously damage the capacities for strategic coordination elsewhere in the German economy. But the political effects of such strategies may be more deleterious. They drive a wedge between insiders with relatively secure jobs and outsiders in precarious employment.[33] That makes it more difficult for social or Christian democratic parties to retain the support of a cohesive coalition in the electorate and opens up opportunities for parties on the fringes of the political spectrum to mount appeals tailored to those in precarious employment. In Germany and France, parties on the radical right and radical left have been doing precisely that. The result is centrifugal pressure that further erodes the capacity of mainstream parties to take bold measures to address their nations' problems.

In these countries, the class compromise that underpinned post-war institutions is fraying at the edges, and governments face problems that are as intractable in political terms as they are in economic ones. More is at stake than economic performance. The effort of the European Union to find a new legitimating ideal in a commitment to open markets is failing in the large economies at its heart, even as that commitment makes it difficult for their governments to experiment with alternative formulae. Unless another wave of prosperity lifts Europe's boats, the result is likely to be a new era of political conflict that will once again shake, if not reform, its VoC.

NOTES

I am grateful to Jan-Emmanuel de Neve for efficient research assistance, to Tom Cusack, Torben Iversen, and Tim Smeeding for sharing their data, and to Cathie Jo Martin, Bo Rothstein, and Mark Thatcher for comments. This chapter benefits from what I have learned in joint work with Kathleen Thelen and support from the Wissenschaftskolleg, Berlin.

1. When this chapter speaks of Europe, the reference is to Western Europe and references to Germany are to West Germany up to 1989 and reunified Germany thereafter.
2. This is a problem to which Polanyi (1944) directs our attention.
3. New classical economists would attach more importance to the level of real wages, while post-Keynesian economists put more stress on levels of aggregate demand, whether domestic or international.
4. For important efforts to do so, however, see Acemoglou, Johnson, and Robinson (2004) and endogenous growth theory more generally (Aghion and Howitt 1988; cf. Liebenstein 1978 on X-efficiency).
5. Of course, some analysts contend that market competition is the only viable route to efficient performance. For a telling account of how strategic coordination can deliver equally good results in some spheres, see Finegold and Soskice (1988).
6. In the 1940s and 1950s, for instance, many analysts and policymakers were highly critical of the strategies pursued by British firms and the *malthusienisme* of French firms (cf. Landes 1949; Baum 1958; Shonfield 1958).
7. For a classic overview, see Shonfield (1969).
8. See Rosanvallon in Hall (1989) and Manow (2001).

9. Compare Beer's account (1969) of the ways in which post-war British institutions reflected new understandings of collective purpose and of how economic and political institutions serve such purposes.

10. The 'replacement rate' is the proportion of previous wages that a worker on unemployment benefit receives.

11. On Fordist modes of production, see Boyer (1990) and the references there. My approach to these issues is deeply influenced by the efforts that he and other founders of the 'regulation school' have made to link the institutions of the macroeconomy to production regimes. See also Amable (2003).

12. These were in the inflows of 'guest workers' between 1959 and 1971. By 1980, there were about four million of these workers and their family members in the country.

13. This feature of the model was influenced by the bargaining system developed amidst labour scarcity during the 1930s, when employers and unions in the export sector joined with employers in the construction sector to negotiate at the peak-level of the economy (Swenson 1991).

14. Around such central tendencies, of course, the strategies adopted by firms in any one country also vary substantially.

15. Of course, the growth of the overseas dollar balances that contributed to the collapse of Bretton Woods also fed these inflationary conditions.

16. A second shift of employment from industry to services that began on a large scale during the 1960s reduced the rate of growth of productivity further, because the productivity gains available in services tended to be smaller than those available in industry.

17. As the Irish case indicates, however, it is not impossible to establish a durable social partnership in LMEs.

18. The average size of a plant in Sweden increased by 23% from 1971 to 1988 (Pontusson 1997).

19. Industrial employment in Germany shrank by 11% between 1970 and 1975 (Kreile 1978).

20. However, these measures indicate that the experience of cutbacks to social benefits, which many see as a recent phenomenon, goes back twenty years.

21. For Germany, of course, the collapse of communism was especially consequential since the reunification of East and West Germany that followed was also an immense economic shock for the political economy. See Streeck (1997).

22. The reorientation of the large German banks is a striking example. Many have reduced their equity stakes and involvement in the management of domestic enterprises in order to focus on global markets. The law of 1999 abolishing capital gains tax on the sale of inter-corporate shareholdings was designed, in part, to allow them to do so.

23. For analyses of why these nations entered into monetary union, see Eichengreen (1997), McNamara (1998) and Dyson and Featherstone (1999).

24. Honoured in the breach as well as the observance, this pact nonetheless inhibits governments from taking exceptionally reflationary steps, thereby also altering

their capacity to assure firms that domestic demand, so crucial to investment, will remain robust.

25. On current trends, 30% of the EU population will be over the age of 65 in 2050, up from 17% in 2005.

26. This is reflected in the British current account deficit, which averaged 25 billion USD from 1995 to 2005 compared with an average surplus of 15 billion USD in Germany and France.

27. Employment in private services in Germany increased faster from 1992 to 2002, than in the EU15.

28. Of course, the striking model for this postulate is Denmark. See Boyer (2005*b*), Campbell, Hall and Pedersen (2006).

29. Hall and Soskice (2001) acknowledge this point, observing that coordinated economies are coordinated *market* economies.

30. I owe this point to Kathleen Thelen.

31. Between 1970 and 1996, a social democratic party held on average 43% of the legislative seats in Germany and 64% in Sweden, while Christian democrats held 41% of the seats in the former and 2% in the latter (Iversen 2005: 251).

32. At 2.6% of GDP, Sweden is spending more an active labour market policy than any other European country.

33. Rueda (2006) reports that respondents with more job security are less likely than those with less security to support increases in taxes designed to advance job creation.

Part II

Macro-Adjustment and Varieties of Capitalism

3

Macroeconomics and Varieties of Capitalism

David Soskice

3.1. INTRODUCTION

There are three motivations behind this chapter. The first arises from the perception that LMEs manage aggregate demand more flexibly than many CMEs, both as far as monetary and fiscal policy is concerned. The core argument of the chapter, which is set out in Section 3.2, is that powerful complementarities tie aggregate demand management regimes (ADBRs) into the nexus of complementarities linking production regimes with welfare states and political systems. As an aide-memoire, these linkages are shown in simplified form in the following table.[1]

Table 3.1 relates to the pattern of complementarities in the 1990s and more recently. My argument is, essentially, that aggregate demand regimes in particular countries changed sharply in line with developments in their production regimes during the 1980s.[2]

The second motivation for the chapter is to demonstrate how developments in modern macroeconomics in the last decade or so help in providing a positive answer to the following question: Do these differences in ADMRs enable us to understand unemployment developments in this recent period? The increasingly dominant New Keynesian paradigm offers a framework in which differences in fiscal and monetary policies may be able to account for some of the variations in unemployment between the large CMEs, Germany and Japan, and the LMEs, the UK and the USA, while also explaining how many small CMEs have relatively low unemployment. This is set out in Section 3.3.

The New Keynesian argument is that prolonged unemployment can arise if adverse demand shocks cannot be offset by ADMRs (or, in the case of small countries, by real exchange rate changes). Lack of offsetting normally only occurs if adverse shocks are large and ADMRs are conservative. This combination held for Japan and Germany throughout the 1990s and more recently—while the UK and the USA, with their discretionary ADMRs—could

Table 3.1. Complementarities between demand management regimes, political systems, welfare states, and production regimes

Production regime	Liberal market economy	Coordinated market economy
Political system	Majoritarian	Consensus
Welfare state	Liberal	Social democratic/continental
Aggregate demand management regime	Discretionary/Delegated, centralized	Rules-based/negotiated contract

brush these shocks aside by rapid interest rate responses augmented by massive discretionary fiscal injections.

This raises the question, which is a central concern of this book, of what has been the response of different types of capitalist systems to a range of major shocks in the last two decades? In this chapter, these shocks are adverse demand shocks, and a third motivation for the chapter is to explore the idea that CMEs react differently to LMEs to major, but not to minor, shocks.

Specifically the proposition, explored in Section 3.4, is this: the complementarities in CMEs which link production regimes with welfare states, political systems, and ADMRs damp down minor but amplify major adverse shocks. To understand properly this dysfunctional amplification requires an understanding of the micro behaviour of households. Much research has been done in comparative political economy into the differences in skill acquisition, labour market participation, and employment patterns of individuals in CMEs and LMEs, contrasting in particular specific and general skills. By contrast, there has been little research on the savings behaviour of specific versus general skill households. Placing the individual in the nexus of complementarities above, it is argued that if welfare state benefits are perceived as difficult to sustain because of major adverse demand shocks, this will differentially increase savings in specific skill households and thus amplify the shock. Thus complementarities may be dysfunctional under certain circumstances.

Behind the chapter lies an intriguing puzzle in the intellectual history of comparative political economy, at least as done by political scientists. The macroeconomics of unemployment and inflation in different types of advanced capitalist systems was a central preoccupation of the neocorporatist literature of the 1970s and the 1980s (see the useful survey by Molina and Rhodes 2002), and on the then research frontier of comparative politics. Low unemployment and inflation were argued to be major benefits of corporatist systems—the consequence of agreements between governments and centralized unions, in which the latter traded wage moderation for expansionary Keynesian employment policies from the former.[3] Moreover, it was the inability of non-corporatist economies to maintain this type of agreement for other than short periods that lay behind the relatively high unemployment of the UK and the USA.

However, the last two decades present a quite different picture. In terms of research in comparative political science macroeconomics has become a minority interest, at least compared to the neocorporatist literature of the early 1980s. Moreover, LMEs, notably the UK and the USA, are now associated with low unemployment—while the two largest CMEs, Germany and Japan, have suffered prolonged high unemployment in the last fifteen years. For many observers, the centralizing or coordinating capacity of unions no longer connotes the benefits it did in the corporatist era. The CMEs are seen, if anything, as associated with higher rather than lower unemployment. While this problem of intellectual history is not central to the chapter, it can be seen that addressing the estrangement of most political scientists from serious macroeconomics—perhaps as a result of the dazzling effects of the shooting star of New Classical economics with its received message that neither aggregate demand nor aggregate demand management could affect unemployment—may be a starting point in its solution.

3.2. AGGREGATE DEMAND MANAGEMENT REGIMES AND VARIETIES OF CAPITALISM

In this section, a theory is sketched of how ADMRs might be incorporated into a broader VoC framework. The intention is to suggest why—or rather under what circumstances—we might expect to see more conservative management of both fiscal and monetary policy in CMEs as opposed to LMEs. This involves, first, spelling out the relationship between production regimes, welfare states, and political systems; second, it will be suggested that there are complementarities between these systems and aggregate demand management.

3.2.1. Complementarities between Production Regimes, Welfare States, and Political Systems

The original VoC literature (Hall and Soskice 2001) was concerned with understanding how *production regimes* worked and with the complementarities of their key institutions (education and training systems, labour market regulation, corporate governance and financial systems, and the governance of inter-company relations in terms of market competition and technology transfer). Neither political systems nor welfare states played a major role in the original development of the VoC framework. Since then, much work has been devoted to analysing the relationship between production regimes and welfare states, and there has been some research into how both of these tie into political systems. Since these linkages have not been set out in convenient form elsewhere, they are summarized in this subsection.

(1) *Welfare states*: What might be described as a VoC view of the welfare state has been developed by Estévez-Abe, Iversen, and others (Estévez-Abe et al. 2001). Here, a strong welfare state underwrites specific skills; in so far as companies located in CMEs build specific assets which need these skills, then a strong welfare state is likely to be associated with CMEs (Iversen 2005). Put simply, and focusing on human capital, the argument is that a precondition for skill specificity, especially if acquired through deep investments early in a career, is the need for extensive guarantees: of wage protection, against the possibility that the returns on the skills acquired will decline over time; of employment protection, against the possibility that employment in which the specific skills are needed will be lost; and of unemployment protection, that there will be adequately compensated time for the unemployed to find appropriate re-employment. The strong welfare state now becomes a guarantee that it is safe to invest in specific skills.[4] Hence CMEs, with their strong emphasis on vocational training and hence specific skills, should be associated with strong welfare states. As Huber and Stephens have pointed out (2001), this affords a bridge to Esping-Andersen's classification (Esping-Andersen 1990) of types of welfare states. The CMEs have either continental or social democratic welfare states—but not liberal. By contrast in LMEs, where flexible labour markets are important to the production regime, the welfare state is liberal.

The welfare state in a CME thus provides the guarantees needed for a workforce to invest in specific skills. This has critical implications for voter and group interests. It implies that the CME constituency which supports the welfare state may stretch across the voting population. By contrast to LMEs such as the UK and the USA—in which skills are primarily general, and where the median voter is typically hostile to welfare state expenditures, which are seen as benefiting low-income groups—the median voter in CMEs with specific skills is typically supportive (Iversen and Soskice 2001). Moreover, as Swenson has shown us in his important historical work, political support for the welfare state is not only to be found in the labour force; business, especially large-organized business, while seldom explicitly vocal, is aware of the importance of welfare state guarantees to the stability of the labour market and training system (Swenson 2002). For businesses also have large specific investments in their workforces. To use Swenson's powerful terminology, where business and unions provide joint support for a particular conception of the welfare state, there is a 'cross-class alliance'. This leads to a discussion of why there might be differences between political systems.

(2) *Political systems: consensus versus majoritarian*: Recent work by Gourevitch, among others, has pointed to a strong correlation between production regimes and the nature of political systems (Gourevitch 2003). The CMEs correspond to consensus political systems, to use Lijphart's term (1984), while LMEs are majoritarian. In general, therefore, government in CMEs has been by explicit coalition or by minority governments with support from other parties, by contrast to single-party government in LMEs. This difference between political systems can be disaggregated into (*a*) differences between electoral systems—PR in the case of consensus systems—versus first past the post in majoritarian; (*b*) representative political parties in which decisions are negotiated out across the different interest groups within the party in consensus systems versus leadership parties in which the leader decides (Iversen and Soskice 2006*a*); and (*c*) effective committee systems versus government decision in public policymaking. Consensus political systems thus play two related roles in CMEs and their associated welfare states. First, they provide a framework for interest groups to take part in policymaking. The importance of this is reflected in the many areas of institutional policymaking in which the major business and union groups have broadly shared goals (training systems, employee representation, collective bargaining, etc.) but often sharply different ideal points within those areas; and where some degree of standardization nationally is called for. The cross-class alliance behind a strong welfare state is an example. There is broad agreement that workers with specific skills need employment, unemployment, and wage protection, but sometimes sharp disagreement over the ideal institutional frameworks and rules within which protection should be embodied. Many disputes are settled outside the political system, but they are typically settled within these broad institutional frameworks. Second, a consensus political system allows negotiated change over time which at least partially takes account of the specific investments individuals and businesses have made in the past. Guarantees that the implied group interests will be represented in future negotiations is based both on the inclusion of interest groups in the process of policymaking and on the nature of parties as representative of groups, and hence acting as a long-term guardian of their interests. From this point of view a majoritarian system is quite unpredictable: policymaking is dominated by single-party government and reflects the concerns of the median voter; thus unless the specific investments are owned by the median voter no account of them

will be taken. But in an LME, with a preponderance of general skills, and/or short-term specific skills, and with innovation systems not geared to long-term incremental innovation and modification, the majoritarian system is not problematic. Moreover, in an LME, the major problem with interest groups is that they seek to create protection for their interest; if government is geared towards the interests of the median voter, the ability of interest groups to buy into the political system is diminished.[5]

There is a second, quite different, relationship between political systems and welfare state types, which reinforces the production regime, political system, and welfare state nexus. Systems of PR empirically favour left of centre coalitions, while majoritarian systems favour the centre-right. There is no accepted reason why this is so, but one argument is that, under PR, with a left, middle and right party, middle-class parties will prefer to govern with left of centre parties since they can jointly tax the rich; yet it does not pay the middle-class party to ally with the rich since this leaves little to be extracted from low-income groups. By contrast, in the two-party centre-left/centre-right world of majoritarian electoral systems, the risk-averse middle-class voter—never sure of whether a government once in power will not move towards its more extreme supporters—will generally prefer the centre-right party which, at worst, will lower taxes, to the centre-left which, at worst, will raise taxes on the middle class and redistribute them to lower-income groups (Iversen and Soskice 2006a). Thus welfare state strength in CMEs reflects both directly the need to insure specific skills and indirectly the redistributive consequences of PR in consensus political systems. These contrasts are nicely drawn by Kitschelt (2006) and Stephens (2006) in a symposium on Iversen's *Capitalism, Democracy and Welfare*(2005).[6] Thus far the argument is summarized in Figure 3.1.

3.2.2. Bringing Aggregate Demand Management Regimes into the Nexus

The basic argument of this section is that where governments are powerful and unified, and where individual agents are 'small', governments can generally take decisions on fiscal and monetary policy without being concerned that discretionary behaviour may weaken their bargaining position. If governments *ceteris paribus* gain from discretionary behaviour, and if they have the power to select ADMRs, then we should expect them to favour looser monetary and fiscal arrangements.[7] We argue below that this characterizes LMEs since the early 1990s—though not necessarily before, when ur-LMEs confronted and wanted to break the power of powerful unions. By

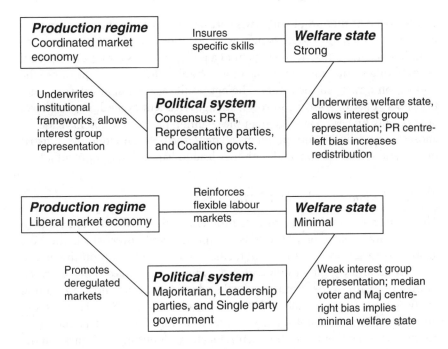

Figure 3.1. Production regime, welfare state and political systems: LMEs and CMEs compared.

contrast, when the authorities confront a small number of powerful unions—this will be referred to as the Small-N case—they are likely to prefer conservative monetary and fiscal arrangements. This is also likely to hold in a coalition government when the prime minister or minister of finance is confronted by powerful coalition partners. These 'non-encompassing' situations can lead to inefficiencies when ADMRs are discretionary, and we argue that it is usually in the interests of the key actors to support conservative monetary and fiscal regimes. This corresponds to nearly all CMEs since the early 1990s—but not necessarily earlier when some ur-CMEs, notably Sweden and Denmark, had encompassing labour and business organizations. The main current exceptions to the Small-N case are Norway and less clearly Iceland, both of which have maintained more discretionary ADMRs.

The two problems faced by CMEs (but not by LMEs) are well known. The first comes from the literature on wage bargaining. In the Small-N case, sectoral bargainers can often raise relative wages and prices in large sectors because of demand inelasticity (absent external sanctions, here in the form of a conservative monetary authority); so absent such sanctions an economy composed of a small number of bargainers is likely to have a lower level of competitiveness than would otherwise prevail. The second, the common pool problem, is often associated as here with coalition policymaking, where the coalition partner gains the full benefit of a policy but pays for it out of general taxation or government borrowing, thus spreading the cost over the rest of the population now or in the future. The net result (again absent external sanctions, here of strong fiscal control) is that government expenditure and taxes are typically higher on average than the coalition partners would have ideally chosen cooperatively. Both problems relate to the political economy of distribution and redistribution, and both may lead to Pareto-inferior outcomes.

3.2.2.1. *Unions in LMEs and CMEs*

The LMEs are vulnerable to neither problem while CMEs are vulnerable to both. Before explaining why this is so, the timescale over which the VoC analysis is meant to apply is set out, since there is confusion on this point. The VoC analysis applies to the different types of economies which emerged in the aftermath of the profound shocks which hit the advanced economies in the period from the late 1960s to the mid- to late 1980s. There is still much disagreement about the key drivers of change and the dynamic interrelation between them, but three central factors, all putting into question the organization of labour markets and skill systems, were (*a*) the IT revolution, implying a move towards more skill-intensive systems of production, (*b*) the growing inability of a number of countries to control the power of semi-skilled workers in Fordist plants, and (*c*) the great improvement over time in the educational levels of those entering the labour market in all countries. Together they led to the end of protection of traded goods, in turn spelling the end of Fordism, both of which were fiercely politically contested events. Fordism and mass semi-skilled workforces were more important in those economies which became LMEs; long distinguished by lack of vocational training systems, and by lack of the coordinated employer movements and cooperative unions needed to create such systems, these mainly Anglo-Saxon economies moved strategically towards flexible labour markets. Based on a labour force with general education and competences, and giving businesses the ability to reposition themselves rapidly, flexible labour markets, and the full exposure of companies to world competition were seen as the only feasible way of developing competitive advantages in world markets. Critical to our argument, the success of the LME strategy (and its conflictuality notably in the UK and New Zealand) depended on the elimination of powerful unions.[8] Thus LME production regimes have increasingly moved to flexible labour markets in which the bargaining and political power of unions has been substantially extinguished.

Those economies which had effective vocational training systems, coordi-nated employers, and cooperative unions in the 1970s took the CME strategic path, developing specific skilled workforces with both industry-occupational and company skills. Because CME workforces have strong company- and industry-specific skills, they are in principle in a strong bargaining position in relation to their employers. First, their specific tacit knowledge means that they are difficult to monitor; instead, employers seek long-term coop-erative agreements with employee representatives whereby skilled employees are given considerable responsibility—the management to non-management ratio is relatively small in CMEs compared to LMEs. Thus industrial disrup-tion, if it comes, is costly to employers. Second, the specific skills are costly to replace, and probably impossible to do so in the short run.

This has implications for union bargaining structures and leads to what we call the Small-N union system in current CMEs:

(a) Companies do not want wage bargaining primarily located at the com-pany level. This is for two reasons. First, in transaction cost terms, employees with strong company-specific skills would then be in a position to hold the company to ransom; for instance, if the company introduced new machinery and it was costly to train employees to use it, they would be in a strong bargaining position *ex post* to demand higher wages. Second, if wages were determined at company level, it would be difficult for an employer to make a credible commitment to a potential new employee that future wages would not fall below the industry average[9] (unless the company already had a strong reputation). So hiring good apprentices would become harder, at least if once hired their specific skills partially lock them into the company. Hence companies in CMEs, with specific skilled workforces, want unions with wide bargaining jurisdictions.[10]

(b) How wide is the optimal jurisdiction from the employer's point of view? Not too wide: Centralized economywide bargaining has become increas-ingly unattractive to companies relying on highly skilled and experienced workforces. This is because it is associated with egalitarian wage agreements (Wallerstein 1999). While there is no agreed theory, the intuition is as follows: because bargaining is centralized, the union central represents both skilled and unskilled workers; it is harder for the union central to persuade the employer side that unskilled workers will strike because unskilled workers, being easily replaceable, are typically in a much less secure employment position, hence less prepared to strike. Thus unskilled workers need greater compensation from any potential strike to make it credible to employers that they will be prepared to strike if called to do so: this is provided by the union central adopting egalitarian wage demands. But this is a problem for companies needing skilled experienced workforces. For egalitarian wages make it harder for employers to fashion career incentive structures; and the more the employer relies on skilled workers the more important internal incentives become. In consequence, as Pontusson and Swenson (1996) have argued, leading Swedish employers in the advanced export sectors, in cross-class alliance with export sector unions representing relatively more highly skilled workers, overturned the pre-existing centralized bargaining structure.

In terms of wage bargaining structures, no CMEs fall into the flexible labour market category. But, equally, the few countries which had still had centralized wage bargaining in the 1980s, notably Sweden and Denmark, had moved to a more pluralist system in the 1990s, albeit with a limited number of bargainers. Thus CMEs have typically a Small-N bargaining system. However, there are a handful of CMEs which still have important elements of centralization: Norway and Iceland outside EMU, and Finland and Belgium within EMU (in all four cases with some form of optout from the extreme egalitarianism which characterized pre-reform Sweden and Denmark).

3.2.2.2. Monetary Institutions and Small-N Bargaining

What are the consequences for monetary and fiscal institutional arrangements? Why are monetary institutions more conservative in countries with a small number of powerful unions than either in countries with a single centralized union or in countries with flexible labour markets?

Why does it pay to have a conservative monetary authority in the Small-N case? We can illustrate this in a simple game, where it is assumed that in a two-sector economy each sector has a monopoly union. The two unions set wages independently of each other (e.g. simultaneously), though, of course, any amount of discussion may have taken place between them. Both sectors export and produce for the domestic market. Thus, if the real wage is held constant in sector 2, an increased real wage in sector 1 has two consequences for that sector: it increases the consumption real wage in the sector since sector 1 workers can now buy more sector 2 goods; but it reduces the competitiveness of sector 1 in both export and domestic markets. In this simple example, each union can either raise the real wage or hold it constant in their sector. We make two assumptions about monetary policy: first, we assume that it is accommodating so that if real wages are increased—requiring an increase in money wages and hence prices—real interest rates will be held constant. The result is shown in Table 3.2.

To see the outcome of this game we need to understand the preferences of the two unions. The union in the Small-N case is concerned both about real wages and employment. It may be more accurate to say that it has two broad

Table 3.2. Small-N case with accommodating monetary policy

		Union 1	
		Raise	*Constant*
	Raise	Both lose competitiveness; and lose exports; with 'foreign' real wage gains only	1: competitiveness constant and no loss of exports but loses 'domestic' real wages and domestic demand
			2: loses competitiveness but gains 'foreign and domestic' real wages
Union 2			
	Constant	2: competitiveness constant and no loss of exports but loses 'domestic' real wages and domestic demand	No change
		1: loses competitiveness but gains 'foreign and domestic' real wages	

constituencies: core-skilled workers in profitable sectors who are unlikely to lose their job even with the high real wage option with accommodating demand management, and whose interest is thus in raising real wages; and workers in less profitable companies, as well as less secure workers in profitable companies whose interest is primarily in employment security. In the game above the union will be under considerable pressure to go for the high real wage option. In this classic prisoners' dilemma, whatever the other union does, the sector 1 (2) union can always get higher real wages by moving from moderate to high: If the other sector's real wage remains moderate, sector 1 workers' income rises both in terms of the cost of purchasing sector 2 products and of the cost of imports (similarly for sector 2). Hence if sector 1 workers are more concerned about increasing real wages than employment losses at the starting point, they will vote for high real wages if sector 2 real wages remain moderate (similarly for sector 2). If sector 2 wages are raised, the argument for sector 1 also to go for a high real wage is stronger, since the moderate alternative implies that sector 1 workers will face higher sector 2 prices if their wage remains moderate. So both sectors will choose the high real wage: this implies both lose competitiveness, but their purchasing power of domestic goods does not increase since wages have risen in both sectors.

Conservative monetary authorities change this outcome. The conservative monetary authority reacts sharply to inflation by raising interest rates and hence exchange rates: this weakens competitiveness sharply and puts core jobs at risk. Each union knows that if it chooses a wage increase, it will itself generate enough inflation—whatever the other union does—for the monetary authority to respond proportionately to the resulting increase in inflation.

Hence such a move puts at least some core jobs at risk. And hence it is plausible that the sectoral union will choose moderation rather than the high wage route. In which case both unions will choose moderation in this equilibrium with a conservative monetary authority.

Thus conservative ADMRs change the trade-off between real wages and employment: the same real wage increase now becomes more expensive in terms of employment losses. If a major concern of the union is the employment of its members, a conservative monetary authority will always be able to adopt a tough enough policy in terms of interest rates and the exchange rate in the Small-N system to make moderation an optimal policy choice by the union independently of the other union. In that case both unions will choose moderation. Sufficient monetary toughness thus converts a prisoners' dilemma game into a cooperative one.

In the Small-N wage bargaining system, conservative monetary authorities will not necessarily be unattractive to unions with wide jurisdictions and a concern with real wage moderation to preserve employment. Moreover the preservation of competitiveness and profitability which derives from real wage moderation makes non-accommodation in the interest of employers. Thus, given the Small-N wage bargaining system, non-accommodating monetary authorities are likely to be maintained or moved towards. And since as we have seen the Small-N wage bargaining system is a likely consequence of CME production regimes in the 1990s, we can also argue that CME production regimes are likely to lead to non-accommodating monetary authorities. The exception is when collective bargaining takes place under more centralized conditions in CMEs; here we would expect more discretionary ADMRs.

The situation with LMEs is quite different. LMEs, at least by the 1990s, have had flexible labour markets and/or at least a very large number of wage bargaining units. Hence a switch from an accommodating to a non-accommodating monetary authority does not increase the incentive for moderation for the individual wage or price setter. In so far as a government benefits from a rapid response to an unemployment shock, then it may want to have some direct or indirect understanding that its monetary authority will react in that way. Thus it is not surprising that LMEs have central banks with closer links to the government than those in CMEs.

3.2.2.3. *Fiscal Policy and the Political System*

Why should we expect CMEs to have tougher fiscal policy regimes than LMEs? We believe that the degree of discretion which governments allow themselves to have over fiscal policy depends on whether the fiscal authority faces powerful bargainers making demands on government expenditure. There are three reasons why this is more likely to occur in CMEs and LMEs.

The first and major reason is that CME political systems are consensus-based, while LMEs are majoritarian. As noted earlier a consequence of CME consensus-based political systems is that CMEs typically have coalition governments (or implicit coalitions in which minority governments rely on a stable set of parties for support on agreed policies). Moreover, the parties which make up the explicit or implicit coalitions are normally representative parties, where the party represents a more or less well-defined social group or groups. By contrast, the majoritarian electoral systems of LMEs produce in general single-party government. And the governing party is typically a leadership-based party in which the party leader (prime minister) decides policies.

This field was opened up by von Hagen, who argued that coalition governments will work out ways to remover discretion from fiscal policy in order to solve the common pool problem (Hallerberg, Strauch, and von Hagen 2001). Without such arrangements and following the standard Laver–Shepsle model, coalition governments imply that different parties make decisions about government expenditure in different areas. If these decisions are taken independently but financed out of general taxation, the common pool problem arises.

So it is in the interest of each member of the coalition to accept an external discipline to maximize the interest of the group they represent. Obviously one way to do this would be to impose a tax on each group equal to its expenditure; in practice that is very difficult to do unless groups are defined by region (or perhaps by income). So the most obvious constraint is that the government is required to bargain out a complete programme to which individual coalition partners then have to stick. A common way in which this is done is to give the Finance Ministry the role of monitoring and sanctioning expenditures along the lines of the programmatic 'contract'.

This logic, that we should expect to see tough finance ministries in consensus political systems with little room for discretionary expenditure, is reinforced by a second argument. This is that tough monetary authorities require tough fiscal authorities for their own credibility. Monetary policy uses interest rates to operate on aggregate demand; this is what drives changes in unemployment relative to equilibrium and hence changes in inflation. Fiscal policy also operates on aggregate demand, so in principle an expansionary fiscal policy can nullify a contractionary monetary policy. Thus, if monetary policy is to be effectively conservative, fiscal policy must eschew an aggregate demand role, and simply ensure fiscal stability.

The third reason why governments may prefer a conservative fiscal policy relates to the nature of representative parties and the public policy formation process in a consensus political system. Representative parties represent interest groups, in particular labour and business. Thus Small-N unions and business associations operate through political parties to press their interests.

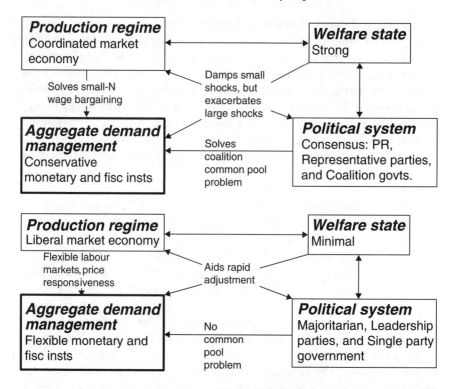

Figure 3.2. Production regime, welfare state, political system and aggregate demand management: LMEs and CMEs compared

They also typically have direct access to the process of public policy formation. This is not necessarily a problem with an encompassing union and business organizations: for it will pay them to bargain out between themselves a pareto-optimal agreement. But particularly if the groups are individually powerful but imperfectly coordinated (as is likely in the Small-N case) the common pool problem will be reinforced if fiscal control is weak. We may sum up this section in Figure 3.2.

3.2.3. Empirical Evidence on Aggregate Demand Management Regimes

As explained in the introduction, a main motivation for the chapter is to explain why major adverse demand shocks have led, in some economies but not others, to persistent unemployment in recent years. This section shows that a key necessary condition for dampening major shocks is that monetary and fiscal authorities are concerned to engage actively to stabilize output gaps as well as to keep inflation on target, a characteristic often loosely referred to as 'discretion'. The optimal way to measure the discretion of authorities is by examining the estimated coefficients of a properly specified econometric model, and this is an intention of future research. Here, however, we follow the standard practice of measuring discretion by properties of institutions, which is outlined below.

3.2.3.1. *Central Banks and Monetary Policy*

In the case of central banks discretion has been interpreted as dependence on government, and although this definition is not ideal it will be adopted here. The most widely used indices on central bank independence date to 1990 (Grilli et al.) and 1992 (Cukierman). These are criticized for their treatment of the USA and Japan (Japan is classified as having low independence since it was controlled directly by the Ministry of Finance, but the Japanese Ministry of Finance is strongly conservative). Moreover, since 1990 many changes have taken place, notably with the advent of the ECB, and changes in the con-stitutions of the UK, New Zealand, and Japanese central banks. The CMEs outside EMU are Denmark, Sweden, Norway, Iceland, and Japan, and the LMEs Australia, Canada, New Zealand, the UK, and the USA.

Here we show that there are significant differences between the role of government in formulating the criteria under which central banks operate. Following the New Zealand central bank's recent comparative work, we sug-gest two criteria are important. First, whether the government is involved in setting the target rate of inflation (inapplicable only to the Danish central bank, which pegs the Danish krone to the euro). The second criterion is not so clear cut: whether employment and/or output are part of the goals of the bank. We do not discuss national central banks within EMU, but we record the rules for the ECB.

Table 3.3 suggests that central banks are 'responsive' to government con-cerns in LMEs with flexible labor markets, and in CMEs with quasi-centralised wage bargaining systems. But they are 'non-responsive' in CMEs with small-N wage bargaining systems.

3.2.3.2. *Fiscal Policy*

As explained above, the major work which has been done in this area is by von Hagen and associates. In recent work, based on questionnaires covering the period 1998–2000, they classified EU governments according to whether there was (*a*) a contract formed across coalition partners, (*b*) powers were delegated to the finance minister, or (*c*) a hybrid case (Hallerberg, Strauch, and von Hagen 2001). This work indirectly suggests an answer to the question of the degree of discretion governments enjoy in stimulating the economy in the face of an adverse demand shock. In the case of (*a*), the contract between

Table 3.3. Aggregate demand management regimes and labour market institutions

Central bank	Government involved in inflation target	Objectives beyond price stability	Shifts 1980s to 1990s/2000s
Liberal Market Economies (flexible labour markets)			
UK	Inflation target set by Chancellor of Exchequer	'To maintain price stability and subject to that to support the economic policy of Her Majesty's government including its objectives for growth and employment'	Tight monetary control by government when unions remained strong in 1980s. Designed to break unions
USA	No formal inflation target. 'Independent within government. Its decisions do not have to be ratified by government, but they must be consistent with overall framework of economic and financial policy'	'Economic growth in line with the economy's potential to expand; a high level of employment; stable prices; moderate long-term interest rates'	
Australia	Inflation target agreed with Treasurer	'To ensure that monetary and banking policy . . . will best contribute to (a) the stability of the currency in Australia; (b) the maintenance of full employment in Australia; (c) the economic prosperity and welfare of the people of Australia'	
New Zealand	Inflation target agreed with Minister of Finance	'. . . maintaining stability of prices'[a] (1988). But 'As New Zealand's PTA has evolved, it has incorporated more references to real economy considerations. In the last six years, additions have included the notion . . . that policy should seek to avoid unnecessary instability in output, interest rates and the exchange rate'[b]	Central bank independence in 1988 during period of Douglas reforms; since then a significant shift of policy has taken place as powerful unions have been replaced by more flexible labour markets
Canada	Inflation target agreed with government	'To promote the economic and financial well-being of Canada'	

Coordinated market economies (Small-N bargaining)			
Sweden	Government, no role	'To maintain price stability'	Tight monetary regime adopted with move to Small-N bargaining
Switzerland	Government, no role	Its primary goal is to ensure price stability, while taking due account of economic developments. In so doing, it creates an appropriate environment for economic growth[c]	
Japan	Government, no role	'Currency and monetary control shall be aimed at, through the pursuit of monetary policy, the development of a sound national economy'	
		'BOJ officials have maintained a devotion to price stability in the post-war period that rivals the MOF commitment to fiscal balance'[d]	
Denmark	n.a.	To ensure a stable krone' 'Other aspects than the exchange rate—e.g. cyclical developments in Denmark—are not considered'[e]	Switch to Small-N bargaining; and switch from more accommodating monetary regime
ECB	Governments, no role	'To maintain price stability'	
Centralized market economies (Quasi Centralized)			
Norway	Government sets inflation target	'Monetary policy shall also contribute to stabilizing output and employment'[f]	Bargaining system more decentralized early 2002 on, though substantial centralized component remains
Iceland	Government agrees inflation target	'The Bank shall support the economic policy of the Government as long as it does not deem it inconsistent with the objective of price stability'[g]	

Sources: New Zealand Central Bank report for columns 2 and 3 except where stated (report does not cover); italics are either from the report or refer to quotes from central bank websites. Column 4 are author's comments.

[a] In initial legislation establishing independent NZ Central Bank in 1988.
[b] NZ Reserve Bank briefing note 2002.
[c] SNB home page.
[d] Vogel p. 47.
[e] Danish Central Bank report on monetary policy 2003.
[f] Norges Bank website.
[g] Central Bank of Iceland website.

Table 3.4. Ranking of degree of delegation or centralization in budgetary implementation by the Finance Ministry: 4 = highly centralized; 0 = low

Score	EU member-state
4	UK, *France*, Austria
3	Ireland, *Italy*
2	Denmark, Germany, Luxembourg
1	Belgium, Finland, Netherlands
0	Sweden

coalition partners, the freedom of movement of governments may be limited because of the difficulty of delegating power to a single player; and in fact (*c*) may be a shadow case of (*a*) in which minority governments (Denmark and Sweden) have to commit credibly to an implicit coalition agreement. So the best measure of discretion using the von Hagen et al. approach may be the case in which power is delegated to a single actor (the Ministry of Finance). They measure the power of the Ministry of Finance in planning the budget, in the legislatory process and in implementation, and provide a composite index. But, since the most precise questions are posed in the latter stage, we use their ranking of delegation (or centralization) in the implementation stage. This index gives scores from 0 to 4 and the data is presented in Table 3.4. The only surprise in this list is Austria. Otherwise, it conforms reasonably well to the LME–CME division. The LMEs have more discretion (on this measure) than CMEs.

A quite different measure is provided by the OECD at a more aggregated level. Figure 3.3 shows the contemporaneous correlation between the change

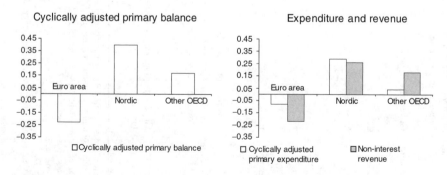

Figure 3.3. Contemporaneous correlation between the change in the cyclically adjusted primary balance and the output gap, 1981–2005

in the cyclically adjusted primary balance and the output gap over the period 1981–2005 for the countries that now make up the eurozone, the Nordic countries and 'other' OECD. Finland is included with the Nordic group. The results indicate that fiscal policy has tended to be pro-cyclical in the eurozone countries but counter-cyclical in the two other groups. The Nordic group is biased towards counter-cyclicality on account of public sector employment tending to rise in recessions as women seek to return to work. The Euro group is largely CME: so the figure confirms our broad hypothesis. The third group consists primarily of the LMEs, the USA and the UK, and the CME Japan. There is independent evidence that the Japanese government has generally had a tight fiscal policy, see Vogel (2006: 46–8). So the counter-cyclicality over this period probably reflects the USA and the UK.

3.3. MODERN MACROECONOMICS

Since the early 1980s comparative political scientists have paid little attention to macro demand management. One reason for this is the perception among many political economists that macro demand management can have no impact: this reflects the success of Alesina's application of New Classical economics in demolishing Hibb's position that governments could choose their preferred unemployment-inflation trade-off (Hibbs 1977; Alesina 1989). This is not a particular argument to be engaged in here; Hibb's own exposition of Keynesian macroeconomics is, to current thinking, flawed—but so too is Alesina's implication that Keynesian economics and macro demand management is no longer relevant. Modern macroeconomics has moved a long way from the New Classical paradigm in which only short-term mistakes about the current money supply could explain temporary movements away from equilibrium unemployment. A second reason is that the research frontier of modern macroeconomics has been technically difficult for much of the last two decades; few developments percolated to the undergraduate level; and only recently has the basic New Keynesian model—increasingly the paradigm—been set out in simplified form. Section 3.3.1 sets out this current standard model.[11]

3.3.1. New Keynesian Macroeconomics

This section outlines some of the main propositions of mainstream modern macroeconomics, often referred to as New Keynesian macroeconomics or the three-equation model and associated with such economists as Ball, Bernanke,

Blanchard, Clarida, Gali, Gertler, Layard, Mankiw, Nickell, D Romer, and Svennson (see references in Carlin and Soskice 2006). Unlike the New Classical approach, the New Keynesian model assumes that markets are not perfectly competitive and that prices and wages take time to adjust. The model is at the core of modern central bank practice and graduate-level macroeconomics. The large forecasting models used by central banks, international organizations, and governments are disaggregated forms of it. It explains how economies respond to demand and inflation shocks, with monetary policy playing a key role. (It is noteworthy that, although this approach is increasingly the new orthodoxy and although it implies that governments can have a strong effect on the real economy, it is rarely used by political scientists.)

Most work on New Keynesian economics has focused on the closed economy, doubtless because it has been primarily developed in the USA, and we will set out the closed economy model first. We will see later that the open economy operates to give aggregate demand movements more potential importance than the closed. In the three-equation closed economy model, the first equation determines aggregate demand or economic activity. Aggregate demand depends on three major factors: the real short-term rate of interest controlled by the central bank; fiscal policy, controlled by the government; and exogenous private-sector expenditure. Leaving fiscal policy aside for the moment, this equation says that aggregate demand depends positively on exogenous private-sector expenditure and negatively on the interest rate. The time-lag structure is important: There is usually assumed to be an average lag of a year before interest rates affect demand. This is the broad assumption that is made by the Bank of England and built into a widely used version of the three-equation model referred to as the Ball–Svensson model (see Carlin and Soskice 2005). This equation is called the IS or aggregate-demand equation. Because unemployment is closely inversely related to the level of economic activity, we can also think of the equation as determining unemployment.

The second equation is the short-run Phillips curve, which determines inflation relative to expected inflation. Excess demand in the labour market, the difference between unemployment and equilibrium unemployment, takes about a year to impact the rate of inflation. It pushes up inflation relative to what wage and price setters expect the rate of inflation to be. The logic here is that excess demand for a particular good or service leads the relevant price setter(s) to try to raise its expected relative price, by increasing its price faster than the expected rise in the general price level; repeated throughout the economy, the general price level rises faster than its expected increase. Empirically there is strong evidence that the expected increase in inflation is simply its pre-existing rate. Hence inflation rises faster than its pre-existing rate if unemployment is below equilibrium, and it rises more slowly if there is excess aggregate supply. Combining the IS and Phillips curve equations shows, for example, that a cut in the interest rate in 2001 reduces unemployment in 2002 which in turn raises inflation relative to its existing rate in 2003. The third equation is the monetary rule, sometimes called the Taylor rule, and it shows how the central bank sets current short-term real interest rates to respond to the deviation of inflation from its target rate and/or to the deviation of unemployment from equilibrium. It therefore closes the model. Imagine that in 2001 unemployment rises above equilibrium, with inflation falling below the bank's target rate. The central bank responds using the Taylor rule by lowering the interest rate. Via the IS curve, the lower current (2001) interest rate boosts activity levels in 2002, pushing down unemployment and creating excess demand in the labour market. Using the Phillips curve, we can see that inflation then begins to rise in 2003, as a result of the excess supply in the labour market in 2002. How fast it rises back to the target rate depends on how wage increases respond to the excess supply in the Phillips curve.

That at least is the theory: the three-equation model has been widely accepted as showing how, in the absence of automatic market mechanisms for bringing unemployment back to its unique equilibrium level, a well-functioning interest rate policy based on an inflation target could do just that. But there is considerable evidence that much depends on how inflation targeting is carried out, and even then that sole reliance on it is for fair weather not foul. The next step sets out some of these limitations of inflation targeting (it is confined to a closed economy with a unique equilibrium unemployment rate).

(a) Much depends on the CB objective function. Its degree of 'conservatism' is important in three main respects: A *low inflation target* may be difficult for private sector actors to attain, especially in the presence of non-wage cost shocks: this is an under-theorized area, but there is some empirical evidence which suggests that a reduction in inflation at low positive levels—around 2 per cent—is difficult because it typically entails cutting money wages for some proportion of employees; this can be a signal for coordinated resistance by employees. A conservative CB may also attach a *high weight to inflation deviation* compared to unemployment deviations from target. And, most significantly, the CB *response function may be asymmetric*— it may respond by raising interest rates to inflation above target but not to cutting them when inflation falls below its target. In the latter case, there is simply no policy available to act on increased unemployment, even when the higher unemployment has pushed inflation below target—policy only moves when inflation is above target.

(b) Much depends also on the responsiveness of unemployment to interest rates. A critical assumption is that, after an adverse demand shock, there will be *some* change in the real short-term interest rate which will restore aggregate demand back to the level needed for equilibrium unemployment. There are two issues here. The first is the responsiveness of aggregate demand to a unit cut in the short run real interest rate. The second is the limit to which it is possible to cut the short-term real rate. 'Well-behaved' households using rational expectations and able to borrow on future income movements will infer that a credible central bank will keep the interest rate below that needed to restore demand to a level consistent with equilibrium unemployment until unemployment is decreased again and inflation pushed back up to its target level. Hence they will infer that their future income will be improving and therefore increase consumption. But this optimistic picture has many flaws: borrowing on future income prospects may be difficult (liquidity constraints and bank nervousness), as was the case in Japan; or a major adverse shock may induce greater pessimism about the future, including fears for the welfare state in Germany and employment security in Japan (Section 3.4). In any case, the nominal interest rate is bounded below by zero: suppose the inflation rate is 2 per cent so that the real interest rate is—2 per cent, but that this generates insufficient aggregate demand for equilibrium unemployment; then, via the Phillips curve inflation will keep falling so long as unemployment remains above equilibrium; that implies that the real rate of interest falls and goes on falling, with unemployment therefore increasing. This is sometimes described as the modern version of Keynes' liquidity trap.

Thus in the closed economy it is far from evident that major adverse demand shocks can be neutralized in a relatively short period by interest rate rules. This brings in the need to add fiscal policy to the demand management repertoire when monetary policy is unable to work by itself. This was the (more or less) explicit response of the administration in the USA and the tacit response of the UK government to the sharp 2001–2 recession. In the 1990s as a whole the German government remained hostile to discretionary use of fiscal policy and insisted that it was de facto ruled out by the Maastricht Treaty; and the Japanese Ministry of Finance had to be dragged into accepting it as the Japanese crisis worsened.

3.3.2. Equilibrium Unemployment in Closed and Open Economies

A key element of the New Keynesian approach to the closed economy is that there is a unique equilibrium rate of unemployment. The same is of course true of the New Classical model, but there union bargaining and wage restraint can have no role. By contrast in the New Keynesian model equilibrium unemployment depends on the implications for real wages which come from wage-setting on the one hand and price-setting on the other. Both wage-setting and price-setting are nominal operations, but the goal in the first is some level of the real wage and in the second of real profits. Wage-setting can be carried out by employers alone ('efficiency wages') or as a result of bargaining—we focus on wage bargaining. Unions bargain for an expected real wage. The lower the level of aggregate unemployment, the higher the bar-gained expected real wage, w^B. But real wages are also set implicitly as a result of price-setting: Take the simplest case of unit labour productivity, so that nominal unit cost is simply the money wage W. And suppose product markets enable businesses to set a mark-up of $1 + \mu$ on unit costs (where the mark-up covers fixed costs as well as a monopoly element), so that the price level $P = (1 + \mu)W$, implying a (price-setting) real wage of $w = W/P = 1/(1 + \mu)$.

Equilibrium is defined as a constant rate of inflation. In equilibrium, the bargained real wage w^B must equal the price-setting real wage w. This because if, say $w^B > w$ by 1 per cent, wage bargainers will believe they can raise the real wage by 1 per cent; so if pre-existing inflation is 2 per cent, this implies that unions will individually set nominal wage inflation at 3 per cent, in the belief that the real wage will increase by 1 per cent. However, this implies that businesses will raise prices by 3 per cent to restore their mark-up. And if this process continues nominal wage inflation and price inflation will subsequently rise to 4 per cent, and so on. So, for equilibrium, the bargainable real wage w^B needs to be equal to the price-setting real wage. If the unemployment rate is too low, $w^B > w$; if too high $w^B < w$, so the equilibrium unemployment rate brings w^B into line with w.

Some useful consequences are as follows. Union bargaining power tends to be higher the lower the elasticity of demand in the (aggregated) product markets which correspond to union bargaining coverage, since an increase in the bargained real wage implies a smaller fall in employment; hence equilib-rium unemployment needs to be higher to bring down w^B into line with w. Since the more aggregated the product market is (i.e. the more sub-sectors it covers) the more inelastic will be product demand, and at the same time the smaller will be the overall number of unions: so, *ceteris paribus*, the smaller the number of unions the higher the equilibrium unemployment rate. (There is a double whammy here, for the more inelastic product demand is the larger will be the pricing mark-up μ, and hence the smaller the price-setting real wage— also pushing up the equilibrium rate of unemployment.) But *cetera* are not necessarily *pares*: wage restraint, the foregoing of bargaining power, allows the equilibrium unemployment rate to fall, and small numbers of unions may be better able than larger numbers to organize wage restraint.

Unfortunately, for comparative political economy much less work has been done in open economies. There is, however, a persuasive argument that in open economies there may be many unemployment equilibria: We follow Layard, Nickell, and Jackman (1990). In the open economy equilibrium unemployment is determined as in the closed by the requirement that the bargained real wage, w^{WS}, is equal to the real wage implied by price-setting, w^{PS}. The bargained real wage is determined as before, and we will keep with the simple case in which it declines as unemployment rises. But w^{PS} is different. This is because the price level is now a weighted average of domestic costs of production (W) and world prices (P^*). World prices are important since they directly affect import costs and indirectly impose limits on mark-ups as a consequence of potential competition. If P^* is high relative to P, that reduces the real wage for two reasons—it implies a high real cost of imports and it enables domestic companies to set a high profit mark-up. The ratio P/P^* is the real exchange rate;[12] a high real exchange rate means a high price-setting real wage (low cost of imports and low-profit mark-up), and vice versa. Thus a high real exchange rate allows a high bargained real wage and hence a low equilibrium level of unemployment, and vice versa.

How is the equilibrium rate of unemployment chosen? In the following diagram, Figure 3.4, the real wage is on the vertical axis, with unemployment on

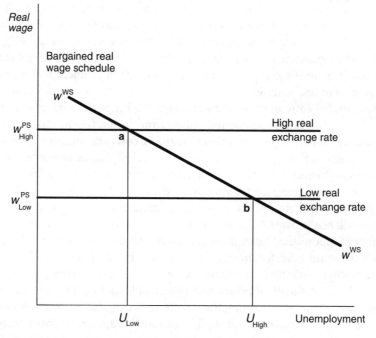

Figure 3.4. Open economy model (1): Real exchange rates, wage bargaining, and equilibrium unemployment

the horizontal. The downwards sloping relationship shows how the bargained real wage, w^{WS}, declines as aggregate unemployment increases.

The real wage implied by price-setting is high when the real exchange rate is high, w^{PS}_{High}, since the real cost of imports is then low and the profit mark-up is subdued because of the competitive effects of low world prices. So when the real exchange rate is high, the high price-setting real wage means that the bargained or wage-setting real wage will also be high in equilibrium; and that allows equilibrium unemployment to be low, U_{Low}, as shown by the intersection at **a**.

By contrast, a low real exchange rate implies a low price-setting real wage, hence a low bargained real wage and a high unemployment rate in equilibrium, indicated by the intersection at **b**. The actual equilibrium unemployment rate is determined by aggregate demand. Figure 3.5 shows how the mechanism works.

Assume the economy is initially in equilibrium at **a** with low equilibrium unemployment and a high real wage $w^{WS} = w^{PS}_{High}$, with high aggregate

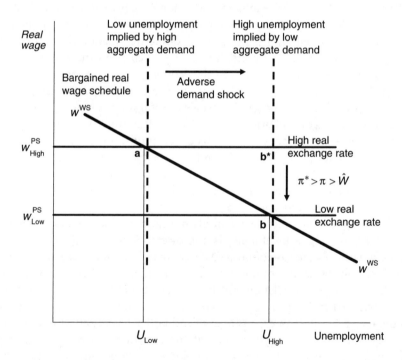

Figure 3.5. Open economy (2): Equilibrium unemployment and adverse demand shocks

demand implying low equilibrium unemployment. There is then an adverse demand shock, shown in the diagram by the rightward shift of the vertical aggregate demand dashed line. This pushes up unemployment and pushes down the bargained real wage, so that the actual real wage (w_{High}^{PS}) is now above the bargained real wage (say by 2%). The consequence is that employers bargaining with unions will be able to push down the real wage. Suppose initially that world inflation, domestic inflation, and nominal wage inflation are all 3 per cent, implying a constant real exchange rate (since domestic inflation is equal to world inflation) and a constant real wage (since nominal wage inflation is equal to domestic inflation). Then if wage bargainers in year one believe domestic inflation will continue at 3 per cent, money wage inflation will fall to 1 per cent to engineer an expected real wage cut of 2 per cent. What do price setters do in consequence of these 1 per cent money wage increases? Domestic inflation is a weighted average of money wage inflation and world price inflation, so the fall in money wage inflation will reduce domestic inflation relative to world inflation and this will reduce the real exchange rate. Thus if, for example, domestic inflation (π) is composed half of money wage inflation ($\hat{W}$) and half of world price inflation (π^*), domestic price inflation will fall to 2 per cent ($\pi = 0.5\hat{W} + 0.5\pi^* = 0.5 \times 1\% + 0.5 \times 3\% = 2\%$). Hence the real exchange rate will fall by 1 per cent, since domestic inflation of 2 per cent is 1 per cent below world price inflation of 3 per cent; and the real wage will have fallen by 1 per cent as well. So the economy will have moved half way down the vertical line between **b*** and **b**. The next year, a similar process will be repeated in wage bargaining (since the real wage is now 1% above the bargained real wage), and price-setting, and it will continue until the economy is eventually at **b**. (In fact with rational expectations, this process could take place immediately, with $\hat{W} = -1\%$ and $\pi = 1\%$ for just one period while π^* remains at 3%; with all three rates reverting back to 3% the next period; so the real wage and the real exchange rate both fall by 2%; the economy then moves at once to its new equilibrium at **b**.)

This argument has potentially radical implications. If demand management is conservative (e.g. if fiscal policy is non-discretionary and monetary policy inoperative, as in the case of post-EMU Germany), then an adverse demand shock simply raises the *equilibrium* unemployment rate: after a period of inflation below world inflation, inflation restabilizes at the world rate, though at a lower real exchange rate. If, by contrast, fiscal policy is discretionary, as in the UK in 2001–2, an expansionary fiscal policy has the effect of reducing the equilibrium unemployment rate at the cost of an increase in the real exchange rate. This can then explain the success of consumption-led booms, where aggregate demand pushes down unemployment over a prolonged period, raising the real exchange rate to accommodate the higher real wages demanded by an ever-tighter labour market, but not generating accelerating inflation.

3.3.3. Wage Restraint in Large and Small Open Economies

The analysis of Section 3.3.2 is useful for understanding the differential effects on unemployment of wage restraint in large and small open economies. Leading unions in CMEs represent export sectors; anticipating the discussion of their objective functions in Section 3.4, we assume here that they respond to an adverse demand shock by wage restraint.

In Figure 3.6 both large and small economies are in equilibrium initially at **a** with $w = w^{WS} = w_0^{PS}$ and $U = U_0$. The relevant bargained real wage schedule is labelled 'initial'. The only, but critical, difference between the large and the small economy lies in the slope of the aggregate demand curves. The aggregate demand schedule in the small economy has long dashed lines and in the large economy short dashed lines. A cut in the real wage has two opposite effects on aggregate demand. On the one hand it improves international competitiveness by lowering the real exchange rate, increasing exports and reducing imports

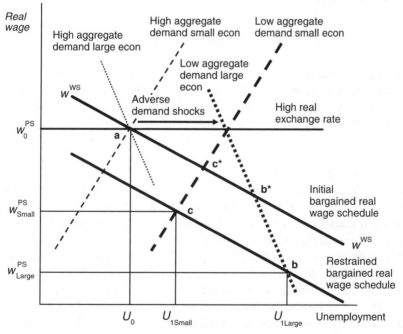

Figure 3.6. Open economy model (3): Demand shocks, wage restraint, and unemployment in large and small economies

and hence raising aggregate demand and lowering unemployment. If this was the only effect the aggregate demand curve in the diagram would be upwards sloping. But a cut in the real wage also lowers consumption. In a small and therefore more open economy, we assume the first effect dominates so that a lower real wage leads to an economywide improvement in unemployment; and vice versa in a large economy (in both cases employment in the export sectors should improve).

Now imagine that there is an adverse demand shock affecting the export sectors. That pushes both aggregate demand schedules to the right, the post-shock aggregate demand lines being in bold. Equilibrium unemployment in both economies rises, by more in the large—which moves to **b***—than in the small economy—**c***, but significantly in both. Facing unemployment in the export sectors, unions then decide on wage restraint, thus shifting down the bargained real wage schedule to that labelled 'restrained'. The final equilibria are at **c** for the large economy with $U = U_{1\,\text{Large}}$ and at **b** for the small economy with $U = U_{1\,\text{Small}}$. Thus wage restraint worsens unemployment in the large economy, but reduces it in the small economy.

3.4. IMPLICATIONS FOR MODERN MACROECONOMICS

The discussion of modern macroeconomics in the last three subsections was designed to make three points. First, that the standard New Keynesian model says that in a closed economy a central bank with a flexible and symmetric interest rate policy can be relied on to correct normal demand shocks. Second, in an open economy a conservative central bank especially with an asymmetric interest rate policy would not be adequately equipped to deal with major adverse demand shocks; and if fiscal policy was also non-discretionary, there would be a danger of such shocks translating into medium-term higher unemployment. Third, this would be worsened in a large open economy if leading unions were in the export sector and if they responded with real wage restraint in this situation—since the negative aggregate demand effects on consumption could outweigh the positive demand effects from the trade balance; and the contrary would be the case with wage restraint in a small open economy where the trade balance effect could outweigh the consumption effect. And finally, this initial adverse shock, uncorrected by the ADMR, may change household expectations about the future adversely—for example that welfare state guarantees might be thought to be put at risk. In that case the dampened effect on household consumption, as households sought through increased savings to build up precautionary assets, could prolong the inability of the economy to recover. Section 3.4.1 suggests that this is particularly likely to be the case in CMEs where specific assets make welfare state arrangements important to households. It will focus on Germany as a large open CME economy with conservative demand management and export unions responding to adverse demand shocks with wage restraint in order to preserve competitiveness, but with appropriate modifications the argument of Section 3.4.1 can also be applied to Japan.

3.4.1. Specific Skills and Consumption

The final section of the chapter looks at the proposition that the CME welfare state acts to dampen small adverse shocks but to amplify large ones. This applies to large CMEs—especially Germany and Japan. We have explained why small CMEs can use the real exchange rate to dampen shocks (and the Nordic countries can use public sector employment in addition). With a small shock, employment protection means that few face unemployment; those few that do have a relatively high and secure unemployment replacement rate; and wage protection holds up the wages of those who remain employed. So even if the ADMR is conservative in a Small-N CME, the perturbation is dampened; and since only limited pressure is put on the welfare state workers do not worry that the future of the welfare state is at risk. The argument rests heavily on the importance of specific skills in CMEs which Iversen has forcefully underlined (Iversen 2005).

Here is the basic argument in relation to Germany: Germany went through major deflationary shocks in the 1990s. In no previous decade in the second half of the twentieth century have the German authorities engaged in such sustained deflationary policies. The Bundesbank reacted by 1994 against the inflationary and deficit effects of reunification, and the revaluation of the mark led to a substantial shake-out of less-skilled employees—itself exacerbated by longer-term technological change and low rates of return; further, as a result of Maastricht and the conditions of EMU entry, fiscal policy in Germany and across Europe remained sharply non-accommodating. The consequences of these sustained deflationary shocks were an increase in unemployment and a slowdown of growth. Both Maastricht and rising unemployment, together with increasing early retirement and additional demographic pressure on the pensions system, caused the public finances to fall below target and led successive governments towards welfare state reform. Three implications can be drawn from this.

(1) *Specific skills and consumer behaviour: amplifying adverse demand shocks*: Employees with specific skills can be expected to react with particular concern

to the slowdown in growth, the rise in unemployment and the fear of welfare state reforms to unemployment benefits and to pensions. For workers with specific skills it will generally be harder to find appropriate re-employment if they lose their jobs. Moreover, there is a negative externality in a labour market dominated by specific skills. If most of the workforce has long-term employment, the number of vacancies within a given category of employment is likely to be limited; and companies may anyway seek to fill vacancies via apprenticeships. Thus mid-career labour markets for many categories may be quite limited or 'illiquid'. The most obvious comparison is with life-time employment in Japan: in the relevant categories, mid-career labour markets do not exist, short of accepting a position in a subsidiary company.

In Germany, as in Japan, illiquidity of mid-career labour markets applies more to the relatively more highly skilled—since companies have already invested more in them and, since it pays companies to invest more in them, they have longer tenure; less-skilled workers, but still with apprenticeship certificates, face more open occupational labour markets—which is what portable qualifications should equip them for. We return to this distinction below. In any case, given serious concerns about unemployment and with governmental pressure for welfare state reform in unemployment benefits and pensions (in Japan equivalently ending 'lifetime' employment), the great majority with specific skills who remain employed respond by building up savings. In economic terminology, savings results not from an interest rate incentive to *substitute* future for present consumption but from *precautionary* savings, and in response to actual recent cuts in state pensions entitlements *life-cycle* savings.

(2) *The welfare state and the political system*: Iversen's analysis (2005) of the guarantor-insurance role of the welfare state for those with deep specific skills in a CME explains why this substantial proportion of the workforce should feel insecure as its welfare state benefits start to be questioned. Many employees factor in the possibility of early retirement or part-time work from their mid-50s should economic conditions become difficult—both schemes which depend on welfare state provision. By contrast to CMEs such as the UK or the USA where a workforce with more general skills could imagine at a similar age responding to economic difficulty by finding alternative employment, labour markets for older workers do not exist on any substantial scale in Germany.

These fears are exacerbated by the consensus nature of political institutions in CMEs. As discussed in Section 3.2, this reflects an economic environment in which institutional change requires wide agreement if the environment is to continue to encourage investments in specific assets. That in turn implies that to generate sufficient support for significant institutional change, any government has to persuade those adversely affected that the crisis is one of great severity. Government rhetoric in much of the late 1990s and subsequently has been dominated by emphasis on the critical nature of the welfare state. Thus the perceived need by those employed to build up their savings is increased. Ironically, in this domain of welfare state reform, consensus-based political institutions aggravate the problem.

(3) *Consumption as a driver of modern business cycles.* A critical component of the story is the reaction to a more uncertain world of the consumption of employees with specific skills. This mirrors a marked shift in the behaviour of business cycles in large economies over recent decades from investment and sometimes export-driven cycles to cycles driven by consumer expenditures—the largest component of GDP demand. The growth in the UK and the USA in the 1990s, to take the most evident examples, was driven by consumption growth, accompanied by debt accumulation and exceptionally low rates of household savings. To take the latest OECD data for 2005 on the ratio of net personal savings to household incomes the USA ratio is −0.2, the UK ratio is 5.1 (but this is gross not net), while Germany's is 10.6 and Japan 6.7; in other LMEs, the figures are −2.2 in Australia and −0.4 in Canada; and in other large CMEs: Italy is 12.1 and France 11.6.[13] Thus in comparative terms, the insecurity-driven slowdown of consumption in Germany (and Japan and Italy) plays an important part in understanding different employment performance between the liberal market Anglo-Saxon economies and the large CMEs. The specificity of skills, aggravated by uncertainty about the future of the protective welfare state, itself generated by the consensus nature of the political system, is the analytic tool which enables us to understand this.

3.5. CONCLUSION

This chapter has attempted to cover a lot of ground. Its main contribution is hopefully to show that, and explain why, CMEs are typically associated with conservative ADMRS and LMEs with more discretionary ones. More specifically, the aim has been to develop the following points.

First, that monetary and fiscal policy regimes are not given by long-term cultural considerations but reflect the requirements of governments faced by the problems thrown up by powerful wage bargainers, on the one hand, and the demands of consensus politics, on the other. Both of these in turn reflect the nature of capitalist systems at the turn of the twenty-first century. This may hopefully contribute to an important and growing debate in political economy on the endogeneity of institutions.

Second, that ADMRs matter as a result of changing orthodoxies in modern macroeconomics. The New Keynesian economics of open economies explains how conservative ADMRs can fail to dampen large adverse shocks, and this may explain persistent high unemployment in Germany and Japan, big CMEs exposed to larger adverse shocks in the 1990s than they had previously faced. This should serve to explain the demise of neocorporatist theory linking wage coordination and low unemployment.

Third, that small shocks can be absorbed by CME welfare states but large shocks cannot. Thus the complementarities between CME production regimes, strong welfare states, consensus political systems, and conservative ADMRs may be functional for small perturbations but not for large ones.

NOTES

1. The typologies for production regimes are from Hall and Soskice (2001), for political systems, Lijphart (1984), and for welfare states, Esping-Andersen (1990); the discretionary/rules-based distinction was introduced by Barro and Gordon (1983) in application to monetary policy, while the analogous delegation (centralized)/negotiated contract distinction relating to fiscal policy is from Hallerberg, Strauch, and von Hagen (2001).
2. The chapter does not cover Greece, Italy, Portugal, or Spain. France is discussed in the conclusion.
3. This picture is idealized (see Flanagan, Soskice, and Ulman 1983 for detailed analyses of individual Western European countries in this period). Germany and Japan, for instance, never had such a bargain. And Scharpf (1991) showed the conditions under which the arrangement was time-inconsistent.
4. This literature incidentally makes it plain that there is no clear-cut split between the institutions of production regimes and those of welfare states: e.g. wage bargaining systems both help sustain implicit long-term agreements within companies guaranteeing cooperation in CME production regimes and provide wage protection within the corresponding welfare state.
5. This does not apply fully when the executive does not fully control the legislature or its own party, as in the USA.
6. This is, of course, an idealized account of the relationship between political systems and VoC. Behind its functionalist flavour a historical account is needed of why at the critical periods in which political systems were fashioned (in the case of electoral systems in the early twentieth century) embryonic coordinated economies chose PR; for putative explanations, see, Cusack, Iversen, and Soskice (2005) and Iversen and Soskice (2005).
7. It will be noted that the standard argument for the choice of 'independent' central banks—namely that they can solve the time-inconsistency problem of

monetary policy—plays no role here in the ADMR choices which governments make. The reason for this is explored at length in Iversen and Soskice (2006*b*): given the empirical time lags in modern macroeconometric models it would not pay *opportunistic* politicians to set up independent central banks (it is not the free lunch implied by New Classical macroeconomics); and there is no reason to believe that politicians (Thatcher, Mitterrand, and Reagan) were opportunistic in the Barro sense. Discretion here refers mainly to using fiscal and monetary policy to exit recessions without inflationary consequences, not to buy short-term output increases at the expense of accelerating inflation.

8. During the conflictual period in the 1980s both the UK and New Zealand maintained tough macroeconomic policies. Our argument is that it is only with flexible labour markets and the elimination of powerful unions that governments have been able to move to macroeconomic policies in which they de facto have more discretion.

9. The new employee (or apprentice) typically contemplating a long-term career at the company.

10. Companies facing difficult economic circumstances may want optouts from industry agreements; but these are explicitly bargained as optouts.

11. Much of the following is a simplified and non-mathematical account derived from Iversen and Soskice (2006*b*); see Carlin and Soskice (2006) for an extensive treatment.

12. This assumes that the nominal exchange rate is fixed at 1; if the nominal exchange varies then the real exchange rate is P/P^*e.

13. The argument needs more detailed empirical work. In particular, the savings data needs to be examined at micro panel data level.

4

Wage Bargaining and Comparative Advantage in EMU

Bob Hancké and Andrea Monika Herrmann

4.1. INTRODUCTION

The introduction of the Euro in 1999, and the adjustment process since the signing of the Maastricht Treaty in 1991 that preceded it, has profoundly changed the macroeconomic regime that members of EMU face. While the growing literature on the effects of EMU has taught us much about the inter-action between different elements of the macro-political economy (see Allsopp and Artis 2003 for an assessment of those debates), few studies have examined the micro-level effects of these shifts, especially those that follow from changes in wage-setting regimes. Such causal links between changes in macroeco-nomic regimes and their micro-effects are largely ignored in conventional economics. The broader political economy literature that has emerged since the early 1980s and which found a strong culminating analytical statement in Hall and Soskice (2001), however, has put these links between broad macro-institutional regimes and company organization and performance at the cen-tre of debates (see Piore and Sabel 1984; Dore 1986; Streeck 1991; Soskice 1999; Aoki 2000 for debates on the effects of institutional frameworks on the organization of the firm). This chapter builds on that literature and examines the effects of broad shifts in wage-bargaining systems on the organization of firms in EMU member-states. We argue that the move to coordinated wage bargaining induced by the Maastricht criteria has led firms in EMU member-states to align their product market strategies with the existing institutional framework. In countries where wage bargaining became (or was) centrally coordinated, firms increasingly pursued high-end product market strategies, while firms in countries where wage bargaining followed a decentralized coor-dination path opted for low-end strategies. By exploring these relations, our paper develops a research agenda that links macro- and micro-level through the institutional complementarities on the basis of the VoC framework.

We develop our argument in four steps. We start in Section 4.2 by presenting the theoretical basis for our argument on shifts in wage bargaining across Europe in the 1990s and their most important consequences for competitiveness. Section 4.3 analyses aggregate data on comparative advantage and wage bargaining. This correlation analysis supports our contention that shifts in the wage-setting regime have led to shifts in competitive strategy at the firm level. Section 4.4 unpacks these correlations and explores the causal links between shifts in wage-bargaining systems and central elements in company organization. We complete our analysis in Section 4.5 by comparing the interest constellations on the basis of opposite developments in Italy and Spain in the 1990s. Section 4.6 concludes.

4.2. EMU, MACROECONOMIC REGIMES, AND COMPETITIVE STRATEGIES

The main effect of the 1991 Maastricht Treaty was that it generalized, throughout the EU, or more precisely across all the member-states that had signed up for entry into EMU at the end of the decade, the mode of interaction between central banks and wage setters that prevailed in the deutschmark (DM)-block. Against the background of a fixed exchange rate regime that precluded competitive devaluations as an adjustment tool, centrally coordinated wage-bargaining systems produce wage increases commensurate with the tacit or explicit inflation target of the (independent) central bank. International wage coordination attempts by trade unions and (more importantly, we think) relative competitiveness concerns within a highly integrated European economy have led to profound shifts in the mode of wage setting: wages across EMU member-states increasingly are set between a floor given by past inflation and a ceiling set by labour productivity, thus resulting in low and stable (or falling) wage inflation rates. In the countries of the DM-block in the 1980s—Austria, Belgium, France, Germany, the Netherlands, and Denmark—wage-setting systems had been reorganized during that decade to accommodate the restrictive stance of national central banks that were forced to follow the Bundesbank under the ERM's fixed exchange rate regime. The effect of the Maastricht Treaty was that it imposed this disinflationary wage-setting regime on all prospective members of EMU, including the high-inflation Mediterranean countries. In some of these countries that were forced to adapt their wage-setting systems in the 1990s, such as Italy, social pacts were concluded and wage setting increasingly followed centrally coordinated guidelines. In others, such as Spain, coordination took on a decentralized pattern, in which firms internalized both the inflation and productivity constraints (Herrmann 2005). To a large extent, these moves were conditioned by the ability of employers and trade unions to build on previously existing 'proto-institutions' that could be reconfigured to meet these new goals (Hancké and Soskice 2003; Hancké and Rhodes 2005).

Such shifts in wage-setting systems (can) have important micro-level consequences. As students of the post-war German and Swedish economies (Martin 1984; Soskice 1990; Streeck 1992) have pointed out, centrally coordinated wage-setting systems such as the one analysed above, significantly constrain the adjustment possibilities of firms. Unable to lower wages, denied recourse to quick massive lay-offs as a result of strong trade unions, and constrained by a hard currency regime that precluded competitive devaluations, German business has been forced to adopt two coping strategies: a permanent rationalization of production, especially in the traded goods sector, and an orientation towards product market niches that are relatively insensitive to cost competition. The coordinated wage-bargaining system, relying on strong trade unions and employer associations, provided the organizational means for such moves. On the one hand, it made poaching of skilled workers impossible, or at least very unlikely, and created the basis for extensive inter-firm cooperation in other areas as well (Soskice 1999).

Our argument builds on this insight. The shifts in wage-setting systems in the current EMU member-states (in response to the Maastricht criteria) have led to parallel shifts in the competitive strategies of their firms. In centrally coordinated systems, firms have increasingly adopted or retained high-value-added product market strategies, while firms in decentrally coordinated systems—with similar effects on inflation—have adopted low-cost-based product market strategies. The argument consists of four related sub-points. First, it is important to see that centrally and decentrally coordinated wage-bargaining systems have very different effects. Coordinated wage-setting systems that adopt a proximate wage target of 'nominal wage growth equals inflation plus aggregate productivity' impose a wage floor on employers and a wage ceiling on trade unions: the floor for employers is set by the inflation rate, while for unions the ceiling is set by productivity. The difference between centrally and decentrally coordinated systems is that in the former, a single industry or (directly or through *erga omnes* extensions) nationwide wage target is adopted, which is applied to all companies in the sector or economy. A decentrally coordinated system allows for the inflation plus productivity target to be set at the level of individual companies. Ultimately, they both lead to the same aggregate outcome of nominal wages rising with labour productivity (and therefore stable relative unit labour costs). However, there is one important difference: a centrally coordinated wage-setting system in fact acts as a productivity whip, since it forces companies who have lower than average productivity either to improve their productivity rapidly in order to be able to pay the agreed tariff wages or to exit the market, while rewarding companies with above-average productivity with lower relative wage claims. Decentrally coordinated wage-setting systems do not have this effect, since wages reflect company-level labour productivity. As a result, poorly performing companies are neither forced to raise productivity nor to exit the market.

Shifts in wage-bargaining systems also have different effects on labour unions. Centrally coordinated systems provide strong incentives for labour unions to enter local productivity coalitions: given relatively low and stable inflation, labour productivity ultimately determines the effective nominal wage claims. Rising labour productivity therefore allows unions to claim higher wages without endangering the competitiveness of the company. While similar incentives might operate in specific cases in decentrally coordinated systems they are, on aggregate, considerably weaker. Poorly performing firms do not face the strong pressures they would do in centrally coordinated systems, and the workers in those firms do not necessarily face unemployment, since the firm passes on the weak performance to workers in the guise of lower wage growth. We therefore expect, *ceteris paribus*, labour productivity growth to be higher in centrally coordinated systems than in decentrally coordinated systems as a result of these constraints. In large measure this is linked to the contribution of firm-level supply-side institutions: labour productivity levels are, other things being equal, determined by skill levels and forms of work organization.[1] Under this assumption, labour unions (and employers) in centrally coordinated systems will pay more attention to company-level 'soft' issues such as skill provision through continuous training, pay-for-knowledge, and new forms of work organization. While most of these productivity-enhancing issue areas have become (or remained) decentralized after the decentralization wave of the 1980s (Katz 1993; Katz and Darbishire 1999), equally often they remained under the control of labour unions within the companies.

As a result of this combination of constraints and opportunities that employers and trade unions face, firms are both pushed upmarket by the constraints that result from a centrally coordinated wage-setting system (the wage floor), and enabled to do so by the new division of labour within the trade unions, which furthers local involvement in productivity-improving work organization and skill provision (the wage ceiling). In decentrally coordinated systems, in contrast, companies have neither the incentives to move upmarket nor the opportunities to do so, since both the wage floor and ceiling are considerably more flexible, and supportive micro-level institutions are often absent.

Sections 4.3, 4.4, and 4.5 explore the empirical basis for this argument. We start in Section 4.3 with a correlation analysis which demonstrates that shifts in wage-bargaining regimes of the EMU member-states have led to shifts in the competitive strategies of companies. Section 4.4 which follows this explores the firm-level mechanisms through which these shifts took place. Comparing developments in Italy and Spain in the 1990s, Section 4.5 explores the politics underlying the adjustment processes.

4.3. DISINFLATIONARY WAGE-BARGAINING REGIMES AND COMPARATIVE ADVANTAGE

We link wage-bargaining systems to competitive strategies in two steps. In line with Porter (see Porter 1985: 11, 12–14), we start by identifying two different competitive strategies, namely high-quality production (HQP) on the one hand, and low-cost production (LCP) on the other. Each of these two product market strategies is linked to different labour market institutions (Traxler 1997: 31; Estévez-Abe et al. 2001). The manufacturing of high-quality products and customized goods requires a workforce with specific skills. Centralized wage-bargaining systems are a necessary condition for the development of a training system that delivers such skills, since both employers and employees can engage in sophisticated education and training programmes without facing hold-up problems (see Estévez-Abe et al. 2001; Hall and Soskice 2001: 24–5, 36–44). A decentralized wage-bargaining system, in contrast, furthers the success of LCP. Since the wage militancy of unions is reduced at the firm level, a coordinated and decentralized bargaining system potentially allows for the lowest possible wage increases, while maintaining wage differentials across various employment categories within one industry (Suárez Santos 2002). If EMU indeed triggers the changes at the microeconomic level that we hypothesized, we expect to find that firms increasingly pursue a competitive strategy which reflects the institutional environment they are embedded in, with firms in centrally coordinated wage-bargaining systems increasingly pursuing a HQP strategy, whereas firms in decentrally coordinated wage-bargaining systems can be expected to pursue an LCP strategy.

In order to measure the competitive strategy of firms in an economy— which reflects that country's comparative advantage—we draw on standard analyses and assume that differences in prices (unit values) reflect quality differences (see European Commission 1997: 19, 41, 70–83; Porter 1985: 62–4, 127–8). We measure the competitive strategy of firms within one country in terms of the Weighted Relative Unit Value (henceforth WRUV) of a country's relatively most important export sectors. The WRUV is calculated in two steps.[2] First, the relatively most important export sectors in an economy are determined by calculating the Revealed Comparative Advantage (henceforth RCA). For each production sector, the RCA is obtained by comparing the relative export performance of a country to the relative export performance of a group of countries, for example the EU (see Balassa 1965):

$$RCA = \frac{(\text{Exports of Country A in Sector p/Total Exports of Country A})}{(\text{EU Exports in Sector p/Total EU Exports})}$$

The results obtained from these calculations reveal the sectors where a country has a comparative advantage, in that it exports comparatively more than the EU average. For each EMU member-state, we identified the five most important export sectors.

The second step is to calculate the WRUV for these five sectors. To obtain the WRUV, the Relative Unit Value (henceforth RUV) is calculated by comparing the unit prices of a country's sector to EU unit prices in this sector:

$$RUV = \frac{\begin{array}{c}(\text{Value of Exports in Sector p of Country A/Quantity of Exports}\\ \text{in Sector p of Country A})\end{array}}{\begin{array}{c}(\text{Value of EU Exports in Sector p/Quantity of EU Exports}\\ \text{in Sector p})\end{array}}$$

The WRUV, in turn, is obtained by calculating the weighted average (in value added) of these five export sectors. The WRUV thus measures how many percentage points average prices of the considered goods differ from average prices in the EU. Since differences in prices (unit values) are announced to reflect quality differences, the data in Table 4.1 mean that in countries with a positive WRUV firms pursue a HQP strategy, while in countries with an negative WRUV firms pursue an LCP strategy. Table 4.1 demonstrates—in aggregate terms—how product-market strategies of firms in the EMU member-states have developed over the 1990s, and suggests two patterns: aggregate competitive strategies either changed entirely (from positive to negative or vice versa), or existing strategies became more pronounced over the 1990s.[3]

We now need to link these aggregate shifts in product-market strategies to changes in the institutional framework of wage-bargaining structures: are HQP strategies positively correlated with centrally coordinated wage bargaining, while LCP strategies are linked to decentrally coordinated wage-bargaining structures? We measure wage coordination using the measures for wage-bargaining centralization developed by Traxler et al. (2001: 114, 307) because it is considered to be the most valid and reliable indicator (Kenworthy

Table 4.1. Competitive strategy of firms in EMU member-states in 1992 and 2001

EMU member-states	Firms' aggregate competitive strategy	
	WRUV in 1992	WRUV in 2001
Ireland	1,498.0	1,813.0
France	122.5	27.7
Denmark	47.9	65.3
Sweden	43.9	29.8
Germany	24.0	80.4
Italy	17.2	27.1
Belgium	15.9	52.0
Luxembourg	15.9	−32.6
UK	10.2	479.8
Finland	2.1	61.2
Austria	−6.7	4.4
Spain	−11.7	−14.2
Portugal	−12.4	106.2
Netherlands	−23.5	71.9
Greece	−26.2	−60.1

Source: OECD online database 'ITCS—International Trade by Commodity; SITC Rev.3'.

2001: 70; Kenworthy 2003: 15).[4] Table 4.2 summarizes the values for 1992 and 2001. It demonstrates, first of all, that only a few changes have taken place in the degree of wage-bargaining centralization over 1990s. It also suggests that most moves in wage centralization have been downwards rather than upwards.

These descriptive statistics allow us to explore the correlations between institutional frameworks for wage-setting and competitive strategies adopted by firms in these economies. However, this way of measuring ignores an important dynamic element: by the early 1990s, several EMU member-states had relatively highly centrally coordinated wage-bargaining systems (often as a result of their earlier membership of the DM-block (see Hancké and Rhodes 2005). A measure that takes into account changes in wage-setting systems will not reflect the fact that these countries either cannot increase the degree of central coordination of their wage-bargaining systems, or that top-level centralization is not necessary for a coordinated outcome (Soskice 1990). We therefore calculate three separate correlations, which capture different dimensions of our argument. The first of these reflects the 'tightness of fit' between the centralization score and WRUV for 1992 and for 2001. If the difference between the correlation coefficients for 2001 and 1992 is large and positive, the fit between competitive strategy and the institutional framework of wage bargaining has improved during that period. The second addresses one aspect of the causality in our argument and answers the

Table 4.2. Degree of wage-bargaining centralization in the EMU member-states

EMU member-states	Degree of centralization in 1992	Degree of centralization in 2001	Scores of wage-bargaining centralization, as defined by Traxler, Blaschke, and Kittel (2001)*	
Ireland	12	12	1	Company and plant, with group-specific bargaining
Finland	11	11	1.5	Company and plant, with all groups and group-specific bargaining equally important
Germany	6	6	2	Company and plant, with all groups bargaining jointly
Italy	6	6	3	Combination of industry and company and plant, with group-specific bargaining
The Netherlands	6	6	3.5	Combination of industry and company and plant, with all groups and group-specific bargaining equally important
Portugal	6	6	4	Combination of industry and company and plant, with all groups bargaining jointly
Greece	12	6	5	Industry, with group-specific bargaining
Austria	5	5	6	Industry, with all groups bargaining jointly
Denmark	5	5	7	Combination of central, industry, company, and plant, with group-specific bargaining
Sweden	5	5	7.5	Combination of centr., ind., comp., and plant, with all groups bargaining jointly at central level and group-specific bargaining at all other levels
France	4	4	8	Combination of central, industry, company, and plant, with all groups bargaining jointly
Spain	6	4	9	Central and industry, with group-specific bargaining
Belgium	3	3	10	Central and industry, with all groups bargaining jointly
Luxembourg	3	3	11	Central, with group-specific bargaining
UK	2	2	12	Central, with all employees bargaining jointly

Source: Traxler, Blaschke, and Kittel (2001: 114, 307), updated as reported by the EIRO (http://www.eiro.eurofound.ie).

*The Traxler et al. scores have been reversed so that the lowest score indicates the lowest degree of wage-bargaining centralization, and vice versa.

Table 4.3. Wage coordination and competitive strategy

H1	$R_{WRUV1992} \to$ centralization$_{1992}$	$R_{WRUV2001} \to$ centralization$_{2001}$	Δ (Difference)
EMU-11 (without Eire)	−0.424	0.348	+0.772

H2	$R_{WRUV1992} \to$ centralization$_{2001}$	$R_{WRUV2001} \to$ centralization$_{2001}$	Δ (Difference)
EMU-11 (without Eire)	−0.261	0.348	+0.609

H3	$R_{WRUV(1992–2001)} \to$ centralization$_{2001}$	Strong corr.
EMU-11 (without Eire)	0.547	>50%

question: Have firms adapted their competitive strategy (expressed in WRUV) to the institutional framework or the other way around? We measure the extent to which the competitive strategy fits the institutional framework better in 2001 than in 1992, by holding constant the institutional framework of wage-setting at 2001 scores. The basic idea is that if the value is higher for the 2001–2001 correlation, companies adjusted their product-market strategies anticipating (as it were) shifts in the institutional framework or, at the very least, reinforcing those when no changes in wage bargaining occurred. The third analysis, finally, correlates the shifts in WRUV with the centralization scores for 2001. Again, we hypothesize that positive shifts in comparative advantage reflect the type and level of centralized wage bargaining at the end of the period. In other words, if the correlation between $\Delta WRUV_{1992–2001}$ and the scores on wage centralization is positive and high, the competitive advantage of countries moves in line with the position in terms of wage bargaining that these countries were choosing in the 1990s. If these three ways of analysing the relation between wage-bargaining institutions and competitive strategy follow our predictions, we treat the basic hypothesis as confirmed. Table 4.3 recapitulates the hypotheses and the results in condensed form; all three coefficients take the form that we predicted.

4.4. COMPANY REORGANIZATION UNDER RESTRICTIVE MACROECONOMIC REGIMES

Having found that the aggregate indicators on wage bargaining and comparative advantage evolve in the direction we predicted, we now turn to analyse the mechanisms underlying these strong correlations. In this section, we will rely on comparisons of means between centrally and decentrally coordinated economies in EMU to explore the evolution of (aggregate) firm-level indicators. Even though such data are scarce and we therefore often have to rely on imperfect proxy indicators, the ones we deploy here clearly illustrate one point: they all suggest that adjustment in centrally and decentrally coordinated economies over the 1990s followed very different paths.

Prior to the signing of the Maastricht Treaty, countries in the DM-block had already adopted disinflationary wage-setting systems. Keeping unit labour cost (ULC) growth in line with Germany (in order to keep exchange rates fixed within the ERM) implied a ceiling on nominal wage growth given by labour productivity. Therefore, firms and labour unions faced strong incentives to increase productivity so that real wages could grow while inflation rates were stable against the DM. After the adoption of the Maastricht convergence criteria in 1992, a second group of countries adapted its micro-level institutional framework as well, though often by very different means from the front-runners in the DM-block. While historically these countries had not been able to produce the type of collective or club goods of the type generally found in CMEs (Hicks and Kenworthy 1998), decentralized forms of labour–management cooperation and of inter-firm skill provision and cooperation existed. As Hancké and Rhodes (2005) suggest, these were used as a basis for firm-level reorganizations. The steps in the argument for this group would thus be the same as for the DM-block group, but with a prior condition: micro-organizational change builds on existing 'proto-institutions' (Hancké and Rhodes 2005); followed by a rise in skill levels, an increase in the presence of cooperative workplace institutions and practices, and an upwards shift in career perspectives.

In other countries, however, which lacked such beneficial and often local proto-institutions, wage coordination took a decentralized form. Unable to build new micro-level institutions with their beneficial effects in terms of training and skills, companies in these countries primarily embarked on a path that emphasized cost-based advantages, which was expressed in shifts towards low-end product-market strategies. Where this was already the dominant product-market strategy, renewed emphasis was given to LCP. In these cases, we would expect to find relatively few upwards shifts in skills, cooperative workplace institutions and practices, and in careers. In addition, we would also anticipate that labour productivity growth would be slower than in the other two groups, for the reason given earlier: in decentrally coordinated wage-setting systems, wage setting varies directly with firm-level labour productivity.[5]

None of the wage-setting indicators that we know (European Commission 2004; Traxler et al. 2001; Kenworthy 2003) distinguish between central

Table 4.4. Competitiveness, productivity, and wages in the manufacturing sector

	Avg. 1990–9 ULC growth	Avg. 1990–2000 L productivity growth	Avg. 1990–9 real wage growth
Central wage coordination avg. score	1.3	2.7	1.1
Decentral wage coordination avg.	5.4	2.3	1.9

Source: OECD STAN indicators.

forms of coordination, where wage bargainers de facto follow centrally set wage targets by directly introducing them into wage setting, and decentral modes, where these targets are adopted company by company. While most centralization and coordination indices capture part of this distinction, they tend to emphasize organizational characteristics at the expense of outcomes. The logic of our argument could be operationalized by analysing which part of the final wage is set at national inter-industry and national industry level (as opposed to being set at company level), but we have no knowledge of data that systematically make these comparisons. The distinction between centrally and decentrally coordinated systems in the analysis that follows therefore builds in part on an analysis of social pacts and central coordination in the run-up to EMU, and in part on EIRO (2005) data on collective bargaining for the ten EMU member-states analysed in the paper (i.e. without Ireland and Luxembourg). Economies with centrally coordinated systems include Austria, Belgium, Germany, Finland, The Netherlands, France (through pattern-setting large firms and *erga omnes* extensions), and Italy. Decentrally coordinated economies are Spain, Portugal, and Greece. We excluded Ireland because of its outlier status in the correlation analysis.[6] Luxembourg, in turn, is not included both on the basis of its small size and of its heavily finance-based export sector.

4.4.1. Wage Setting, Labour Productivity, and Competitiveness

The core of our argument revolves around the effects of the type of wage coordination on labour productivity and, through that, on competitiveness which, in turn, is supported by micro-organizational changes. We therefore expect to find that centrally coordinated wage-setting systems have a higher labour productivity rate than decentrally coordinated systems. This is, precisely, the central message of Table 4.4 which confirms that labour productivity has been higher in centrally coordinated wage-setting systems throughout the Maastricht period.

The ULC growth therefore was higher in the decentrally coordinated economies, but as Table 4.5 demonstrates they converged significantly in the latter half of the 1990s (the standard deviation drops sharply) and on a lower

Table 4.5. Unit labour cost growth in business sector, 1990–4 and 1995–9

	1990–4	1995–9
Austria	2.5	−0.6
Belgium	3.5	0.7
Denmark	0.0	1.3
Finland	−1.1	0.4
France	0.9	0.2
Germany	3.1	−0.2
Italy	3.6	1.3
The Netherlands	2.3	1.4
Portugal	10.9	2.5
Spain	5.7	2.6
Average	3.1	1
Standard deviation	3.4	1.1

Source: OECD Economic Outlook.

level. This reflects the need for all prospective EMU members to bring (wage) inflation in line with the best performers, as the Maastricht Treaty prescribed. Having established that the basic data evolve in the direction we anticipated, we can now turn more directly to the underlying mechanisms for the differences in labour productivity growth.

4.4.2. Skills

A large part of our argument implicitly and explicitly hinges on shifts in skill levels. Unfortunately, we have not been able to find systematic data which allow us to conclude that companies in countries with centrally coordinated wage-setting systems on average rely on higher skills among their workers. The data in Table 4.6, however, help us explore our argument. If we assume that workers have to be retrained more often when companies adjust their product-market strategies upwards, the increase in the adoption of continuous vocational training (CVT) schemes for existing workers is a good indicator of the increased reliance of companies on workers' skills. These data suggest that CVT has both increased more strongly in countries with centrally coordinated wage-bargaining systems and remained at a significantly higher level than in countries with decentrally coordinated systems. As a result, the gap in CVT between the two types of bargaining systems has increased over the last decade.

4.4.3. Workplace Cooperation

Parallel to an increased reliance on skills, another aspect of micro-level changes is the cooperative nature of workplaces in centrally coordinated

Table 4.6. Continuous vocational training programmes in centrally and decentrally coordinated wage-setting systems, 1993 and 1999

	1993	1999
Percentage of all companies reporting CVT		
Central wage coordination avg.	53.2	69.6
Decentral wage coordination avg.	33.3	25.3
Employees covered as a percentage of all companies		
Central wage coordination avg.	77	87
Decentral wage coordination avg.	50	57

Source: 1993 data, First Continuous vocational training survey, Statistics in Focus, 1996; 1999 data: Second Continuous vocational training survey, Office for official publications of the European Communities, 2002.

wage-setting systems. The absence of conflict is a first precondition for cooperation. Table 4.7 shows that strike activity has declined everywhere, but also that the level and the changes in the level are considerably more pronounced in the centrally coordinated wage-setting systems. Importantly, however, the variation around the average for that group is much wider than in the other group.

Absence of conflict is, of course, not the same as presence of cooperation in the workplace. Since very few studies systematically assess the evolution of cooperative and participative practices in OECD–EU economies, we have to rely on single point data for the mid-1990s. The EPOC survey (Benders et al. 1999; see also OECD Employment Outlook 1999) is the main recent source of comparative information on such practices as group work and decentralization of decision-making authority across EU member-states and beyond. Table 4.8 presents the data from the EPOC survey reorganized along the lines of our distinction between centrally and decentrally coordinated wage-setting systems, the results of which are striking. Centrally coordinated

Table 4.7. Working days lost due to strikes per 1,000 employees, all industries, averages 1991–3 and 1998–2000

	Average 1991–3	Average 1998–2000
Central wage coordination avg.	60	32
Decentral wage coordination avg.	254	101

Source: Joanne Monger, 'International Comparisons of Labour Disputes in 2000', *Labour Market Trends*, January 2003.

Table 4.8. Delegation of responsibility in companies

	Proportion of workplaces reporting presence of	
	Individual delegation	Group delegation
Central wage coordination avg.	55	37
Decentral wage coordination avg.	33	26

Source: OECD Employment Outlook (1999: table 4.1, p. 186).

wage-setting systems score considerably higher on both indicators of decentralized decision-making.

4.4.4. Careers

A higher reliance on skills, and more devolved company-level decision-making, implies an investment from both the employee's and the employer's side in firm-specific competencies. The resulting potential hold-up problem is usually resolved through longer-term career structures that mutually tie worker and employer. Since centrally coordinated systems invest more in skills and have more cooperative workplaces, we ought to find that centrally coordinated systems have higher employee tenure rates and decentrally coordinated systems lower ones. Unfortunately, longitudinal data are not easy to obtain, but the data in Table 4.9, which present tenure rates for the mid-1990s, offer a useful proxy.

When reading these data, it has to be kept in mind that employment protection legislation interferes with the pure micro-foundation logic that we follow (see Estévez-Abe et al. 2001 for elaborations of that argument). Many countries in the decentralized group have had very strict employment protection which often made dismissals difficult. While the differences between the two groups are less pronounced than for other indicators, there is still considerable variation between the two types of systems. Both indicators that we used—average and median tenure rates—confirm our

Table 4.9. Employee tenure rates, 1995

	Average tenure in years	Median tenure in years
Central wage coordination avg.	10	8
Decentral wage coordination avg.	9	6

Source: OECD Employment Outlook (1997: table 5.5, p. 138).

hypothesis. In centrally coordinated systems the averages of both indicators are higher than in decentrally coordinated systems, and especially the median tenure rate is significantly higher.

The different indicators of micro-level changes that we have used in this section not only support our argument that these institutional adjustments differed systematically across the two wage-setting regimes. They also allowed us to unpack the correlation results presented in Section 4.2. First of all, they show that the competitiveness profile of centrally versus decentrally coordinated systems was very different: while ULCs converged between both groups, labour productivity was higher in centralized systems. That, we argued, was related to the micro-level incentives and institutions which allow companies in centrally coordinated regimes to move upmarket, and thus to rely on a high-productivity model. Accordingly, centrally coordinated wage-setting systems score differently—and higher—than decentrally coordinated systems on three core indicators: they rely more on employees' skills, and they have more cooperative workplaces; in part as a result of this different micro-organizational strategy, employees are more often employed on a long-term basis. Companies in decentrally coordinated systems continue to have a different micro-organizational profile: they rely less on skills and cooperation, and employment tenure rates are lower. As a result, adjustment strategies have been more of a low-productivity type in decentrally coordinated systems, and competitiveness resulted primarily from wage moderation to reflect lower productivity.

Section 4.5 introduces material on the dynamics and outcomes of the reorganization of wage-bargaining institutions in Italy and Spain, which allows us to explore the calculations that employers (and trade unions) made when facing the need for a move towards disinflationary wage-setting. As we see, the wage-setting systems adopted in both cases—central coordination in Italy and decentral coordination in Spain—reflected the dominant product-market strategies of firms in these economies. The decentral wage-setting regime in Spain ultimately reinforced the low-cost orientation of Spanish manufacturing and exports, while the centrally coordinated system in Italy was articulated with attempts by Italian business to leave low-cost markets and move into higher value-added segments.

4.5. WAGE-BARGAINING INSTITUTIONS AND COMPETITIVE STRATEGIES IN ITALY AND SPAIN

At the beginning of the 1990s, both Italy and Spain suffered from high inflation rates. They therefore faced similar pressures to reform their wage-bargaining system in order to meet the EMU convergence criteria by the end of the 1990s. Despite these similarities, both countries—and, most importantly, companies and employers within them—chose different paths. While Italian employers tended to secure stable ULCs through the pursuit of high-quality manufacturing, Spanish employers oriented themselves towards LCP. This, we argue, is the result of differences in the degree of bargaining centralization.

Centralized and decentralized bargaining systems differ crucially in the extent to which industrywide employment categories exist that define both wage and skill levels for the employees in a given industry. In centralized systems, the social partners define employment categories for the entire industry. These categories specify the skills an employee needs to have in order to be attributed to one category, as well as the pay he obtains in return for these skills. Consequently, wage levels for equally skilled workers are fairly homogeneous in centralized bargaining systems.

Italy provides a good example of such centralized wage homogeneity. In Italy, the social partners regularly negotiate an industrywide agreement, the so-called Contratto Collettivo Nazionale di Lavoro (henceforth CCNL), which determines a large variety of work-related issues that equally apply to all companies of the industry. With regard to remuneration, the CCNL distinguishes—depending on the industry—between five and six employment categories (*categorie professionali*), for which it determines the minimum wage employers have to pay. In so doing, the CCNL fixes a wage floor for each employment category of an industry. Of course, employers can and do pay wages above the CCNL floor. Such wage top-ups differ according to individual parameters, for example the employee's work experience, the company's current economic situation, or the regional cost of living (Chiriatti 2006).

Despite such individual wage parameters, the existence of an industrywide pay floor leads to fairly homogeneous income levels throughout Italy. Comparing average earnings per hour paid in the manufacturing sector in different groups of Italian regions, Table 4.10 provides an overview wage differentials in Italy's manufacturing industry.[7] These data show that for almost nine of ten Italian employees in manufacturing, i.e. those working in north-east, north-west, and central Italy, income differentials are small: 7 per cent above the Italian average in Italy's richest north-western regions, and only 4 per cent below the Italian average in central Italy.

The opposite holds for decentralized wage-bargaining systems. In decentralized bargaining systems, industrywide employment categories determining equal pay for equal skill levels usually do not exist. Accordingly, wage differentials are often substantial, as in Spain. Like their Italian counterparts, the Spanish social partners regularly conclude collective agreements which

Table 4.10. Italy: regional differences in average earnings per hour paid in the manufacturing sector

Region	Absolute earnings per hour (€)	Relative earnings per hour (compared to national average) (%)	Manufacturing employees per region (as % of overall manufacturing workforce)	Added % of employees
1. North-west	14.35	107	43	
2. North-east	13.33	99	30	73
3. Centre	12.94	96	16	89
4. South	10.72	80	9	98
5. Islands	11.49	86	2	100
National average	13.43	100	Σ = 100	

Source: EuroStat (2002): *Earnings Structure Survey*, available at: http://www.istat.it

determine both contents and conditions of employment—including wages. However, contrary to the industrywide agreements in Italy, only a small minority of the collective agreements in Spain are concluded at the national-sectoral level (1.8% in 2001). The large majority of agreements are concluded at the provincial-sectoral level (22.6% in 2001), and the level of the company (72.9% in 2001). Most Spanish employees (75.2% in 2001) are therefore covered by collective agreements concluded at a decentral level (EIRR 2002*b*: 29).

Wage levels are therefore highly heterogeneous throughout the Spanish economy. Table 4.11 compares regional differences of average earnings per hour paid in the manufacturing sector and demonstrates that wages vary considerably between the three employment-richest regions, in which 50 per cent of the manufacturing workforce is engaged. While wages are 15 per cent below the Spanish average in the Valencian Community, they are 19 per cent above average in Madrid and 8 per cent in Catalonia. Similarly, strong wage differentials exist within the second (and the least) employment-richest group of regions, offering work to another 37 per cent (for the former) and 13 per cent (for the latter) of employees in manufacturing. The decentralized bargaining system in Spain thus leads to high wage differentials throughout the economy, while bargaining centralization in Italy produces comparatively homogeneous wage levels.

The importance of bargaining centralization for Italy's manufacturing industry is reflected in the development of the Italian wage-setting system since December 1991. Shortly after the Maastricht conference, the Italian government proposed a social pact with the aim of decreasing inflation through wage-bargaining coordination. The central provision of this pact consisted of a wage formula according to which wages are negotiated successively at two

Table 4.11. Spain: regional differences in average earnings per hour paid in the manufacturing sector

Region	Absolute earnings per hour (€)	Relative earnings per hour (compared to national average) (%)	Manufacturing employees per region (as % of overall manufacturing workforce)	Added % of employees (per employment density of region)
Catalonia	9.34	108	26	
Valencian Community	7.3	85	13	
Madrid	10.23	119	11	50
Andalucia	8.06	93	9	
Basque Country	9.84	114	8	
Castile and Leon	8.41	97	6	
Galicia	7.36	85	6	
Aragon	8.49	98	4	
Castilla la Mancha	6.84	79	4	37
Murcia	6.74	78	3	
Asturias	9.07	105	2	
Canary Islands	7.14	83	2	
Navarre	9.1	105	2	
Ballearic Islands	6.82	79	1	
Cantabria	8.53	99	1	
Extremadura	6.25	72	1	
La Rioja	7.51	87	1	13
National average	8.63	100	Σ = 100	Σ = 100

Source: EuroStat (2002): *Earnings Structure Survey*, available at http://www.ine.es

different levels every two years. First, pay is increased at the national-sectoral level according to the inflation target of the ECB (EIRO 1999). Secondly, wages can be topped up at the firm level according to the company's productivity growth rate (EIRO 1998). The social partners in Italy accepted this pact in July 1993, which was facilitated by the fact that industrywide employment categories were already in place. Since then, Italian employers have also supported centralized bargaining: Despite the possibility to top-up wages at the company level, productivity premiums are rare and only negotiated in large companies. For the large majority of Italian employees working in small and medium enterprises, final income increases are determined at the national-sectoral level.[8] Importantly, this entails a homogeneous raise of homogeneous wage levels.

The preference of Italy's employers for centralized bargaining illustrates the logic linking training systems to product-market strategies. Homogeneous wage levels support a HQP regime as it makes both employers and employees willing to engage in sophisticated education and training programmes (see Estévez-Abe et al. 2001; Hall and Soskice 2001: 24–7). Employers know that highly skilled workers—once trained—are unlikely to leave their company as financial incentives are limited, while employees are assured 'that they are receiving the highest feasible rates of pay in return for' their commitment to invest in specific skills (Hall and Soskice 2001: 25). Secondly, overarching employment categories reflect the needs of an industry for specific employee qualifications. In so doing, employment categories have an important signalling function which enables the responsible government officials to tailor professional education and training programmes to such skill requirements. A centralized bargaining system thus assures that future employees are taught the (often highly sophisticated) skills that employers rely on for HQP.

The opposite seems to have happened in Spain. The preference of Spanish employers for decentralized bargaining (see EIRR 1992a: 20, 2002a: 24) is reflected in the development of Spain's wage-bargaining system after the Maastricht conference. As the Italian government did, the Spanish government also proposed the conclusion of a social pact, both in 1992 and 1993, in order to 'bring the Spanish economy into line with the requisites agreed at the Maastricht summit, for entry into (...) EMU' (EIRR 1992b: 12). However, contrary to their Italian counterparts, the Spanish social partners rejected these proposals. While opposition at that time mainly came from the unions, Spanish employers were also reluctant to reform the bargaining process because they feared that this would result in wage-bargaining centralization (Suárez Santos 2002). As a result, the Spanish government unilaterally decreed two important labour market reforms in 1992 and 1994 (EIRR 1992b, 1994).

The 1994 reform 'clear[ed] the (...) way for the complete reorganisation of industrial relations' (EIRR 1993: 19) as it declared all labour ordinances void. A legacy of the Franco years, these ordinances had regulated a large variety of work-related issues for the majority of Spanish employees. By urging the social partners to replace the (mostly outdated) ordinances with collective agreements, the Spanish government provided a unique opportunity to reorganize the collective-bargaining system entirely. Employers, however, never seized this opportunity to centralize the bargaining process (EIRR 1994: 24), but made sure that collective bargaining remained decentralized (see EIRR 1992a: 20, 2002a: 24). When asking for the reasons for such preferences, Spanish employers stated that the introduction of industrywide employment categories was considered impossible in view of the pronounced wage and skill differentials throughout the economy. In particular, employers were concerned that the central determination of pay increases would deprive firms of the necessary flexibility to set wages according to their individual needs (Suárez Santos 2002; see also EIRR 1993: 19).

The importance of wage flexibility as a means of securing stable ULCs through wage control is also visible in the 2001 reform of Spain's collective-bargaining system. Following the government's threat to impose reform uni-laterally, the social partners concluded a national pay-moderation agreement in December 2001. This pact constituted a landmark in that it coordinated the Spanish wage-bargaining process for the first time in seventeen years. Yet, in contrast to the Italian pact of 1993, the Spanish 2001 agreement does not give a concrete figure that wage setters should adhere to during the year, but instead states that pay agreements should take as their first reference point the Spanish government's inflation forecast for 2002, which is 2 per cent. The text also limits above-inflation settlements to productivity growth (EIRR 2002a: 24). In other words, while coordinated in the sense that they require *ex ante* agreement on targets, wage negotiations after December 2001 remain decentralized, whereby negotiators are invited, but not bound to increase wages in line with inflation and productivity. This pay-determination guideline was carried over into the 2003 and 2004 wage-bargaining rounds and has become the corner-stone of wage bargaining in Spain (EIRR 2004: 22). By not setting an industry-wide wage floor, such coordinated but decentralized bargaining structures leave firms the necessary flexibility to secure competitiveness through wage control. This, in turn, explains why Spanish employers increasingly seized the opportunity to remain internationally competitive by pursuing a low-cost, low-value-added strategy (see also Herrmann 2005: 305–6).

In sum, the constraints and opportunities related to different bargaining structures illustrate how our empirical results of Sections 4.2 and 4.3 are related: on the one hand, the productivity-whip constraint and the high-skill opportunity related to bargaining centralization meant that employers in countries with a centralized bargaining system increasingly pursued a high-quality strategy in the course of the 1990s. On the other hand, the low-skill constraint and wage-control opportunity resulting from decentralized bargaining push employers in these countries to pursue a low-cost strategy.

4.6. CONCLUSION

In this chapter, we analysed the effects of changes in wage-bargaining systems on product-market strategies. This builds on an older but recently ignored literature on the German and Swedish economies in the 1980s, which argued that centralized wage-bargaining systems impose a set of direct constraints, and through their operation—easily conceptualized as complementarities in the VoC framework—indirect opportunities for companies to upgrade their product-market strategies. We examined these basic theses against the background of those changes which took place in many European wage-bargaining systems in the 1990s following the adoption of the Maastricht criteria.

We found, first of all, that the fit between product-market strategies and wage-bargaining systems became stronger throughout the 1990s: the comparative advantage of prospective EMU member-states reflected the type of wage-bargaining system more strongly in 2000 than in 1992. We also demonstrated that the extent of wage-bargaining centralization influences shifts in comparative advantage rather than the other way around. We then examined a set of micro-level changes across the different EMU member-states. These analyses suggested not only that labour productivity and skill levels are higher in centrally coordinated systems, but also that workplaces in these systems are more cooperative while tenure rates of employees are longer. In conclusion, our analysis in this chapter suggests strongly that shifts in the macroeconomic regime—expressed as changes in the wage-bargaining system—have entailed changes in the organization of companies which enabled the latter to exploit different product markets. Such constraints in the institutional framework of an economy are beneficial to the extent that they force companies to reassess and, possibly, change their competitive strategy in order to exploit institutional opportunities (Streeck 1992).

This argument, when applied to the Maastricht period and EMU, has two important implications. First of all, it sheds light on what we would call the macroeconomic foundations of microeconomics: companies adjust their strategies not only in response to textbook competitive environments, but also—and probably more than we have been led to believe—to changes in macro-institutional environments. The emphasis on 'micro-foundations' in economic theory over the last few decades has pushed this approach somewhat in the background. However, a further development of this argument, building on the strong micro-institutional literature in such areas as organization economics (Aoki 2001) would allow us to enrich debates in economics and revive the institutional economics literature. Interestingly, whatever else we take away from this paper, there seem to be strong links between the macro-institutional framework of economies and the microeconomic effects, and we think that they pass through the way wage-bargaining systems operate as a set of incentives on companies to adjust their internal operations because of the central role that wage bargaining plays in this process. These links between micro- and macroeconomic environments can easily be captured in terms of complementarities (see Hall and Soskice 2001: 17–21; Soskice, this volume).

The second implication is related to the economic policy debates in EMU, especially those surrounding the Lisbon process and the OECD jobs strategy. One of the underlying assumptions of that debate is that labour markets in most Western European economies are too rigid. More flexibility in the labour market, including a decentralization of wage-setting, is often seen as a crucial remedy which will allow Europe to improve its economic performance. Our analysis, however, suggests the opposite: the economies that adopted a high-skill, high value-added product-market strategy in the course of the 1990s are those with a centrally coordinated wage-setting system characterized by 'strong' labour unions. Decentrally coordinated systems, which are presumably closer to the flexible type that the OECD and Lisbon agendas advocate, seem to have the opposite effect: they reduce pressures for companies to improve productivity. If both the OECD and the European Commission are as serious about developing high-skill, high value-added economies as they claim they are, they would be well advised to think carefully about the foundations of such a system.

NOTES

We thank the participants in the workshops that led to this volume, as well as Gianmario Candore, Sotiria Theodoropoulou, and Eric Verdier for their help and advice. The Hans-Böckler-Foundation and the European University Institute provided financial and institutional support.

1. We are not discarding the role of investment in raising labour productivity, but we assume this to be determined by two macroeconomic variables—interest rates and growth expectations—which cannot be influenced directly at the level of companies.
2. For a better understanding of how the RCA has been calculated, four points have to be clarified: First, the data for calculation have been downloaded from the OECD online database 'ITCS—International Trade by Commodity; SITC Rev.3' (available at: http://www.sourceoecd.org). Second, all export figures required to calculate the RCA are expressed in value (rather than in units). Third, the RCA has been calculated for all secondary, i.e. production sectors (SITC classes 5 to 9) because differences in the skills of workers have a notable impact upon the quality of *manufactured* goods, whereas they are unimportant for the quality of *agricultural* goods. Accordingly, primary, i.e. agricultural sectors (SITC classes 1 to 4) have not been considered. Finally, the considered SITC classes (5 to 9) have been detailed to the 2-digit level.
3. It is important to note that Ireland constitutes an outlier case due to its extremely high WRUV values. In order not to obtain spurious correlation results, we have removed Ireland from all subsequent analyses.

4. We updated the Traxler et al. (2001) data for Luxembourg and Greece for 1998 and for all for 2001 on the basis of the most recent EIRO reports on wage-bargaining development in the EMU member-states (see http://www.eiro.eurofound.ie). In so doing, the classification schemes used by Traxler et al. have been copied literally. In most cases the classifications for 2001 remain the same as for 1998—except for Spain where a slight decrease in the degree of wage-bargaining centralization can be observed.

5. Since the focus of this paper is on the evolution of comparative advantage, expressed as shifts in product-market strategies, we will—where the data allow us—concentrate on firms in the manufacturing sector. The reason is that we assume the latter to be a good proxy for the tradable goods sector.

6. Including Ireland would not radically alter the results of this analysis. Ireland scores very high on wage coordination; on many of the indicators in this section it would also support the group of centrally coordinated economies, since the scores are often at or slightly above the average of that group of countries.

7. Regional-level data do not exist. Economic conditions (most notably the level of unemployment and living costs) are fairly homogeneous within north-west, north-east, central, and southern Italy. Accordingly, these four groups of regions constitute the units of analysis which are commonly used for intra-Italian comparisons because significant variations exist between, rather than within these groups.

8. According to the most recent survey, 90% of Italy's employees are covered by contracts concluded at the national level (EIRO 2005).

Part III

The Single Market, Regulation, and Firms

5

Reforming National Regulatory Institutions: the EU and Cross-National Variety in European Network Industries

Mark Thatcher

5.1. INTRODUCTION

Regulatory institutions offer a powerful means to coordinate firms governments and public policymakers, and hence create institutional advantages. They can take different forms, thereby offering sectoral equivalents to national 'varieties of capitalism'. Their reform raises important issues about how nations with diverse institutions for coordination respond to common pressures for change.

This chapter examines how and why sectoral regulatory institutions in three countries in Europe (Britain, France, and Germany) have been reshaped in the face of European integration. In particular, it investigates the implications of the development of supranational regulation that is based on a liberal market economy (LME) model of regulatory institutions and runs counter to other state-led and industry-led models. It thus considers the uses and limits of the VoC approach to explain institutional change at the sectoral level.

It follows four central lines of analysis. First, it looks at how the VoC approach can be extended to sectoral and regulatory institutions. Second, it compares institutional responses to pressures for change, both domestic and international, but excluding supranational regulation. Here it finds strong support for VoC's claims of diverse institutional reform paths. Third, it investigates the effects of European Union supranational regulation on formal sectoral institutions. It shows how and why European regulation aided national policymakers to break out of previous institutional arrangements and indeed in France and Germany to adopt sectoral arrangements that differ sharply from national-level institutions. It also argues that, partly due to EU regulation, France and Germany adopted similar formal institutions to those in

Britain, based on regulated competitive markets. These marked a clear break with traditional institutions. Hence it suggests that integrating EU regulation has important implications for VoC's analysis of institutional continuities and cross-national differences. Finally, however, it also shows how existing institutional arrangements condition the timing, mechanisms, and strategies of national reform paths, and continuing informal institutions or norms. Thus it suggests that even when formal sectoral institutions converge, the VoC approach can add explanatory value.

The chapter studies regulatory institutions that coordinate 'national champion' firms and national governments in 'network industries'— telecommunications, stock exchanges, energy, railways, airlines, and postal services. These are economically and politically vital sectors. They offer sharp examples of the coordination problems between governments and firms. They also provide different models of regulatory institutions to respond to those problems. Finally, they have seen the growth of detailed EU regulation since the late 1980s, allowing investigation of its effects on national regulatory institutions.

The chapter begins with a brief summary of the institutional position from the mid-1960s until the mid-1980s. It argues that by the late 1980s, network industries in the three countries offered a prime example of how nations enjoyed different institutional complementarities arising from formal and informal institutions, ones that were consistent with those predicted by the VoC literature. Thus Britain had moved towards a regulated competitive model of coordination, France a state-led one and Germany an industry-led one, producing an increasing divergence among the three countries. It then outlines the development of EU sectoral regulation, which ran counter to the institutional frameworks and relations that had developed in France and Germany. Finally, it looks at reforms in the three countries, including both key formal regulatory institutions (ownership, rules governing competition and the allocation of regulatory powers), and informal rules and norms that actors generally follow (cf. Hall and Soskice 2001*b*: 9). It shows that, in Britain, changes took place without much reference to Europe, but in France and Germany the new EU regulation provided an important force for change through a combination of new pressures, opportunities, and legitimation for reform. The reforms of formal institutions not only broke with the past but also led all three nations towards a competitive regulated market (albeit at different speeds and to diverse extents), weakening traditional coordination mechanisms in France and Germany. However, the timing of reform, national strategies and informal institutions, remained very different. The result is thus the evolution of *formal* regulatory institutions of coordination between governments and firms towards LME-type regulatory structures across different nations, but the maintenance of diverse *informal* ones. The concluding section then offers a broader discussion of the strengths and limits of VoC approaches for understanding changes in regulatory institutions.

5.2. REGULATORY INSTITUTIONS, COORDINATION AND INSTITUTIONAL COMPLEMENTARITIES

The VoC literature offers a relational analysis of the firm and economic institutions. It underlines firm institutions (defined as a set of rules, formal or informal, that actors generally follow) develop to and the coordination of firms and other actors (Hall and Soskice 2001a). A key relationship is that between firms and governments. The two sets of actors are highly interdependent and hence need to coordinate their actions (or at least can benefit from so doing). However, their relationship faces many problems, such as different time horizons, constraints, objectives and incentives.

Interdependence between governments and suppliers and problems in coordinating their actions are particularly acute in network industries.[1] At least five reasons can be given. First, governments face problems of 'credible commitment' vis-à-vis private investors (cf. Levy and Spiller 1996; Gómez-Ibáñez 2003). On the one hand, these industries require large-scale capital investments, which then generate returns over long periods—often 20–50 years. On the other hand, once networks are built, investors face the danger of 'expropriation' of returns through government price controls or other regulation. This is a particular risk because network industries are essential for the lives of citizens who, as voters, seek both good services and low prices. Hence governments are often under considerable pressures to ensure low prices, at least for residential users, which may mean damaging the profits of suppliers. Thus long-term promises by governments lack credibility.

A second problem is the existence of major externalities in network industries. Key examples that are highly relevant for governments are pollution, congestion, regional development, or broader economic growth. As a result, the decisions of network suppliers can have important consequences for governments that will not be reflected in market prices. Specific sectoral regulation is needed to ensure that externalities are taken into account in the decisions of firms. This relates to a third issue: information asymmetries between governments and suppliers. Network industries are highly technical and problems are worsened if there is a monopoly or oligopoly, which limit independent sources of information and comparators governments.

A fourth problem is that most network industries are in whole or part natural monopolies or at best oligopolies. Hence suppliers have market power and can drive up prices above marginal cost. Moreover, monopoly means that even if part of a network industry can be open to competition—usually services—those firms face monopoly providers (usually of the infrastructure on which they must supply their services). The interests of different suppliers can thus be in conflict.

Introducing new technologies represents a fifth issue, relating to coordinating several interdependent actors who have diverse interests and risks. Governments need new technologies, which offer higher-economic growth and may have knock-on effects on other industries, especially given the widespread use of networks by other sectors. New technology often involves the definition of standards: suppliers need to adopt a common standard to allow interoperability of equipment and services. But these standards can create de facto monopolies thereby creating market power for some firms and preventing effective competition. In addition, infrastructure suppliers, equipment manufacturers, users and service providers need to invest in the new technology, but each is dependent on the others for its successful implementation. Thus, for instance, manufacturers depend on network providers to place orders and invest in new services and equipment to be used on that network, but the latter fear that, having invested, they may find themselves prisoners of manufacturers' proprietary standards and timetables. Equally, users and service providers want to be reassured that the infrastructure will be available at the appropriate price, quality and time, before they will invest in equipment and services, but unless network suppliers are confident of demand from users, they will not place orders for new technology nor will equipment manufacturers invest in research and development.

Potentially, there is an almost infinite number of regulatory institutions to respond to these coordination problems. However, for simplification, five are particularly prominent in Europe: ownership, rules governing supply, the allocation of regulatory powers, informal linkages between suppliers and the state, and norms governing decision-making. Although potentially a very high number of combinations of these institutions are possible, there are strong complementarities between different institutions—for instance, between competition and the allocation of powers to an independent regulatory agency. For simplification, three stylized models can be set out that are highly relevant for Europe.[2] No country conforms totally to one, but they provide a yardstick to compare sectoral regulatory institutions across countries and to assess change over time.[3] Moreover, they offer a sectoral equivalent to the national models developed by Hall and Soskice (2001a) and Vivien Schmidt (2002). Each model combines formal and informal regulatory institutions that complement each other.

The first is an *industry model of coordination*. Large parts of the sector are publicly owned, especially providers of services, and networks but equipment manufacturers, who represent a minority of the sector, are (equipment manufacturers privately owned). Publicly-owned suppliers also enjoy a broad monopoly over supply to final users. But, formally or informally, regulatory powers lie with the industry or industry associations. The industry sets standards and ensures coordination over matters such as developing new forms of equipment or investment programmes. This involves close linkages between network and service suppliers and equipment manufacturers, either through vertical integration in one company or via close formal and informal mechanisms for cooperation ranging from industry standard-setting bodies to common recruitment of an elite group of managers. Thus the industry has strong internal networks that link suppliers. Although suppliers may be in close contact with the government, especially through industry associations, they have considerable relational distance from—for instance, through their top managers being recruited from different socio-professional groups. Moreover, there are strong informal norms that the government will follow the industry's lead, aiding the latter's autonomy. Equally, there are norms of providing a 'public service' and ensuring long-term technological development of the sector. In the industry model, regulatory institutions aid in dealing with problems of credible commitment and innovation by allowing industry actors to lead and largely excluding the government from many policy decisions. However, public ownership is designed to ensure that monopoly positions are not abused, externalities are taken into account and profit-seeking private companies are not able to exploit information asymmetries to evade regulation.

The second model is a *state-led model of coordination*. Here network providers and sometimes equipment manufacturers are publicly owned and the former have a monopoly over supply to final users. Programmes for investment and the development of new equipment and services are planned by state officials and funded by the state or by state-guaranteed borrowing. State officials lead coordination between service suppliers, infrastructure operators, and equipment manufacturers. The sectoral norms are of state leadership, albeit in pursuit of 'public service', and long-term technological and economic development of the industry. Equally regulatory powers both legally and in practice lie with the state, which decides matters such as choice of technology, standards, investment and pricing levels. Government officials have strong informal networks with suppliers and the central policymaking norm is that they are closely involved in almost all major decisions in the industry. Thus a combination of public ownership, monopoly, and a central role for government is used to coordinate diverse actors, prevent private exploitation of monopoly and take into account externalities.

A *regulated competitive market* offers a third institutional model of coordination. Here the government operates at arm's length from suppliers who are privately owned. There is little government role in the internal workings of the privately owned suppliers. However, competition is allowed. This does not mean disengagement by the state as a whole. Instead, detailed formalised rules may cover a host of matters such as prices, quality, or universal service. Typically these rules are largely set and enforced by independent regulatory agencies. Coordination between firms occurs through competition. Thus infrastructure suppliers choose equipment manufacturers freely rather than being tied to selected long-term partners. Equally, decisions about investment and new technology will be made by privately owned suppliers. Key norms are ensuring 'fair and effective competition' and, for firms, maximizing profits and stock market valuations. Independent regulatory agencies make and enforce rules for competition, creating further separation between politicians and suppliers. Coordination takes places through competition and rules governing supply that seek to maintain or mimic a competitive market. Thus the industry has many of the features of competitive sectors in LMEs (Table 5.1).

Table 5.1. Key institutional features of the three models of regulatory institutions

Institutional feature	Industry-led model	State-led model	Regulated competitive market model
Ownership of suppliers	Public (except equipment manufacturers)	Public (except some equipment manufacturers)	Private
Rules governing supply	Monopoly for supply to final users	Monopoly for supply to final users	Competition; re-regulatory rules designed to ensure 'fair and effective' competition
Allocation of regulatory powers	Formally or informally, with industry associations	Formally and informally with state officials	Independent regulatory agencies and governments
Relations between governments and suppliers	Industry managers and government are distinct groups	Strong informal networks between government and suppliers; government closely involved in major decisions of suppliers	Distant- little government role in internal workings of suppliers
Norms	Government will follow industry's lead; pursuit of public service and long-term technological development	State officials lead coordination of actors, and decisions over services and technology; pursuit of public service and long-term technological development	Public officials seek 'fair and effective competition', suppliers seek maximization of profits and stock market value

5.3. DIVERSE NATIONAL REFORM PATHS FOR REGULATORY INSTITUTIONS: MID-1960s–MID-1980s

A well-established European 'model' that was close to the industry model of coordination existed in network industries in the late 1960s. In most sectors, publicly-owned suppliers enjoyed legal or de facto monopolies over network infrastructures and most services to final users. Examples of these suppliers for Britain, France, and West Germany included:

— telecommunications and postal services: the Post Office, the Direction Générale des Télécommunications (DGT)/La Poste, and the Deutsche Bundespost;

— electricity and gas: the Central Electricity Generating Board (CEGB) and British Gas, Electricité de France (EdF), and Gaz de France (GDF);[4]

— railways: British Rail, Société Nationale des Chemins de Fer (SNCF) and the Deutsche Bahn for railways; and

— airlines: British Airways, Air France, and Lufthansa.

Suppliers frequently had a special status, either as part of the civil service or sometimes as particular forms of public corporations, often subject to public rather than private law. They had close formal and informal links with governments and with national equipment manufacturers, who were mostly privately owned (e.g. Siemens, Alcatel, GEC). Regulatory powers were almost entirely in the hands of governments, as there were no sectoral independent regulatory authorities and general competition law was not applied to public sector monopolists.

A mixture of formal and informal norms governed policymaking. The *raison d'être* of public ownership and monopoly was to provide a public service, sometimes formalized as a judicial doctrine of '*service public*'. Key elements included supplying services across the country, even when this meant making losses, and protecting poorer users. Thus another related element was cross-subsidisation—between services and also between types of user; typically, business users cross-subsidized residential ones. Suppliers such as EdF/GdF or the Post Office often developed their own organizational cultures, taking pride in their delivery of a service, far-removed from (and indeed often in opposition to) the aim of making profits. At the same time, suppliers formed part of national industrial policies. Their orders aided and promoted privately-owned equipment manufacturers; they themselves developed long-term technologies such as nuclear power or digital switching. Finally, politicians used publicly-owned suppliers for short-term political and economic policies such as maintaining employment, reducing inflation or as part of fiscal policy.

Table 5.2. Summary of the European model of regulation in the mid-1960s

Institutional feature	
Ownership	Public
Rules governing supply	Monopoly
Allocation of regulatory powers	Governments
Relations between governments and suppliers	Close, although sometimes mediated through industry associations
Norms over objectives of suppliers	Public service; fiscal and political aims of governments; long-technological and economic development

Table 5.2 summarizes key institutional features of regulatory institutions for network industries.

From the mid-1960s onwards, this general European 'model' faced a number of pressures for change. Technological and economic developments began to transform many network industries. But introducing new technologies often required high capital investment in projects such as digitalizing telecommunications networks, setting up nuclear power plants or creating high-speed rail networks. Demand for services such as telecommunications, energy, and airlines rose sharply. Domestic dissatisfaction grew as supply failed to follow suit. The traditional European model was questioned—in part as new economic ideas were developed that challenged natural monopolies, but also as the US restructured industries such as airlines or telecommunications, offering a powerful example of a competitive regulated market. Faced with these pressures, Britain, France and West Germany took different paths in institutional reform (cf. Hayward 1995; Thatcher 2007).

Britain moved furthest away from the traditional European 'model towards a regulated competitive market. During the late 1960s and 1970s, British policymakers were often unable to coordinate government departments, state suppliers, and private equipment manufacturers (cf. Cawson et al. 1990). Public services suffered from increasing problems in the 1970s—reduced investment, increased prices to ensure profitability, and loss of public esteem. The 1980s saw dramatic reforms in Britain. First, most publicly owned suppliers were privatized (e.g. British Airways, British Telecom, British Gas, and most of the electricity industry). Second, independent sectoral regulators were introduced: Oftel for telecommunications, Ofgas for gas, Offer for electricity.[5] Competition was permitted. Although initially, it was limited—for example, being restricted to advanced telecommunications services or large energy users—the aim of governments and sectoral regulators was to extend it. The norms of policy also altered: from public service to the promotion of 'fair and effective competition'; towards cost-based prices, with cross-subsidises being regarded as anti-competitive; towards formalization of the requirements placed on suppliers, through licences, and the ending short-term 'intervention' by elected politicians. It is, however, noteworthy, that privatization and competition were accompanied by greater regulation—i.e. 'more rules', notably over licensing, pricing, and interconnection (cf. Vogel 1996).

In contrast to Britain, France followed a state-led coordination strategy, best known as one of *'grands projets'* in several network industries including telecommunications, electricity, and railways (Cohen 1992). Policymakers sought to closely coordinate the decisions of public network suppliers, private equipment manufacturers, and governments, in order to pursue long-term objectives. The public suppliers developed new technologies such as nuclear power, the high-speed train (Train à Grande Vitesse-TGV), or digital switches, in close cooperation with equipment manufacturers. They enjoyed long-term spending programmes that allowed planning and provided a large domestic order base. French firms sought to develop world leads in these new technologies and hence hoped for exports of equipment and expertise. Within France, consumers were to benefit from high quality, modern technologies. Programmes were largely financed through borrowing by the state-owned suppliers, backed by state guarantees. The leadership for *grands projets* was provided by the state—both directly by the government and indirectly through the *grands corps of* elite civil servants who also took senior posts in suppliers and whose tentacles stretched across public and private sectors.

Between the mid-1960s and the mid-1980s, West Germany largely followed an industry model of coordination in most network industries. On the one hand, close long-term relationships existed between the publicly-owned suppliers and the private equipment manufacturers. On the other hand, powerful state leadership was lacking. Thus West Germany did not develop large-scale industrial projects in areas such as nuclear power or telecommunications. Instead, it relied on high quality equipment and innovation produced by the privately-owned equipment manufacturers. Moreover, attempts to alter the status of publicly-owned suppliers—for instance making the telecommunication side of the Deutsche Bundespost or the Deutsche Bundesbahn, into private-law companies, were unsuccessful and were dropped as they failed to achieve consensus among political parties and with the trade unions. Instead, problems with public services were usually dealt with through a combination of extra public funding and cooperation between the public and private suppliers.

Thus by the mid-1980s, sectoral institutions in network industries in Britain, France, and West Germany appeared to bear out the claims of

VoC: faced with common pressures, each had chosen its own path. Moreover, each had followed a sectoral equivalent of its national-level variety or model: Britain by moving towards a regulated competitive market, France by adopting a state-led strategy and Germany by remaining with an industry-led model. However, from the mid-1980s onwards, a new factor emerged: EU regulation.

5.4. EU REGULATION AND THE SINGLE MARKET

Until the mid-1980s, the EU was largely absent from the regulation of network industries.[6] Almost no EU sectoral legislation was passed. Moreover, EU general competition law and rules on state aids were almost never applied to state suppliers.

This position changed from the mid-1980s onwards. The EU began to pass legislation regulating supply (cf. Schmidt 1997; Larouche 2000; Thatcher 2001, 2007).[7] Initially (the late 1980s), it focused on certain parts of telecommunications, notably advanced services and terminal equipment. However, during the 1990s it extended its reach to the entire telecommunications sector. Moreover, it began to pass legislation for parts of the energy sector, namely large users in electricity and gas, some of the postal sector, and the railways. Finally, during the late 1990s and then after 2000, it passed increasing amounts of legislation, notably for the remaining parts of electricity and gas, and the railways.

The central feature of EU sectoral legislation was 'fair and effective competition'. Member-states were obliged to end national monopolies ('special and exclusive rights') over supply. They were not permitted to prevent entry to liberalized market segments (with a few exceptions due to capacity shortage, such as mobile communications). Tariffs were to be based on costs. Regulation was to be organizationally separated from supply—i.e. different bodies were to undertake these functions. When competition seemed impossible, EU law required separation, at least in accounting terms, between the infrastructure and supply of services on it (eg. in railways). General EU law on public procurement was extended to network industries, who now had to follow rules such as publication of tenders and non-discrimination in equipment purchasing. EU law did not require the creation of independent sectoral regulatory authorities, but the European Commission strongly promoted them.

The European Commission also increasingly applied general competition law to network industries, including publicly-owned suppliers. The most visible examples were in the airline industry, where it attacked subsidies as illegal state aid. In addition, although under the Treaty of Rome the EU cannot alter ownership in member states (Article 119[222]), the Commission greatly 'encouraged' privatization of suppliers, notably through negotiations on state aid in which it linked approval to privatization.

Although the 'public service' aspects of network services were recognized, they were severely circumscribed. First, the Commission and EU legislation required that they were exceptions to the general rule of competition that had to be costed and justified. Thus for example, the provision of 'universal service' was accepted, but national policymakers had to show additional costs in a transparent manner. Second, public service tasks were limited—for instance, universal service referred to the provision of basic services; other tasks such as long-term industrial policy goals were not accepted. Finally, public service tasks were not to be used to promote specific suppliers—on the contrary, they were to be implemented in a transparent and non-discriminatory manner. The bulk of EU sectoral legislation remains based on liberalization and regulation to ensure that competition is fair.

Three major points are worth underlining in analysing EU regulation. First, the EU's framework ran strongly counter to both the industry and state-led models of coordination as they had operated in West Germany and France during the 1970s and 1980s. It outlawed or threatened key elements of these models such as legal monopolies, cross-subsidies between services, favoured equipment suppliers, or state aid to national champions. In contrast, it was very much aligned with the 'regulated competition' model that had developed in Britain.

Second, despite the apparent conflict between national regulatory models in France and Germany and EU law, the two countries largely supported the expansion of EU regulation. The extent of Commission 'imposition' on member states (supported by the European Court of Justice) as against national acceptance, is debated in telecommunications (see Schmidt 1996; Sandholtz 1998; Thatcher 2001). However, most directives were passed by the Council of Ministers. They involved long negotiations but were accepted by governments after significant compromises over the timing of liberalization rather than the principles of competition and EU-level regulation.

Third, EU regulation altered the potential dynamic of European markets. If implemented in practice, it offered the possibility that national champion suppliers could expand into other markets, taking advantage of liberalization and EU rules for 'fair and effective competition'. By the same token, it threatened the domestic monopolies of those national champions. Thus the new European 'single market' offered opportunities for cross-border expansion but also dangers of new domestic or overseas competitors entering home markets.

5.5. NATIONAL RESPONSES TO EU REGULATION[8]

5.5.1. Britain

During the late 1980s and 1990s, Britain largely continued its path of liberalization and privatization.[9] Thus for instance, it sold off remaining shares in British Telecom, energy suppliers (including nuclear power) and then broke up and sold British Rail. By 2005 the only major network in public hands was the Post Office. Competition was extended into the residential market for gas and electricity in the 1990s and then into postal services. Liberalization was accompanied by much greater detailed formal rules—over retail prices, terms of interconnection between networks, use of infrastructures, information, quality of service, trading arrangements for energy and internal pricing within integrated suppliers, to name but a few. Further independent regulatory agencies were set up, notably in the railways and postal services. Relations between suppliers and the government saw increasing separation. Governments were rarely directly involved in 'commercial decisions' of companies. Nor did they protect British firms from overseas takeovers—indeed, the 1990s saw a string of acquisitions and mergers, notably by US and French companies. Yet this did not mean disengagement by the state: on the contrary, the independent regulators, created many detailed rules for incumbent suppliers. Relations between regulators and incumbents were initially often conflictual but, over time, the key policy norms which centred on ensuring 'fair and effective competition' became widely accepted (cf. Coen 2005*a*).

Thus by 2000, Britain had moved very clearly towards regulated competitive market institutions for network industries. The period after *c.*2000 saw some interesting and perhaps unexpected shifts in regulation, especially concerning the formal framework and role of the government. The latter intervened to deal with failing infrastructure suppliers. In electricity, it rescued the privatized nuclear electricity generator (British Nuclear). In the railways, it forced the railway infrastructure provider Railtrack into liquidation and replaced it with a not-for-profit company (Network Rail) guaranteed by the state— a backdoor form of nationalization. Moreover, it greatly increased public subsidies for railway investment and is currently engaged in restructuring the rail regulators to increase its direct role. Nevertheless, the dominant model has remained that of institutions based on private ownership, competition, and regulation.

EU regulation played almost no visible part in developments in Britain during the 1990s or after 2000. Britain had little adjustment to make to incorporate EU legislation: it had liberalized and privatized before EU action took place and its new reforms were compatible with the EU's regulatory framework. British policymakers justified their regulatory approach based on private ownership and competition in terms of economic principles and protecting the 'consumer interest' through choice. In so far as they looked elsewhere, it was to the USA rather than the EU.

However, at the EU level, in network regulation, Britain was far from being an opponent of supra-national rules—on the contrary, it was a strong supporter of EU and Commission regulation to liberalize markets and expand EU competencies. Thus it led 'liberal' member-states which favoured the use by the Commission of Article 86[90] to issue directives ending monopolies in telecommunications (Thatcher 2001). It also enthusiastically backed the Commission in expanding its activity into electricity, gas, railways, and postal services (cf. Geradin 2002; Cameron 2005). British governments and regulators devoted their energy to seeking to export the UK model of regulation and arguing that liberalization in Continental Europe was too slow. They saw liberalization in other EU member states as offering opportunities for UK-based companies and more generally, that the EU was following the British lead in regulatory reform.

5.5.2. France[10]

French policymakers might have been expected to oppose EU regulation, since it ran counter to the traditional state-led model of regulatory institutions, notably state financial support, cross-subsidies between services, monopolies over infrastructures, and privileged relationships between national champion infrastructure and equipment manufacturing suppliers. At the level of rhetoric, France opposed 'liberalism imposed by Brussels'. Yet the reality was much more complex. French governments, in conjunction with national champion suppliers, accepted the principle of ending national monopolies— notably in telecommunications, energy, and postal services. However, they fought the Commission and 'liberal' member-states such as Britain over other matters. One was timing, as France sought to delay liberalization; thus for example, in discussions in 1993–4 on telecommunications and on electricity in the 1996–2003 period, it sought to delay EU legal requirements for full competition in the infrastructure. Another was re-regulation: French governments sought to balance increased competition with EU measures to allow member-states to protect objectives such as 'universal service' or rural development. The third was the constitutional position of liberalization directives: France bitterly resisted the use of Article 86(3) (ex-Article 90) which permits the Commission to issue its own directives to enforce competition rules over public enterprises or enterprises to which member-states have granted 'special and exclusive rights' (e.g. monopolies) (Schmidt 1998). It lost this legal battle in telecommunications, but the Commission did not use Article 86(3) for liberalization directives in other domains such as energy or postal services. France's stand was linked to a fourth element in its approach to EU regulation: negotiations with the Commission to obtain quid pro quos for its acceptance of EU liberalization. Thus for instance, it accepted liberalization of telecommunications in the mid-1990s in return for the Commission approving an alliance between France Télécom and Deutsche Telekom (Thatcher 2001). Finally, despite French government rhetoric opposed to EU liberalization, French suppliers have turned to Brussels when faced with overseas obstacles to expansion.[11]

While France was accepting or negotiating change at the EU level, at the domestic level formal institutional frameworks were considerably modified from the 1990s onwards. The organizational status of state network suppliers was altered towards private law companies (for instance, France Télécom in 1990 and then EdF and GdF 2004–5; in railways, services were separated from infrastructure in 1997). Partial privatizations (coyly termed 'openings of capital') followed for some suppliers (for instance, France Télécom and Air France, which by 2005, were majority privately owned, while EdF and GdF were partially privatized). Legal monopolies were ended, although France has usually gone no further than required by EU law. As competition has been permitted, detailed regulatory rules have also developed. New independent sectoral regulators were established for telecommunications, energy and postal services.

Thus France altered several of the formal regulatory institutions that underpinned its state-led coordination approach, notably state monopolies, publicly-owned suppliers with a special public law status, and regulatory powers lying in the hands of the government. It moved partially towards the formal institutions of a regulated competitive model of regulation. Why was this done?

In part, institutional change arose from factors unrelated to European regulation of network industries (cf. Quélin 1994; Bauby 1997; Rouban 1997; Thatcher 1999). The *grand projet* strategy came under attack in the 1980s and 1990s (e.g. in electronic services or nuclear energy). France faced fiscal deficits that made privatization very attractive to governments and limited the state's capacity to fund large-scale investment. In some sectors, notably telecommunications, policymakers saw international markets altering to make competition and internationalization of suppliers as inevitable and hence sought to prepare French suppliers.

Nevertheless, the reforms were far from defensive. A modified French strategy of creating European or international champions emerged (cf. Cohen 1995). This had two related strands. First, French suppliers such as EdF,

France Télécom, GdF, Air France and even the train operator SNCF expanded abroad—by exporting directly, taking over foreign companies or creating alliances with overseas suppliers. Thus in telecommunications, France Télécom formed an alliance with Deutsche Telekom and the US firm Sprint in the 1990s, took over the mobile telephone company Orange in 1999 and bought shares in Italian consortia. In electricity, EdF became the most expansionary supplier in Europe, supplying electricity to Italy, Spain, and Britain, and buying stakes in overseas operators in several European countries. In the 1990s Air France formed an international Skyteam alliance to compete globally.

Overseas expansion was closely related to a second strand: ensuring that French suppliers had a solid domestic base for overseas operations. The organizational position of operators such as EdF, GdF, or France Télécom was altered, so that they could issue shares and were permitted to take over foreign companies; hence one of the reasons for privatization was to provide capital and also to allow suppliers' shares to be used for overseas purchases. Policymakers have sought to ensure that the domestic market is profitable and hence produces cash to finance overseas 'adventures'; thus for example, France Télécom has gradually been able to pay-off some of its huge debts incurred in the purchase of Orange through profits on its French networks, while Air France has been able to take over domestic competitors such as Delta or Air Inter to enjoy an effective monopoly over the domestic market. Technological advances and large markets in France have offered a protected base for overseas supply. In particular, EdF has exported excess nuclear energy to neighbours, helped by the low-variable costs of generation (and not bearing the full-fixed costs of power stations). Similarly, Air France's position is aided by high-quality infrastructure for the Paris Charles de Gaulle airport, which offers a good hub for its operations. A further element has been protection of the home market from overseas competition through a range of measures, from use of re-regulatory instrument such as licensing or universal service obligations to re-balancing of tariffs by suppliers to reduce profitable opportunities for newcomers.

European integration has been central to the French strategy of creating international champions. First, EU liberalization measures open up national markets for expansionist companies such as EdF. They provide weapons to attack overseas monopolies and attempts to restrict the foreign ambitions of French suppliers, who have often been larger and better capitalized than other European suppliers, notably in Italy, Spain, and Germany, and hence well placed in a liberalized European market. Second, European regulation has offered a valuable tool to legitimate controversial changes such as privatization or altering the organizational status of suppliers. Trade unions remain powerful in France, especially when they enjoy public support. Reformers have been able to argue that they have little choice but to alter institutional arrangements—otherwise national suppliers would be disadvantaged in the new competitive European market 'imposed by Brussels' (cf. Henry 1997; Rouban 1997; Commissariat du Plan 2000; Thatcher 2004*a*, 2004*b*). These have been useful arguments for breaking down the previous political coalition that supported public ownership and monopolies, and instead creating a new one composed of governments, the top management of suppliers and the 'nationalistic Right' (and sometimes also the 'nationalistic Left'), leaving trade unions and employees often isolated with only the extreme Left as allies. Third, the gradual nature of European integration has aided France's strategy. Liberalization has been clearly signalled, allowing French suppliers time to prepare. Moreover, transposition of EU liberalization measures has often been late in France (e.g. for electricity or postal services) helping to delay overseas entrants to the French market and hence protect the domestic market for French suppliers.

Thus EU regulation has aided both strands of the French strategy. At the same time, it has permitted the continuation of informal institutions of coordination between governments and suppliers. Strong links between the two though have remained, buttressed by social and political networks and the use of government appointment powers. The heads of network suppliers have enjoyed very close relationships with elected politicians and senior civil servants, helped by all three groups being largely drawn from the *grand corps*.[12] European integration has not prevented those strong relationships from being used to the advantage of French international champions. The French government has strongly supported suppliers abroad and participated in crafting deals that aided overseas expansion. Thus for instance, it offered the European Commission accelerated liberalization of telecommunications infrastructure in return for approval of France Télécom's alliance with Deutsche Telekom and then Sprint. In electricity, it put strong pressure on the Italian government to abrogate the law designed to prevent EdF controlling an important domestic electricity supplier (Montedison) and ultimately promised that by selling a share of an EdF company, the Italian supplier ENEL would gain a set share of the French electricity market! Equally, re-regulatory instruments have been open to use (and abuse) to protect the French market. Third generation mobile licensing provides an excellent example. The EU law insists that licensing methods must be non-discriminatory but allow member-states the choice between allocating through auctions or beauty contests, and also are silent on the cost of licences. France ran a high cost 'beauty contest', which first led most overseas bidders to seek a French partner and then withdraw when the costs were too high; finally, three French bidders emerged, and the French government greatly reduced the costs of the licences for them. In addition, provisions over universal service have been available to ensure that

payments can be made to La Poste or France Télécom. Favourable accounting practices, such as the allocation of the costs of nuclear power between
the government and EdF, or the transfer of SNCF's debts to the infrastructure supplier Réseau Ferré de France (RFF) have offered another means of
ensuring financial support. Although independent regulators have sought to
extend competition, they have found themselves hampered by lack of political
support; hence for example, in 2005, attempts by the telecommunications
sectoral regulator the Autorité de Régulation des Télécommunications (ART)
to question France Télécom's increase in rental charge were swiftly overcome
by an alliance between the Prime Minister and the supplier. Even naked state
bailouts of suppliers (e.g. to Air France or France Télécom in 1994 and 2002)
were not stopped by the European Commission, which at best has undertaken
lengthy investigations or sought assurances that state suppliers would undertake 'restructuring' to justify the state aid.

The result is that while France has moved a significant distance from the
formal institutions of a state-led model of regulatory institutions towards a
regulated competition model, it has been able to adopt a modified state-led
policy of creating French international champion firms abroad and protecting
them at home through the use of re-regulatory instruments and informal
networks.

5.5.3. Germany

At the EU level, Germany[13] was often initially reluctant about EU liberalization measures during the late 1980s (cf. Schmidt 1997; Eising and Jabko 2001).
However, its position altered, so that by the early 1990s, it not only accepted
EU legislation to extent competition but was frequently an ally for Britain at
the EU level. Germany supported EU regulation that ran directly counter to
many German traditional institutional arrangements—for instance, monopolies or the role of industry associations in setting standards and dividing up
markets.

At the same time as EU regulation was being developed, major reforms were
introduced in Germany from the 1990s onwards. These were made gradually
and after lengthy debates that involved government and opposition political
parties and trade unions. The incremental and consensual nature of reform
was particularly strong when constitutional reform was required (for instance,
the 1994 Postreform II legislation that allowed privatization of Deutsche
Telekom). The organizational position of suppliers was changed. Some major
publicly-owned network suppliers were privatized. The most striking example
was Deutsche Telecom, which was made into a form of public corporation
in 1995, 25 per cent privatized in 1996 and by 2001 was majority privately

owned. Other suppliers moved towards becoming market organizations as forms of private law companies, albeit entirely state owned; thus for instance, the railway operator, the Deutscheßahn, was made into a private law company and then in 1993 infrastructure and service provisions were separated (Lodge 2002). Competition was gradually extended by law into different sectors— from telecommunications to energy (Eberlein 2000; Böllhoff 2005; Coen and Héritier 2005; Héritier 2005). The general competition authority has extended its role to include reviewing industry association agreements. Although independent regulatory agencies run counter to German administrative traditions, several sectoral regulators were created.[14]

The result of the reforms is that Germany's formal regulatory institutions have moved a long way from the industry model. The previous closed regulatory structure in which industry associations had many powers and faced relatively few other actors or legal constraints has been ended. Instead, the associations must deal with sectoral and general competition authorities, and new entrants, as well as the government and incumbent operators.

How can Germany's reform strategy be analysed in the context of European integration? Why were major reforms introduced into formal institutions after years of little change? Why did Germany accept EU regulation that largely ran counter to traditional institutional arrangements?

On the one hand, German policymakers faced powerful forces for change that were largely unrelated to EU regulation. The most important was the effect of reunification, which left many German network suppliers with enormous debts and large modernization programmes. Thus for instance, after West and East Germany's telecommunications operators had been merged, Telekom faced debts of DM100 billion, and debt servicing costs represented 12 per cent of its income of DM54 billion in 1992, and an estimated DM60 billion was required between 1990 and 1997 (*The Economist* 30 October 1993; Werle 1999). Moreover, reunification left the federal government short of money, and hence less able to finance network development and instead looking for new sources of revenue, notably from privatization. Another significant factor was the influence of overseas examples, particularly the UK: German policymakers were attracted by the UK regulatory model, including competition and independent regulatory authorities (cf. Eising and Jabko 2000; Lodge 2002). Domestic dissatisfaction also played some role, notably from business users in telecommunications and electricity, who attacked high prices for large users, poor service and cross-subsidies. A final factor, notably in energy and telecommunications, was fear of loss of competitiveness for Germany, especially in the context of slow growth and high unemployment in the 1990s and 2000s.

On the other hand, European regulation played several important roles in reform. It offered an additional source of pressures for change. The

European Commission exerted direct pressures on German policymakers to modify regulatory institutions, through court cases based on general competition law for liberalization, the ending of association agreement and against 'state aid' and more subtle encouragement to create independent regulatory authorities, especially in energy. Overseas companies from other European nations began to enter the German market—either directly as suppliers or through alliances and takeovers. The most spectacular example was the hostile takeover of Mannesmann by the UK-based firm Vodafone in 2000, which ran counter to German traditions of consensual mergers. German policymakers worried that large overseas companies such as BT or EdF with considerable capital and experience would overwhelm domestic firms. They were particularly concerned about energy, where German firms were small and fragmented, lacking a powerful 'national champion' company. Without reform, EU regulation left German suppliers open to being swallowed by larger predatory companies.

However, European integration was not just a source of pressures: it also offered opportunities for domestic actors. First, EU liberalization aided some German firms to expand abroad. Thus for instance, Deutsche Telekom formed an international alliance with France Télécom and then the US firm Sprint in the mid-1990s, which was approved by the Commission in exchange for agreement on rapid liberalization of the telecommunications market (Thatcher 2001). Equally, in postal services, Deutsche Post sought to expand in other countries thanks to the introduction of competition. Second, the 'demands' of European integration allowed larger domestic firms to seek changes to improve their position within Germany. Thus for instance, in energy, larger suppliers sought to break down the protection given to municipal suppliers and hence expand their domestic market share (Eising and Jabko 2000). Equally, large users saw that competition could lower prices and increase their choice of suppliers. However, a third reason was perhaps the most important: EU regulation represented an important external source of legitimation for reforms that were designed to allow German network suppliers to adapt to both EU and non-EU pressures. It was argued to make reforms urgent and indispensable, aiding governments and network managers to overcome opposition, especially by trade unions and employees. Thus for instance, it was used to justify controversial reforms such as privatization of Deutsche Telekom (Thatcher 2004*b*) or transforming DeutscheBahn into a private law company. These reforms were desired for many non-European reasons, including raising finance for the German budget and adapting German farms to 'inevitable' changes in an altered world market, such as increased competition and the spread of internationalized companies (for telecommunications, see Schneider 2001). After years of domestic blockage to reform, the EU provided an important 'external' source of impetus and justification for change.

Yet change in formal regulatory institutions also left much scope for the continuation of traditional informal institutions. Although the role of industry associations has been weakened by the arrival of new entrants and competition, they remain significant in energy and railways (Coen 2005*b*; Héritier 2005). Thus for example, they continue to strongly influence third party access to the energy infrastructure, a key element in competition (Böllhoff 2005; Coen 2005*b*). Equally, although independent sectoral regulators have been created, their autonomy in practice has often been limited. Hence for example, the RegTP for telecommunications and postal services has appeared to be strongly 'shadowed' by the federal government, helped by the fact that most of its employees are former ministry officials (Coen and Héritier 2005). In energy and railways, pro-competitive regulation has been hindered by the lack of an independent sectoral authority and the lack of resources of the general competition authority (five to eight staff assigned to the energy sector and one for railways—Coen 2005*b*; Héritier 2005).

Thus while German formal regulatory institutions moved towards those of a 'regulated competitive market', they did so gradually and leaving in place many informal institutions of a industry-led model of coordination. European integration played an important part in the evolution, acting as a source of pressure but perhaps more importantly, as part of a strategy of adaptation for network suppliers and the state to a new domestic, European, and international environment that was much less favourable to traditional institutions.

5.6. CONCLUSION

Regulatory institutions—formal and informal—provide a means to coordinate firms with other actors. Different combinations of regulatory institutions are possible, allowing for sectoral equivalents to varieties of macro-level capitalist institutions. An analysis of the institutional reform paths in Britain, Germany, and France between the mid-1960s and 2006 reveals both change in these combinations and interesting cross-national patterns, that can be divided into two main periods.

After a relatively similar starting point of industry-led regulatory institutions in the mid-1960s, Britain, France, and West Germany introduced different institutional reforms at the sectoral level to deal with pressures on network supply in the period until the mid-1980s. Moreover, those reforms increasingly matched those expected at the macro or national level by the literature on varieties or models of capitalism. Britain greatly enhanced the role of competition and private markets to coordinate the different actors, as expected in an LME (cf. Hall and Soskice 2002). France took the opposite direction, reinforcing the direct role of the state (cf. Schmidt 1996, 2002; Hancké 2001). West Germany largely retained the industry model of coordination, remaining closest to the traditional European model, due to the importance of consensus and the lack of a strong central group of policymakers to take the lead in creating new projects. For each country, the influence of institutional complementarities can be seen, as policymakers drew on existing institutional constraints and resources in choosing their differing national paths.

The second period runs from the late 1980s onwards. It saw the development by the EU of a wide-ranging regulatory framework that conflicted with, and often outlawed, regulatory institutions in France and Germany, such as monopolies, cross-subsidies, or closed privileged relationships between network infrastructure suppliers and equipment manufacturers. In contrast, the EU's framework was close to the regulated competitive market model adopted by Britain. Perhaps surprisingly, national governments largely accepted the EU's regulatory framework. The period also saw major reforms that considerably reversed the increasing diversity among Britain, France, and Germany. All three countries moved their formal institutional structures towards the regulated competition model, with the privatization of suppliers, the ending of monopolies and the creation of independent sectoral regulatory authorities. The speeds and extents varied of the movement varied—as predicted by a VoC model, Britain moved furthest and fastest. Nevertheless, the changes represent considerable convergence compared with the position in the mid-1980s.

Yet despite convergence in formal regulatory institutions, three sets of important differences existed between Britain, France, and Germany. First, the role of EU regulation in domestic institutional reform varied. In Britain, it was negligible as reforms often preceded EU regulation and in any case were undertaken with little reference to Europe. In contrast, in France and Germany, European regulation played an important part in creating additional pressures for change, in offering advantages for firms and large users and in legitimating reform in the face of opposition. Thus the nature of 'Europeanization' varied.[15]

A second and related contrast concerns the strategies of policymakers in the three nations concerning both institutional reform and the EU. In Britain, policymakers sought the extension of competition and accepted foreign entry, including overseas firms buying British companies, with little regard to Europe. In contrast, French policymakers aimed at creating strong French international champions that would expand abroad, aided by a good domestic base. EU regulation was crucial for their approach, since it ensured that other markets would be opened to French suppliers. At the same time, they implemented EU regulation domestically slowly and/or in ways designed to aid French firms. German policymakers faced great domestic pressures, and hence used EU regulation to adapt to problems such as fiscal constraints, inefficiencies of networks, and sometimes fragmentation of suppliers. Thus EU regulation formed part of a more defensive adaptation strategy than in France.

Finally, despite a common EU regulatory framework, informal regulatory institutions continued to differ greatly across the three nations—both informal norms and linkages between governments and suppliers. In Britain, norms of seeking 'fair and effective competition' and non-interference by governments in the internal decisions of suppliers went hand-in-hand with considerable distance between most suppliers and government. In contrast, policymakers in France sought to promote French suppliers abroad and protect them at home, a policy helped by close links between elected politicians, civil servants, and the heads of suppliers. In Germany, there were norms of adaptation to a new environment and gradual change, whilst industry associations continued to play a significant role.

The overall outcome thus is convergence in formal regulatory institutions, but with continuing differences in the mechanisms of reform, national strategies and informal institutions. This is summarized across the three countries in Table 5.3.

What are the implications of these findings for VoC, and especially the utility of the approach in explaining institutional change and responses to supranational regulation? First, the cases indicate that it is possible to apply the VoC approach to sectoral institutions. Indeed, interesting sectoral equivalents to national-level varieties can be found. Second, the findings from the period between the mid-1960s until the mid-1980s strongly support the VoC divergent national paths of institutional reform thesis. From the mid-1960s, international pressures for change grew, notably transnational technological and economic developments and new ideas that called into question traditional sectoral regulatory institutions. But the three countries adopted different sectoral models. A major reason was indeed the influence of variation in coordination at the national level. Thus the inability of British policymakers to coordinate key actors, notably the government, state-owned suppliers, and privately owned equipment manufacturers, was important in the move during the 1980s towards a competitive market model of sectoral coordination. In contrast, coordinating institutions such as networks of the *grands corps* spanning public and private sectors in France or industry associations in West Germany were important in the former following a state-led model and the latter in staying with the industry-led model of regulatory institutions. Hence, nations responded to pressures for change by following their own VoC path at the sectoral level, linked to differences at the national level of reform.

Table 5.3. Sectoral regulatory institutions in 2005 and features of institutional change

	Britain	France	Germany
Formal regulatory institutions	Regulated competitive model–private suppliers, liberalization of supply, independent regulatory agencies	Regulated competitive model–privatized (majority or minority) suppliers, liberalization of supply, independent regulatory agencies	Regulated competitive model–privatized (majority or minority) suppliers, liberalization of supply, independent regulatory agencies
Informal regulatory institutions/ norms	Aim of 'fair and effective competition', separation of commercial decisions of suppliers and government	Promotion of French suppliers, strong informal links between politicians, civil servants and suppliers	Gradual change and adaptation, continuing role for powerful industry associations
Role of supranational regulation in institutional reform	No role for EU regulation	Use of EU to legitimate formal institutional reform, offer advantages, and increase pressures for change	Use of EU to legitimate formal institutional reform, offer advantages, and increase pressures for change
National strategies towards supranational regulation	Support for rapid EU legislation to liberalize markets—'export' British regulatory model	Use EU regulation to create international champions and open other EU national markets; slow or biased implementation to protect domestic market	Use EU regulation to adapt to new conditions (EU, domestic, and non-EU), aid development of strong firms domestically to meet foreign competition and some help for overseas expansion

However, when supranational regulation by the EU developed, a more nuanced picture emerges of the application of the national-level VoC approach to sectoral change, offering a third set of general observations. On the one hand, all three countries adopted the formal regulatory institutions of a regulated competitive market: neither diverse national-level institutions nor different previous histories prevented this convergence. At least at the sectoral level, policymakers broke out of the previous sectoral regulatory model. In France and Germany, they adopted formal sectoral institutions that differ sharply from the national-level variety of VoC—i.e. an LME-type 'regulated competition model'. The cases show how and why supranational regulation gave them the opportunities to do so, notably by legitimating changes and increasing pressures for reform.[16] At the same time, national policymakers accepted and indeed created these pressures through decisions at the EU level, as this EU 'two-level game' then allowed them to use EU regulation to reform domestic institutions for both EU and non-EU reasons. Supranational regulation provided much greater freedom to reshape sectoral institutional arrangements than anticipated in nationally centred VoC analyses.

On the other hand, the VoC approach proves useful in explaining cross-national differences in the timing, mechanisms, and strategies of institutional reform, and in informal institutions. Thus for instance, Britain had greater incentives than France or Germany to adopt regulated competitive market institutions because failures of coordination had contributed to difficulties in supply in the 1960s and 1970s. France and Germany had fewer reasons to do so until the late 1980s due to the success of their coordinating institutions in earlier decades and the existence of powerful trade unions and industry associations. Instead, from the late 1980s onwards, the two countries needed EU regulation to legitimate reform and overcome domestic opposition to changes such as privatization or liberalization. Finally, the VoC analysis helps explain the coexistence of these similar formal institutions with continuing differences in strategies and informal norms across the three nations. Thus for instance, strong networks in France gave the state the capacity and the ambition to use EU legislation to both promote French (inter)national champions abroad (be these privately or publicly owned) and to implement European legislation domestically so as to protect the home market or at least utilize it as a bargaining chip in the foreign expansion strategies of firms. Germany has been keen to maintain its strong industry associations whilst also preparing its domestic firms for overseas expansion and domestic competition. In contrast, Britain's institutional arrangements, notably its existing LME and moves towards a regulated competitive market before EU legislation, are important in explaining why British policymakers have largely ignored EU regulation in domestic reform, welcomed entry by foreign firms and instead focused on opening up overseas markets through EU legislation.

Overall, the cases suggest that at the sectoral level the VoC approach has mixed explanatory power in analysing formal national institutional responses to international forces for change: strong when dealing with transnational technological and economic factors or new ideas, but much weaker when supranational regulation intervenes and offers opportunities for policymakers to move beyond the constraints of existing institutional frameworks. However, its value in understanding cross-national differences in informal institutions and the processes of institutional change seems very high, as it allows linkages between existing institutions and adjustment strategies towards supranational regulation. Existing national institutions condition these features more than formal institutional changes in the face of supranational regulation.

NOTES

1. For economic analyses of network industries, see for instance, Newbery (1999), Armstrong, Simon, and Vickers (1994), Gómez-Ibáñez (2003); for a legal analysis, see Prosser (1997).
2. The three models are not exhaustive—for instance, the industry-led model has an interesting variant, seen in some US networks, of privately-owned industries with an independent regulatory commission.
3. For a similar analysis based on airlines, see Lehrer (2001), although he focuses more on the internal workings and commercial of suppliers than regulatory institutions.
4. West Germany was an exception in that a mixture of publicly-owned and privately-owned suppliers existed; moreover, many suppliers were regional or municipal.
5. The Office of Telecommunications, the Office of Gas Supply, and the Office of Electricity Regulation.
6. The chapter refers to the European Union although, legally, decisions were taken under the European Community pillar of the EU.
7. Key liberalizing directives include Commission (1988, 1990, 1994, 1995, 1996) European Parliament and Council (1996, 2003*a*) for electricity, European Parliament and Council (1997 and 2002) for postal services, European Parliament and Council (1998, 2002), and European Parliament and Council (2003*b*) for gas.
8. For cross-sectoral and cross-national comparative studies that discuss network industry reform, see Thatcher (2007), Henry (1997), Coen and Thatcher (2000), Henry, Matheu, and Jeunemaitre (2001); for energy, see Cameron (2005), for telecommunications, see Schneider (2001), Thatcher (2004*a*, 2004*b*), for postal services, Geradin (2002), for airlines Staniland (2003).
9. For analyses and overviews of reform of British network institutions, see Foster (1992), Newbery (1999).
10. For cross-sectoral studies, see Bauby (1997) and Henry (1997).
11. One prominent example was Italian electricity, where the government passed a law to prevent EdF from using its purchase of a controlling stake in a large domestic supplier, Montedison, leading to legal action before the European Court of Justice.
12. The most prominent examples include Thierry Breton (head of France Télécom 2004–5 before becoming finance minister) or Bernard Attali (brother of Jacques Attali, Mitterrand's close adviser), who was head of Air France in the 1990s.
13. For cross-sectoral studies, see Coen and Héritier (2005).

14. For example, the RegTP for telecommunications and postal services (1996) and the Bundesaufsichtsamt für den Wertpapierhandel—BAWe for stock exchanges in 1995 (Döhler 2002; Böllhoff 2002, 2005); in 2005, Germany established a cross-sectoral regulator, for telecommunications, postal services and energy, the Bundesnetzagentur.

15. For wider discussions of Europeanization, see for instance Featherstone and Radaelli (2003), and Schmidt (2002).

16. cf. Thatcher (2004a) for a detailed analysis of the example of telecommunications.

6

Institutional Variation and Coordination Patterns in CMEs: Swiss and German Corporate Governance in Comparison

Alexander Börsch

6.1. INTRODUCTION[1]

One of the most important insights of the VoC approach is that national institutions shape economic specialization patterns by influencing the structure and the strategies of firms. Complementarities link the single institutions of a political economy which results in coherent incentive structures for firms and in two ideal-types of market economies: coordinated (CME) and liberal (LME). Corporate governance systems mirror the overall patterns of coordination in a political economy. Stakeholder systems of corporate governance are found in CMEs and shareholder systems in LMEs. Whereas the differences between the prototypes of CMEs and LMEs and their respective corporate governance systems—Germany versus the USA and/or the UK—have been examined in depth (Hall and Soskice 2001; Vitols 2001), corporate governance in CMEs other than Germany has been less intensively studied from a VoC perspective.

This chapter tries to fill this gap, because the VoC focus on Germany implies three shortcomings. First, differences in institutional arrangements among CMEs tend to be overlooked by assuming that their coordination mechanisms mirror the ones in place in the German political economy. Second, due to the lack of comparative work on CMEs from a VoC perspective, most changes taking place within the German system are either interpreted as trivial or as indicating the convergence of the German model—and CMEs more generally—towards the LME model (Jürgens et al. 2000*a*; Höpner 2001; Börsch 2007; Lane 2003; O'Sullivan 2003). Third, it is assumed that the different—complementary—institutions in Germany are equally important for the outcome, namely Diversified Quality Production (DQP).

In this chapter, I examine the link between the institutional framework and economic specialization patterns by comparing the corporate governance systems of Germany and Switzerland. These two CMEs with stakeholder systems of corporate governance have the most similar economic specialization among all CMEs—the outcome of corporate governance arrangements in the VoC approach. Both have comparative advantages in medium-high-tech industries, which are characterized by incremental innovation patterns and DQP. Given this similar specialization, the VoC approach lets us expect that the Swiss institutional infrastructure should resemble that of Germany. The crucial question with regard to complementarities is whether there needs to be a high degree of institutional similarity or whether different forms of coordination are possible.

The chapter demonstrates that Germany and Switzerland have different frameworks for corporate governance, despite their very similar economic specialization. The Swiss corporate governance system mixes LME- and CME-type institutions in the different subsystems. Whereas there are strong similarities between German and Swiss corporate governance—for example regarding ownership concentration, the absence of a market for corporate control, the structure of the training systems, and the organizational capacities of employers—Swiss corporate governance is closer to shareholder systems with respect to financial market development, the importance of institutional investors, and labour market set-up.

How is then possible that Swiss technological and product market specialization is in DQP, given that the literature argues that Germany's DQP is based on its whole set of complementary institutions? I argue that the mix of LME- and CME-type institutions in Switzerland is not random and also that Swiss corporate governance is not based on market coordination. However, Swiss corporate governance follows a different pattern of coordination compared to Germany. Coordination in Switzerland is more informal and voluntary in nature—also because of a lower level of public regulation—and thus the corporate governance system is more differentiated than the German variant. Swiss companies are able to build arrangements—especially with regard to industrial relations—conducive to DQP if they are following this product market strategy. Coordination in Switzerland mainly results from bargaining at the industry and especially company level. In sectors characterized by incremental innovation and DQP, Swiss firms are able to construct arrangements with the workforce that very much resemble those of German firms, despite the considerable differences on the macro-level. The institutional conditions for DQP are created at the industry and company level, less so at the national level.

The reason why Swiss firms can build these institutions at the industry and company level, while firms from shareholder systems find this hard to do, lies in two enabling conditions that render coordination possible. First, the training system in place—based on the coordination capacities of employers—supports the formation of firm- and industry-specific skills on the part of the employees and hence allows Swiss firms access to a qualified and specialized workforce. Swiss firms invest heavily in the national training system because they are dependent on the skills it generates for their product market strategies. Second, the concentrated ownership structures and the missing market for corporate control shelters them from capital market and shareholder value pressures to a high degree—despite well-developed financial markets—and allows those kinds of commitments on the part of management necessary for DQP strategies. Long-term relationships with stakeholders and employees are possible that would not be sustainable if stakeholders feared the breach of implicit contracts in the case of a hostile takeover. Hence, the institutional mechanisms and the levels of coordination do differ in German and Swiss corporate governance, but Swiss firms have found a functionally equivalent way to form the institutional requirements of DQP strategies.

The comparison between the Swiss and German models presented in this chapter is structured along the lines of the VoC model. The first section discusses the varieties approach and how it relates to corporate governance. I then present evidence on the dominant modes of innovation and company strategies in Germany and Switzerland which result in the technological and product market specialization of these two countries. Following that, I compare the organization of capital markets, patterns of corporate control, the organization of labour markets and the education and training systems. Lastly, I deal with coordination patterns in Germany and Switzerland.

6.2. VARIETIES OF CAPITALISM, CORPORATE GOVERNANCE, AND ECONOMIC SPECIALIZATION

The VoC approach sees firms as the central actors in the political economy (Hall 2001: 225). The dominant mode of coordination—market or non-market—in a political economy facilitates or hinders the development of organizational competencies in firms that are necessary to compete in different markets. Firms capitalize on the institutions available and derive distinctive competitive advantages from them (Hall 2001: 225).[2] Consequently, LMEs and CMEs excel in those industries whose requirements fit their institutional framework (Soskice 2000: 179). In short, different institutional settings shape company strategies and the resulting technological specialization of countries.

Following from the focus on firms and their relationships with the institutional environment, the corporate governance system is of central importance. There are two broad categories of corporate governance systems—distinguished by the dominant mode of control—shareholder and stakeholder systems. Shareholder systems are characterized by highly developed and fluid financial markets, market-based corporate finance, widely dispersed ownership, flexible labour markets, arm's-length industrial relations, weak unions, and a CEO-dominated board. Stakeholder systems are characterized by poorly developed financial markets, bank-based corporate finance, concentrated and cross-ownership patterns, regulated labour markets, cooperative employee–management relations, strong unions, and a consensus-oriented management board. The distinction between shareholder and stakeholder systems of corporate governance corresponds to the distinction between LMEs and CMEs, that is shareholder systems are found in LMEs and stakeholder systems in CMEs.

The type of corporate governance system in place shapes innovation processes, which in turn reinforce countries' specialization patterns (Casper et al. 1999: 11). Incremental innovation—the small scale upgrading of established products or cumulative improvements in production processes—is characteristic of stakeholder systems due to the prerequisites of long-term relationships between management, financiers, and employees. Radical innovation—the development of new products and processes—is the dominant innovation pattern in shareholder systems, because radical innovation requires high autonomy for management and access to liquid financial markets.

A central building block of the VoC approach is the concept of institutional complementarities. Complementarities imply that in well-performing economies there needs to be a fit between the individual institutions, which leads to a coherent system with an identifiable institutional logic. This institutional logic shapes actors' choices and increases overall efficiency or the ability of actors to reach their objectives (Deeg 2005). Whereas complementarity is an attribute of the relationships between the various elements of a system, consistency refers to the system itself. A system is consistent if the values of the various elements 'fit together', that is they encourage a similar behaviour in different spheres of action and therefore realize the potential of complementarities (Schmidt and Spindler 1999; Schmidt 2004). In the framework of the VoC approach, complementarities imply that the patterns of coordination in the different subsystems all follow the same logic and type of coordination (Hall and Soskice 2001: 18). In the following sections I take issue with this

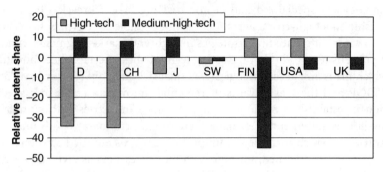

Figure 6.1. Relative patent specialization in 2002

Source: German Federal Ministry of Education and Research (2005: 21).

claim by investigating patterns of coordination in the two stakeholder systems with the most similar production profiles.

6.3. GERMAN AND SWISS PRODUCTION PROFILES

The economic specialization of Switzerland and Germany is highly similar. Both countries tend to specialize in medium-high-technologies and products, while both have weaknesses in genuine high-technology industries.[3] Looking at the distribution of patents, the following pattern emerges (Figure 6.1).

The specialization of Germany and Switzerland, with their comparative advantages in medium-high-tech industries, is an almost perfect mirror image of the comparative advantages enjoyed by the USA and the UK and fits therefore very well the CME–LME classification (German Federal Ministry of Education and Research 2005: 21).[4] Congruent with patent specialization, the Swiss and German shares of world trade are almost twice as high in medium-high-technology products as in high-technology products (German Federal Ministry of Education and Research 2004: 755).

The similarities are not only in the type of industries in which Germany and Switzerland have comparative advantages, but also in the patterns through which the comparative advantage in these industries is created. The strength of German industry lies in well-established products, which are based on complex production processes and extensive after-sales services; these products are characterized by modest rates of technological change (Porter 1990: 356–75; Casper et al. 1999). This production model has been characterized as DQP, meaning that German firms tend to compete in high-quality markets with technologically specialized and customized products (Streeck 1991). Cost-leadership in a high-cost environment is not possible, so German firms gravitate towards differentiation strategies in high-end market segments. Innovation patterns tend to build on existing technologies in established industries, in which firms aim at technological and quality leadership (Porter 1990: 356–75). DQP and the bias towards incremental innovation result in a specialization in established medium-high-technology industries with cumulative know-how requirements. Germany therefore has comparative advantages in industries in which incremental innovation patterns are the key success factor; these are mostly medium-high-tech industries such as civil engineering, transport, engines, and chemicals. It has disadvantages in high-tech industries characterized by radical innovation such as biotechnology, semiconductors, and information technology.

   Diversified quality production is also characteristic of Swiss industry: 'Most products are small-batch, customer-oriented specialized items of high quality and reliability, supported by prompt delivery and excellent after sale service' (Fluder and Hotz-Hart 1998: 263). The basic competitive advantage of Swiss firms lies in their ability to combine established products and processes with new technologies while offering a high-quality standard; the focus being on market niches in traditional markets. By contrast, Swiss firms are under-represented in new and fast-moving high-tech markets (Fluder and Hotz-Hart 1998: 264–5). In other words, Swiss firms pursue DQP strategies based on incremental innovation. The overall economic structure of Switzerland also resembles that of Germany; small- and medium-sized enterprises dominate, even though both countries have a sizeable proportion of multinational enterprises.[5]

   Hence, the '. . . composition of the Swiss economy is like that of the German economy in a number of respects. Both have strengths in chemicals, machinery, machine tools, precision mechanical tools, optical products, and textiles. Switzerland's position in these industries, however, tends to be more specialized and focused on the most sophisticated segments. German companies tend to offer broader lines, though they also usually compete via differentiation' (Porter 1990: 318).

   In the framework of the VoC approach, the DQP strategies of German firms and the overall specialization of the economy are seen as the outcome of institutional arrangements and their effects on firm behaviour (Hall 1997: 298). Underdeveloped financial markets, long-term bank-based financing patterns, bank monitoring, concentrated ownership, a missing market for corporate control, specialized human capital formation through the education system and long-term employment patterns, as well as co-determination work together in enabling and sustaining DQP strategies. Management will take advantage of the prevailing institutional conditions by choosing long-term DQP strategies based on incremental innovation patterns. Firm strategies therefore fit the institutional environment. The guiding question of the rest of the chapter, which will compare the institutional features of corporate governance in Germany and Switzerland, is in how far Swiss corporate governance resembles the German institutional setting and how the Swiss system developed coordination patterns that facilitate DQP.

6.4. SWISS AND GERMAN CORPORATE GOVERNANCE IN COMPARISON

In the present context, national systems of corporate governance are defined as the institutional and legal arrangements which influence the behaviour of firms (Dufey et al. 1998: 46; Schmidt 2004: 388). Those elements of the institutional framework with the greatest impact on the behaviour and the strategies of firms are the organization of the capital market and corresponding patterns of control, the organization of the labour market and industrial relations, as well as the education and training system.

German and Swiss corporate governance are clearly not of the shareholder system type, both are accurately classified as stakeholder systems. However, they also differ in many respects from each other. Switzerland combines German-style institutions with elements that resemble Anglo-Saxon corporate governance patterns. The institutions they have in common are concentrated ownership, the absence of a market for corporate control, bank monitoring, the modest use of stock options, the training system, the coordinating capacities of employers, and interlocking directorships. In contrast, there are wide differences in financial market development, the importance of institutional investors and labour market-related issues such as the extent of statuary co-determination, union strength, the centralization of wage bargaining, the structure of labour markets, as well as the formal organization of firms.

Table 6.1 gives an overview of the institutional infrastructure for corporate governance in Germany and Switzerland in comparative perspective. Despite the apparent differences in the institutional set-up, firms from both corporate governance systems could specialize in DQP. In the following sections, I analyze these indicators in detail and advance the argument that the differences in the institutional infrastructure of corporate governance between Switzerland and Germany are offset by different forms of coordination.

Table 6.1. Comparing the institutional infrastructure for corporate governance

	Germany	Switzerland
Capital markets and corporate control		
Stock market capitalization	Low	High
Importance of institutional investors	Low	High
Ownership concentration	High	High
Monitoring by banks	High	High
Frequency of hostile takeovers	Low	Low
Use of stock options	Low	Low
Board structure	Two-tier system	One-tier system
Frequency of interlocking directorships/corporate networks	High	High
Industrial relations and labour markets		
Extent of co-determination	High	Low
Coordination capacity of employers	High	High
Strength of unions	High	Low
Centralization of wage bargaining	High	Low
Coordination of wage bargaining	High	High
Flexibility of labour markets	Low	High
Education system		
Skill base/specialization of the workforce	High	High

6.4.1. Capital Markets and Corporate Control

The most basic indicator that distinguishes between stakeholder and shareholder systems of corporate governance is stock market capitalization. Shareholder systems show a much higher market capitalization and they give a prominent role to institutional investors, which results in a prioritization of their preferences in company strategy. Stock market capitalization in the USA and Great Britain has exceeded Germany's three- to fourfold since the 1970s. In 2004, Germany's market capitalization as a percentage of GDP was 44 per cent; the corresponding figures for the USA and the UK were 139 and 132 per cent respectively. However, Switzerland's stock market capitalization is also among the highest worldwide. Over the 1990s, it has been constantly higher than the market capitalization of the USA, and was only slightly behind the UK's. In 2004, Swiss stock market capitalization amounted to 230 per cent of GDP, more than five times higher than Germany's (OECD 1998; IMD 2004: 668). Also institutional investors in Switzerland have a more significant role than in the Anglo-Saxon economies and far more so than in Germany. In 2001, the last year for which comparable data are available, the assets of Swiss institutional investors amounted to 233 per cent of GDP, those of British and American institutional investors accounted both for 191 per cent of GDP, whereas German institutional investors managed assets worth 81 per cent of GDP (OECD Institutional Investors database).[6]

Despite the huge differences in financial market development, Switzerland and Germany show similar structures in terms of ownership concentration. Ownership concentration is one of the crucial features of corporate governance because it shapes the exposure of firms to capital market pressures. Ownership concentration in Germany is extraordinarily high. Two-thirds of the 650 largest companies have a single owner holding more than 25 per cent of the equity stock, 51 per cent have a majority owner. In Switzerland, almost half of the biggest Swiss companies have an owner controlling at least 25 per cent of the equity stock and a third of the largest companies are controlled by a majority owner. In the USA, none of the largest firms has a majority owner with more than 50 per cent, 0.1 per cent have an owner with a stake of more than 25 per cent; 95 per cent of all shareholdings in firms are smaller than 5 per cent (Windolf 2002: 38).[7]

Both countries run a bank-based financial system with universal banks. Their role in company financing in Switzerland is significant. About 30 per cent of the financing of industrial companies comes from bank loans (David and Mach 2001: 11). German firms raise 25 per cent of their financing in the form of credits (Jürgens et al. 2000b: 7). However, comparisons of company finance are plagued by measurement problems. The question of which measurement approach is most appropriate is largely unresolved in the finance literature, with each approach leading to quite different results for corporate finance patterns (Corbett and Jenkinson 1998; Hackethal 2000).[8] Nevertheless, agreement prevails that internal finance is by far the dominant form of finance in all corporate governance systems. However, banks can influence companies through more channels than simply providing credit. For Germany, it has been argued that proxy voting and supervisory board representation are the main instruments for banks to exercise control.

In this regard, the two national systems have remarkably similar institutional features. The German proxy voting system, in which banks vote on behalf of the shareholders at the General Meeting, making them the most influential actors there, is business practice in Switzerland, too.[9] Thus, banks also have a very effective channel of control in Switzerland. Furthermore, banks are represented on companies' boards in both countries. In Germany in 1996, the big three banks were represented on the supervisory boards of twenty-one of the twenty-four non-financial DAX companies and they provided eleven chairmen (Prigge 1998: 959). Also, in Switzerland banks are represented extensively on the boards of companies and they are—as a group—the most important outside members (David, Mach 2001: 11). Generally, corporate control in Germany and Switzerland is predominantly exercised by corporate networks via interlocking directorships, not by financial markets. In these two countries '... the networks are relatively highly centralized, with dense interlocks incorporating virtually all the large companies of a country ... and with a high proportion of relationships consisting of multiple representation ...' (Windolf 2002: 49).

The commonalities between Germany and Switzerland regarding ownership concentration and the networks of managers and bankers have one crucial implication. A market for corporate control is virtually absent in both countries. Mergers and acquisitions in both countries increased over the 1990s, but hostile takeovers are largely unknown. In the period from 1990 to 1998, the transaction value of announced hostile takeovers has been 2.2 per cent of the world total in Germany and 0.7 per cent in Switzerland. The figure for the USA was 63 per cent, and for the UK 17.5 per cent (Guillen 2000: 196). Hence, management in both countries does not have to prioritize shareholder value and profitability because it is not exposed to the danger of a hostile takeover bid to a significant degree.

Concerning internal company organization, there are wide differences again. German companies are governed by a two-tier board system with a clear separation between the management board that runs the day-to-day operations and the supervisory board, whose main role is to monitor management. In contrast to the Anglo-Saxon CEO-dominated boards, decisions are taken in consensus in the management board and the supervisory board. Owing to co-determination, half of the supervisory board consists of employee representatives; other groups heavily represented include bankers, former CEOs, as well as representatives of other companies and suppliers. The structure of Swiss companies is different. Swiss corporate law requires a 'unitary board' similar to the Anglo-Saxon one-tier system. The board of directors consists of executive (internal) and non-executive (external or independent) board members. The main duties of the board of directors are matters of strategic management. Traditionally, the majority of directors are non-executive members, currently the ratio is 83 per cent, a situation similar to the USA (Ruigrok 2002: 7). Moreover, there is no legal obligation to separate the roles of the CEO and the chairman of the board; over 30 per cent of Swiss-listed firms have a CEO serving both functions (Ruigrok 2002: 7).[10]

Both corporate governance systems lack a crucial feature of Anglo-Saxon corporate governance, namely highly powered monetary incentives for management to tie strategic decisions to the firm's share price through stock options. Holmström and Kaplan have argued that the most important factor in the transformation of the American corporate governance system from a managerial to a capital-market-oriented system has been the introduction of stock options following the 'leveraged buy out' (LBO) wave: 'Thanks to lucrative stock option plans, managers could share in the market returns from restructured companies. Shareholder value became an ally rather than an enemy' (Holmström and Kaplan 2001: 3). Thus, if management's compensation is closely tied to share prices, it can be expected that their attention will be focused on boosting it.

According to a compensation survey, Germany and Switzerland are way behind the USA when it comes to the use of stock options. In 2001, 61 per cent of the total compensation of American CEOs was variable pay, for German CEOs the figure was 36 per cent and for Swiss CEOs 16 per cent. The components of variable pay differed even stronger. In the USA 161 per cent of basic compensation was paid as long-term incentives, usually stock options. In Germany, long-term incentives amounted to 30 per cent of basic compensation and in Switzerland absolutely no long-term incentives were paid (Towers Perrin 2002: 26). This indicates the complete absence of stock options in the compensation packages of Swiss CEOs. Thus, the personal incentives for management to pursue a strategy focused on promoting share price are very limited in Germany and particularly in Switzerland compared to the USA. Partly related to this, CEO compensation in Germany and Switzerland is also considerably lower, in absolute terms, than in shareholder systems, such as Great Britain. Measuring CEO compensation as a multiple of an average manufacturing worker's pay, German and Swiss CEOs earned eleven times more than a worker in 2000; the salary of British CEOs was twenty-five times higher. This ratio has been almost unchanged since 1980 for German and Swiss CEOs, whereas it increased more than 2.5-fold for British CEOs in the same period (see Söderstrom et al. 2003: 19).[11]

In sum, stock markets are much more developed in Switzerland than in Germany and resemble those in shareholder systems. The same is true for the importance of institutional investors. However, ownership concentration and the network-type character of the relations among managers and between managers and bankers display strong similarities, which prevent a market climate receptive to hostile takeovers. In terms of formal firm organization, Swiss companies run an Anglo-Saxon-type one-tier system without labour representation, whereas German firms have a two-tier system where labour has a strong influence on the supervisory board. Management remuneration in both systems relies only to a very minor degree on stock options.

However, despite the similarities between Swiss corporate governance institutions and those found in shareholder systems management autonomy and its capacity for coordination is equally high in Germany and Switzerland. The concentrated ownership structures shelter Swiss management to a high degree from financial market influence and, due to their remuneration patterns, Swiss managers have a very low incentive to pursue shareholder value strategies. Moreover, the dense network of managers and bankers, evident in the prominence of interlocking directorships, also contributes significantly to a relationship-based system in which coordination is possible. This implies that ownership concentration, the absence of a market for corporate control, and managerial networks—the bases for stakeholder governance in the financial realm—are feasible even if financial development is high.

6.4.2. Industrial Relations and the Labour Market

Switzerland and Germany differ considerably in the institutional set-up of their labour markets and industrial relations structures. Germany has the most extensive formal system of employee representation worldwide. There are two levels of co-determination: at the board and plant level. First, companies with 2,000 or more employees are obliged to include employee representatives on their supervisory boards.[12] In these firms, employees must have 50 per cent representation on the supervisory board, while the other 50 per cent are shareholders. In case of a deadlock between these two blocks the chairperson, who is elected by the shareholders, has a casting vote.[13] Hence, employee representatives have a say in almost all strategically important decisions, which is seen as the '... key mechanism compelling firms to look for smart ways of employing the skills of their expensive though extremely productive and sophisticated workers' (Guillen 2000: 181–2).

The second level of co-determination is at the plant level. Every plant with at least five full-time employees is entitled under the Works Constitution Act 1952 (*Betriebsverfassungsgesetz*) to elect a works council. The works councils are entitled to participate in issues such as the hiring of new employees, introduction of new technologies, and use of overtime and short-working time; in case of mass redundancies, they have the right to bargain with management about social plans covering redeployment, severance payments, and early retirement. Thus, management has to bargain with the works councils over most issues that are of immediate concern to the workers. Furthermore, there is normally a personal interdependence between plant and supervisory level co-determination since the head employee representative is typically a leading works council member.

Labour's strong role at the firm level corresponds to union strength at the macro-level. The unions have a well-organized counterpart in business associations with a high coordinating capacity (Wood 2001). Wage bargaining is highly centralized and coordinated (OECD 2004: 151) and takes place at the industry level between unions and employers' associations. Despite an only moderately high union density of 25 per cent, companies are bound to these agreements because their outcomes are usually made obligatory for non-members by the Federal Ministry for Labour and the Economy. The collective bargaining coverage is 68 per cent (OECD 2004).[14] Centralized bargaining also results in a highly regulated labour market with limited labour mobility, which in turn encourages the formation of firm-specific human capital.

By contrast, unions in Switzerland are weak. Unionization rates are low and although the political system rests on social consensus, unions have played a subordinate role in the Swiss social coalition (Fluder and Hotz-Hart 1998: 268). The absence of centralized corporatist structures in the Swiss economy—due to the fragmented character of the federal state and its weakness—led to a minor role for the unions in public policy compared to most other European countries (Armingeon 2000: 393). Furthermore, the unions themselves are politically divided. There is no effective coordination of confederations, which leads to the absence of efficient union organization at the workplace (Fluder and Hotz-Hart 1998: 271). Moreover, the industrial structure, which is dominated by SMEs, is not favourable to unionism. In several respects, Switzerland bears striking similarities to the Anglo-Saxon LMEs. Union density is 18 per cent and the degree to which employees are covered by collective agreements is below 42 per cent (OECD 2004). In this respect, Switzerland belongs to the same cluster as the USA, Great Britain, Canada, and New Zealand, the archetypical LMEs. The legal position of the unions at the firm level is as unfavourable for Swiss unions as it is for those in Great Britain, Ireland, Japan, Canada, New Zealand, and the USA (Armingeon 2000: 397). Accordingly, Swiss labour markets are highly flexible; Switzerland ranks second among the industrial countries in terms of the flexibility of wage determination, just behind the USA (Jaeger 2003: 111).[15]

However, the weakness of unions is not mirrored on the employers' side. Swiss employer's associations are significantly more powerful and their coordinating capacity is much higher. Their degree of organization is about twice as high as the unions and ideological differences among them are—as opposed to the unions—minor. Collective bargaining takes place at the sectoral level, with the peak employer association playing a coordinating role (Fluder and Hotz-Hart 1998: 273). Thus, even if the centralization of wage bargaining is low, the degree of coordination in wage bargaining is high—owing to the high coordination capacity of employers. In fact, the coordination of wage bargaining in Switzerland matches Germany's, even if it is achieved by more informal means (OECD 2004: 151). This reinforces the VoC argument that business associations are crucial actors in the organization of market economies, but at the same time it shows that labour market arrangements in CMEs can be highly diverse.

Formal employee co-determination is, in comparison to Germany, relatively poorly developed in Switzerland. Until 1994, there were no legal regulations on co-determination. Co-determination itself was rejected in a 1976 referendum (Armingeon 1994: 215). In 1994, a Cooperation Act (*Mitwirkungsgesetz*) was approved, which authorizes cooperation committees in firms with over fifty employees. Their primary competencies concern the right to be consulted in cases of takeovers and mass lay-offs, as well as in safety and health matters (Fluder and Hotz-Hart 1998: 278). Co-determination through collective agreements by unions and employers is more important than legal regulations. A third of the collective agreements at the sectoral level and two-thirds of those at the company level foresee work committees (Fluder and Hotz-Hart 1998: 278). These voluntary forms of co-determination result in widely differing levels of employee influence between sectors and companies. Employee influence primarily concerns matters of working time; institutionalized influence over investment decisions and general business strategy issues is limited (Hotz-Hart et al. 2001: 62). However, the influence of employees over strategic decisions can be of an indirect nature, because co-determination in even narrowly defined areas provides many options for issue-linking and for blocking strategic decisions.

Despite the low degree of institutionalized co-determination, industrial relations are extraordinarily peaceful, helped by the general political focus on consensus, compromise, and social partnership. Strikes are virtually unknown in Switzerland. A historical breakthrough was the 1937 agreement in the engineering and watch industry. Central to the agreement was the commitment of employers and employees to the peaceful solution of industrial conflict and the introduction of procedures for conflict resolution. This agreement has remained in force since then, and has been elaborated and renewed continuously. It has become the model for collective agreements in other sectors and regulates many aspects of industrial relations that are determined by law elsewhere, for example parts of social welfare or benefits for parents.

All in all, the set-up of Swiss labour markets resembles in several respects those of shareholder systems; wage setting is highly decentralized, employee influence at the firm level mainly voluntary, and yet industrial relations are peaceful and cooperative. The industrial relations literature therefore characterizes Switzerland as stable neocorporatism through social promotion, where the strength of organized labour is low, but the coordinating capacity of labour and, especially, capital is high (Crouch 1994: 216–7). Since labour does not threaten stability, employers prefer cooperation with weak unions to a situation without unions. German labour markets are very different. A strong statuary form of co-determination gives employees considerable influence in matters of strategic management, wage setting is centralized, unions play an important role, and the labour markets are highly regulated. Despite these differences, both countries have managed to build up very peaceful industrial relations. Also the job tenure in Germany and Switzerland is comparable; 9 years on average for Swiss employees and 9.7 years for German employees in 1995 (OECD 1997: 138).[16]

Hence, both countries were able to build up peaceful and long-term-oriented industrial relations, but by different means. Coordination between capital and labour in Switzerland is possible, but is based less on mandatory forms of regulation, and more on industry- and firm-level bargaining. This results in a much more differentiated system than in Germany, but it allows firms and industries that are dependent on close cooperation with employees and on their specialized skills to establish bargained forms of capital–labour cooperation. Hence, Swiss firms are able to find forms of coordination that can resemble those of German firms at the micro-level, even if their macro-level industrial relations institutions are different. In this sense, it is not only mandatory forms of co-determination and the formal influence of labour that enable capital–labour coordination conducive to DQP; the self-interest of employers can also foster a similar outcome, assuming that they can credibly commit themselves.

6.4.3. The Education System

One additional key variable in the VoC approach is the education system. Its importance lies in the fact that it forms the skill base of workers and shapes the background of managers. Differences in skills make different company strategies more or less difficult to pursue. For example, in industries which require a high degree of industry-specific human capital, an early education of the workforce with a focus on this industry will help companies to build up the necessary human capital.

The German educational system supports its particular economic specialization because it stresses technological competencies. The German university system has its strengths in technological and scientific disciplines, whereas it has been less successful in the social sciences and in management (Porter 1990: 369).[17] The system is complemented by the universities of applied sciences (*Fachhochschulen*), which stress practical education. They are open in their specialization to the demands of local industry and often work together with local firms. Furthermore, the majority of German managers hold engineering, not business, degrees, so that technical improvement often enjoys priority over entrepreneurial capabilities (Eberwein and Tholen 1993: 173).

Of crucial importance is the dual apprenticeship system, consisting of practical training in a company and theoretical training in vocational schools, which forms the skills base of the German labour force. This system rests on cooperation between business associations, firms, trade unions, and public authorities. These actors organize the dual system and negotiate the skill categories and the content of training in order to meet the needs of firms in each sector. The regulations are drawn up at the federal level and the states oversee the vocational schools. Two-thirds of the costs of the dual system are financed by companies, and the rest by state authorities. More than 60 per cent of each age group are trained in the dual system (Federal Ministry of Education and Research 2003). Workers are therefore well-trained in specialized fields and have a theoretical basis for further skill development within the firm. In this sense, the dual system enables specialized human capital formation and high levels of company investment in initial vocational training.

The Swiss educational system is very similar to its German counterpart. Swiss researchers have been at the forefront in disciplines such as chemistry or physics.[18] Their leading position in the former has been of great value to the Swiss pharmaceutical industry. Generally, there is close collaboration between universities and industry (Porter 1990: 320). Switzerland also runs a system of *Fachhochschulen*. Their main goals are practical research, know-how transfer to local enterprises, and the education of employees for the regional small- and medium-sized enterprises (Hotz-Hart et al. 2001: 338). Another similarity to the German system is the bias towards managers with a technological educational background (Porter 1990: 320). Switzerland also runs a dual apprenticeship system, which resembles its German counterpart very closely. The Confederation regulates the vocational training system, the cantons implement the regulations and run the vocational schools, and the employer associations largely determine the content of the apprenticeship programmes. Also in Switzerland the enterprises contribute to the costs of the dual system to a high degree; their gross spending in the mid-1990s was roughly two-thirds of total costs (OECD 1999: 19–20). More than 50 per cent of each age group receive their training in the dual system (Backes-Gellner 2003). One difference between the dual systems in Germany and Switzerland is that unions are not involved in running the system in Switzerland, consistent with their subordinate role in the Swiss political economy. Nevertheless, the strong coordination capacities of employers enable the system to function, so that the working of the training system and its outcomes in terms of a high workforce qualification and the resulting skill profiles of employees are very similar in Germany and Switzerland.

6.5. VARIETIES OF COORDINATION IN CMEs AND FUNCTIONAL EQUIVALENCE

Diversified quality production in the VoC framework is based on the commitments of employers and employees, which facilitate long tenure and investment in firm-specific human capital and are supported by the overarching institutional infrastructure. Incremental innovation patterns are dependent upon firm- and industry-specific skills of employees, which have to undertake specific investments in their human capital to acquire these skills. Labour market institutions such as co-determination and collective bargaining in Germany support these investments by giving employees the security of knowing that they will not be pre-emptively laid off by employers after having undertaken those investments. In other words, German labour market institutions give employees a strong incentive to acquire firm and industry skills, because they have a say in corporate strategy and their investments are to a considerable degree protected. Given these institutions, employers have an incentive to calibrate their corporate strategies according to the institutional incentives. Stable ownership patterns, long-run finance, protection from capital market influence, and an education system providing workers with suitable skills facilitate management's commitment to their workers and support DQP strategies.

The situation in Switzerland is different. For example, Swiss employment legislation gives '. . . management in Switzerland considerable discretion to pursue "hire-and-fire" strategies' (Sousa-Poza 2004: 34). However, management largely refrains from pursuing hire-and-fire strategies. Tenure in Switzerland is relatively long and industrial relations very peaceful. Switzerland has developed patterns of coordination which deviate from German patterns in that they are more informal and voluntary in nature, but nevertheless facilitate efficient coordination between capital and labour. Also in the field of corporate governance, Katzenstein's finding with respect to the overall character of the Swiss political economy is valid: 'Switzerland relies on private coordination' (Katzenstein 1985: 92).

Private or voluntary coordination is possible or necessary because the density of public regulation in Switzerland is—compared to Germany— much lower. Hence, coordination is less a result of the overarching institutional infrastructure, but results instead from bargaining at the industry and especially the company level. This implies that Swiss corporate governance arrangements are more diverse than those in Germany. In sectors that are characterized by incremental innovation and DQP, this diversity allows Swiss firms to construct arrangements with their workforce that very much resemble those of German firms, despite the differences at the macro-level.

For example, in the engineering industry—the showcase for incremental innovation patterns and DQP—union density in Switzerland is much higher than the national average, the coverage rate is the most extensive, and collective bargaining is strongly established. Work committees in the engineering industry are much more influential than in other sectors. Their rights go beyond the normal information rights of works committees; they have, for example, the right to negotiate with management over working time and wages. Also the social benefits of metalworkers are more generous for Swiss than for German workers (Fluder and Hotz-Hart 1998: 271, 276, 278). The sectoral differences in employee co-determination are due to the voluntary character of co-determination, which is mainly regulated by collective agreements at the sectoral and the company level. If firms and sectors are dependent upon the specialized skills of their employees they can give them a greater role in decision-making and therefore enter credible commitments. Hence, firm-specific skills can be protected and the institutional conditions for DQP created on the industry and company level.

However, why are Swiss employers able to enter credible commitments with their workforce and construct arrangements conducive for DQP while employers in LMEs find it hard to do this, despite the similarity between Switzerland and LMEs across several elements of corporate governance? The difference lies in the structure of the Swiss training system and in the capital market exposure of Swiss firms. In common with the German variant, the system of vocational training in Switzerland allows the formation of industry- and firm-specific skills on the part of the employees, which is a precondition of DQP. Employers invest heavily in this system because it provides them with the skilled workers indispensable for their economic specialization and product market strategies. The coordination capacities of Swiss employers are crucial for the working of the entire training system.

Regarding Swiss capital markets, their similarities with Germany in the organization of some of their features are key to an explanation of why Swiss employers find it easier to enter credible commitments than managers in shareholder systems. Although Swiss capital markets are highly developed and institutional investors very important players in quantitative terms, their direct influence on firm behaviour is minor compared to shareholder systems. The reasons for this are found in other features of Swiss corporate governance: ownership is concentrated, a market for corporate control is absent, and the personal interest of management in shareholder value strategies is due to the minor importance of stock options in management compensation very weak. In other words, management is to a high degree sheltered from capital market pressures and cannot be forced to focus on shareholder value. Especially the absence of a market for corporate control facilitates long-term relationships with stakeholders that would not be sustainable if stakeholders feared the breach of implicit contracts in the case of a hostile takeover. Also the accumulation of firm-specific human capital is more likely because employees can be confident that it will not be destroyed in the event of a hostile takeover. The missing market for corporate control also facilitates other crucial elements of stakeholder corporate governance, for example higher spending on R&D and investment, a market share instead of a pure profit orientation, and a focus on segments with lower returns and lower risk (Höpner and Jackson 2001: 12).

Hence, although the locus and the mechanisms of coordination differ between Germany and Switzerland, coordination is feasible in both cases. Swiss firms have greater autonomy due to a less-regulated environment, which results in more diverse firm and industry arrangements depending on the industry in question. However, they have the capacity to build the institutional preconditions for DQP, because they are to a similar degree as German firms sheltered from capital market influence on corporate strategy and have access to a highly qualified workforce through the training system in place.[19] In other words, Swiss firms have the capacity to build functionally equivalent institutions at the company level—especially with regard to industrial relations—that allow patterns of incremental innovation and DQP.

6.6. CONCLUSION

The institutional frameworks and the coordination mechanisms for corporate governance differ significantly in Germany and Switzerland, but there are different institutional roads to the same outcome, namely DQP strategies. From a VoC perspective, the Swiss corporate governance system seems less coherent than the German variant because some subsystems do not function according to a 'pure' CME logic. The DQP strategies in Switzerland are compatible with highly developed financial markets, fluid external labour markets, decentralized wage-setting, weak formal employee representation, and weak unions. Tight integration of all subsystems in the sense of a logic of similarity or synergy (Deeg 2005) across subsystems is not present in the Swiss corporate governance system. However, even if Swiss corporate governance deviates in important respects from its German counterpart, its institutional infrastructure still facilitates DQP, because the structure of the training system and the protection management enjoys from capital markets enables coordination for those firms that wish to pursue DQP strategies. Consequently, the Swiss corporate governance system is more differentiated than the German variant. Coordination is more of a voluntary nature and located on the company level with institutions serving as necessary conditions. Institutions that are not directly related to these two enabling conditions—access to a suitably qualified workforce and protection from capital market pressures—seem to be of secondary importance for DQP.

This variation in institutional frameworks between two countries with a very similar economic specialization has implications for issues of institutional stability and change in CMEs. If not all elements of corporate governance need to be complementary and certain institutions across spheres of a political economy can be more loosely coupled and compensated for by industry- or firm-level bargaining, then we should not necessarily expect snowball effects resulting from institutional change as long as the core institutions are not affected. For example, the emergence of global finance and the rising importance of institutional investors have often been cited as being the string that might unravel CMEs. However, the structure of Swiss corporate governance shows that highly developed financial markets can go hand in hand with, for example, concentrated ownership structures, which are themselves the basis of stakeholder systems. Since cross-ownership and the resulting missing market for corporate control are the basis for coordination capacities and long-term DQP strategies, their persistence is likely to be the key for the survival of CME-type political economies. Therefore, the proposition that the hybridization of stakeholder systems results in unstable and temporary systems that will sooner or later be completely replaced by shareholder systems due to the inevitable strain for system coherence (Lane 2003: 6–7) is likely to be premature. It depends on which elements in stakeholder systems are changed. Financial market development and the rise of institutional investors per se do not necessarily result in dispersed ownership structures and the emergence of a market for corporate control.

The goal of this chapter has been to explore the variation in coordination mechanisms in CMEs and to draw attention to the agency of firms and their capacity for developing coordination by themselves, given certain key institutional preconditions. To identify different coordination mechanisms in CMEs is also important for the question of what kinds of reforms (and especially in which areas) may undermine the capacities for strategic coordination in CMEs. Of course, this chapter can only be a first step in achieving this goal. Further comparative research is needed to investigate the corporate governance frameworks of other CMEs with the complementarities perspective in mind in order to get a more subtle understanding of the institutional effects at work and the agency of firms.

NOTES

1. I would like to thank Peter Hall, Bob Hancké, Martin Rhodes, David Soskice, Mark Thatcher, and all participants of the EUI and LSE workshops for very helpful comments, criticisms, and suggestions. Remaining errors are of course mine.

2. The relevant institutional elements are the structures of the capital and the labour markets, the education system, and inter-company relations.

3. According to the OECD classification, high-tech industries include aircraft and spacecraft; pharmaceuticals; office accounting and computing machinery; radio, television, and communication equipment; medical precision and optical instruments. Medium-tech industries include electrical machinery; motor vehicles, trailers, and semiconductors; chemicals; railway equipment and transport equipment; machinery and equipment.

4. These patterns have a high degree of stability. The values in 1991 were −47 and 5 for Germany and −44 and 14 for Switzerland (German Federal Ministry of Education and Research 2005: 21).

5. Considering the size of the country, the number of Swiss MNCs is extraordinary. Among the ten largest firms in Europe, in terms of market capitalization, there are three Swiss firms; among the fifty largest firms, Switzerland is represented with five firms. Germany has seven firms in the top fifty, but none in the top ten. See *Financial Times* 2004.

6. The high market capitalization and the importance of institutional investors are, to a large degree, due to the Swiss pension system. Contrary to the German pay-as-you-go pension system, the Swiss pension system heavily relies on private provision of retirement income, which leads to a high accumulation of assets under the management of pension funds. Their financial assets amounted to 113% of Swiss GDP in 2001. British and American pension funds manage assets worth 65% of GDP, German pension funds assets add up to 3.3% of GDP (OECD Institutional Investors Database).

7. There are slight differences in the identity of the owners. In Germany, corporations are the most important shareholders, owning over 30% of the shares in non-financial firms, followed by individuals (15%), insurance companies (13.7%), investment funds (12.9%), and banks (10.3%) (Jürgens et al. 2000*a*: 3). In Switzerland, the most important groups of shareholders are: individuals (20%), non-financial enterprises (16.4%), institutional investors (13.4%), and banks (4.7%) (David and Mach 2001: 10). A striking difference is the degree of foreign shareholdings. It was 35% in Switzerland already in the early 1990s and 11% in Germany; during the 1990s foreign shareholdings in Germany rose to 16% (Decker and Lukauskas 2000; David and Mach 2001: 10).

8. The main divides in the debate are whether gross or net sources of finance, stock or flows data, data from national income accounts or from company accounts should be used.

9. For Germany, in a 1992 sample Baums and Fraune report that an average of 84.09% of shares were associated with a bank. 60.95% consisted of proxy votes, 13.02% of bank equity ownership and 10.11% of dependent investment companies. The votes of the banks at the general meeting are only 13% due to the banks' shareholdings. Ten per cent are due to the bank-owned investment funds, but 61% are based on the exercise of proxy votes. See Baums (1995).

10. A speciality of Swiss corporate law is the requirement that the majority of members of the board of directors must be Swiss nationals and resident in Switzerland.

11. The average salary of American CEOs in 2001 amounted to US $1.9 million, whereas it was US $455,000 for German, and US $405,000 for Swiss CEOs (Towers Perrin 2002: 20).

12. A stronger form of co-determination applies for companies mainly involved in steel and coal mining, whereas a weaker form applies to most companies between 500 and 2,000 employees.

13. The number of supervisory board seats are to total 12 in companies between 2,000 and 10,000 employees, 16 in companies with between 10,000 and 20,000 employees, and 20 in companies with more than 20,000 employees. Moreover, in companies with between 2,000 and 20,000 employees, two employee representatives can be union functionaries, in companies with more than 20,000 employees three may be union functionaries. Union functionaries means that they need not be employees.

14. Although there have been attacks on the part of some employers on the centralization of wage bargaining, reforms have been modest at most and try to achieve more flexibility within the parameters of the existing institutions (Thelen 2001: 85; Vogel 2003: 320).

15. Nevertheless, it should be noted that, although the strictness of employment protection legislation in Switzerland resembles LME standards, unemployment protection—mainly due to the generosity of unemployment benefits—is very high (Estévez-Abe, Iversen, and Soskice 2001: 164–9).

16. Data are from 1995. The USA and the UK had an average job tenures of 7.4 and 7.8 years respectively. The lowest tenure was found in Australia.

17. For a detailed analysis of the German scientific specialization, see Fraunhofer Institut für Systemtechnik und Innovationsforschung (2004: 7).

18. An analysis of Swiss scientific specialization can be found in Fraunhofer Institut für Systemtechnik und Innovationsforschung (2004: 13).

19. Factors that ease coordination in the Swiss economy include the size of the country as well as the general consensus orientation. Due to the smallness of Switzerland, the economic—and political—elites share a similar socialization and very often know each other from school, army, or university. The consensus orientation is deeply ingrained in the Swiss culture, as Hanspeter Kriesi argued: 'For Switzerland it is indeed true that (almost) everybody cooperates with (almost) everybody' (Katzenstein 1985: 124).

7

Capital Mobility, Varieties of Institutional
Investors, and the Transforming Stability
of Corporate Governance in
France and Germany

Michel Goyer

7.1. INTRODUCTION[1]

Will the globalization of finance and investment lead to convergence across
European systems of corporate governance along the lines of the American
model? The topic of corporate governance—the system by which firms are
controlled and operated, the rules and practices that governs the relationship between managers and shareholders, and the overall process by which
investment capital is allocated—has become an important issue for policymakers and scholars in recent years in the wake of financial scandals in
Europe and in the USA (Coffee 2002, 2005; Shinn and Gourevitch 2002).
The increasing importance of corporate governance in Europe, however, goes
beyond the advent of recent scandals. It reflects the importance of critical
trends in advanced European capitalist economies and has serious political
consequences (Roe 2000; Gourevitch and Shinn 2005). Continental European
systems of corporate governance have long been associated with concentrated
ownership structures, banks, and non-financial firms as stable owners, low
market transparency, underdeveloped securities markets, reliance on bank
loans as a source of external finance, and the absence of hostile takeovers (see
Zysman 1983; Roe 1993; Deeg 1999 for reviews). Now, however, tremendous
changes have pushed these systems towards the pursuit of greater shareholder
value in company strategy in recent years (Höpner 2001; Goyer 2003; Jackson
2003; Clift 2004).

This chapter deals with the rise of foreign ownership and its diverging
internal characteristics in France and Germany—and the consequences for the
evolution of the two systems of corporate governance. I focus on the period

lasting from the mid-1990s to 2005, an era of tremendous change in European finance. A critical methodological consideration serves as motivation for these research questions: how does one assess the advent of institutional change in corporate governance? As Campbell (2004) reminds us, we often mistake evolutionary shifts for more revolutionary developments, and vice versa. The absence of an analytical framework to distinguish between patterns of institutional change leaves us powerless to understand their consequences. Institutional changes in corporate governance might be a relatively recent development in Continental Europe, but advanced capitalist economies underwent substantial institutional change in many other areas in the past twenty-five years without resulting in either internally revolutionary transformation or cross-national convergence (Berger 1996; Hall and Soskice 2001).

The argument presented in this chapter is the following. First, an assessment of the consequences of the rise of foreign ownership in France and Germany requires a sophisticated differentiation between types of investors—primarily between pension and hedge/mutual funds. Pension funds are long-term investors that acquire an equity stake in corporations primarily for diversification purposes; hedge/mutual funds seek to maximize assets under their management as they possess shorter term horizon since they face greater liquidity constraints. The importance of this distinction is primarily its implication for the mode of coordination of firms in advanced industrialized economies. As Hall and Soskice (2001) have argued, access to patient capital is a key feature of CMEs, as opposed to LMEs that rely on short-term, risky capital. The different investment strategies and time horizons of investors have particular consequences for the sustainability of national models of European capitalism. The short-term preferences of hedge/mutual funds are typically seen as being more compatible with the LME of the USA. Second, I argue that the firm-level institutional arrangements of workplace organization constitute the most significant variable to account for the diverging ability of French and German firms to attract funds from Anglo-Saxon institutional investors. Mutual and hedge funds pursue short-term investment strategies and possess short-time horizons. They also exhibit firm-specific preferences since the performance of their portfolio is shaped by the behaviour of a smaller number of companies than is the case for pension funds. The degree of fit between their preferences and the firm-level institutional arrangements of advanced capitalist economies reflects the ability of the CEO and top managers to reorganize the workplace in a unilateral fashion.

I draw on notions from the VoC theoretical perspective (Hall and Soskice 2001) to illustrate continuing differences between contemporary capitalist economies. This perspective emphasizes the critical importance of patterns of institutional complementarities across the various sub-spheres (finance and corporate governance, industrial relations, innovation systems, and inter-firm relations) of the economy that lead to diverging forms of behaviour by economic actors. The key insight is that the impact of an institution cannot be studied in isolation as it is mediated by its interaction with other features of the national institutional framework, thereby implying that different types of institutional fit are possible (Milgrom and Roberts 1995; Hall and Soskice 2001). In other words, each institutional feature fits with the others and makes them more effective than they would be on their own. The outcome of this is that developed economies are distinguished by their specific configuration of interdependent institutions. The VoC theoretical perspective has come under attack in recent years. For some scholars, the theoretical insights of the concept might be quite useful in accounting for stability, but they are far too static to account for institutional discontinuity (Howell 2003; Crouch 2005*a*; Morgan 2005). Moreover, it has been argued that the sustainability of institutional frameworks cannot be assumed to occur in an automatic fashion simply because it is economically efficient. Instead, it requires active maintenance by actors in order for institutions to adapt to environmental changes (Deeg 2005; Streeck and Thelen 2005: 24). Finally, scholars have also argued that the environment faced by firms is increasingly characterized by the presence of institutional hybridization, with the consequence that advanced capitalist economies might no longer fit neatly into a single model (Pieterse 1995; Regini 2000*c*). This process of hybridization can result from firms borrowing from the features of different models as the process of institutional adoption tends to be piecemeal rather than full scale. The theoretical contribution of the VoC perspective would be seriously eroded if it was not able to account for institutional change to the same extent that it has provided insights for the study of institutional diversity.

What does my analysis of the investment patterns of institutional investors in France and Germany entail for the VoC theoretical perspective? The argument presented in this chapter testifies to the importance of national institutional frameworks for the study of institutional change. First, domestic institutional arrangements interact to complement each other and consequently cannot be studied in isolation regardless of whether one is analysing the presence of stability or the occurrence of change in the broader institutional framework. The effects of a single institutional variable vary accordingly with the presence of other institutions in the economy (Hall 1994; Hall and Franzese 1998). This is particularly the case since institutional change is almost invariably piecemeal rather than full-scale, thereby highlighting the importance of the interaction between the new institutions and those already in place. Second, institutions are characterized by an element of latency, their effects, and importance changing over time. In the case of France, for example, a central element such as the concentration of power in the CEO had little impact on the provision of finance before the advent of financial deregulation. It was with the advent of the international strategy of Anglo-Saxon institutional investors that the stable institutional property of power concentration became an important factor in the provision of short-term, impatient capital. Third, this chapter highlights the need to distinguish between institutions and the mode of coordination that follows from these institutions (Hall and Thelen 2005: 30). Institutions have gone through tremendous changes in the two countries but their effects on an important dimension of the mode of coordination, namely the role of employees in the building of innovative capabilities of large blue-chip firms, have been marginal. The discussion of the shortcomings of hybridization is particularly insightful in this context. I recognize that processes of institutional hybridization can, and do, occur. Nonetheless, their occurrence still requires an argument to assess whether hybridization constitutes a revolutionary or evolutionary transformation. The notion of interaction among the various elements of an institutional framework represents a very helpful indicator in assessing the consequences of institutional transformation.

The road map for this chapter is the following. First, I provide an overview of the changes in the external environment in which French and German companies are embedded. Second, I empirically analyse the transformation of these two systems of corporate governance by highlighting the distinctive nature of foreign capital attracted by companies in the two countries. Third, I demonstrate how the institutional arrangements provide significant theoretical insights to account for the direction of change of corporate governance by highlighting the critical importance of the institutions of workplace organization. Fourth, I conclude by presenting the theoretical implications for the analysis of institutional change that emerges from the study of French and German corporate governance.

7.2. STRUCTURAL CHANGES IN EUROPEAN FINANCE

The French and German systems of corporate governance have experienced some important transformations resulting from a series of cumulatively far-reaching changes. These developments have decreased the importance of debt as a source of external finance and have heightened the importance of stock markets. Three features previously characterized the two systems of corporate governance. First, corporations had a high debt-equity ratio, that is bank loans were more important than stock issues as a source of external finance (Zysman 1983). Firms' stock market capitalization was of secondary importance to managers after market share. Second, the ownership structure of blue-chip companies was highly concentrated in the hands of friendly cross-shareholdings among companies, with a single large owner in the form of a family firm, banks' direct share and proxy voting in Germany, coexisting with, in the French case, an extensive public sector (Morin 1974; Edwards and Fisher 1994). Third, as a result of the other two factors, the market for corporate control was fairly restricted (Franks and Mayer 1997). In particular, hostile takeovers were a rarity.

The bank-based financial system of corporate governance in the two countries crumbled under the impact of several developments. First, their financial system underwent a massive process of deregulation: the use of credit ceilings as a mean to control inflation has been replaced by the discipline of central bank independence and of high real interest rates. Capital controls have been removed under pressures from the EMS and the suspension of the dollar's convertibility into gold, and the bond market has been deregulated (Loriaux 1991; Goodman 1992; Story 1996). Moreover, the liberalization of financial markets has seen interest rates rise as banks were forced to compete for deposits with new competitors. It also removed impediments to the developments of direct finance that led to the introduction of new financial instruments for raising capital.

Second, the transformation of corporate governance in France and Germany is the result of developments that have raised the importance of equity capital. Two key factors account for a rise in the importance of firms' stock market capitalization. In the first place, the removal of capital controls by European policymakers enabled Anglo-American investors to pursue a strategy of international diversification of their assets. The growth of foreign equity held by American institutional investors increased from US$128.7 billion in 1988 to US$1,787 billion in 2000 (Conference Board 2002: 39). The average percentage of total assets held in international equities by the largest 25 American pension funds increased from 4.8 per cent in 1991 to 18.0 per cent in 1999 (ibid. 2000: 43). The impact of these developments on the strategy of large companies should not be underestimated. Anglo-Saxon institutional investors have expressed clear preferences for the adoption of shareholder value practices that maximize return on equity.

The growing prevalence of equity swaps, whereby companies issue additional stocks to pay for the shares of the target firm during takeover bids, has also increased the importance of securities markets in the USA. In 1988, nearly 60 per cent of the total value of deals over US$100 million in the USA was paid for entirely in cash. The similar figure for deals paid in stock was less than 2 per cent. By contrast, about half of the value of large deals in 1998 was paid entirely in stock—and 17 per cent was solely financed in cash (Rappaport and

Sirower 1999: 147–51). The importance of takeover activity in the USA for European corporate governance is intimately related to the process by which firms build their innovative capabilities. Large French firms are engaged in a process of institutional arbitrage (Hall and Soskice 2001: 57). They have sought to pursue radical types of innovation, thereby gaining access to new innovative capabilities, through the acquisition of companies in the USA via takeovers. Firms with higher stock market capitalization possess a substantial advantage in the global merger marketplace in using equity swap as a mean of payment (Coffee 1999: 649). A concern for the valuation of the value of equity capital has become a necessary condition if French and German companies want to be able to acquire others.

7.3. THE TRANSFORMATION OF FRENCH AND GERMAN CORPORATE GOVERNANCE: AN EMPIRICAL EVALUATION

A key development in the transformation of corporate governance in France and Germany has been the rise of foreign ownership, that is how Anglo-American institutional investors are operating in the new European financial environment, which is characterized by the importance of stock market capitalization for blue-chip companies. Section 7.2 has highlighted the growing importance of Anglo-American institutional investors in Europe. The greater mobility of capital and the strategy of international diversification of Anglo-American institutional investors have been associated with a rise of foreign ownership in France and Germany. Foreign investors have become key shareholders in the capital structure of large firms in the two countries (see Tables 7.1 and 7.2).

The significant foreign presence in both French and German blue-chip companies, however, masks substantial divergence between the two. First, foreign ownership in France has grown significantly during the 1990s while the

Table 7.1. Foreign ownership of selected French blue-chip companies (in % of equity capital) (2002)

Accor 51.7	Air Liquide 37.1	Alcatel 50.0*	Alstom 48.0
Aventis 60.6	AXA 80.0	BNP-Paribas 67.0	Cap Gemini 63.9
Danone 42.0	Lafarge 54.9	Lagardere 48.1	L'Oreal 20.0*
LVMH 17.5	Michelin 47.0	Publicis 59.4	SocGen 50.8*
St-Gobain 40.5*	Total 64.0	Vivendi 53.4*	Vivendi. Envi. 27.0

Source: Annual report of companies (various years).

* Data is for 2000.

Table 7.2. Foreign ownership of selected German blue-chip companies (in % of equity capital) (2002 unless otherwise indicated)

Adidas 57.0	Allianz 32.0	Altana 20.0	BASF 35
Bayer 39.0 (2001)	Commerzbank 35.0	Daimler-Chrysler 29.9	Deutsche Bank 46.0
D. Telekom 59.0	E.ON 57.9 (2000)	Fresenius 49.1	Linde 60.0
Lufthansa 29.1	MAN 19.0 (2001)	Munich Re 37.0	RWE 15.0 (2001)
SAP 57.6	Schering 52.0 (2003)	Siemens 54.0 (2000)	Volkswagen 23.1 (2001)

Source: Annual report of companies (various years).

German picture is best characterized as stagnation. The foreign penetration of the French market increased from 17.4 to 36.1 per cent from 1990 to 2000. The growth of foreign ownership in Germany, by contrast, remained largely stable from 22.7 to 23.6 per cent for the same period (Gourevitch and Shinn 2005: 105). Second, an analysis of the causes and consequences of the growing importance of Anglo-American institutional investors in Europe requires a nuanced understanding of the preferences and strategies of interests groups. Theoretical inferences cannot be drawn simply because of the growing importance of capital mobility across borders since Anglo-American institutional investors do not constitute a monolithic bloc. I distinguish here primarily between hedge/mutual and pension funds. These categories of investors possess preferences and time horizons that either clash or fit with the institutions of European companies. Pension funds constitute long-term investors that acquire an equity stake in corporations primarily for diversification purposes. The incentives of managers of pension funds lie in generating minimum revenues so as to cover regular payments to retirees with a long-term horizon. Hedge and mutual funds, by contrast, possess shorter term horizon and seek to maximize assets under their management by picking firms undervalued in financial markets.

The growth of foreign ownership in France and Germany has been characterized by substantial divergence in regard to its composition. Both French *and* German firms have been a favourite destination for the international diversification strategies of pension funds.[2] This reflects the fact that corporate law in the two countries provides an adequately acceptable level of financial transparency and a sufficient level of protection for minority shareholders. Moreover, the quality of law enforcement is excellent (Roe 2002). Hedge and mutual funds, on the other hand, have primarily chosen France *over* Germany as a site for investment in Continental Europe. I argue in Section 7.4 that the degree of fit between their investment strategies and the institutional arrangements of advanced industrialized countries reflects the ability of CEOs and top managers to reorganize the workplace in a unilateral fashion. It fits well with the decision-making and adjustment process in France, which is management-led with the workforce excluded from the decision-making process. French workers possess fewer opportunities to block managerial initiatives (Schmidt 1996; Hancké 2002; Rebérioux 2002). French firm-level institutions are characterized by the concentration of power in the CEO that, in turn, allows for a rapid reorganization of the workplace under the guidance of a small number of corporate officials. The strategies of hedge/mutual funds, by contrast, do not fit well with the firm-level institutions found in Germany. Firm-level institutions impose several constraints on the ability of management to unilaterally develop and implement strategies. How German firms adjust to external pressures is the result of negotiation between management and employee representatives as there are several legal obstacles to a rapid and unilateral reorganization of the shop floor (Thelen 1991; Streeck 1992; Soskice 1999). The rest of this section is divided in two parts. First, I provide an overview of the differences between mutual and pension funds. Second, I present data on the presence of mutual funds in France and Germany.

7.3.1. Hedge, Mutual, and Pension Funds

Three critical features set apart these three groups of institutional investors, with systemic consequences for comparative corporate governance. They are the mode of collecting funds and issuing payments, time horizon and liquidity constraints, and the process of picking portfolio companies. First, a key difference between these types of institutional investors lies in how they collect funds and issue payments 'held in trust' for the beneficiaries. Defined benefits (DB) schemes guarantee the level of benefits the fund will pay and the method of determining those benefits, but not the amount of the contributions. The DB schemes guarantee a fixed payment in the future. The level of contributions in the current period is determined actuarially on the basis of the benefits expected to be paid to the retirees who contributed to the fund and the assumed rate of return. Defined contribution (DC) schemes, on the other hand, specify the level of contributions but not the amount of the benefits to be paid. The amount available to the beneficiaries depends on both the portfolio performance and the amount initially invested.

The relationship between the method of collecting funds and the type of institutional investors is almost perfectly correlated. Pension funds—public and private alike—rely substantially on DB schemes to collect and distribute assets (Pensions & Investments 26 January 2004: 16). The assets of mutual funds, by contrast, are managed almost exclusively on a DC basis (see Pozen 1998: 397–423). This is not surprising since mutual funds are investment companies that pool funds from individuals and corporations with the proviso that the money invested is redeemable on demand.[3] The funds paid to investors are dependent on the market performance of the mutual fund. Moreover, it is also important to note that pension funds directly manage only a small percentage of the assets collected by them—mutual funds serving as external fund managers. The pension fund industry is increasingly dominated by reliance mutual fund managers for asset management since 401 (k) plans allow corporations to more easily outsource direct contribution pension plans to external DC fund managers.[4]

Second, the time horizon of institutional investors diverges considerably with regard to their patterns of trading. The annual average turnover rate of American public pension funds in 1997 was 19.3 per cent (Conference Board 1998: 11). The equivalent figure for mutual fund managers and external money managers was 42.5 per cent. The average amount of time a share is held for Fidelity and Templeton (mutual funds) were respectively 2.63 and 2.22 years in 1999 (Bandru, Lavigne, and Morin 2001: 125). By contrast, most public pension funds have a longer-term horizon as witnessed by their turnover rates: Florida state (12.5 years) and California State Teachers (7.6 years) (ibid. 126). Pension funds do not face the same liquidity constraints as mutual funds and external money managers since payments to retirees are regular and predictable. Mutual funds managers do have liquidity concerns since the funds provided by investors are redeemable on demand.

Hedge funds are also reliant on short-term trading, albeit in a different way from mutual funds (Ackermann, McEnally, and Ravenscraft 1999). The investment strategies of hedge funds revolve around rapid turnover and aggressive trading on short-lived information which entails a statistical arbitrage that involves balancing positions in assets (equity, government bonds, and national currencies) that are believed to be undervalued against others whose value is expected to fall—an intrinsically short-term strategy.

Third, the criteria and processes by which funds select companies for investment also differ, resulting in a different composition of the stock portfolio. The composition of the stock portfolio for the great majority of pension funds is increasingly based on an index strategy. By late 1995, the percentage of assets managed on an index by American pension funds was 60 per cent and climbing (COB 1998: 15). This figure is even higher for some of the most activist funds. For example, around four-fifth of the stock portfolio of CalPERS and TIAA-CREF were indexed in 1997 (Del Guercio and Hawkins 1999: 302). The growing recourse to indexing by pension funds reflects their assessment that active management of the equity portfolio produces results inferior to market indexing. Pension funds in the UK and in USA often lack the firm-specific knowledge to take actions aiming at transforming the strategy of portfolio companies (Black 1992: 853).

Mutual funds, by contrast, do not acquire an equity stake in a corporation because it is part of an index. Managers are in stiff competition with other funds for the assets of investors that, in turn, can be redeemed at any moment. The structural characteristics of the mutual fund industry compel managers to achieve high returns, not simply match an index. Mutual funds behave like stock pickers and are the mirror image of DB pension funds (Pozen 1994; Monks and Minow 1995: 163). As a result, it is not uncommon for mutual funds to spend significant amounts of money to acquire firm-specific information. Finally, the compensation of hedge fund managers is based on the amount of assets under management and on incentive fees, the latter being paid only in the event of a positive return. The typical remuneration of hedge fund managers is characterized by 1 to 2 per cent of assets under management and 5 to 25 per cent of profits realized (Brown and Goetzmann 2001:2). The *raison d'être* of hedge funds is to pursue flexible and aggressive strategies that entail above-normal risks for potentially high returns.

The importance of specific firms for the overall financial performance of the fund also illustrates the differences in the composition of the portfolio of mutual and pension funds. The use of an index as an investment strategy by pension funds means that their aim is to reproduce as closely as possible the economic profile of a sector/country. The investment strategy of mutual funds, by contrast, is about picking undervalued firms that are likely to out-perform the market in the short term. These particular investment strategies, in turn, entail diverging degrees of dependence on the performance of specific portfolio companies. The top portfolio companies for mutual funds account for a greater percentage of their overall investment than the top portfolio companies for pension funds.[5] The financial returns of mutual funds are more dependent on the performance of a selected number of portfolio companies than they are for pension funds.[6]

7.3.2. Presence of Hedge and Mutual Funds in France and Germany

In this subsection, I compute data on the presence of hedge and mutual funds in France and Germany with the use of two indicators. The first is related to the disclosure requirements of listed companies. The EU regulation requires anyone who owns 5 per cent or more of the outstanding equity capital of a corporation to notify the national securities regulator. I recorded data on equity stakes above the 5 per cent threshold from September 1997 to December 2006 for both France and Germany.[7] I also recorded every instance of acquisitions of equity capital over the 5 per cent threshold by American and British institutional investors under the following conditions. First, I discarded acquisitions above the 5 per cent threshold by subsidiaries of both non-financial firms and asset management investors from the database. Second, my sample is composed of domestically based corporations in France and Germany. Third, I also discarded movements of capital above and below the 5 per cent threshold within a thirty-day period. Some mutual funds have adopted a policy of automatic sale of stocks if their equity stake goes above the mandatory disclosure requirement. Moreover, movements above and below the 5 per cent threshold might reflect a share buyback programme by a portfolio corporation rather than an intended strategy by an institutional investor. Fourth, I selected equity capital in a firm rather than voting rights as an indicator of movement of capital above the 5 per cent threshold. Finally, I cross-checked the data collected by relying on two national business directories: DAFSA Annuaire des Sociétés for France and Rudiger Liedtke's Wem Gehort die Republik for Germany. These two publications serve as useful reliability check mechanisms.

Data on the presence of hedge/mutual funds in France and Germany reveals striking patterns of divergence.[8] Hedge/mutual funds have invested massively in France as measured by the overall number of equity stakes over the 5 per cent threshold. For the top twenty French firms by market capitalization, ten of them recorded twenty-seven instances of investment over the 5 per cent threshold by Anglo-Saxon institutional investors. Because a firm can receive more than one investment from Anglo-Saxon institutional investors, the number of investments is always higher than the number of companies receiving investment. For the top twenty German firms by market capitalization, only six of them recorded sixteen instances of investment over the 5 per cent threshold by Anglo-Saxon institutional investors. For the top forty firms in the two markets, twenty-six French firms recorded 77 instances of investment over the 5 per cent threshold; the corresponding figures for Germany were 16 firms and 33 acquisitions. For the top 60 companies, 41 French firms recorded 122 instances of investment over the 5 per cent threshold; the corresponding figures for Germany were 27 and 52. For blue-chip companies, therefore, the overall number of acquisitions in French firms was twice as important as those recorded for German companies.[9]

The second source of data concerning the presence of mutual funds in France and Germany is taken from analysis performed by Morningstar Inc., the Chicago-based rating agency. Morningstar Inc. is the leading provider of independent research on American mutual funds and is highly influential with investors as an improvement in the rating of a fund is associated with significant new inflows of capital (Del Guercio and Tkac 2001). Data on the

Table 7.3. Number of times countries appear among the top three foreign investment destinations of individual mutual funds

Year	Germany	France	UK
1997	9	24	39
1998	22	39	56
1999	7	26	48
2000	10	29	52
2001	11	22	50
2002	6	31	46
2003	8	20	53
2004	8	25	53
2005	3	20	51

Source: Morningstar, *Morningstar Funds 500*, various years.

importance of mutual funds is collected from *Morningstar Funds 500*, an annual publication that evaluates the performance of the biggest 500 funds in the USA. Most of the funds covered in this annual publication have assets invested in domestic stocks and bonds. About seventy-five funds per year are involved in international equity. For each of these internationally oriented funds, *Morningstar Funds 500* lists the five top countries of exposure.

I compiled data on the importance of the French and German markets by computing the number of times they appear in the top three countries in terms of international exposure for mutual funds. I also collected for comparability purposes data for the UK, an LME with a system of corporate governance very similar to that of the USA. The results are presented in Table 7.3. The attractiveness of the French market compared with Germany for mutual funds is further confirmed. Internationally oriented American mutual funds are almost three times more likely to invest in France than Germany.

7.4. FIRM-LEVEL INSTITUTIONS IN FRANCE AND GERMANY

The argument presented in this section is that the firm-level institutions of French and German companies provide different degrees of fit with the preferences and strategies of this group of investors. The degree of fit between the investment strategies of mutual funds and the firm-level institutions of advanced industrialized nations reflects the ability of the CEO and top managers to unilaterally reorganize the workplace. The degree of concentration of power is a crucial influence on its patterns of adjustment, as well as on the interaction between companies and investors. I argue that the divergence in the institutional arrangements of firm-level organization between France and Germany impacts on the ability of top management to unilaterally implement reorganization schemes, thereby providing specific incentives for the managers of hedge/mutual funds. The short-time horizon of mutual funds fits well with the decision-making and adjustment processes of large French firms—which are management-led as the exclusion of the workforce from decision-making gives them fewer opportunities to block managerial initiatives (Schmidt 1996; Hancké 2002; Rebérioux 2002).

The diffusion of power inside German firms, by contrast, means that securing the consent of works councils as well as top management is necessary for the introduction of new strategies (Hall 1997; Goyer 2002; Culpepper 2003). The legal rights of works councils and the regulations regarding training provide employees with the means to derail unwanted measures (Thelen 1991; Streeck 1992). Moreover, the lack of managerial autonomy over how unit activities are performed militates against radical changes in the organization of the workplace. The involvement of employees in many activities, combined with the absence of carefully designed formal rules from management, makes it unlikely that the elaboration of performance standards can be decided centrally (Whitley 1999*b*).

The rest of this section is organized in the following manner. First, I identify the institutional arrangements of firm-level organization which illustrate the concentration of power at the top of French companies and the constraints on managerial autonomy in Germany. I discuss three areas of firm-level organization—skill certification and formation, segmentation of activities, and the autonomy of employees in problem-solving tasks. Second, I analyse how these institutional arrangements shape the adjustment process of companies which, in turn, provide for different degrees of fit with the preferences and strategies of mutual funds.

7.4.1. Training and the Building of Firm Competencies

The first set of key firm-level institutions is related to the process of skill formation and certification of the workforce, that is training. The matching of jobs and worker competencies in the two countries shapes the ability of management to implement restructuring measures in a unilateral manner in different ways. The German economy requires that the majority of employees possess certifiable skills so that firms can develop their capabilities. By contrast, French companies build their competencies around mid-level management and technical specialists rather than investing in improving the skills of the bulk of the workforce.

The divergent methods of coupling tasks and competencies are reflected in the role of training in the two countries. Vocational training, in particular, is prominent in Germany and relatively neglected in France. The German system of occupational training is both prominent and autonomous—all in contrast to the French situation (Soskice 1994). A substantially higher proportion of workers in Germany have received some vocational training. In 1995, the average number of trainees for large German firms (over 500 employees) was 6 per 100 workers with a retention rate of 85 per cent. The corresponding figure for large French companies was 2.2 per 100 workers in 1996 with a retention rate of 35 per cent (Culpepper 1998: 286, 301).

The different patterns by which competencies and jobs are matched in the two countries are also visible throughout the entire career of employees—and not simply limited to the vocational training. The qualifications of German employees determine the definition of their jobs. Access to a majority of jobs in large firms requires a recognized diploma or qualification—most often acquired as part of a vocational or on-the-job training programme. Training is invariably a prerequisite for employment and promotion (Maurice, Sellier, and Silvestre 1986: 65–73). The influence of firm-level works councils is paramount as they insist that different types of occupations be associated with different levels of skills. Managers cannot move employees within the firm without prior appropriate training. It is also interesting to note that mid-level managers and foremen must undergo specific training in order to be appointed and promoted. As a result, the promotion process in German firms reflects the acquisition of the required technical expertise and completion of the relevant training. This process ensures that the authority of project managers rests on technical competence and is not based on their access to higher levels of managerial authority. By contrast, French employers use their own criteria to define jobs to which employees adapt either in training programmes (blue collar) or through obtaining university diplomas (white collar)—the promotion system of French firms being a reflection of a change of status unilaterally decided by top management rather than the acquisition of technical expertise. The relationship between training and promotion is reversed in France. Management selects workers to be promoted and then provides them with the appropriate training (ibid. 77). French firms provide in-house training for employees who usually have substantial experience in the firm. Attempts by state officials to impose the recognition of training (vocational or on-the-job) as a prerequisite for holding jobs have encountered strong opposition from employers (Culpepper 1998; Marsden 1999: 98).

The German training system, moreover, is well established and autonomous from managerial interference—in addition to being prominent. The presence of a majority of workers with certifiable skills in the German economy is legally based and protected from outside intervention (Muller-Jentsch 1995: 70–1; Culpepper 1998: 276). First, a high number of jobs require certifiable skills that are acquired in vocational training programmes. Second, industrial or regional chambers must certify the training programmes of firms, and any change in the content of training certification—such as the modification of an existing certification or the introduction of a new one—requires the approval of a body of experts in which national industrial unions (not works councils) occupy half of the seats (Culpepper 1998). In turn, works councils have been instrumental in setting training standards as well as overseeing the implementation of training programmes in the firm. The veto power of employees on the boards of the industrial and regional training commissions prevents significant modifications of the system and ensures a stable demand for certified employees. Third, firm-level works councils possess full veto power over hiring, thereby constraining managerial ability to rely on outside experts (Streeck 1989: 129; Goyer 2002: 26). New jobs must be offered first to the current members of the workforce. The position of organized labour and the works councils in the training system has enabled them to impose significant constraints on hiring new employees when a company scaled back its activities to a few core competencies: since new training programmes have to be approved by an expert body in which organized labour holds half of the seats, they have de facto veto power over these programmes. The institutions of German training constrain management on several fronts: skills are a prerequisite for jobs; management must provide the relevant training to employees; the content of these programmes must be certified by an outside body where labour possesses a veto; and the hiring of new employees with the requisite skills is subject to the approval of works councils.

By contrast, the development of the core competencies of French firms is not based on the skills of the bulk of the workforce. The educational system remains the primary mechanism by which employees are assigned to skilled positions, with vocational and on-the-job training occupying an inferior status (Marsden 1999: 121–38). The French case is characterized by the absence of a legal requirement to assign specific jobs to workers with certifiable skills. First, attempts by state officials to impose the recognition of vocational training as a prerequisite for holding specific jobs have been defeated by French employers (ibid. 98). Managers use their own criteria to define the jobs to which employees adapt either through participation in training programmes (blue collar) or through obtaining university diplomas (white collar). The content of training and the place of employees in the production process represent areas of pure managerial prerogative (Maurice, Sellier, and Silvestre 1986: 74–9; Linhart 1994). Second, boards of experts (business associations and employee committees) on training play a simple consultative role (Culpepper 1998: 278). At the firm level, works councils possess only information rights as employers must specify how funds raised from tax levies will be spent. On the specific issue of vocational training, moreover, it is the Ministry of Education that is responsible for the elaboration of standards. Third, firm-level works councils possess limited information rights on the hiring of new staff—not a full veto power that could prevent employers from replacing current workers with new employees (Goyer 2002: 25). Relying on outside experts has in fact proven to be a privileged strategy of adjustment for French companies (Hancké 2002: 57–82).

7.4.2. Work Organization and the Segmentation of Activities

The second major difference in the organization of the workplace between France and Germany concerns the extent to which activities are segmented, that is the degree of managerial control over the organization of the production process and especially the extent to which employers rely on the bulk of the workforce in organizing and carrying out tasks (Whitley 1999: 38–44). The French case is characterized by the segmentation of production activities and responsibilities between blue-collar employees and managers, a rather rigid system of rules, and an emphasis on narrow and specialized skills (Sorge 1991; Linhart 1994; Marsden 1999). Firms rely on the presence of rules that regulate the nature of the tasks to be accomplished—rather than the functions to be performed—to organize the production process (Maurice, Sellier, and Silvestre 1986: 60–5; Marsden 1999: 103–4). The implementation of this business strategy is accomplished through numerous sets of carefully defined rules designed to specify the terms of exchange among parties. The organization of work is divided into fragmentary tasks (Sorge and Warner 1986). Highly qualified engineers elaborate the conception of products and employees carry out the tasks following detailed instructions (Linhart 1994; Boyer 1995). This results in a high supervisor-to-worker ratio and a strict division of authority between management and employees (Maurice, Sellier, and Silvestre 1986: 69–80; Lane 1989: 40–2; Sorge 2005: 160–2). The separation between planning and execution limits the involvement of blue collar in the conduct of the firm's business strategy since they possess a limited view of its operations, which contributes to the concentration of power at the top of the managerial hierarchy.

The initial rationale for French workplace organization is best explained by Crozier's notion of the avoidance of face-to-face relationships and Hofstede's classification of France as a country in which individualism ranks high as a value (Crozier 1963; Hofstede 1980). The French propensity for uncertainty avoidance, combined with the antagonistic nature of industrial relations, has led firms to adopt mechanisms designed both to prevent the involvement of employees in the conduct of firm's strategies as well as to protect them from unpredictable and unwarranted intrusion. However, the advent of firm-level flexibility and the increasing importance of microprocessor technology have raised the costs of maintaining this separation between elaboration and implementation of tasks. The need for companies to adapt quickly to a changing environment requires a change of attitude of workers (Streeck 1987). Employees must enter into a dialogue with management and different functional departments in order to achieve flexibility, quality, and speed. The avoidance of face-to-face dialogue is no longer sustainable in this context. Consequently, greater levels of participation by employees in modifying their environment have taken place inside large French companies in the past fifteen years (Linhart 1994: 23–47; Hancké 2002: 57–87). Employees are given a greater choice of tasks by management. They have become more involved in problem-solving and have greater input into monitoring and evaluating performance as more is expected of them from management (Linhart 1992).

Nonetheless, the separation between planning and execution is still predominant and the organization of work has not lost its key Fordist component (Linhart 1994: 48–64; Culpepper 1998, 2003). Shop floor restructuring in France in the past fifteen years might have provided for greater employee involvement in monitoring and evaluating performance, but it does not grant them much influence over what tasks they perform and under what conditions. Hierarchical relationships are still predominant inside French firms despite the greater involvement of employees.

The organization of work in Germany, on the other hand, is more straightforward and is characterized by the application of rules to broad functions, rather than by trying to predict all contingencies on the shop floor through reliance on explicit instructions (Maurice, Sellier, and Silvestre 1986: 65–73; Sorge and Warner 1986; Kristensen 1997; Whitley 1999b: 509–12). The predominance of employees with certifiable skills and the subsequent reliance of management on the bulk of the workforce as a strategy for developing firm's capabilities are critical factors that have bridged the gap between conception and implementation in Germany (Whitley 2003: 669–79). The role of training is particularly important in this process as employees are grouped according to the types of qualifications they possess, with tasks organized according to their skill requirements (Marsden 1999: 38). The outcome is one where the institutional arrangements of the workplace are characterized by: blurred organizational boundaries and reduced segmentation; the delegation of control over the nature of work processes resulting in the involvement of employees in many tasks; and low reliance on formal rules in evaluating performance (Sorge 1991: 166; Kester 1992).

7.4.3. The Autonomy and Competencies of Workers in Problem-Solving Tasks

The third firm-level institutional difference between France and Germany is to do with the degree of autonomy that employees have on the shop floor. I distinguish here between the separation of task execution and implementation (covered in the previous subsection) on the one hand, and the extent to which workers exercise discretion over how tasks are performed and their ability to contribute to problem-solving for two reasons. First, as noted by Kumazawa and Yamada (1989) in their study of skills formation in Japan, institutional arrangements in large Japanese firms give employees a degree of influence over the standardization process—however they are powerless to shape the conditions under which work takes place once job tasks are standardized. A similar argument has been made for France since the greater involvement of employees there has not been matched by a corresponding willingness of management to share authority (Linhart 1992). Second, the ability of employees to contribute to problem-solving is not independent of the development of their organizational careers. The case of France illustrates well the shortcomings of the partial reform of the institutions of workplace organization. The narrow skills of French employees limit their contribution to problem-solving and the fulfilment of the organizational goals of the firm, despite greater managerial expectations.

The autonomy and competencies of employees in problem-solving tasks in large companies also exhibit stark contrast between France and Germany. The institutional arrangements of workplace organization in Germany provides for substantial autonomy in the definition of tasks and autonomy in their implementation (Maurice, Sellier, and Silvestre 1986: 90–100; Sorge 1991; Kester 1992; Kristensen 1997). High levels of authority sharing, the development of firm competencies via the institutions of training, and the involvement of workers beyond the managerial hierarchy in the elaboration of the firm's strategies mean that the fate of employees is linked with that of management (Whitley 2003: 669–79). Skilled employees possess strong incentives for developing problem-solving capabilities given the firm-specific stakes of their organizational career development. Moreover, the capabilities of German employees are profoundly shaped by the content of their skills. The involvement of employer associations in the certification process ensures that skills are relevant to their strategic needs (Culpepper 2003). The involvement of national union representatives in the certification process, on the other hand, ensures that skills will be of a general character and fit with a broad job description (Streeck 1989: 131–2).[10] The content of the skill certification of employees is not tightly connected to specific jobs. National industrial unions, and the metalworkers union IG Metall in particular, have been adamant in insisting that skills should be broad rather than narrowly firm-specific or task-connected. Finally, the use of job rotation enhances the degree of polyvalence of German employees, thereby increasing their ability to engage in problem-solving task (Maurice, Sellier, and Silvestre 1986: 79–84; Sorge 1991). Job rotation allows companies to rely on employees with broad skills to tackle shifts in work demands (Marsden 1999: 133). German employees are open to job rotations across departments and divisions since their career development is linked to their ability to contribute to the success of the firm (Whitley 2003: 674). The degree of polyvalence of workers is high since the organization of the workplace favours the acquisition of broad-based skills (Maurice, Sellier, and Silvestre 1986: 69–73; Streeck 1992).

The institutional arrangements of workplace organization in France, by contrast, do not significantly contribute to the development of the firm-specific problem-solving capabilities of employees. First, job rotation in French enterprises is lower than in Germany (Maurice, Sellier, and Silvestre 1986: 79–84; Marsden 1999: 130–1). The working life of employees tends to be associated with specific tasks, which leads to substantial segmentation of work roles and greater functional specialization. Second, job demarcations are stricter. The segmentation of the activities of the firm between elaboration and execution and the narrow skills of French employees entails that they possess a limited view of the totality of the operations of the firm and rely on top management for coordination. Their capabilities to develop firm-specific problem-solving capabilities are seriously limited since they only have a partial view of the operations of the firm (Sorge 1991). The process of problem-solving is management-led, with the involvement of a few highly qualified technical specialists.

7.4.4. Firm-Level Institutional Arrangements and Paths of Adjustment

The firm-level institutional arrangements of German firms place serious constraints on the ability of managers to unilaterally dictate the firm's business strategy. Nonetheless, companies have exhibited flexibility in adjusting inter-nally to shifts in demand on world markets—although not in a manner that fits well with the preferences of short-term, impatient investors. German firms have traditionally responded to the volatility of markets by redeploying the capabilities of employees to new uses—instead of relying on firings and other types of market-based adjustments (Sorge 1991; Streeck 1992). This adjust-ment process is possible because the skills of employees are broad enough to accomplish a wide range of tasks in a context where labour laws make it difficult to proceed to dismissals. Broad skills and blurred organizational boundaries provide employees with a fairly complete view of the operations of the firm. There is substantial scope for the involvement of skilled workers in problem-solving activities (Maurice, Sellier, and Silvestre 1986). Training curricula and regulations are broadly defined to avoid overspecialization in narrow skill assignments and the blurring of boundaries and responsibilities allows employees to switch between different functions. The skills of employ-ees shape their ability to solve problems that, in turn, present management with opportunities to reorganize the production process. The volatility of markets punishes firms where the skills of the workforce cannot be applied to a wide range of rapidly changing and previously unknown tasks. The possession of broad skills by employees provides German companies with the capacity for retooling in response to new market demands (Sorge 1991: 170; Streeck 1992). This strategy, however, does not fit well with the preferences and tac-tics of hedge/mutual funds. The redeployment of the skills of employees to new economic circumstances involves a process of experimentation to ensure that the certified skills are relevant to the production needs of companies. This learning-by-doing strategy is unlikely to be accomplished as rapidly as external mechanisms of adjustment that rely on dismissals and other types of market-based adjustment. This is particularly true in times of rapid product and technological change requiring a radical transformation in skill content. The German system is plagued by serious rigidities, as the introduction of a new product or technology invariably gives rise to jurisdictional disputes between various employees (Herrigel and Sabel 1999). The respective role to be performed by each of the skill categories in the introduction of new products must be bargained out.[11]

The centralized and functionally differentiated work organization of large French firms, on the other hand, militates against experimentation with skill redeployment. It instead entails a separation between categories of workers: a small number of highly qualified employees sealed off from the imple-mentation process, and the bulk of the workforce composed of low-skilled workers with narrowly specialized tasks that cannot be redeployed to respond to unpredictable shifts in demand (Streeck 1992*b*: 256). The importance of the failure of state officials to impose the recognition of training as a prerequisite for holding specific jobs becomes apparent in this context. Differences in training between France and Germany are not simply a quantitative issue— that is more workers possessing certified skills in the latter. Despite state regulation that imposes a legal obligation on French firms to spend a percentage of their wage bill on training, flows of funds have been concentrated on managerial staff with already high levels of skills, not for the improvement of the general skills of the majority of employees (Culpepper 2003: 57). The sharp segmentation of production activities and responsibilities between blue-collar employees and managers, a rigid system of rules, and the emphasis on narrow and specialized skills limit the ability of workers to participate in the conduct of the business strategy, thereby lessening the dependence of management on the skills of the bulk of the workforce.

7.5. CONCLUSIONS AND IMPLICATIONS

The argument presented in this chapter provides several implications for the study of comparative corporate governance. The issue of accounting for institutional change (and its effects) has become critical for comparative political economists given that the field has long focused on using institutions to account for divergence across countries. Critics have argued that institutional theories associated with the VoC perspective perform a better job at accounting for stability than institutional discontinuity (Howell 2003; Crouch 2005*a*; Morgan 2005). The argument of this chapter, by contrast, has highlighted the continuing usefulness of VoC in taking seriously domestic institutional frameworks as an independent variable for middle range theoretical projects. I argue that key institutions (workplace organization) constitute the single most important variable to account for the presence of institutional change (ownership structure). This outcome is driven by three factors.

First, institutional arrangements interact to complement each other and consequently cannot be studied in isolation whether analysing the presence of stability or the occurrence of change in the broader institutional framework of countries.[12] The introduction of a profound institutional change in the ownership structure of French and German companies does not annul the theoretical importance of institutions since substantial institutional differences remain in other areas, and these persisting cross-national differences form a distinctive constellation that produces different outcomes across nations. The impact of institutional change on the overall operation of the political economy depends on the interaction of the new institutions with those already in place, as institutional change is almost invariably piecemeal rather than full-scale.

Second, the theoretical importance of the degree of power concentration associated with the institutions of workplace organization as an explanation of the ability of companies to attract foreign capital is contingent upon its resilience and its ability to sustain cross-national comparisons. The research design of this chapter and its ability to draw causal inferences would find themselves on shaky ground if both the degree of power concentration inside companies and the ownership structure of large firms had changed in recent years, given the problem of over-determination. The degree of power concentration of large French and German companies and the process by which they develop their innovative capabilities have been both relatively stable while exhibiting striking differences between the two countries for the past thirty years, despite changes in ownership structure.[13] A key insight of this chapter is that one must distinguish between the character of coordination and innovation of firms from the institutional framework that supports it (Hall and Thelen 2005: 30). Change in the former does not entail a modification in the latter. Power concentration has remained stable over a period of time in which the ownership structure of French and German companies underwent a significant transformation.[14] Institutional hybridization does occur, but the concept is not particularly useful for capturing the dynamics and consequences of institutional change.

Third, the institutions of workplace organization in the two countries were characterized by an element of latency prior to financial deregulation and have become more salient in the new context of financial globalization.[15] The long-term cross-national differences in work organization have contributed to the differences in the patterns of economic specialization of the two countries, but they had nothing to do with the ownership structure of large domestic companies given the lack of international diversification of Anglo-Saxon institutional investors prior to the early to mid-1990s.

The last point about latency illustrates quite well the importance of the interactive effects associated with an institutional matrix, namely the presence of institutional complementarity. Prior to the mid-1990s, France and Germany were two bank-based financial systems with long-term patient capital despite differences in the institutions of workplace organization. The provision of patient or long-term capital in France was previously made possible through a combination of state regulation of the banking sector that facilitated access to long-term capital through bank loans and cross-shareholdings among large companies (Zysman 1983; Schmidt 1996). The deregulation of the banking sector and the decline of cross-shareholdings in France mean that the provision of long-term capital in the form of debt finance is no longer available; it has instead been replaced by the presence of short-term, impatient capital (Loriaux 1991). A key insight is that while the institutions of workplace organization have not fundamentally changed, the external environment in which they are embedded has. The concentration of power in top management was previously interacting with state policies and patterns of cross-shareholdings that enabled firms to have access to long-term capital. The arrival of mutual funds in France has not been the cause of the deregulation of the banking sector, nor has it been responsible for the decision of French blue-chip firms to sell their equity stakes in other companies. Nonetheless, it must be mentioned that the concentration of power in the CEO in French firms, if not supported by state regulation of the banking sector and patterns of cross-shareholdings among firms, is highly receptive and supportive of the investment strategy of short-term oriented institutional investors. The concentration of power in the CEO of French firms is compatible with both the presence and absence of long-term capital.

NOTES

1. Different versions of this paper were presented at the 2004 annual meeting of the American Political Science association and at the workshop on Institutional Change in Contemporary Capitalism, London School of Economics, 3–4 June 2005. I wish to thank Suzanne Berger, Peter Gourevitch, Peter Hall, Bob Hancké, David Soskice, and Mark Thatcher for their comments.
2. See Table 4 in Goyer (2006*b*).
3. Hedge funds, on the other hand, are traditionally set up as limited partnerships that are limited to a restricted number of wealthy individuals (500) with personal assets of at least US$5 million who are willing to adopt highly risky short-term strategies and borrow on financial markets in exchange for high potential returns. Hedge funds are managed on a DC scheme with investors not certain to recover their investment since fund managers are typically given mandates to make an absolute return target regardless of the market environment. But, in contrast to mutual funds schemes, hedge funds impose initial lock-up periods of at least one year as funds are not redeemable on demand. This difference aside, hedge and mutual funds constitute two forms of short-term, impatient capital. For an overview, see Stephen Brown and William Goetzmann, 'Hedge Funds with Style', NBER working paper #8173 (Cambridge, MA: 2001).
4. However, pension funds do retain some form of control by issuing specific guidelines on investment decision to external money managers (Del Guercio and Hawkins 1999: 299–301). Moreover, they often change external money

managers that deviate from investment guidelines by taking excessive risks even for superior financial performance (Del Guericio and Tkac 2002: 525–30).

5. See Table 5 in Goyer (2006*b*).

6. Hedge funds do not have to reveal the composition of their portfolio and materials distributed to investors are often available on a restricted basis and published at irregular intervals. Their low profile and secretive nature are designed to minimize regulatory and tax oversights. As a result, it is often impossible to acquire credible data on the holdings of hedge funds. On the other hand, however, financial regulation in the European Union obliges shareholders to disclose equity stake above the 5% threshold. Thus, it becomes possible to track the investment targets of hedge funds when their equity stake exceeds this threshold. Data on the presence of hedge funds in France and Germany is provided in the next section.

7. I recorded data from the two official governmental databases: http://www.amf-france.org and http://www.bawe.de

8. The full compilation of data on the presence of mutual funds in France and Germany is presented in Goyer (2006*b*).

9. A similar divergence characterizes the investment patterns of Anglo-Saxon institutional investors in the two countries outside the blue-chip company category (Goyer 2006*b*). If we deduct the top 60 companies from the analysis, 114 German firms recorded 156 instances of an investment over the 5% threshold by an Anglo-American hedge/mutual funds from September 1997 to April 2006. The corresponding figures for France are 200 companies recording 367 instances above the 5% threshold.

10. Moreover, skilled employees possess strong incentives for developing problem-solving capabilities given the firm-specific stakes of their organizational career development, since training is a prerequisite for progression within the company.

11. e.g. thirty-one new occupations were defined and ninety-seven were updated and modernized between 1996 and 1999 (Rubery and Grimshaw 2003: 130).

12. See Hall and Franzese (1998), Hall and Soskice (2001: 17–33), and Milgrom and Roberts (1995) for a full discussion of the concept of institutional complementarity.

13. Compare Boyer (1995), Culpepper (2003), Maurice, Sellier, and Silvestre (1986), Marsden (1999), and Whitley (2003) for an analysis of the continuing differences in the processes by which institutions of workplace organization enable large firms to develop their innovative capabilities in France and Germany.

14. I demonstrate in this chapter how the transformation of one aspect of French corporate governance (increasing importance of foreign ownership in the ownership structure) did not affect the process by which large firms build their innovative capabilities. In other papers, I analysed how other developments in French corporate governance (focus on core competencies

and adoption of financial transparency) also led to the continuing exclusion of employees from the decision-making process and, as a result, left unaffected the development of innovative capabilities (see Goyer 2003, 2006).

15. See Thelen and Steinmo (1992: 16–18) for a discussion of the concept of latent institutions.

Part IV

Labour Market and Welfare State Adjustment

8

The Political Economy of Adjustment
in Mixed Market Economies: A Study
of Spain and Italy

Óscar Molina and Martin Rhodes

8.1. INTRODUCTION

Critics of the VoC approach, as defined in Hall and Soskice (2001), have
focused on its alleged weaknesses—its neglect of the state, its divorce of the
firm from national contexts, an over-concern with institutional equilibrium
rather than dynamics of change and its incapacity for dealing with non-
LMEs and CMEs. But as the editors argue in their introduction, none of these
problems present fatal flaws. To some extent, it is true, VoC theory seems to
be caught in a trade-off between parsimony and explanatory capacity. It provides high heuristic value-added for analysing countries where performance-
enhancing complementarities rely on clearly different patterns of actor interaction and forms of coordination. It appears more difficult to extend to
'deviant' cases where there is a mix of logics, a high degree of institutional
incoherence and an apparent absence of complementarities.

Yet that is the task we undertake in the following analysis. We use the tools
of VoC to explain how mechanisms of market and non-market coordination
work and change in two 'mixed market economies' (MMEs)—Italy and Spain.
We focus in on the relationship between production regimes and welfare
systems, and specifically the wage–labour nexus and employment protection.
In doing so we are responding to Hall and Soskice's call for analyses (2003:
249) that move beyond the insights of their original argument and 'develop
more complete models of the coalitional dynamics that underpin institutional
stability and change, using contemporary and historical cases to trace the
complex interplay between action in the political and economic arenas'.

In Section 8.2, which follows, we consider how VoC's focus on the asset-
investment strategies of actors and institutional complementaries can be

adapted to the analysis of MMEs. We also present a two-tiered framework for understanding the interaction between the political and economic arenas. We are especially concerned (see also Iversen, this volume) with the ways in which the nature of the political system—majoritarian versus proportional—will shape and constrain economic change. Section 8.3, which focuses on our two case studies, is concerned with two puzzles. The first is theoretical and concerns the role of the state in these economies. In contrast to arguments for a distinctive form of state capitalism alongside 'market' and 'managed' varieties (Schmidt 2002), we argue, in line with the editors' introduction, that the state's role is distinctive in the Mediterranean countries but not unique and has also undergone considerable change.

That process of change presents us with our second puzzle: does 'market liberalization', and the redefinition of the state mean a shift in these MMEs towards the LME model; or do their institutional characteristics demand new kinds of coordination for managing 'market liberalization' and the withdrawal of the state? Hall (this volume) argues that measures commonly described as 'liberal' can have different economic or institutional effects: some are corrosive of strategic coordination elsewhere in the economy; others enhance it. We argue similarly that two different trends can be perceived: the growth of 'autonomous coordination' in which actors seek to govern the economy with new kinds of non-market coordination; and 'market colonization', a process whereby market modes of coordination emerge and prevail. Section 8.4 concludes with some reflections on the destinies of our cases: convergence on either of the LME or CME archetypes, or continued hybridity?

8.2. COMPLEMENTARITIES, COALITIONS AND CHANGE IN MMEs

The conventional template for analysing political economies close to the LME and CME types (see Soskice, this volume) relies on the following linkages: LME = liberal market production regime + liberal welfare state + majoritarian political system; CME = coordinated market production regime + social democratic/continental welfare state + consensus political system. Following on from Soskice (1990, 1999), Hall and Soskice (2001) signal the existence of institutional spillovers within these systems that influence economic and employment performance. They suggest a series of institutional complementarities and positive feedbacks between protection systems (the welfare state and labour market legislation) and production regimes (the dominant form of competition among firms, forms of corporate governance) and forms of specialization in international market competition.

But analysing Europe's MMEs requires that attention is paid—as one would expect—to their 'mixed' character and the complexities of their institutional systems. The production systems of Europe's Mediterranean MMEs tend to be more fragmented than either LMEs or CMEs by large firm/small firm, public–private, and territorial divides. They also therefore contain different logics of coordination and forms of actor interaction, making it difficult to talk of one national production model with a single form of comparative advantage. These cleavages underpin two causally related features of these MMEs: the organizational fragmentation and politicization of interest associations and the greater role of the state as a regulator and producer of goods. Welfare systems, as understood by a long tradition of analysis (e.g. Rhodes 1997*b*) also map imperfectly on to the standard liberal versus social democratic/Bismarckian continental division. They too are fragmented, unevenly developed, subject to politicization and clientelism and mix Bismarckian (pensions) and liberal (health system) characteristics. Electoral systems range from the more majoritarian (Spain, Portugal, and Greece) to the proportional (Italy), and further complicate attempts to generalize correspondences between production regimes, welfare states, and political institutions.

In order to extend VoC to such MMEs we need to innovate conceptually in two directions: understanding the complex links between production regimes and welfare states and their consequences for coalition formation, asset investment, and institutional complementarities; and providing a framework for analysing the interplay between the political and economic arenas.

8.2.1. Production Regimes and Welfare Systems

Analyses of the relationship between production regimes and welfare systems have tended to concentrate on the degree of fit between them (Soskice 1990; Hollingsworth and Boyer 1997; Huber and Stephens 2001; Iversen 2005). Huber and Stephens (2001:119) argue that 'within each country, certain—though not all—aspects of its welfare state and production regimes do "fit" each other'. They refer to the need for wage and benefit levels to fit and for labour market and social policies to be aligned so that they do not create perverse incentives for economic actors. In line with basic VoC insights, they also argue that protection regimes and production systems link up in ways that enhance the performance of firms and the efficiency of the national economy, thereby contributing to comparative institutional advantage (Rhodes 2005).

The VoC literature conceptualizes 'fit' in terms of institutional complementarities, whereby the efficiency of one institution is increased by its interaction with another (Aoki 1994). One would expect the potential for *misfit*, by contrast, to be considerable in those economies that do not conform closely to the LME or CME types for, in theory, their sub-systems should be much less well-calibrated (though see Boyer 1998; Crouch 2005 for counter-arguments). This perception lies behind the reasoning of Hall and Gingerich (2004) for whom 'hybrid' systems—such as those of southern Europe—will *ceteris paribus* under-perform 'purer' types. Amable (2003) also argues that MMEs lack the pre-conditions for beneficial complementarities and positive spillovers. Thus southern European welfare systems typically have less social protection and more employment protection; low levels of social protection deter investment in specific skills; and, in turn, low-skill levels impede engagement in high-technology activities. In the production regime, lower competitive pressures due to high levels of product-market regulation and state intervention help maintain stable bank–industry relations and constrain the growth of financial markets. Together, these features produce a pattern of industrial specialization based on small firms competing mainly on price and heavily constrain movement of the economy on to a high-wage/high-skills development path.

The institutional lock-in effects of this combination of protection system and production regime are as important in MMEs as they are in the LME and CME models. One of the core insights of VoC is that the institutions of a nation's political economy will tend to encourage investment by firms and other actors in particular kinds of assets—specific or co-specific assets (dependent on cooperation and strategic interaction) in CMEs and switchable assets in LMEs (Hall and Soskice 2001: 17). Actors will become committed to the continuation of a given activity where such assets are applied (O'Neil and Pierson 2002: 13). Actors that have invested in particular institutional arrangements are likely to mobilize more readily to protect their investment by opposing change (Gourevitch 2000) or to pursue incremental changes that maintain a high return on those investments.

These forms of actor interaction are relatively well understood for CMEs and LMEs. The capacity to defend specific or co-specific investments is determined to a large extent by the organizational characteristics of interest groups, that is trade unions and employer organizations. In CMEs, well-organized socio-economic actors have invested in institutions that produce a range of collective goods. An example is Germany's co-determination system and sectoral industrial relations framework, the resilience of which is underpinned by the strength of the labour movement and an employer–employee, cross-class consensus, and coalition (Thelen 2001). Both employers and employees share an interest in protecting their comparative institutional advantage and maintaining the complementarities it produces for firms. Neoliberal deregulation will be resisted. In LMEs, by contrast, weaker employer and union organizations cannot produce as easily the collective goods or autonomous forms of coordination that support investment in specific assets. Complementarities come instead from the opportunity structures of more fluid markets. Coalitions in favour of higher levels of institutional regulation find it hard to mobilize support and reform is more likely to be driven by a market-making logic.

The MMEs, however, will typically combine both market and non-market forms of coordination. While unions and employers tend to have stronger organizational structures than in LMEs, they tend to be more fragmented and weaker than in CMEs. Thus, while they are unable to deliver the same collective goods or create strong autonomous forms of coordination (in collective bargaining, for example) they frequently do have the power to veto change and/or demand compensation from the state. Levels of direct state intervention, via company ownership, for example, have been heavily reduced in European MMEs in recent years. But there has been a reluctance to abandon the protection of national firms from foreign predators. The role of the state as a compensator 'of first resort' is also still strong, depending on the access of vested interests to policymaking power.

Some (notably Schmidt 2002) argue that the state's centrality in such systems warrants identification of a third type of 'state capitalism'. Crouch (2005) also suggests that the state can introduce, extend, and consolidate complementarities between institutions in countries considered 'hybrid cases'. Our view is that such state activity is a form of 'non-market coordination' found in many economies. It is obviously characteristic of CMEs, where state social policies, for example, act as a guarantor of employers' investments in workers' skills (Mares 2003: 237). It also varies significantly in form and extent across LMEs and MMEs. A strong state role does not in itself create a different 'type' of capitalism. What matters is the kind of coordination it imparts alongside regulation by markets and social actors. Thus, the benefits of protection systems for employers can outweigh the costs they incur from state policies, corporate taxes, and employers' contributions or not. The absence of complementarities in MMEs, where state intervention has been pervasive, is therefore related more to the *degree* and *form* of the latter than to its presence per se.

This has important implications for the analysis of complementarities (and non-complementaries) in MMEs. First, the exertion of strong veto powers by organizationally weak socio-economic interests has limited investment in specific or co-specific assets and created serious coordination failures—in wage bargaining, the regulation of the workplace, and the management of social and employment protection. Second, since coordination failures have often been met by state intervention, processes of adjustment are frequently dependent on the gate-keeping role of the state. Third, although the incentives for specific and co-specific asset investment are limited, there have been strong incentives to invest in one kind of asset—political power—creating strong clientelistic links or mutually supportive relations between political parties and their flanking organizations, including trade unions. Fourth, the state's role in correcting for coordination deficits will therefore often be accompanied, and sometimes subverted by, 'compensation' (subsidies, protection) demanded by interest organizations in return for cooperation.

Institutional stability in these systems can quickly degenerate into sclerosis, producing durable 'non-complementarities' between the production regime and the social protection system. State regulation will tend to perpetuate long-term inefficiencies because of the collective action (e.g. prisoner dilemma) problems that ensue. In the absence of mechanisms for collective goods provision, or a state independent and powerful enough to resist vested interest demands, actors will tend rationally to pursue their independently defined interests. Complementarities—the outcome of coordination between freely contracting actors—will prove extremely difficult to build.

Table 8.1 and Figure 8.1 contain a schematic presentation of the differences in organizational logics and complementarities between the three models. The critical importance of employers and trade union organization is presented in Figure 8.1. The more employers are coordinated within strong organizations, and the more trade unions are articulated—both horizontally across sectors and vertically between levels of representation—the more likely it is that cross-class coalitions will emerge. Such coalitions will be able to develop long-term horizons and invest in specific and co-specific assets. It then becomes possible to produce collective goods (e.g. wage moderation, skills, and training provision) and the complementarities that bind them together.

8.2.2. Bringing Politics Back In: A Two-Tiered Framework for Analysis

The interaction between micro (company—local production) and macro (political system) levels in VoC is important for the propensity of actors to invest in specific assets. Asset specificity is positively correlated with the capacity of political systems to make credible the maintenance of certain lines of policy and to diminish the probabilities of radical departures from them. Sharp swings of policy make specific-asset investments risky, while stable policies protect them. In turn, institutional complementarities and asset specificity help condition mobilization by corporate actors and the development of reform coalitions.

Table 8.1. The three varieties of capitalism

	CMEs	LMEs	MMEs
Dominant form of coordination of micro-interactions	Autonomous coordination	Market; arms'-length interactions	Mixed (autonomous + market) with a higher impact of regulation and state mediation
Source of complementarities	Bottom-up induced	Market-induced coherence across policy arenas	State regulatory changes aimed at correcting coordination failures may be dysfunctional
Re-enforcing mechanisms (mechanisms of stability)	High permeability of political system to domestic coalitions	High penetration of policymaking by exogenous economic forces	Gate-keeping role of the state: veto power of domestic actors.
Time horizons	Long-term	Short-term	State regulation may perpetuate long-term inefficient equilibriums
Investment in specific assets	High	Low	Medium-low
Organizational characteristics of interest associations	Employers: strong and well-organized in sectors Unions: politically strong and well-articulated organizations	Employers: fragmented Unions: strong firm-level, but fragmented and politically weak	Employers: fragmented Unions: politically strong but fragmented and weakly articulated
Role of the state	Enabling: protects collective goods	Minimum state: guarantees the effective functioning of the market	Pervasive state: direct production and regulation + correction of coordination failures
Expected reform coalitions	Cross-class	Producer groups, multinational industrial, and financial groups	Class-conflict; fragmented cross-class coalitions (sectoral reform coalitions)

Systems with many veto points (e.g. in consensual/proportional polities) diminish the risk of radical policy change. Majoritarian systems, by contrast, tend to magnify the impact of small shifts of votes, allowing large swings in policy to occur (Hall and Gingerich 2004; Gourevitch and Shinn 2005: 76–7).

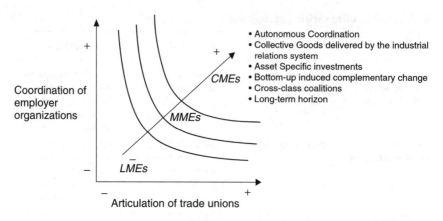

Figure 8.1. The organizational logic of complementarities in varieties of capitalism

Political/institutional frameworks also define the authority of government and hence its leeway for reform. They also determine which other actors can influence policy and to what extent. The LMEs or shareholder systems are typically characterized by majoritarian systems where power tends to be concentrated in the hands of the executive and social actors are by and large excluded from policymaking. The CMEs are typically consensus-based systems in which both the parliament and the executive share power and social-economic actors enjoy de facto (and sometimes *de jure*) veto influence in many policy arenas (Iversen and Soskice, this volume; Iversen 2005). Dedicated assets between interest groups and parties are less likely in majoritarian systems as electoral losses will more readily erase the value of the investment (O'Neil and Pierson 2002: 20).

Two related factors are therefore important for the analysis of MMEs: domestic demands from reform coalitions trying to gain access to the policymaking process and to impose formal and/or informal vetoes upon it; and the degree to which executive action is vulnerable to such pressures. The relative importance of these factors in driving change will be mediated by the structural features of the political system.

We argue that a 'two-tier' approach provides useful insights into the nature of these dynamics and the factors underpinning the degree of 'fit' (i.e. complementary links) and/or 'misfit' (dysfunctional relations) between protection and production. Amable (2003: 34–5), elaborating on Aoki (2001), defines a two-tier or nested game structure for analysing agents' strategies. Institutions provide the rules of the game. The upper tier, the 'meta-level', defines the framework for the lower-tier game. A situation of relative institutional stability

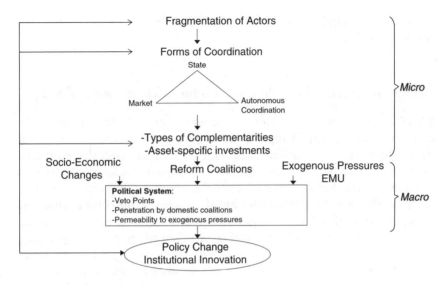

Figure 8.2. A two-tier analytical framework

is preserved in so far as the rules of the game are not significantly altered by the individual strategies devised by lower-level, individual agents.

The two-tier perspective's utility lies in its differentiation of two spheres of action (Figure 8.2). The micro level is important for understanding coordination among economic actors. Here the relevant variables are the fragmentation of interest associations and state intervention. Since MMEs are characterized both by a higher degree of interest fragmentation and state intervention than CMEs, the resulting coordination dilemma impedes the autonomous provision of collective goods. Fragmentation also impedes the consolidation of a stable framework for integrating socio-economic actors into the macro-level policymaking system, making it difficult to build a complementary form of regulation across sub-systems.

This framework allows us to examine the mechanisms whereby lower-level demands are transferred to and negotiated at the macro-political level. While the fragmentation of corporate actors and state intervention helps explain many coordination differences between countries, the character of the political framework is critical for explaining system dynamics (i.e. policy and institutional change). 'State permeability' to vested-interest demands will depend on the involvement of interest associations in socio-economic governance and the character of political institutions. The disruptive effects of 'exogenous pressures' will depend on the 'goodness of fit' between domestic conditions and exogenous requirements and their mediation by political institutions and domestic coalitions.

8.2.3. Institutional Conditions for Adjustment in Italy and Spain

We now turn to the application of the above template to our two MME cases: Italy and Spain. Changes observed in the institutions governing the wage–labour nexus and welfare states of these countries over the last decade or so have attracted the close attention of scholars seeking answers to a series of puzzles: the achievement of macroeconomic stability allowing EMU entry despite apparently intractable initial imbalances; the consolidation and re-organization of collective bargaining systems that have resisted pressures for decentralization, a gradual loss of trade union strength notwithstanding; and renegotiation of the welfare state without delivering across-the-board retrenchment and substantial cuts in benefit entitlements (e.g. Adam and Canziani 1997; Cebrián et al. 2001; Herrmann 2003; Molina 2005). The emergence of novel forms of macro-concertation between employers, unions, and governments has been especially intriguing (e.g. Rhodes 2001; Royo 2002; Regini 2003; Hancké and Rhodes 2005; Molina 2006).

Different analytical tools have been deployed in this venture, but none has been entirely successful in explaining Mediterranean 'exceptionalism'. Neocorporatist theory finds it difficult to explain corporatist-type agreements in countries lacking the organizational capacities for successful concertation. The emergence of social pacts in these and other economies has led to a re-consideration of the theory itself (Siaroff 1999; Regini 2000a; Rhodes 2001; Molina and Rhodes 2002; Siegel 2005). The emerging literature on Euro-peanization has also sought explanations based on the role of the exoge-nous pressures from European integration and EMU (Ferrera and Gualmini 2004; Hancké and Rhodes 2005). But it has been difficult to move beyond a characterization of these pressures as 'catalysts' for domestic change. Their precise nature and the endogenous dynamics they trigger have still fully to be explored.

We argue that an adaptation of VoC theory can help clarify the domestic dynamics of change associated with exogenous shocks. The experience of MMEs in the 1990s has been characterized by the search for new forms of domestic coordination—both market and non-market—conditioned by the existing organizational capacities of socio-economic actors, their veto powers and the coalitions they manage to create. The recalibration of production and protection systems has been carried out through complex processes of political conflict and exchange in several policy arenas that have weakened or accommodated veto actors to varying degrees.

Because these countries share with European continental CMEs a social insurance-based welfare system, protection and production are a priori much more closely coupled than in LMEs. This occurs first through the wage–labour nexus that links protection and production via the industrial relations system and corporate governance practices (Ebbinghaus and Manow 2001: 13; Ferrera, Hemerijck, and Rhodes 2003); and second, through the character of social protection delivered via labour market policies (Martin and Swank 2004). The nature of interest organizations and their mediating role between protection and production, and the opportunity structure for influence provided by the political/electoral system, determine the extent to which either 'market colonization' or new forms of 'autonomous coordination' will result.

We make several related propositions concerning the dynamics behind these processes. First, where the veto powers of trade unions cannot be ignored, employers will search for new forms of 'autonomous coordination'. Second, when the labour movement is weaker, employers will be able to engage in 'market colonization'. Third, in proportional systems there is greater opportunity for unions to become partners in shaping new forms of non-market coordination. Unions in majoritarian systems will have less opportunity to gain access to decision-making and exercise 'positive veto powers'. They may, however, as demonstrated by Greece and France, be able to exert 'negative veto power' in obstructing rather than constructively contributing to institutional change (Natali and Rhodes 2004; Rhodes 2007).

Italy and Spain are interesting cases for examining these propositions. They share numerous institutional features: similar structural cleavages that derive from their MME production regimes; certain common characteristics in their Bismarckian-type social protection systems; and similar (fragmented) forms of interest-group organization. State involvement in the economy has been pervasive in both. And yet their political systems are distinct: more proportional in Italy, closer to majoritarian in Spain.

These factors matter a great deal in explaining policy dynamics and institutional change. So too do the characteristics of interest representation and the potential for inter-class conflict or coalitions. Sectoral cleavages in the production structures of Southern Europe's MMEs are a major source of interest fragmentation. These include a public–private cleavage, due to a large (though now diminishing) state-owned business sector; a cleavage between industries with different levels and intensities of skills; and the cleavage between small and large firms. Differences in the preferences and behaviour of firms have been partly determined either by over-regulation (large firms) or under-regulation (small firms), producing a primary sector of enterprises where unions are able to influence policy through collective bargaining, and a secondary sector of small- and medium-sized enterprises (SMEs) where union organization is weak or nonexistent and management has greater scope for discretion.

These fractures place a serious constraint on both employer and labour organizations. Because their respective associations have to accommodate a large number of differentiated demands, their capacity for creating well-articulated structures of interest representation and delivering collective goods in the industrial relations arena is heavily reduced. Fragmentation also impedes the development of autonomous non-market mechanisms of coordination across sectors and levels in the economic system (Martin and Swank 2004: 593), and augments centrifugal pressures from particularistic demands. Fragmentation therefore profoundly shapes the nature of reform coalitions and their mobilization, either in support of the status quo or for change.

As shown in Table 8.2, Italy and Spain share many associational characteristics, yet they differ on one important dimension: union versus employer membership density. The organization rate of Italian employers is 51 per cent, compared with a 34 per cent union density rate, and is based largely in manufacturing industry. In Spain, however, the employer organization rate of 72 per cent is much higher, with representation spread across industry, finance

Table 8.2. The organizational fragmentation of socio-economic interests in Italy and Spain

	Italy	Spain
Trade Unions		
Main inter-confederal unions	CGIL, CISL, UIL	CCOO, UGT
Main lines of organization	Sectoral-regional	Sectoral-regional
Inter-confederal fragmentation	High	Low (unity of action 1988–2005)
Main divisions in organization	Political–religious	Political
Main divisions affiliates	Sector	Sector
Formal centralization score (*)	2	4
Organizational articulation	Medium	Low-medium
Union density	34%	16%
Employers		
Peak confederation	Confindustria	CEOE-CEPYME
Main lines of organization	Regional-sectoral	Sectoral-regional
Number of affiliates	110	148
Organization rate	51%	72%
Main constituencies	Industry	Industry, finance, services
Formal centralization score (**)	3	3

Sources: Ebbinghaus (2003), Ebbinghaus and Visser (2003), and European Commission (2005).

(*) Austria 7, Denmark 1.

(**) Denmark 6, Japan 1.

Table 8.3. Structural features of the Italian and Spanish political systems

	Italy	Spain
Type of democracy	Consensual democracy; elites perpetuate power relations within the system (until 1992).	Competitive democracy; alternatives in the executive respond to changes in voter's opinions
Predominant institutions	Strong legislature with an increasingly important role for the executive.	Strong executive and limited role of the parliament in the legislative process
Party system	Polarised multi-party system (1980s) Moderate multi-party system (1990s)	Bi-polarism with regional multi-partyism (moderate multi-party system)
Evolution in the 1990s	Change in the party system (+ Majoritarian): increasing strength of the executive	Party alternation in power; increasing importance of parliament
Political cohesion (1)	1.52	0.56
Counter-majoritarian constraints (2)	3	2
Veto-player index (3)	7	6

(1) Gourevitch and Shinn (2005: 73). Index ranked from most majoritarian (lowest value, Canada = 0.04) to most consensual (highest value, Switzerland = 2). Mean value for a country sample of 38 observations is 0.77.

(2) Schmidt (1996). High-values indicate a large number of counter-majoritarian constraints; low values indicate a small number of counter-majoritarian constraints and thus a larger room for manoeuvre for central government.

(3) Schmidt (2000). The higher the value, the higher the number of potential veto players.

and services, while at 16 per cent the union density rate is very low. We explore the consequences of these power differentials below.

The differences are even clearer between the two political systems (Table 8.3). Although there is some disagreement as to the consociational or consensual character of Italian democracy during the so-called pre-1992 'First Republic', (Zucchini 1997; Lijphart 1999; Powell 2000), political parties and the executive regulated conflict through compromise and mutual concessions. Spain is unambiguously associated with a competitive type of democracy. Developments in the 1990s took different directions. While the role of parliament has been strengthened in Spain (Pérez-Díaz 1999), developments in early 1990s Italy initiated a transition from a consensual to a more competitive democracy. Nevertheless, the Italian system contains more veto points and constraints on the government than does that of Spain, which, exacerbated by *partitocrazia*—the domination and exploitation of the state by political parties (LaPalombara 1987)—have severely impeded institutional change.

The number of veto players within constitutional structures, partisan influences, electoral pressures, and practices of co-determination and consensus-creation all combine to shape the content of public policies and domestic responses to exogenous challenges (Tsebelis 2002; Frege and Kelly 2003: 16–17). We argue in the next section that these differences have contributed to rather different solutions to distributive struggles in the two countries. Thus, while both have experienced privatization and the liberalization of goods and services markets (including factor markets such as labour), this process has been more rapid and profound in its consequences in Spain than in Italy, particularly with regards to the liberalization of social protection and labour and financial markets.

But regardless of the different characteristics of the two systems, we argue that both reveal an MME-specific logic of adjustment that is quite different from that found in either LMEs or CMEs. As we know from extensive comparative research (e.g. Swank 2002), LME reform can be rapid due to majoritarian political systems and the relative absence of veto players. In CMEs, institutional change—even when exogenously induced—will proceed slowly and incrementally to accommodate veto constraints and re-calibrate institutional sub-systems. The consensus-based, inter-associational governance that is characteristic of CMEs in the lower micro-level tier (see Figure 8.2) tends to produce a 'bottom-up' accommodation of preferences into the macro-level tier of national policymaking.

In MMEs, however, the weaker (and less productive) linkages between sub-systems make them more vulnerable to the disruptive effects of exogenous shocks and reduce the likelihood of concerted efforts to manage them. Their logics of adjustment will differ accordingly. In the Italian and Spanish cases, deep-rooted industrial relations conflict, which has typically prevented stable, autonomous, inter-associational coordination, makes it very difficult to produce consensus 'from below'. Instead, the dominant logic, we argue, is one of top-down conflict governance, whereby governments resort—pragmatically rather than routinely—to political exchange to accommodate in the macro-tier of policymaking the distributive conflict that emerges from the micro-tier of industrial relations. The weakness of foundations for coordination at the micro- and meso-levels impedes the formation of stable cross-class alliances either across or within sectors. Sporadic concertation provides a mechanism for governments and socio-economic actors to resolve distributive conflict, partially compensates for coordination deficits and increases the overall governability of the system.

8.3. THE EMERGENCE OF NEW FORMS OF COORDINATION IN ITALY AND SPAIN

Below we explore three areas of institutional development and change. The first concerns the mechanisms available for coordination in these MMEs. Pervasive state intervention in the Mediterranean MMEs compensated for the inability of socio-economic actors to provide collective goods and create stable frameworks for autonomous regulation. But that role has changed substantially in the last two decades. The second concerns the differences in the capacity of economic actors to fill the consequent institutional vacuum. Even though a shift can be observed in both countries from an active to a more passive role for the state, the degree and quality of this change has differed significantly. Privatization and market liberalization have gone further in Spain, especially in reforms of social protection, labour markets, and financial markets (Martinez Lucio and McKenzie 2004). The third area concerns the emergence of new forms of coordination for governing policy change and institutional transformation.

8.3.1. Spain: State Retrenchment, Weakly Organized Capitalism, and 'Market Colonization'

Under the Franco dictatorship, the Spanish production system was characterized by high levels of protection and state intervention. The state enterprise sector remained preponderant among large firms and the social protection system remained highly statist well into the 1980s, with little scope for an autonomous regulation of the collective bargaining system by employers and employees (Rhodes 1997*a*).

Spain entered a period of profound transformation after the industrial crisis of the early 1980s and its industrial structure became more polarized. Many sectors were composed of a large number of SMEs specializing in labour intensive manufacturing. They were afflicted by weak and declining demand and lacked the kind of technological and managerial resources required to engage in high-technology, quality-based, rather than price-based competition. The few large publicly owned companies with strategic positions were highly inefficient. Close ties between banks and family-owned firms, and control of the banking system by a small number of commercial banks tightly linked to government officials in the economics ministry were hardly favourable to a different economic development path (Pérez 1997, 1998; Crespí-Cladera and García-Cestona 2001). Access to credit was expensive and the scope for capital accumulation (especially on the part of small firms) was limited. A low level of competition in capital and product markets reduced the incentives for firms to innovate and develop demand for skilled labour (Aguilera 2004). Firms were led to pursue external flexibility in the labour market and support policies to contain labour costs.

A rapidly changing production structure from the 1980s onwards, and the organizational fragmentation of employers and trade unions, both contributed to high levels of social and industrial conflict (Rigby and Marco 2001). After a sudden increase in unionization and mobilization following the death of Franco, difficult economic conditions and the politicization of the confederal unions subsequently led to a similarly rapid decline in both indicators (Jordana 1996; Molina 2006). Employers' organizations, which were still weak, adopted a confrontational approach to union militancy. Despite its monopoly of employers' interest representation, the Confederación Española de Organizaciones Empresariales (CEOE) lacked full negotiating authority due its incoherent organizational architecture and the increasingly important role of multinational companies (MNCs) with their own forms of lobbying and access to the policy process (Heywood 1995: 255–6). These conditions frustrated the consolidation of autonomous, 'bottom-up' coordination as an alternative to state intervention. Although sectoral industrial relations frameworks soon developed at the provincial level, they took the form of narrow collective bargaining mechanisms, subordinate to the dictates of peak-level organizations, rather than firm-based regulatory frameworks facilitating the delivery of collective goods such as training.

The state's role was predominantly one of providing passive forms of assistance to both workers and firms (state aids to industry, early retirement, the extension of unemployment benefits) and the externalization of the costs of adjustment on to workers (via wage moderation and labour market flexibility). Due to the absence of CME-type micro- and meso-level mechanisms of strategic coordination, state retrenchment after the mid-1980s left a vacuum filled in many instances by liberalization and an extension of market principles. The strategy of economic recovery based on FDI inflows followed by the Socialist government from the mid-1980s onwards increased the influence of foreign capital. Attracted by a relatively well-developed infrastructure, low-labour costs and the integration of Spain into the European Community, many MNCs moved the labour-intensive parts of their production chains to Spain. Increased FDI from the second half of the 1980s helped sustain a low-cost labour market and boosted the number of firms whose labour relations were 'sheltered' from the surrounding system.

As for social protection, the Spanish welfare state incorporates elements of both the breadwinner-centred continental model and the citizenship-centred liberal model (Moreno and Sarasa 1992). The state traditionally sought to extend and consolidate a residual and fragmented welfare state, expanding significantly unemployment subsidies and early retirement schemes and deepening the country's budget deficits. From the late 1980s onwards, welfare reform produced a shift away from its original passive, conservative-corporatist character towards a greater emphasis on creating new employment through ALMPs (Moreno and Sarassa 1992: 15; Rhodes 1997*a*).

But the extent of real 'activation' has been limited by the weak capacity of employers and unions for joint coordination. Even though ALMPs have increased since the 1980s, both in terms of funding and in the number of initiatives, the weakness of social partner representation at local levels— demonstrated, for example, by the disappointing results of attempts to draw up local employment agreements—has limited the implementation and utility of these policies (EIRO 1997). A key problem is the lack of organization among small businesses which have paternalistic labour relations and provide little in the way of technical and vocational training (Muñoz 2002). A second factor hindering the success of activation and a managed reorganization, CME-style, of the labour market has been the flexibilization of the labour market at the point of entry through the introduction of new contract types and the extension of temporary employment (Encarnación 2001). Third, under the Socialists, employment policy initiatives—such as the Rural Employment Plan—focused on maintaining income levels rather than training and skills enhancement. Subsidized employment has also been used as an active labour market measure (Fravega 2004).

The first important labour market reform of 1984 established a two-tier model of labour market segmentation (Adam and Canziani 1997; Polavieja and Richards 2001). The higher employment registered in the upturn of the late 1980s relied heavily on the extension of fixed-term employment. In the economic crisis of the early 1990s, Spain used these contracts as a major mechanism of adjustment: it was easier, politically, for the Socialist government to introduce measures to increase entry flexibility than to remove exit barriers which, following the practices of the Franco period, continued to protect full-time, permanently employed core workers (Flórez Saborido 1994: 120; Rhodes 1997*a*; Saint-Paul 2000).

But the perverse consequences of this massive use of fixed-term contracts soon became evident, especially the disincentives they created for specific-skills investment and their detrimental impact on productivity levels. The SMEs used such contracts more than larger companies which could more easily resort to internal forms of flexibility. The SME reliance on temporary employment compounded their low-wage, price-based, medium-to-low technology production orientation. They found labour-intensive strategies to be cheaper at a time of relatively high interest rates than investment in new equipment and technology. The SMEs also paid little attention to on-the-job training, thereby reducing the sunk costs incurred on hiring and minimizing the incentives to keep on employees in an economic downturn. Although more heavily unionized, larger firms also relied on labour market segmentation to discipline the workforce and limit the demands of unions in collective bargaining (Lopez and Verd 2004). They have used internal promotion systems to retain skilled workers and preserve their specific investments (Bayo-Moriones and Ortín-Ángel 2006).

How do we explain a policy mix that has been so unfavourable to workers and employees, and apparently so favourable to firms? Spanish business, though fragmented, has been able to build two parallel coalitions in support of its own regulatory agenda.

First, the existence of a similar pattern of productive specialization in large firms and SMEs has allowed Spanish business, regardless of its fragmentation, to create a single and rather stable class coalition vis-à-vis the labour movement. The latter, weakened by the erosion of its constituency and interconfederal divisions, was forced to adopt a defensive strategy around the interests of protected insider workers. Only in the 1990s have unions adopted a different approach, consisting of a more active strategy based on permanent social dialogue with employers and sporadic, more expedient negotiations with government, with the aim of improving industrial relations governance and introducing consensus-based change in the system of employment protection.

Second, the large industrial and service companies (at the beginning those owned by the state, but from the end of the 1980s also multinationals establishing plants in Spain) formed a coalition with the main banks and the financial sector to speed up the process of product market and financial market liberalization and privatization as well as de-regulation in the labour market (Pérez 1997; Arocena 2004). This 'capital coalition' was assisted in its ambitions by the low degree of trade union access to the national policymaking arena, the erosion of union links with the Socialist Party from the 1980s onwards, the comfortable parliamentary majority and capacity for wielding state power enjoyed by the Socialists, and close links between the ministries of economics and finance. The Socialist government therefore proved to be more open to the demands of the financial sector than the labour movement. The vulnerability of the government to external economic pressures is also an important factor, as the FDI-oriented strategy of the Socialist government required an economic environment attractive for MNC relocation. The process of financial deregulation, though a priori contrary to the interests of Spanish banks, which obtained higher rents from protection (Lukauskas

1997), was nonetheless considered indispensable for attracting capital into the country.

8.3.2. Italy: State Resilience and the Struggle for Autonomous Coordination

The structural conditions under which Italy faced adjustment in the 1980s were similar to those of Spain but also differed in key respects: the existence of a more developed and consolidated industrial structure (at least in the centre and north); better-organized socio-economic actors with a comparatively higher level of representation and influence at local and firm levels; a stronger sectoral framework for collective bargaining; a more developed system of social protection; and the greater resilience and pervasiveness of state regulatory intervention in the production and protection systems (Della Sala 2004).

Adjustment policies in Italy have consequently also been rather different in both speed and orientation. The 1980s–2000s have largely been characterized by policy stagnation punctuated by sporadic, consensus-based reform (Lodovici 1999). Although Italian unions also suffered from organizational erosion, the more proportional electoral system provided them with greater influence and sometimes veto powers over policymaking than that enjoyed by their Spanish counterparts, their inter-confederal divisions notwithstanding. Given the unions' more institutionalized role and higher membership density than in Spain, the left and centre political parties continued to look to them for ancillary support. At the same time, the relative organizational weakness of the employers' confederation, Confindustria, due to pronounced divisions between large and small companies, reduced its influence vis-à-vis both unions and the government.

The state regulatory system in Italy creates an accentuated dualism between SMEs and large firms and produces divergent policy preferences. The 1970 Workers Statute created a highly protective system of labour laws, but only in firms employing more than fifteen workers. This helps explain the resilience of state instruments like the *Cassa Integrazione Guadagni* (CIG), through which the state maintains the wages (and formal employment status) of workers in large companies undergoing restructuring (its Spanish equivalent—Fogasa, or *Fondo de Garantía Salarial*—more narrowly compensates for wages lost by workers due to the bankruptcy or insolvency of companies).

From the 1980s onwards, large firms in crisis asked for CIG help in the form of wage-subsidies as they underwent company-specific restructuring (Franzini 2001). Although imposing high costs on the state, the CIG was (and still is) defended as an employment protection mechanism by the unions and as a conflict-dampening, cost-reducing tool by large firms. It is therefore symptomatic of a limited cross-class coalition in support of the 'compensatory state'. However, SMEs are much less faithful allies of the large companies than in Spain: they have much more limited access to the CIG and their lower levels of unionization make de-regulation and market liberalization more desirable and politically less risky. Thus, Italian SMEs have tried to find their own forms of 'autonomous coordination', given largely dysfunctional state intervention and their relatively weak capacity to influence policymaking.

Given a more even balance of power in the industrial relations arena than in Spain, and greater traction over the policy process afforded the unions by the political system, the extension of numerical flexibility (hiring and firing) in Italy has been gradual and limited compared to other European countries. Regalia and Regini (1998: 464) refer to it as a process of 'articulated de-regulation'. Innovations in labour market policy proceed by consensus and concertation (Regini 2000*b*). Until the mid-1980s, there was a cross-class consensus on the Italian model of flexibility and its limits. Collective bargaining governed the extension of flexibility in hiring practices, working hours, and wages. Unions allowed greater internal flexibility in exchange for a limited extension of external numerical flexibility (Regalia and Regini 1998). Since then, the positions of unions and employer associations have diverged and the introduction of flexibility has followed a sporadic, case-by-case approach. This has prevented employers and the government from implementing more comprehensive market-oriented reforms, and employers and unions from freely and jointly agreeing on coordinated adjustment strategies. It has therefore been difficult to generate positive complementarities by moving closer to LME- or CME-type institutional solutions (Coe and Snower 1997; Belot and van Ours 2004).

Thus, as in Spain, coordination deficits have limited the potential for effective investment in co-specific assets and the development of complementarities between the internal needs of firms (in skilled manpower, for example) and the functioning of the broader labour market. Skills mismatches and bottlenecks have been a major problem for both firms and workers, accounting for a significant proportion of the high rates of unemployment—even in the more prosperous central and northern regions of the country—among the under 25s. As in Spain, the shift towards activation in labour market policies and an expansion of training systems that might have helped correct these problems has been slow, with only a few significant measures introduced in the 1990s.

The two major impediments to the consolidation of ALMPs in Italy mirror those in Spain: the weak coordination capacities of unions and employers and the incentives for maintaining passive forms of state assistance. The *Cassa Integrazione,* or CIG, is a case in point. The use of early retirement schemes (shedding older and employing younger workers) and subsidized employment schemes is also widespread (Contini and Rapiti 1999; Fravega 2004). Again reflecting a more fragile employers' coalition and stronger union countervailing powers, and contrary to Spain, where new forms of flexibility and labour market adjustment policies have reduced social protection, in Italy these new instruments have sustained protection levels. The overreliance of the Italian welfare state on social contributions to finance these and other social expenditures impacts heavily on production by increasing labour costs.

There are two distinctive features of the Italian experience of state intervention in production: its later retrenchment and the consequences for financial markets and corporate governance. The privatization of Italian state-owned companies began in the mid-1980s but only in 1992, with pressure on the budget from the Maastricht criteria, was the first ambitious privatization programme launched (Goldstein 2003). Particularly important was the state-controlled financial sector. Compared to early liberalization in Spain, the non-financial state business sector used its control of the largest financial intermediaries to provide liquidity to industrial holdings. With the exception of the merchant bank Mediobanca, Italy's financial institutions were detached from the corporate governance of the country's private sector (Segreto 1997). Family-control has been perpetuated by cross-shareholdings that strengthen minority positions with a minimum of capital. The pyramidal ownership structures to which they give rise also create formidable barriers to hostile takeovers—locking out both domestic and foreign predator firms (Bianchi, Bianco, and Enriques 2001). For these reasons, regulatory reform outside the financial sector has also advanced at a much slower pace than in other EU countries (Boltho et al. 2001; Deeg 2005).

Under these conditions, the smaller-scale private industrial sector found it much harder to access the financial market than large-scale companies— a factor also creating a strong division within the capitalist camp. The main form of financing for SMEs has been through *commercialisti* and local (often cooperative) banks. *Commercialisti* are accountants or individual business consultants. In order to provide much-needed fiscal advice, they became insiders to the SMEs they were helping and used this position to liaise between client firms and financial intermediaries. In many ways, they became small-scale merchant bankers (De Cecco and Ferri 2001: 77–8). In this respect, the Italian system departs from the bank-based continental model in that banks have never played a central role in corporate governance (Cobham, Cosci, and Mattesini 1999).

Privatization in Italy in the 1990s exerted a positive impact on this situation: by increasing the amount of capital raised on the Milan bourse; by liberalizing the market for financial intermediaries; and by prompting the adoption of new legislative measures to better safeguard the interests of shareholders and increase transparency.

But the divisions between the interests and preferences of SMEs and large firms, the balkanized nature of the industrial-financial sector and the much lower presence of foreign MNCs in Italy combined with the veto powers of the unions and their access to political power to prevent the emergence of the kind of 'capital coalition' that forged a powerful liberalizing agenda in Spain. Nor, until the emergence of *Forza Italia* under Silvio Berlusconi in the early 1990s, was there any equivalent in Italy to either the moderate, market-oriented Spanish Socialist Party (its Italian Socialist counterpart was much smaller and forced into coalition with paternalist-state-oriented Christian Democrats) or the liberal, centre-right Spanish Popular Party.

This socio-economic and political context has consequently led to greater experimentation with 'autonomous coordination' in Italy and to much less 'market colonization'. The creation of new spaces for 'market' forms of coordination has, nevertheless, been important. Given political and legal constraints on labour market flexibility, both firms and workers have sought flexibility via other channels. These include self-employment and exit from the regular sector (covered by collective bargaining) at both ends of the skill distribution: highly skilled workers leave to seek the higher returns to self-employment, while the less-skilled are forced into the more precarious underground economy (Bertola 1990; Erickson and Ichino 1995: 302). Firms have also increased flexibility by sub-contracting to smaller affiliates that operate below the Workers Statute's employment threshold (Ozaki 1999: 10). Since the 1990s they have expanded their use of 'atypical' temporary, fixed-term and part-time workers, as well as so-called Co.co.co (*collaborazione coordinata e continuative*) contracts, which have lower costs and dismissals protection, creating a growing segmentation of the labour market along Spanish lines (Fravega 2004; Graziano 2007).

But the uncertainty created by shop-floor militancy and high-levels of industrial conflict has also driven the search for new spaces and forms of coordination. While these features of the industrial relations system have diminished the propensity of firms to invest in the training of strike-prone workers (Genda, Pazienza, and Signorelli 2001), they have also encouraged the extension of firm-level negotiations—referred to by Regini (2000*a*) as 'micro-corporatism'—to create a more favourable bargaining environment and escape the political constraints of the system's macro-tier. A second mechanism is the development of industrial districts—geographical areas, that is, with numerous productive complementarities: solid vocational training institutions; a flexible and adaptable production system; relatively peaceful labour relations; a close relationship between users and upstream producers of specialized goods; and more cooperative relationships between firms and banks than typically found elsewhere in the economy (Visintin 1999). More recently, the extension of new forms of local and regional concertation under the mechanisms of *programmazione negoziata* has provided the Italian local system of production with yet another form of 'autonomous coordination', although one that is still limited in scope.

8.3.3. Political Exchange and Collective Bargaining

Despite their distinctive adjustment paths, Spain and Italy do share one important similarity: the creation of greater coordination in wage setting. Our indicators of system transformation in Figure 8.3 and Table 8.4 in the appendix reveal that both systems have increased their respective levels of collective bargaining coordination and centralization even if—as argued by Hancké and Herrmann (this volume)—Spanish employers retain greater freedom to differentiate local wage rates in line with their price-based, product-market strategies. Under Single Market and EMU convergence pressures, although in different ways and with different starting points, employers in both countries have sought out new forms of collective coordination with two objectives: the reduction of industrial relations conflict and the institutionalization of wage moderation.

Reflecting the variable veto powers of trade unions and their capacity for mobilization, employers, and governments in both countries have therefore relied on different forms of political exchange—tripartite pacts in Italy, bipartite (employer + union) deals in Spain—as a second-best option to unilateral forms of economic governance. The differences in the processes and outcomes reflect the asymmetries in trade union powers and their respective capacities for influencing the macro-political tier. Although Spanish unions have also relied on political exchange to reach agreements, their weaker political and institutional position has excluded them from making the major inputs into social protection reforms (e.g. pensions) achieved by their Italian counterparts (Natali and Rhodes 2007).

But in both systems, collective bargaining reforms have increased the independence of interest associations as they have moved into the regulatory spaces vacated by the state (Pérez 2000). This process has been more pronounced in Spain, not only because the Francoist industrial relations system was more legalistic and constraining, but because the de-regulation of

Spanish labour relations has gone further. In the 1990s and 2000s, employers' organizations and union confederations in Spain signed several bipartite agreements on vocational training, out-of-court solutions of labour disputes, a re-organization of collective bargaining, and the re-regulation of labour contracts, establishing a quasi-autonomous sphere of labour relations. In Italy, collective bargaining reform agreements have in most cases required the intervention of the state as a third partner.

In both countries, the roles and strategies of employers and trade unions have been transformed in the process. Employers' organizations have sought to strengthen their positions by balancing the interests of small- and medium-sized firms and large companies, hitherto a major source of conflict and divisions. Large companies (with higher levels of unionization) have strengthened the mechanisms for a top-down control by sectoral federations of grassroots organizations. Their SME counterparts have gained a more stable framework for industrial relations.

Trade union trajectories have been more complicated. Concertation in the 1980s had compounded the crises of organization, representation, and mobilization that the labour movements of both countries were facing. In 1980–6 in Spain and 1983–4 in Italy, tripartite social pacts further weakened the position of confederal unions. Wage moderation, the centrepiece of these bargains, was traded for a short-term reinforcement of their role as political rather than industrial actors and this did little to rectify their longer-term problems. By the beginning of the 1990s they were in a critical position. The unions responded by promoting reforms aimed at setting clearer, formalized rules for the industrial relations system. Unity of action among confederal unions was the key for achieving this goal in Italy (Baccaro, Carrieri, and Damiano 2003).

In Spain, unions sought to escape from tripartite social pacts whose costs were immediate and easily perceptible but the benefits diffuse and effective only over the longer-term. Instead, they pursued targeted and specialized social dialogues on collective bargaining reform. Three main aims were pursued: an extension of the regulatory scope of collective bargaining; a formalization of the rules connecting levels within the system; and the consolidation of the national sector as the predominant bargaining level. Their opposition to income policies which were not accompanied by a change in macroeconomic policy led them to abandon discussions in 1993. A change of government in 1997 allowed the unions to reach a successful and favourable deal, thanks to parallel negotiations on labour market reform. Under the 1997 reform the national sectoral federations recovered their bargaining power, but at the same time the capacity of firms to adapt conditions set at higher levels to local conditions was preserved in line with employer preferences. Employers opposed a greater degree of formal centralization, Italian-style, due to pronounced wage and skill differentials throughout the Spanish economy (Hancké and Herrman, this volume).

In Italy, a 1993 reform deal was struck through an inter-confederal tripartite social pact. The unions pursued the consolidation of a bargaining system with strong formal links between higher- and lower-level units of negotiation. They managed to profit from the rather peculiar economic and political conditions pertaining when the pact was signed to formalize and consolidate the two-tier structure: this was the beginning of the EMU-convergence decade, and the old-party system had collapsed, leaving the government in the hands of a 'technical' administration. The reform not only clarified company-level mechanisms of union representation but also established a clear, two-tier distribution of tasks, with the sectoral and company levels pre-eminent. As Hancké and Herrman explain in this volume, because of their greater concern to maintain the productivity-whip constraint and the high-skill/high-quality production opportunities related to bargaining centralization, employers in Italy have been willing to go along with a more homogeneous wage-setting system than that of Spain. In exchange, the unions accepted wage moderation, a restrictive economic policy for EMU entry and the abolition of the *scala mobile* system of automatic wage indexation.

8.4. CONCLUSION: ADJUSTMENT PATHS AND THE SEARCH FOR NEW COMPLEMENTARITIES

To recap our argument, Western Europe's MMEs are more likely than either LMEs or CMEs to experience inter-class conflict under policy adjustment. This is because they lack the micro-foundations for constructing the positive-sum coordination in the lower-tier of the political economy that could eventually sustain a similar partnership at the macro-tier. At the micro-level, employers' organizations and trade unions have been fragmented and disarticulated—characteristics closely related to a pervasiveness form of state intervention in the past: micro-interactions and patterns of coordination were state-controlled and highly regulated, hence compensating for—but at the same time perpetuating—an incapacity for autonomous coordination at local and sectoral levels.

These similarities notwithstanding, the two countries have followed divergent policy paths. Spain has more fully embraced a market logic of reform as the state has withdrawn from its previous paternalist and protectionist modes of intervention. The FDI-oriented growth strategy of Spanish governments (of both colours) since the 1980s has made them more sensitive to calls for liberalization in sectors such as finance. In order to gain the acceptance by domestic financial interests of their liberal agenda, governments agreed to a process of 'controlled deregulation' of the financial sector and the labour market. As revealed by the indicators in Figure 8.3 and Table 8.4, state ownership has declined in both countries, but to a greater degree in Spain. The level of domestic market capitalization as a proportion of GDP has also increased to a higher level in Spain than in Italy. The role of foreign capital in the Italian system has been marginal.

Distributive outcomes differ accordingly. A key difference concerns the distribution of economic adjustment costs. In Spain they have to a large extent been borne by workers, while in Italy they have instead been assumed by the state, translating into higher social contributions for both employers and employees. A case in point is the maintenance of the CIG wage compensation fund. Spain, by contrast, has made it easier and cheaper to make large numbers of workers redundant. Labour market de-regulation has introduced strong elements of flexibility at the margin while at the same time maintaining the privileged positions of insider workers on full-time, indefinite contracts (Toharia and Malo 2000).

Yet, as we also argue, although one can detect more instances of 'market colonization' in Spain than in Italy, both economies are mixing market and non-market modes of coordination in novel ways as they adjust to the challenges to product-markets and wage bargaining that stem from EU-induced liberalization and monetary union. In each case, these innovations are recalibrating the links between the sub-systems of these economies, especially between wage bargaining, employment relations, and production.

As for system trajectories, Figure 8.3 and Table 8.4 present a dynamic picture of change over the 1990s in Italy and Spain vis-à-vis CME Germany and LME UK. In Spain, where there has been a high degree of specialization in labour-intensive, lower-skill, low-technology production, waves of liberalization, and state retrenchment have tended to reinforce sub-system complementarities in an LME direction. The comparative institutional advantage of Spain would seem to rely on numerical flexibility (hire and fire), the expansion of low-paid service sector work, and the growing role of 'impatient' capital. Nonetheless, Spain is still a long way from becoming a pure LME, given its quasi-Bismarckian, insurance-based welfare state, the under-development of the stock market and a relatively well-organized collective bargaining system, compounded by some still very rigid labour market regulations.

Developments in the 1990s and 2000s have also seen a continued search for greater coordination in collective bargaining and vocational training (Royo 2005). These are essential steps if the 'decentral' wage coordination system is to contain inflationary pressures and avoid cost distortions for firms and if general skills provision is to be upgraded in line with both union and firm aspirations (see Hancké and Herrmann, this volume). Even though less anchored in the political system than their Italian counterparts, a full decentralization of collective bargaining, LME-style, is neither possible nor desirable given the influence retained by trade unions in the Spanish system.

The picture is different in Italy where only recently have there been real attempts to liberalize markets and undertake a retrenchment of the state business sector. State resilience has meant the maintenance of a wide range of instruments—both regulatory and financial—of non-market coordination. Dualism continues to characterize the regulatory system and is reflected more profoundly than in the past in the politics of the country. The greater degree of industrial relations influence and political traction of the Italian unions, and the continued fragility of coordination within the employers' camp makes for greater institutional stasis than in Spain and impedes path-breaking shifts in a more market-oriented, LME direction. At the same time, while there has been greater coordination in wage bargaining in the interests of both employers and trade unions, there has been much less consensus on other areas of social protection and labour market reform—a reflection in part of the divisions between the preferences of large and small firms, which has been further complicated by the political developments of recent years. While the former, more closely linked with *Confindustria*, have adopted a strategy of 'equidistance' from the centre-left and centre-right political blocs, and have been cautious in pursuing a strong liberalizing agenda, small firms and younger entrepreneurs have more fully embraced such policies and closely allied themselves with the Northern League and Silvio Berlusconi's *Forza Italia* to achieve them (Lanza and Lavdas 2000).

Consequently, and regardless of the frequently evoked successes of the mid-1990s social pacts (notably in pensions), the level of reform consensus within and across parties and interest organizations in Italy continues to be low, as does the broader legitimacy of economic reform in Italian society. Policy change and institutional transformation are consequently sclerotic and limited—a state of affairs that even the Berlusconi government, in power between 2001 and 2006, was unable radically to depart from. As a result, the institutional incongruencies and misfits found in the Italian production–protection nexus have not been substantially modified over the last twenty years or so.

APPENDIX

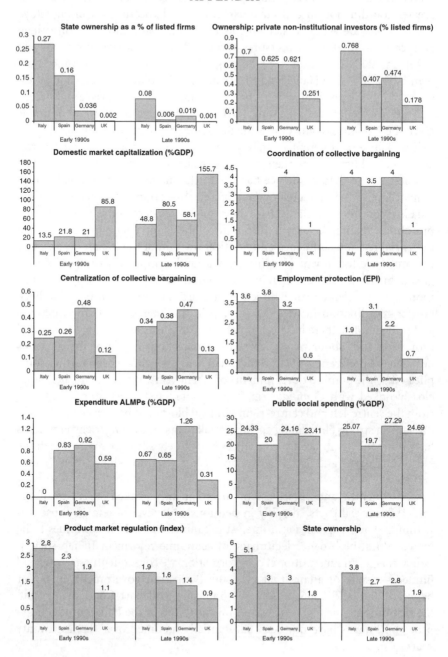

Figure 8.3. Institutional indicators: Italy and Spain versus Germany and the UK, early 1980s and late 1990s

Table 8.4. Institutional indicators in Italy and Spain vs. Germany and the UK, late 1980s and early 1990s

	Italy		Spain		Germany		UK	
	Early 1990s	Late 1990s–2000s	Early 1990s	Late 1990s–2000s	Early 1990s	Late 1990s–2000s	Early 1990s	Late 1990s–2000s
Corporate governance								
Ownership concentration (1)	54.53	na	34.2	na	52.1	na	9.9	na
Ownership concentration (12)	59.6	na	55.8	na	64.6	na	23.6	na
Widely held listed firms (2)	12.98	na	26.42	na	10.37	na	63.08	na
Ownership structure: individuals (% firms listed)(10)	21.8	52.9	35.2	34.6	16.9	15	20.3	16.3
Ownership structure: companies (% firms listed)(10)	20.6	15.8	10.7	5.5	41.6	30.5	2.8	1.2
Ownership structure: state (% firms listed)(10)	27.6	8.1	16.6	0.6	3.6	1.9	2	0.1
Ownership structure: institutional investors (% firms listed)(10)	30	23.2	37.5	59.3	37.9	52.6	74.9	82.2
Minority shareholder: protection index (12)	24	na	50	na	33	na	74	na
Financial system (4)								
Domestic market capitalization (bn$)	148	614	111	726	355	1,079	850	2,460
Domestic market capitalization (% GDP)	13.5	48.8	21.8	80.5	21	58.1	85.8	155.7
Average market capitalization listed firms (Mln $)	579	2,960	259	602	648.4	1,378	436.8	1,294
Listed firms (number)	257	247	429	718	548	1,043	1,946	2,292
Equity raised by initial public offerings (% GDP) (10)	0.18	2.53	0.15	5.07	0.1	1.02	0.93	0.69

(cont.)

Table 8.4. (*cont.*)

	Italy		Spain		Germany		UK	
	Early 1990s	Late 1990s–2000s	Early 1990s	Late 1990s–2000s	Early 1990s	Late 1990s–2000s	Early 1990s	Late 1990s–2000s
Industrial relations								
Coverage collective bargaining (5)	na	70	68	81	72	63	47	36
Coordination collective bargaining (11)	3	4	3	3.5	4	4	1	1
Centralization collective bargaining (5)	0.25	0.34	0.26	0.38	0.48	0.47	0.12	0.13
Coordination bargaining (5)	na	0.42	na	0.48	na	0.43	na	0.19
Labour market								
EPL (6)	3.6	1.9	3.8	3.1	3.2	2.2	0.6	0.7
ALMPs (7)	na	0.67	0.83	0.65	0.92	1.26	0.59	0.31
Social protection								
Index of social protection (8)	0.571	na	0.748	na	0.829	na	0.556	na
Public social spending (7)	24.33	25.07	20.00	19.70	24.16	27.29	23.41	24.69
Unemployment compensation (7)	0.59	0.58	2.62	1.54	1.11	1.31	1.01	0.32
Labour market training (7)	na	0.15	0.17	0.17	0.45	0.33	0.14	0.04
Product market regulation								
Synthetic indicator PMR (9)	2.8	1.9	2.3	1.6	1.9	1.4	1.1	0.9
Indicator of state ownership (9)	5.1	3.8	3.0	2.7	3.0	2.8	1.8	1.9
State involvement in business operation (9)	3.6	2.3	3.5	2.7	2.9	1.5	1.8	1.6
Coordination index (12)	0.87	0.57	0.57		0.95		0.07	

Source: (1) Becht and Roell (1999): data is for the mid-1990s; median size (%) of largest ultimate outside voting block for listed industrial companies. (2) Faccio and Lang (2002); % of publicly traded firms which are widely held, data is for 1996–7. (3) Aguilera (2003): data is for 1996. (4) World Federation of Exchanges http://www.fibv.com: data is for 1990 and 2003. (5) European Commission (2005). (6) OECD (2004): Employment Protection legislation (EPL). (7) OECD Social Expenditure Database, % GDP, data is for 1991 and 1998 respectively (ALMPs = Active Labour Market Policies). (8) Mocetti (2004): data for 1995. (9) Conway, Janod, and Nicoletti (2005): data is for 1998 and 2003 respectively. (10) van der Elst (2000): data is for 1990 and 1999. (11) OECD (2004): periods 1990–4 and 2001–3; data has been updated for the period 2001–3. (12) Gourevitch and Shinn (2005).

9

What Does Business Want? Labour Market Reforms in CMEs and Its Problems

Anke Hassel

9.1. INTRODUCTION

This chapter examines recent reform processes in collective bargaining and training in Germany in the light of the VoC approach. It addresses in particular the interest of business in the reform process. The VoC centres on the capacity of firms to coordinate their activities through either market relations or institutionally based strategic interaction. Both forms of coordination, through markets or institutions, can be equally efficient in securing a successful economic performance by firms. Once a firm is based in one of the two models, it will seek to maintain the comparative advantage which the model provides. With regard to the role of the state, accordingly, business in CMEs is assumed to 'look to the state to protect the institutions of coordination' (Wood 2001a: 251). Firms in CMEs generally have an interest in preserving the institutional capacities that enable coordination to take place, unless the government cannot credibly commit itself to preserving the system. In this case, economic actors are expected to shift towards the model of LMEs because it gives them the flexibility to deal with changing economic conditions (Hall and Soskice 2001). This chapter seeks to address the twin issues of whether, first of all, we find support for the expectation of the VoC argument that business actively supports the institutional structure in a given equilibrium and, secondly, whether recent developments in Germany have altered the preferences of firms towards existing institutions.

Industrial relations, particularly wage bargaining and training, are core institutions of CMEs. Coordinated wage bargaining provides for homogeneous wage levels to be set for given jobs and reduces labour mobility between firms, as better pay is rarely a motivation to change jobs when pay is regulated by central collective agreements. This, in turn, gives employers the reassurance to invest in training since the poaching of skilled labour is uncommon.

Moreover, centralized wage bargaining and the capacity for safe training investments prompt firms to adopt competitive strategies that favour high productivity and quality over low cost strategies (Streeck 1992; Hall and Soskice 2001; Hancké and Herrmann, this volume).

Both wage bargaining and training are embedded in an institutional framework that is partly rooted in legal regulation, and partly results from long-standing patterns of self-regulation of centralized associations on both sides of industry. Moreover, legal regulation and associational self-regulation interact in complex ways, with the structure and competencies of associations being regulated by law and courts. Private actors, individuals or firms, form and mould the associations with their membership; they can, however, not easily escape the effects of these institutions or change them, even if they choose not to belong to those associations. Even though association membership has been shrinking and the effects of institutions have declined, there is no niche within the German economy that can be classified as entirely non-coordinated or completely market based.

The institutional settlement and firms' competitive strategies are therefore complementary: institutions give incentives to firms to follow certain business strategies. The resulting practice by firms leads to investments that are dependent on the capacity that derives from the institutions. This, in turn, gives firms an interest in the maintenance of these institutions. Firms gain their competitive advantages from the institutional settings that allow and support their competitive strategies.

The case of recent reform proposals and changes in the German model, in particular in the area of industrial relations and training, both support and illustrate these arguments. It shows, first, that regulatory changes towards decentralization have been small-scale and generally within the spirit of the existing institutions and, second, that they have not been prompted or lobbied for by business interests. If regulatory reforms occurred or were discussed they emerged within the political arena from actors other than business. In the realm of industrial relations and training, public policy debates and regulatory reforms have only partly coincided with business concerns. Pressures for reform did not stem from business but from mounting public deficits and labour market and social policy inefficiencies that burdened governments. Within the reform processes, business did not pursue radical calls for deregulation.

The chapter thereby follows previous research. Labour market reforms in the 1980s were modest. The Kohl government attempted only a moderate shift in the balance of power towards employers when cutting unemployment benefits for striking workers (Wood 2001a). Firms and employers' associations during that time positioned themselves clearly in favour of centralized bargaining. The German government was very reluctant to deregulate labour markets, despite expert commissions recommending more flexibility and lower social transfers (Wood 2001b: 386–93).

Rather, the chapter argues in favour of a more subtle understanding of current reform processes. Business largely does not want to abandon existing labour market institutions, preferring instead to push for changes that make institutions work in their favour. Business and producer interests are still rooted in the given institutional framework. Their preference is to transform the workings of the institutions towards providing more flexibility for firms but without dismantling them. With regard to collective bargaining, business is mainly interested in increasing the room for unilateral decision-making at the plant level, not in a general decentralization of collective bargaining. With regard to the provision of training, business prefers to continue with existing institutions rather than implementing a training levy, even though this requires business associations to press firms more actively to train.

At the same time, many of the practices of firms and associations in these policy fields have nevertheless changed and, consequently, so has the power balance between business and labour. Without being specific on reform proposals, employers' confederations have started to spend large amounts of money on reform campaigns while they put pressure on the government to keep up labour market and social policy reforms (Kindermann 2005). At the firm level, concession bargaining has spread and has led to major cost-cutting exercises that are not in line with existing collective agreements (Hassel and Rehder 2001). Generally, the ability of associations to generalize and homogenize particular interests vis-à-vis each other and vis-à-vis the political arena has greatly declined. This is not, however, necessarily a sign of an erosion of the coordinating capacity of business interests in the manufacturing sector as implied by the VoC approach. While there is a risk that social partnership—as in its political role—could crumble, and the service sector might suffer from the externalities of existing institutions (Streeck 2001; Streeck and Hassel 2004), the capacity of firms in the exporting manufacturing sector to use these institutions to pursue a high-quality strategy could still be sustained. As a consequence, an increasing dualism can be observed between the high-productivity export sector on one hand and the slow development of a service sector on the other.

For scholars of institutional complementarities and institutional change, this case presents another example of incremental institutional change where, over time, the functioning of institutions adopt a new meaning (Thelen 2004; Jackson 2005; Streeck and Thelen 2005). As in the case of co-determination (Jackson 2005), an examination of wage bargaining shows how the wider political and human aspirations, which were imported into the system up to the late 1980s by the trade unions, gradually faded away and were replaced by a much more narrow conception of the functioning of these institution for business competitiveness. Those who were part of programmes of the 'Humanization of Work' of the 1970s, and the debates about the implementation of these ideas in collective agreements would not recognize the collective bargaining system today any more, even though the structures have hardly changed. Beyond describing patterns of gradual transformation, this chapter also argues that, in order to understand transformation, we need to incorporate the political dynamics of the interest representation of actors and the characteristics of the political process and party competition.

The chapter proceeds as follows: I first recapitulate developments in the area of collective bargaining, particularly after reunification, and discuss recent reform proposals with regard to regulatory reform. Section 9.2 outlines developments in vocational training. Thirdly, I contrast the emerging pictures from these two cases with overall developments, particularly with regard to the egalitarian outcomes of the German model.

9.2. RECONFIGURING COLLECTIVE BARGAINING IN THE 1990s

The LMEs rely on decentralized decision-making regarding wages and working conditions, whereas CMEs tend to have centralized decision-making. However, German collective bargaining was traditionally based on internal flexibility within the framework of high external rigidity. Comprehensive rules in centralized collective agreements were complemented by negotiated flexibility at the plant level. During the 1960s, trade unions negotiated additional agreements at the plant level to capture wage drift (betriebsnahe Tarifpolitik). The implementation of the metal sector wage agreement in Nordbaden-Nordwürttemberg in 1973 required the management and works councils at the plant level to negotiate up to thirty supplementary plant agreements (Billerbeck, Deutschmann, and Erd 1982: 176; Schauer et al. 1984); similarly the framework agreement in 1978 (Sadowski 1985: 244).

The agreements on working time reduction in the metal sector in 1984 opened the way for previously standardized regulation of working hours in central agreements for tailor-made plant-specific working time regimes (Thelen 1991; Bispinck 1997). More than 10,000 plant-level agreements were negotiated following the 1984 collective agreement. Within centrally defined parameters, plant-level negotiations were about finding flexible solutions.

The example of the dispute over working hours highlights the traditional double logic of interest representation on the part of the employers' associations, which is employed until today (Hassel and Rehder 2001): the acceptance in principle of reduced working hours (in spite of the protest of small business) helped to restore social peace at the collective bargaining level while greater flexibility over working time increased the room for manoeuvre at the company level (Wiesenthal 1987: 173 ff.). Employers hoped to compensate for the costs of working time reduction by productivity gains through working time flexibility.

9.2.1. Competitive Pressure in the Early 1990s[1]

Increasing competitive pressures seeded doubt among employers about the collective bargaining system in the early 1990s and forced adjustment processes upon them. The key pressures were the consequences of reunification, the recession in 1992–3, and the increasing internationalization of firms.

First, reunification meant the transfer of wage bargaining institutions from the west to the east. Wages were raised far beyond the productivity of eastern plants, since neither capital nor labour were interested in a low-wage area. Trade unions were afraid of the erosion of the high-wage regime in the west, whereas employers wanted to prevent the emergence of a price-competitive production area (Lehmbruch 1994). Although the reunification process was supported by a massive financial transfer from the west to the east, it could not prevent rising mass unemployment. As a consequence, public debt and labour costs exploded. Moreover, high-wage hikes in the early 1990s did not only affect the east; the west also experienced exceptionally large wage gains, with trade unions claiming their share in what they saw as the unification boom.

In 1992–3 the economy was hit by the worst recession in post-war history, which was accompanied by major job losses, especially in the manufacturing sector. The failures of the past became visible. German business had been deprived of its leadership in quality production and innovation of products. Japanese firms in particular had learned how to produce goods that were both superior and cheaper than German products. As a consequence, German firms had to learn how to improve on price competitive innovations. For instance, the implementation of 'lean production' was accompanied by job losses that could not be compensated for by the reduction of working hours and a social policy which had always been previously a social net for the negative effects of the high-wage strategy (Streeck 1997). Consequently, the costs of social security and labour rose even further.

The declining competitiveness of the German economy was exacerbated by transformations in global production processes. Companies exposed to the world market built up production sites abroad, not only to be present in the most important sales market, but also to benefit from large and high-qualified workforces which they were able to employ for lower and more flexible wages than in Germany. Many companies institutionalized international benchmarking processes that compare production sites continuously in terms of their labour costs and the flexibility of their working conditions (Mueller and Purcell 1992). The plants that come out best are chosen for new investment, whereas others are threatened by closure. Workers who are employed by the same company, but work under different regimes of industrial relations in different countries, compete for investments and job security. The car industry in particular faces this new form of decision-making on investments, as do certain parts of the chemical industry, the tobacco industry and household appliance manufacturing.

The high costs of unification, the recession in 1993, and the internationalization process prompted employers to complain about high and rigid labour costs. As a result, they tried to expand their room to manoeuvre to modify the negative effects of these developments on their firms' performance.

9.3. CONCESSION BARGAINING AS A NEW TOOL

Business, however, did not try to dismantle the centralized bargaining system in response to the competitive pressure it was facing. Rather, it turned to company-level bargaining for a solution. Since the late 1980s, a new type of plant-level bargaining has emerged which goes far beyond the traditional form of company-level bargaining. Rather than implementing or topping up the terms and conditions of central agreements, as in the 1970s, company-level pacts for employment and competitiveness (*betriebliche Bündnisse zur Beschäftigungs- und Wettbewerbssicherung*) have emerged which include a whole bundle of measures to improve competitiveness and job security. The rationale behind the emergence of these pacts is that both groups of actors— management and workforce—suffer from a lack of flexibility in the regulation of firm-specific needs. In this constellation, management and works councils both share the same interest in increased local flexibility, in pursuit of the goal of strengthening the firms' competitiveness and securing jobs.

The transfer of industrial relations institutions to the east in the course of reunification provided a further impetus towards the delegation of bargaining rights to the plant level. The impact of high-wage settlements was felt immediately. In 1993, the coalition of the various political actors which had pushed for the transfer of western institutions to the east fell apart. The east German firms in the metal sector which could not afford to pay high wages any longer denounced the collective agreement (Bispinck 1993; Henneberger 1993). The system was only saved by the introduction of 'hardship clauses' into the collective framework. These meant that companies could apply for exemption from the collective agreement and would be granted this if they met certain conditions. For the first time in post-war history, a German firm which was legally bound by a collective agreement would be allowed to fall short of collective agreement standards in order to survive. Research commissioned by trade unions reported that 181 companies applied for hardship in east Germany between 1993 and 1996 (Bahnmüller et al. 1999).

Hardship clauses in the east were introduced in the midst of the recession. Between 1992 and 1993 more than 0.5 million jobs were lost in German manufacturing. In this context, hardship and exemption clauses spread across all the industries and spilled over to the west in no time. The issues on which exemptions were to be made were similar to those in company-level pacts: flexible and longer working hours, working time reduction with pay cuts, and cuts in pay and basic bonuses. The most generous hardship clause was introduced in the chemical sector agreement in 1995, which allowed companies in hardship a cut in basic pay of up to 10 per cent (Bispinck 1997).

While employers' associations in general aimed to find a peaceful way of introducing flexibility and cost-cutting measures into sectoral collective agreements, trade unions developed a strategy in which they opposed any general concession in principle, but accepted major concessions in individual cases. Hardship clauses therefore emphasize the singularity of the cases by introducing qualifying conditions such as 'in particularly justifiable cases' (as in the 1973 metal sector collective agreement of the powerful region of Nordwürttemberg-Nordbaden). In many cases, these clauses were an attempt to bring the regulations of collective agreements in line with reality, since company-level employment pacts were rapidly being agreed without anyone bothering about the terms and conditions of the relevant collective agreement. Especially in the car industry, company-level pacts had already become a matter of course and preceded the introduction of hardship clauses in the collective agreement.

Concession bargaining at the plant level has led to a deterioration of terms and conditions for large numbers of employees, while leaving others untouched. Today, in a third of companies in the private sector, plant-level agreements exist that provide for terms and conditions that diverge from the industrywide collective agreement. Another 15 per cent of companies simply violate the agreements (Bispinck and Schulten 2003; Seifert and Massa-Wirth

2004). The previous high degree of homogeneity in the labour market has
been reduced.

9.4. DIVIDED EMPLOYERS AND REFORM PRESSURE ON PUBLIC POLICY

Throughout the 1990s, tensions between firms emerged over several issues.
One was the increasing use of plant-level negotiations for lowering costs. This
was a strategy mainly available for big companies, which developed highly
sophisticated work schedules for their large workforces. In particular, the
big manufacturing companies using high-technology equipment were able to
decouple the production process from individual working time arrangements
and thereby achieve high-productivity gains (Silvia 1999). The majority of
small firms continued to keep a standardized working week, while more than
80 per cent of big companies did not, but introduced flexible working time
(Hermann et al. 1999).

The other cause of conflict was over the role of social policy in company
restructuring. Since the early 1970s, early retirement, financed by public
funds, had become the primary tool for organizing mass lay-offs. The stark
increase in numbers of early retirees in the 1990s (see Ebbinghaus 2003;
Trampusch 2005) put an enormous strain on social security funds. Combined with the heavy use of labour market policy and early retirement during
the course of reunification, contributions to social security increased from
35.5 per cent in 1990 to 42.1 per cent in 1998, adding substantially to overall
labour costs (Trampusch 2005a: 80). Again, while big firms benefited from
generous early retirement provisions, small firms were usually not able to
afford the necessary redundancy payments (Mares 2003: 238; Trampusch
2005b: 214).

Thirdly, political strains emerged between industry confederations and
employers' associations, with the industry confederations more publicly critical of existing labour market institutions and the explosion of social expenditure and public debt. Firms, which were usually members of both industry and employers' associations together, were presented with very different
positions in the political arena. In particular, BDI President Hans-Olaf Henkel
steered the industry associations towards a more radical stance on social policy
and the labour market from the mid-1990s onwards (*Sueddeutsche Zeitung*
23.4.1996).

One consequence of the growing rift between employers was a decline
in the membership of employers' associations.[2] The number of firms that
were member of the metal sector employers' association Gesamtmetall halved

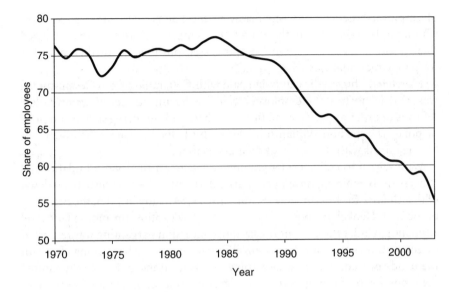

Figure 9.1. Share of employees in the metal sector covered by collective agreements

Note: Until 1991 for West Germany only.

Source: Gesamtmetall (2005), own calculations.

between the mid-1970s and the year 2000 (Gesamtmetall 2005). The share of employees who worked for companies that were members of Gesamtmetall declined from 78 per cent in the mid-1980s to 55 per cent in 2003 (Figure 9.1). Part of that decline was due to the low membership levels in eastern Germany, where only about 20 per cent of employees work for firms that are members of Gesamtmetall. Small employers in particular left the organization as they were critical of its collective bargaining policy, so the regional federations of Gesamtmetall started in the late 1990s to offer firms membership without being bound to collective agreements (OT-Mitgliedschaft). This tool proved to be not only popular, since it created an official free-rider position for small firms, but it also reduced the conflict within the associations. In early 2005, this option was officially recognized by the umbrella organization Gesamtmetall (*FAZ* 1.2.2005).

Also conflicts translated into collective bargaining rounds and were perceived as weakening employers' solidarity, in particular during the metal sector strike in Bavaria in 1995 (Thelen 2000). From the mid-1990s, however, a new compromise emerged within the employers' camp that gave small firms more say in the associations' policy, and this led employers to change their position on social policy. Already from the late 1980s onwards, the leadership of employers' associations was firmly in the hands of medium-sized firms (Trampusch 2005). From the mid-1990s, employers' associations changed their position on early retirement and ceased pushing for further subsidies for public redundancies.

Moreover, a big public campaign paid with €50 million from Gesamtmetall was used to portray the employers' camp as having radical views on policy reforms in order to pacify small firm members without being specific on public policy (Hassel and Williamson 2004). This helped to pacify the discontent of small firms with the policy of their associations.

With regard to collective bargaining, a debate on the legal foundations of concession bargaining developed, particularly after the first near breakdown of the Alliance for Jobs in 1999 (Schulten 1999). Already in 1996, the president of the BDI, Henkel, proposed changes in the law to allow for more plant-level regulation. Under the current legislation, concession bargaining was restricted by court rulings that put the responsibility for collective bargaining clearly in the hands of trade unions and employers' associations and generally limited the scope for bargaining at the plant level to issues that favoured employees (the favourability principle).

While business generally preferred a more decentralized approach, the precise form of a legal change was disputed. The BDI wanted to abolish the clause in the Works Constitution Act that prohibits works councils from dealing with matters that are usually regulated by collective agreements (§ 77 III Betriebsverfassungsgesetz). Without that clause, agreements with works councils could replace collective bargaining. The employers' associations, however, feared a stronger role for works councils and a complete breakdown of the bargaining system. They insisted that plant-level deals should be made easier, for instance by abolishing the 'favourability clause' that rules that plant-level agreements can only be for the advantage of the employee. Generally, employers argued that the main regulatory level should remain the regional collective agreement and works councils should not be able to settle agreements outside this (*FAZ* 27 Jan: 1998).

The debate about the collective bargaining system gained new momentum with Agenda 2010. In a parliamentary speech, the chancellor emphasized the responsibility of the social partners for labour market flexibility and announced: 'I expect the social partners to forge in-company alliances, as is already the case in many sectors. If this does not happen, legislation will have to be passed' (Schröder 2003).

Recognizing the conflict between the unions and the government on this point, the political opposition submitted a proposal for a change in the law. The leader of the opposition, Angela Merkel, of the Christian Democrats

(CDU), persistently claimed that reform of collective bargaining had become the CDU's policy priority on labour market issues. The managing director of the federal employers' association argued vehemently in favour of legal changes in the parliamentary committees. Both announced that the legal changes in the collective bargaining law would be a major issue in the negotiations with the upper house where the government needed the approval of the opposition for other aspects of the Agenda 2010. However, the opposition's proposal was a compromise between the more radical view of the BDI and some industry associations and the concerns of the employers' association that was in itself contradictory (*CDU/CSU-Bundestagsfraktion* 2003). It introduced the possibility for works councils and managers to deviate from central agreements if a vote of two-thirds of the workforce could be achieved, without relinquishing the general rule that works councils should not deal with matters that are regulated by collective agreements.

The attitude of sectoral employers' associations to these proposals was mixed. The chemical employers feared for their cooperative relationship with their sector's union and gave cautious warnings against further political interventions. Metal sector employers publicly backed the opposition, but were also wary about plant-level ballots on collective agreements. Moreover, the legal construction of circumventing trade union approval in line with the constitutionally protected collective bargaining autonomy turned out to be very difficult (Dieterich 2003).

Among firms, surveys reported that 70 per cent of firms were in favour of dealing with wages at the plant level and 80 per cent thought that better solutions could be found if the centralized bargaining system was abolished. However, taking into account the potential conflicts that would also occur, only 23 per cent of firms were in favour of abolishing centralized bargaining, while 73 per cent were in favour of more flexibility within the old system (Köhler 2004).

By the time that the parliamentary horse-trading between the upper and the lower house had been concluded in December 2003, the collective bargaining law had not been touched. Given the legal problems and the mixed support among employers, the opposition did not insist on collective bargaining as a priority in the negotiations with the upper house. However, the pressure on trade unions to support more plant-level bargaining opportunities had increased substantially. The collective agreement in the metal sector that was settled in March 2004 allowed for further plant-level decision-making on working time. The pressure by business to increase firms' room for manoeuvre without making them more vulnerable to union action had succeeded.

9.5. RENEWING THE TRAINING REGIME

The provision of training is an important feature of the VoC approach since it provides workers with a specific type of skill (either specific or general) that is central in shaping the production strategies of firms (Culpepper 2001; Hall and Soskice 2001). The specific skill provision, combined with tight dismissal laws and a generalized wage structure, is a backbone of the incremental production regime of engineering firms in Germany.

At the same time, and in contrast to the collective bargaining regime, vocational training has a high public policy profile, since it is seen to be the most effective policy instrument for keeping youth unemployment at low levels. In Germany, the gap between adult and youth unemployment rates has traditionally been small compared with other OECD countries (Table 9.1). Moreover, a broad range of training places on offer has also reflected the individual right, guaranteed in the constitution, for a free choice of profession. Employers were expected not just to give every school-leaver an apprenticeship, but to ensure that the number of vacancies exceeded the number of job seekers. The challenge of maintaining training numbers is therefore a problem of overcoming sub-optimal investments in training, as identified by Gary Becker from a firm's perspective (Becker 1964), which presents a difficult public policy problem. Therefore, as Culpepper has pointed out with reference to the transfer of training institutions to eastern Germany, it is the combination of public policy and institutional support from other parts of the industrial relations system (i.e. the pressure by works councils and the wage structure) that has traditionally accounted for the high number of training places (Culpepper 1996).

The balance between employers' investment in skills within the framework of a CME and the public policy role of vocational training changed fundamentally between the 1980s and the 1990s. While employers' efforts to train apprentices diminished due to a lack of demand in the 1980s, training in

Table 9.1. Unemployment rates in EU member-states for all age cohorts and young unemployed under 25, 2001

	B	DK	D	FL	F	GB	IRL	IT	NL	AT	P	S
Unemployment rates all age groups	5.4	3.5	7.5	7.4	8.1	3.9	3.2	7.6	2.4	3.6	3.5	4.1
Unemployment rates for under 25-years old	15.3	8.3	8.4	19.9	18.7	10.5	6.2	27.0	4.4	6.0	9.2	11.8

Source: OECD Employment Outlook (2002).

the 1990s was perceived as being in crisis because not all school-leavers were catered for. Tripartite consultation rounds, the threat of introducing a training levy, and a voluntary commitment by business to increase the number of training places all put pressure on business not to neglect the issue.

9.5.1. The Evolution of Training in the 1980s and 1990s

While not perceived as worrying at the time, during the 1980s apprenticeships declined at a rapid rate. From 700,000 new apprenticeships in 1984 the numbers dwindled to 500,000 in 1990 in West Germany (Figure 9.2). The main reason for this decline was the lack of demand by school-leavers. In every single year during the 1980s, supply exceeded demand by several tens of thousands; in the early 1990s more than 100,000 apprenticeships remained unfilled.[3] Numbers of school-leavers declined, while at the same time the higher education system expanded. Apprenticeships had lost their attraction for young people.

With reunification, the situation changed. Apprenticeships had also been part of the East German training regime and they were integrated into the West German system. Within two years, the number of apprentices went up

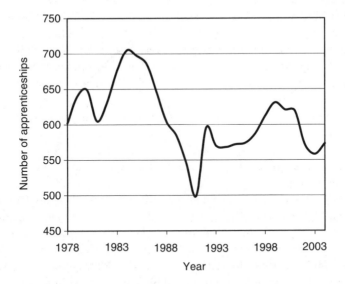

Figure 9.2. Apprenticeships, 1978–2004

Note: Until 1991 for West Germany only.

Source: Bundesinstitut für Berufliche Bildung; BIBB/AB 2.1/J.G. Ulrich; personal communication.

by 200,000. Also as in West Germany after the war when business made extra effort to train the new workforce, even against the resistance of the Allied forces (Thelen 2003), training was seen as a priority in Eastern Germany.

The build-up of training in the east, however, coincided with the recession in the early 1990s as well as with higher numbers of school-leavers there. In the very beginning, training offers in the east just about matched demand. However, from the mid-1990s onwards, demand for training places in Eastern Germany exceeded supply significantly. This process was matched in West Germany, where increasing numbers of school-leavers were unable to find apprenticeships. In stark contrast to the 100,000 surplus training places seen in the early 1990s by September 2003, there were 46,000 young people registered by unemployment agencies as still looking for an apprenticeship.[4] The DGB estimates that in 2002 overall, 200,000 young persons under the age of 25 were still looking for training (DGB 2003). This trend is also reflected in Figure 9.3, which shows the declining share of apprentices among 15-year-old school-leavers.

The crisis of the training system which developed during the 1990s stemmed from an increasing demand for apprenticeships and this coincided with an upsurge in competitive pressures on firms which, together with the

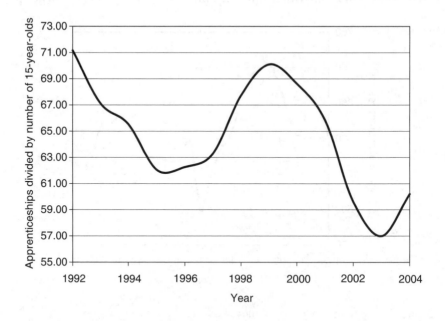

Figure 9.3. Apprenticeships as a share of 15-year-olds

Source: Bundesinstitut für Berufliche Bildung and Statistisches Bundesamt; own calculations.

recession, placed a number of new constraints on firms. In the east, the problem was exacerbated by the lack of big firms that can act as the core in inter-firm networks for the encouragement of training and technology (Carlin and Soskice 1997, quoted after Culpepper 1999*a*: 51).

On the whole, however, there is little indication that the training efforts of private firms have substantially diminished because of a lack of interest by firms in vocational training, as is often claimed in the public discourse as part of a bid to pressurize firms to boost apprenticeship numbers. Between 1996 and 2004, the number of apprenticeships in the non-artisan sector has increased from 260,000 places to 313,000 with a peak of 333,000 places in 1999. The decline of apprenticeships was more pronounced in the artisan sector which has suffered from heavy job losses since the late 1990s.

Also the share of companies offering vocational training places has remained stable over time throughout the 1990s. According to data of the company panel survey by the Institut für Arbeits- und Berufsforschung (IAB), the share of companies that train stands at 30 per cent for west Germany and 26 per cent for east Germany. Between 1996 and 2002, figures have first slightly increased and after 2000 decreased. Roughly 50 per cent of all firms do not have a licence to train.

Moreover, training figures look rather healthy, if seen in the context of the rapid structural change of the German economy and high unemployment. Vocational training takes place primarily in the manufacturing and artisan sector, with the service sector lagging behind. The employment share of manufacturing has declined from 40 per cent in 1990 to 31.3 per cent in 2003.[5] Also the overall number of participants in the labour market has declined during the same period from 37.5 million to 36.1 million active labour market participants (Erwerbstätige). In particular big firms have reduced their workforces within Germany while increasing them abroad. In our study of the 100 biggest firms in Germany, we found that these firms had reduced their workforce by 5.8 per cent between 1986 and 1996 (MPI 2002, S. 16). Taking these structural changes of the workforce into account, the training record of private business has remained substantial, albeit still insufficient to clear the labour market of young school-leavers.

9.5.2. Avoiding the Training Levy

Public policy initiatives have primarily been centred on the issue of deficient numbers of training places for school-leavers. The unsatisfactory training record first became an issue at the Alliance for Jobs in 1998, when business associations committed themselves voluntarily to increase their training efforts. In several rounds of discussing the state of vocational training, new pledges were made from both sides of industry to engage more in vocational training. While the number of training places increased up to the year 2000, they fell again afterwards. Due to the mounting numbers of school-leavers unable to find training places, the tripartite summits on training continued even after the Alliance for Jobs had finally failed in 2003. The effects of the tripartite declarations were however small since they consisted of separate suggestions proffered by both sides of industry with little attempt to reach a consensus on how to handle the crisis.

On 14 March 2003, Chancellor Schröder addressed the issue of training in his parliamentary speech on the Agenda 2010 by exhorting business to keep up their training efforts. He announced that if these expectations were not met, the issue would be dealt with by introducing a training levy that would charge those firms failing to train and subsidize those which did. A training levy had been a policy tool that the youth organization of the SPD had developed in the mid-1990s while still in opposition in order to force companies to increase their training efforts.

Consequently, when the newly confirmed commitment by business to increase their efforts to train made at the summit 2003 did not lead to the expected results, the SPD parliamentary group presented a law on the training levy. The business community was vehemently opposed to such a law and threatened a drastic decline in training if companies had to pay up. The opposition rejected the law as socialist in nature, a new tax for firms and overly bureaucratic. The unions and the left of the SPD were in favour of the law, since they perceived the Agenda 2010 as socially unjust. They saw the levy as a way to force firms to accept responsibility for the labour market situation. Within the government, the law was not well received, and was seen as a concession towards the left. As a compromise to opponents within the government, the law included the promise to not implement the levy if business made a credible commitment to provide more trainin facilities.

After the law passed the lower house and before it was dealt with in the upper house, intense negotiations between the government and business and employers' associations took place. Business associations—in particular the chambers—were overtly upset about the process and were at the same time pressurized by some member organizations and the opposition party CDU not to deal with the government, in order to avoid giving it legitimacy in dealing with the issue of training. The employers' confederation, BDA, which is closely intertwined with the CDU parliamentary group, proposed major changes in apprentices' pay in return for its willingness to sign up. The BDI had initially refused to take part in the deal. The representatives of the chambers, however, sought a pragmatic solution for avoiding an extra charge on companies. The chambers also used the training issue to regain legitimacy, which was doubted by the Green Party and parts of the SPD.

A survey among firms showed that although 68 per cent of them opposed the levy as increasing costs and not solving the problem, only 9 per cent of firms said they would reduce their training efforts when the levy was implemented. A mere 5 per cent of firms stated they would increase the number of training places (Klös 2004).[6] The opposition among firms against the levy was therefore not strong enough to mean that firms would change their training behaviour if it was implemented.

On 13 June 2004, a training pact was signed by all four business associations (the two chambers, the employers' association BDA and the BDI) and the government in which business pledged to provide 25,000 additional training places and the same number of firm placements for school-leavers.[7] In exchange, the government pledged to improve the education levels of school-leavers, to subsidize placements and to make training regulations more flexible. No sanctions were included if business were to fail to live up to its promises.[8] The law on the levy has since not been dealt with in the upper house.

The tension between the political aim of making business responsible for the employment opportunities of school-leavers and the interests of business to preserve the existing skill provision mechanism has been resolved by a compromise that maintains the current system and involves a commitment by business to keep up training. Business could not reject the political responsibility of getting youngsters into training, but it has managed strategically to preserve the mechanisms of skill provision. The business community has not opted to walk out of the training system, even though it had the opportunity to do so. The chambers that are the main coordination device in training were strengthened by new legitimacy in training. The levy could have potentially undermined the vocational training system by shifting the majority of training to public schemes, if companies had reacted negatively against it and reduced their training efforts. In the shadow of the law, the business associations jointly gave renewed support to the existing training institutions. In 2004, the numbers of training places offered by business increased by 4.5 per cent (see Figure 9.2).

9.5.3. The Reform of the Regulatory Framework of Vocational Training

While training numbers have not reached worrying low levels, there is nevertheless growing concern about a serious mismatch between the capacity of firms to provide training and the existing regulatory framework that actually makes it more difficult for firms to train. The regulatory framework is partly based on the Law on Vocational Training (Berufsbildungsgesetz) that lays down the fundamental regulations and procedures regulating job certificates and training standards. It provides for a close cooperation between trade unions and business representatives in the framework of vocational training committees of the chambers of industry and commerce (Industrie- und Handelskammern, IHK). Regulation is also based on collective agreements that regulate pay and working conditions for trainees and in some industries also guarantee further employment for trainees after their training has ended. In some cases, notably the chemical industry and some regions of the metal sector, collective agreements exist that provide financial subsidies for training. Moreover, the pay of trainees is legally fixed by requiring 'appropriate pay levels' that in practice makes collective agreements on pay for trainees mandatory for all firms.

The rising costs of training have been a concern for sometime. Whether costs of training are counterbalanced by benefits has been a controversial issue. The research institute for vocational training (BIBB) has always argued that for any individual employer the benefits of providing training outweigh the costs. However, since the early 1990s the cost–benefits analysis of training firms has been changed by the increasing amount of time apprentices spend in training centres and the above-average increases in pay for apprentices. As Figure 9.4 shows, pay increases for trainees have been above pay increases for

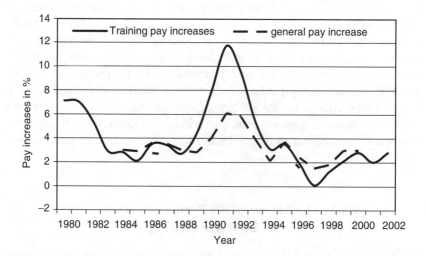

Figure 9.4. Pay increases for trainees and other employees
Source: WSI-Tarifarchiv; own calculations.

adult employees in the 1990s. Between 1984 and 2000, average annual wage increases for trainees were 3.9 per cent, whereas for adult employees it was 3.2 per cent.[9]

Therefore, pay for trainees has become a point of discussion among employers. According to the annual educational report 1998, 45 per cent of employers would like to cut trainees' pay (Culpepper 1999*a*). In a survey by the employers-based research institute IWD on vocational training, 73 per cent of firms agreed or partly agreed with the statement that the costs for training are too high (Nackmayr 2003). The national umbrella organization of the chambers, the DIHK, also lobbies for the abolition of the regulation of pay, while employers have frequently proposed cuts in pay. Employers argue that pay should be lowered to the benefit level that young people on publicly funded training schemes receive (DIHK 2003). Since most apprentices these days are 18 years and over, employers also demand to adjust the rights and duties of apprentices to those of adult employees.

These proposals, among others, were submitted to a major reform of the regulatory framework of vocational training that was negotiated during 2004 and passed in January 2005. The reform is the biggest since the conception of the law in 1969. The liberal party (FDP) and the majority of the state governments in the upper house (Bundesrat) submitted changes in favour of lowering trainees' pay, which were rejected by the majority of the Bundestag.[10] Apart from this, the government coalition and the CDU have largely cooperated on a wide range of issues regarding reform of the vocational training law. In particular, the adjustment process of professions to technical and structural change was speeded up by giving authorities the opportunity to override blockages in training committees. Training schedules are organized on a more modular level by giving the rising numbers of dropouts the opportunity to gain some certificates, if not a full-blown apprenticeship. The legal reform particularly encourages cooperation in training (Ausbildungsverbünde) either between firms or between schools and firms. These cooperative structures have been successfully practised in eastern Germany (Culpepper 1996).

The reform of the law on vocational training occurred during a time (2004) when most of the governments' reform proposals were at an impasse and the social partners were vehemently opposing each other in the public sphere as for example in the area of collective bargaining. This reform, however, was only mildly criticized by the trade unions (among other things for a lack of quality control and the acceptance of completely school-based training), and largely conducted as a large consensus-oriented project. It reflected a degree of cooperation that had already been noted by Wolfgang Streeck et al. (1987), when commenting on the vocational training system: 'Trade unions and employers are far apart when it comes to the question of how training should be financed and to what extent individual employers providing training should be the subject of external supervision.... But the public debate hides the fact that neither side doubts that each school leaver should have access to high quality vocational training and that training should be continually upgraded and modernized. While both sides find the existing system wanting in important respects, neither finds it wanting enough to be willing to let it fall into disuse or decay' (Streeck et al. 1987: 3–4; also Thelen 2003: 49).

9.6. CONCLUSION

The two cases of recent regulatory reforms in collective bargaining and training in Germany examined in this chapter offer valuable insights into the process of adaptation and negotiation of institutional reform. They show distinctly that, despite vehement public debates about the German industrial model, reform steps were taken in the traditional incremental manner that keeps existing institutions intact and adapts their functioning to a new environment (Katzenstein 1985). In both cases, actors aimed to preserve existing regulations rather than to radically change them. The reasons for small-step changes are primarily that existing institutions continue to provide rents for those actors that have a political voice (unions, big firms, and employers' associations) while more radical changes in the regulatory regime create uncertainties which they cannot control. All economic actors therefore erred on the side of changing practices within given institutions. Moreover, none of the actors have had a vision on how a radically different institutional setting would look like and work in the German environment.

In both cases, the practice of the institutions has changed. In collective bargaining, the unions' agenda of shorter working time, humanization of work, and participation has been largely wiped out. Working times for full-time employees have been rising since the mid-1990s. Even the trademark of German trade unionism, the 35-hour week, has been effectively shattered (Statistisches Bundesamt 2002).The majority of white-collar employees in the car industry have returned to a 40-hour week. Working time has become highly differentiated and subject to the competitiveness and productivity of firms.

In training, firms have largely upheld their training records and the regulatory regime of the training system. In order to maintain the system, firms have even grudgingly acknowledged the public responsibility of business to provide sufficient training places for all school-leavers. Complaints about the increasing problems of immigrant youth with low educational records—6 per cent of children dropout of school without any certificate—has not let employers off the hook in providing sufficient training even for those youngsters. In reality, however, these school-leavers end up in further school education and not in an apprenticeship.

9.6.1. Institutional Change and the Policy Process

Categories of institutional change such as *displacement, layering, drift, conversion*, and *exhaustion*, as offered by Streeck and Thelen (2005: 31) point to different underlying mechanisms of change, such as defection in the case of displacement and reinterpretation of institutions in the case of conversion.[11] The problem is, however, that processes of change in national institutional regimes combine elements of all suggested types of change. Defection of firms from the collective bargaining system induces patterns of displacement through other mechanisms of wage regulation as well as a reinterpretation of the bargaining system per se and its exhaustion. In other words, it is not only, and maybe not necessarily, the finer distinctions of forms of transformation that make us understand patterns of change but a better understanding of the driving forces.

Here, we need to sharpen our understanding in two respects: first with regard to the actors that are part of the process of change and second regarding the political process. Actors—particularly firms—have not only different interests depending on their product and labour markets but also different capacities to overcome problems of collective action (Martin 2000). Employers' associations that are organized on industry lines tend to mediate between these different interests in order to keep their affiliates at bay. Unlike small employers in the USA, small firms in Germany are not in a position to voice new policy proposals or induce change but merely to create rifts within associations that lead to blockages in the policy process.

As a response to this problem, employers and business themselves have developed a division of labour by which business associations still advocate more liberalization and deregulation with regard to collective bargaining, but employers' associations have regained control over the issue. Radical proposals on economic and labour market policy that are more in line with small firms' concerns have been voiced in campaigns, such as the New Social Market Economy, but have not been translated into policy proposals. Discontent among small- and medium-sized firms has therefore been largely obscured by good public relations. This process has been helped by the growing weakness of the unions, and the increasing market orientation of the government after Agenda 2010 was launched in March 2003. Thereby, German business was also able to defend existing institutions because of its ability to mute protests from small- and medium-sized firms, which in turn do not have strong independent means of interest representation.

Regarding the political process, we need to be aware of the fact that party competition and vote-seeking behaviour follow a logic that runs independently from economic interests. While policymakers take economic interests into account, they also respond to popular pressure and electoral opportunities (Swenson 2002: 37). Competition between the two major parties has pushed them to adopt opposing positions on the regulation of collective bargaining that created more problems for the conservative CDU than for the governing SPD.

The red-green government was pressurized from the left wing of the SPD and the trade unions to maintain these institutions and not to interfere with their main functions, in line with their own party manifesto. The CDU, however, has pledged a more radical proposal on collective bargaining to prepare the grounds for a possible coalition with the liberal party FDP. Given the antipathy of the employers towards regulatory decentralization, their proposal was, however, contradictory in its attempt to reconcile market rhetoric and employers' concerns. The fear of decentralization and market forces were stronger than the urge to present a cohesive reform agenda.

However, pro-reform forces also existed in the government camp, where existing collective bargaining regulation was perceived as rigid and contributing to high unemployment. In the complex negotiations between the upper and lower house on the reforms of the Agenda 2010, it was possible that collective bargaining rules could have been reformed in exchange for other reforms at the insistence of the prime ministers of some of the conservative *Länder*. The possibility of such 'collateral damage', which would not have reflected the economic interests of the main part of business, should not be ruled out per se. In other words, the dynamics of the political process can induce regulatory changes that in turn trigger off unanticipated and unintended institutional change.[12]

9.6.2. A Less Social-Democratic but Still Coordinated Market Economy

Compared with earlier periods of welfare expansion when the strong protection of skilled workers was accompanied by a general expansion of welfare and an egalitarian distribution, which was accepted by employers, business' interests on social policy, training and collective bargaining today are more narrowly defined around the interests of the core employee. At the same time, the capacity of trade unions to diffuse productivity gains through large segments of the workforce has been confined. While the coordinating capacity of institutions remains, their previous egalitarian distributional outcomes are undermined by cost-cutting measures in social policy, at the plant level and competitive pressure in unregulated parts of the economy. Moreover, the existing institutions did not protect organized labour from a drastic decline in organizational and political power.

Unions have lost considerable power—in the market and in politics. On the surface, their financial resources, legal and organizational structures, and personal political links still assure them a measure of influence on the government and big companies. However, trade unions in Germany have lost more members over the last ten years than any other country in the EU except for the Eastern European transition countries (Eiro 2004). Since the early 1990s, unions have lost more than 4 million members, a third of their membership. Membership as a share of total employment is down to 20 per cent. Union density among young employees is down to 10 per cent (Ebbinghaus 2003: 193).

The labour market that has emerged is less regulated than is commonly assumed and union influence is concentrated on big manufacturing firms and the public sector. One should recall that big manufacturing companies in LMEs also have strong union representation. The regulatory power of the unions in these countries does not, however, extend beyond these plants. It has been a feature of the German model of labour market regulation that agreements were forged that set universal rules for the vast majority of employees. This system is being eroded by company opt-outs and concession bargaining.

At the same time, there are signs that the weak performance of the labour market is related to the core institutions of the German model. Strong employment protection has led to a high degree of labour market segmentation and low degree of labour market mobility. More than a fifth of young workers under the age of 30 (not counting those on vocational training contracts) are employed on temporary contracts which forestall employment security and dismissal protection (Statistisches Bundesamt 2002). Long-term unemployment as a share of the unemployment total is exceptionally high at 51 per cent compared to 33 per cent average in OECD countries. Unemployment among the low-skilled and elderly employees is particularly high and chances for the long-term unemployed to get back into work are particularly low (Benchmarking Deutschland 2001: 80).

High taxation of wages through social insurance contributions crowds out a low-skilled, low paid segment of the labour market. In order to provide job opportunities for the low-skilled, labour market segments were exempted from social security charges through so-called mini-jobs and midi-jobs. In September 2003, there were 6.7 million workers employed in mini-jobs (Hassel and Williamson 2004).

Despite relatively compressed wages in the manufacturing sector, 17 per cent of all German employees receive low wages. Germany comes third in the share of low-paid workers of all workers, immediately after the UK and Ireland (Eiro 2002). Moreover, the incidence of low pay is more closely related to poverty in Germany than anywhere else in Europe. Low-paid workers are most likely to live in poor households. In the UK and Ireland, low-paid workers often live in households with higher incomes.

The evidence suggest that a dualism has emerged within the German economy between a core of the manufacturing exporting-oriented sector where the combination of high productivity, high pay and high skills is still dominant and a fringe sector that comprises services and parts of the manufacturing sector in which employment is insecure—often on fixed term contracts— and pay is relatively low. Moreover, company restructuring, outsourcing, and concession bargaining have led to a complex interaction of core and fringe employment even in the core manufacturing sector. Employment security and high pay for skilled workers is undermined by an increasing share of fringe employment at the expense of core employees. At the same time, core employees are hit by a loss of pay and working conditions through concession bargaining. This process resembles the flexibility drive that has occurred in LMEs during the 1980s (Wood 1989). Centralized wage bargaining and the training regime do little to protect employees from these developments. Rather, they are used as tools by firms under the rationale of social partnership to ensure that this transformation proceeds in a peaceful manner.

These empirical findings do not refute the VoC approach. They direct our attention instead to the rather implicit assumptions of the relationship between production systems and wider distributional outcomes. In the VoC approach, LMEs and CMEs possess not only different capacities for innovation, they also tend to distribute income and employment differently (Hall and Soskice 2001: 21). In CMEs income inequality is lower comparatively, while working hours also tend to be shorter. The correlation with distributive outcomes and even economic performance is however not a central part of the firm-centred VoC perspective. What seems to become increasingly clear is that the link between distributive outcomes and coordinating institutions is not a direct one. In other words, while coordinating institutions help the German manufacturing sector to remain competitive, they do little to preserve the previously egalitarian nature of the German model.

NOTES

1. The next two sections rely heavily on Hassel and Rehder (2001).
2. We do not know much about membership in industry association but do not have any indication that membership also declined there.
3. BIBB/AB 2.1/J.B. Ulrich/Stand: 18.11.2003; personal communication. See also Culpepper (1999a), Table 9.1.
4. Bundesanstalt für Arbeit, Statistik IIIb4, personal communication.
5. Mikrozensus by the Statistische Bundesamt.
6. Survey of 1.018 firms on the training levy in April 2004.
7. National Training Pact. See: http://www.bmwi.de/Redaktion/Inhalte/Downloads/nationaler-pakt-fuer-ausbildung,property=pdf.pdf
8. Unofficially, the government also committed itself to keep the increasing criticism of the obligatory membership in chambers at bay. The Green Party was always suspicious towards the Chambers of Industry and Commerce and pushed for their abolition. At the end of the first term of the red-green government a report was commissioned on the 'efficiency' of the chambers. Also in the Social-Democratic Party there are individual MPs, who would like to remove the coercive nature of chamber membership by firms.
9. The figure refers to pay increases in collective agreements, not to actual changes in nominal wages.
10. See for the proposal by the FDP Bundestagsdrucksache 15/3325, 16 June 2004, and submission by the upper house Bundestagsdrucksache 15/4111, 3 November 2004.
11. The five types of gradual transformation and their underlying mechanisms (in brackets) are Displacement (defection), Layering (differential growth), Drift (Deliberate neglect), Conversion (Redirection, reinterpretation), and Exhaustion (Depletion) (Streeck and Thelen 2005: 31).
12. Another source for triggering off unintended institutional change is the rulings by the supreme court, in particular the supreme labour court, that dominate the interpretation collective bargaining legislation. For instance, a change in the interpretation of the monopoly of representation rights of trade unions can have far-reaching consequences for collective bargaining practices.

10

Economic Shocks and Varieties of Government Responses

Torben Iversen

10.1. INTRODUCTION

There is a widespread perception that the welfare state and policies of the left have been eroding in the past several decades as a result of globalization, technological change, and other forces of change. Also, it has been argued that government responses to these changes are quite similar across institutional 'varieties' (Pontusson 2002). If so, this challenges the idea, central to the VoC perspective, that large welfare states are complements to the system of production (Estévez, Iversen, and Soskice 2001; Iversen 2005). In a VoC framework, exogenous economic shocks are expected to lead to different government responses depending on existing institutional frameworks. Yet there is little in the original versions of this theory that explains the *politics* of how shocks get translated into policy. The focus, instead, is on equilibrium conditions or comparative statics (Hancké, Rhodes, and Thatcher, this volume). This chapter seeks to fill some of the gap by examining the relationship between social spending in different institutional environments and shocks to the income and risk structure. There are two broader objectives: one is to develop a dynamic model of government responses to change—something that the the VoC approach is often accused of being unable to capture (Howell 2003; Hancké, Rhodes, and Thatcher, this volume). The other is to suggest how to understand the relationship between varieties of production systems and political institutions (in particular electoral systems). This is a topic the VoC literature has mostly skirted (Hancké, Rhodes, and Thatcher, this volume).

Building on Iversen and Soskice (2001), the analysis begins at the level of individual preferences, and focuses on two mechanisms linking shocks to policy preferences. It then shows how the translation of these mechanisms into policy, in response to external shocks, is mediated by economic and political institutions. Finally, it suggests some implications of this for the existence of complementarities between political and economic institutions.

The first individual-level mechanism concerns popular preferences for redistribution and takes off from Meltzer and Richard's well-known model in which those with income below the mean prefer at least some redistribution (Meltzer and Richard 1981). Assuming a right-skewed distribution of income, and that the median voter is decisive, the implication is that greater income inequality leads to more redistribution as the gap between the mean and median incomes increases. From this perspective the median voter preference is 'counter-cyclical' in the sense that support for redistribution rises in line with inequality and thus acts as a 'automatic stabilizer' in the face of growing inequality.

The second mechanism is rooted in the notion that support for redistributive spending is at least partly driven by the desire of people to insure themselves against income losses. Even if the intention is not to redistribute, insurance tends to be redistributive because it compensates those who have lost income as a result of unemployment, sickness, etc.[1] Conversely, policies that are deliberately redistributive will at the same time serve an insurance function. The unemployed, the sick, the old, and those with low pre-fisc income more generally will rationally press for redistribution. By doing so many of those who are employed, healthy, young, and enjoying a high income will be insured against the risks of joining the ranks of the unemployed, the sick, etc. There is thus an intimate relationship between preferences for redistribution and preferences for insurance. The former is almost certainly influenced by the latter, and vice versa.

The next step in the analysis is to link differences in popular preferences and their translation into policy to differences in institutions. Preferences are affected by the distribution of skills, which is a function of the national training and production system. Essentially, the more the production system relies on non-transferable, or specific, skills the higher the demand for insurance in response to exogenous shocks.

Demand must be met by supply, and the latter will be affected by political institutions. I focus on the role of the electoral system. There are two parts to the story. One concerns a shock to the income distribution. In a majoritarian two-party system a rise in inequality will (usually) increase the median voter's preference for redistribution. However, if pre-election platforms are not binding, the left party may implement the preferred policy of its poor constituents, and this will hurt the median voter more the greater the level of inequality. By contrast, the rich constituents of the right party will always want taxation to be as low as possible, so the 'threat' from the right to middle-class interests is constant. The actual effect of a shock to the income distribution in a majoritarian system is therefore ambiguous: stronger preferences for redistribution but greater fear of what an 'ideological' left party might do. In a multiparty PR system, by contrast, a rise in inequality will increase the incentives for the centre and left to form a coalition to tax the rich (Iversen and Soskice 2006).

The second part of the institutional story concerns the insurance aspects of social protection. Shocks typically affect only a minority of people, even though compensation of these people can serve as an insurance for the majority. If the current median voter is not among those being affected by the shock, she has an incentive to support compensation *only* if future median voters do the same. The current median voter, therefore, faces a problem of how to commit future median voters. This translates into a *time-inconsistency problem* for the government because it has an incentive to renege on its promise to the current median voter when it seeks to attract the support of the future median voter (Iversen 2005). The PR helps solve this problem in so far as it leads to redistribution since redistribution also serves insurance purposes. Any institution that promotes redistribution thus serves as an (imperfect) solution to the time-inconsistency problem. PR is also closely associated with responsible and programmatic parties, which reduces voter concerns about governments' commitment to the future (Carey and Shugart 1999). A related argument is that PR promotes the effective representation of disadvantaged minorities and therefore facilitates the compensation of such minorities (Katzentstein 1985; Crepaz 1998).

The paper is divided into six sections. The first is a theoretical discussion of how economic shocks are likely to affect the demand for social insurance under different institutional conditions. The next section asks what the implications of such a theory are for the notion of institutional complementarities. Can political institutions be seen as complements to the economy? The third and fourth sections test the theoretical hypotheses on time series on spending data, focusing on the mediating role of institutions. I then asks if the results are consistent with individual-level evidence on policy preferences. The conclusion draws out the implications for studying the politics of adjustment in a VoC framework, and suggests some new frontiers in the study of economic policies and political institutions.

10.2. A FRAMEWORK FOR THE ANALYSIS OF SHOCKS AND POLICIES

In the Meltzer–Richard (M–R) model, a flat-rate benefit paid though a proportional tax implies that those below the mean will prefer redistributive spending up to the point where the benefit to them is exactly outweighed by the efficiency cost of taxation (assuming a typical right-skewed distribution of income). The Iversen–Soskice (I–S) preference model retains this redistributive logic, but it adds an insurance motive by assuming that income (wages and employment-related benefits) can be lost through unemployment and re-employment into jobs where a workers' skills are not fully utilized. The possibility of income loss provides risk-averse workers across the wage scale with an incentive to support redistributive spending. Indeed, if risk-aversion is sufficiently high it is possible for those with higher incomes to prefer more spending because they have more to lose (Moene and Wallerstein 2001).

The I–S model assumes that people are concerned with their material welfare and will favour policies which increase and protect their income. Income, in turn, is derived from the assets that people own, and for the vast majority the most important asset is their human capital, or skills. We can distinguish between two types of skills: general (g) and specific (s). The former are assumed to be fully portable across firms, industries, and occupations, and there is an economywide market wage for these skills. In a perfectly competitive (neoclassical) labour market with only general skills, risks are minimal because the loss of one job is always matched by the availability of another job at exactly the same wage. Specific skills, by contrast, are employable only in a particular firm, industry, or occupation, and losing a job is therefore a serious risk if another job in the same firm, industry, or occupation is unavailable. By implication, when demand for labour in industries or occupations using specific skills declines (because of technological change, foreign competition, or other changes in demand and supply conditions), some workers will find themselves unable to find a job that is suitable for their skills. Of course, in the real world people possess a mix of more or less specific skills. The model captures this by assuming that every worker is endowed with a ratio of specific to general skills (s/g) (or specific to total skills ($s/(s+g)$).

If we now assume that redistributive spending comes in the form of a flat-rate benefit (R) that accrues to all workers regardless of income or labour market status (as in the M–R model), we can account for redistributive preferences as a function of income and exposure to risk. Analytically, it is useful to distinguish between shocks to the income distribution and shocks to the risk distribution. The different possibilities are illustrated in Figure 10.1. *Panel A* shows the relationship between income and the preferred level of redistributive spending (R) for different levels of risk-aversion. The downwards-sloping solid line is the relationship we would expect from an M–R model, and it holds in the general I–S model when the redistributive motive dominates

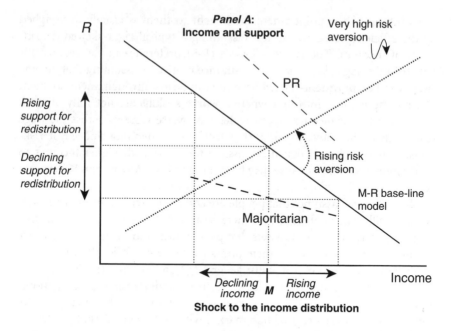

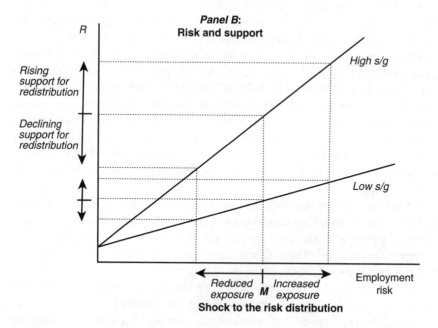

Figure 10.1. Support for redistribution as a function of income and risk

the insurance motive. As risk-aversion rises, the support for redistributive spending among high-income workers will also rise, while it will decline among low-income voters. Higher risk-aversion therefore reduces the class polarization implied by the M–R model. Indeed, if risk-aversion is sufficiently high the relationship between income and preferences turns positive as shown by Moene and Wallerstein (2001). However, the evidence presented below clearly shows that income is always negatively related to the preferred level of spending, so we can exclude this possibility.

My focus is on the dynamic implications of the model. The effect of a shock to the income distribution that reduces income at the low end and raises it at the high end is to increase support for redistribution among those with low incomes and reduce it among those with high incomes. Shocks to the income distribution are likely to have the greatest effects at the tails of the distribution, but if the median voter (M in the Figure 10.1) sets policy, the critical question is what happens to the median voter's income (indicated on the x-axis). Since the median voter is likely to have an income below the mean, a means-preserving rise in inequality would cause relative income to *decline* and redistributive spending to go up.

This simple result is modified if we introduce political parties and if spending is not constrained to a flat-rate benefit (R). Specifically, assume that *any* transfer is possible from the rich to the low and middle classes, or from the rich and middle class to the poor, *subject* to the constraint that net transfers (after taxes and transfers) are not regressive (going from poorer to richer people).[2] This Meltzer–Richard flat-rate benefit constitutes one such transfer, but it also opens the possibility that the poor can take from the middle class. This matters in a two-party majoritarian system if parties cannot fully commit to electoral platforms. Although both parties will seek to cater to the median voter in the election, they might deviate from their platform after the election to please core constituents. This is a well-known phenomenon in the party literature, and there are good reasons why this can happen, including the need of party leaders occasionally mobilize the party base in order to maximize voter turnout among prospective supporters (Schlesinger 1984; Aldrich 1993, 1995: ch. 6; Kitschelt 1994).

Iversen and Soskice (2006) show that under these conditions, the middle class has a bias against the centre-left party because it fears that it might be exploited by the poor, whereas the rich cannot do the same due to the non-regressivity constraint.[3] This does not mean that the median voter will *always* vote centre-right, but if the actual policies of the two parties over time are conceived as the *revealed* preferences of the median voter, these preferences will be more moderate than the median voter's ideal policies. One of the implications of this bias is that centre-left parties in majoritarian systems must seek to convince voters that they are credibly committed to a moderate platform by concentrating power in a leader with a reputation for being moderate or even slightly to the right of centre (think Tony Blair or Bill Clinton). When they succeed they are competitive with centre-right parties, but the platform is of course also correspondingly less redistributive.

Compared to a simple M–R model, where benefits are flat-rate and there is no commitment problem (i.e. parties always represent the median voter), the 'revealed' demand for social spending is thus lower with majoritarian institutions. This is indicated in the figure by the lower dashed line around the position of M. But the preferences of M are also less likely to be sensitive to shocks to the income distribution (hence the 'flatter line'). This is because higher inequality comes with a greater fear by M of heavy taxation imposed by the poor. The poor, if they are allowed to set the policies of the centre-left party, will tax both the rich and the middle class up to the point where the gains from such taxation are outweighed by the efficiency losses of higher taxation. The lower the relative income of the poor the higher the level of taxation before this point is reached (in an exactly analogous manner to a lower income by the median voter in the M–R model). While the middle class will also prefer more redistribution, the effect of its revealed preference is thus muted by a greater fear of what will happen if the centre-left party deviates to the left from its electoral platform.

A very striking set of empirical results consistent with this conjecture has been found in a new study of income and voting in the USA by McCarty, Poole, and Rosenthal (2006). They find that although class voting has actually increased over time, and although inequality has been on the rise, the Republican Party has seen its electoral fortunes among middle class voters *improve*. Although middle-class voters have reason to vote for more redistribution from the rich as inequality rises—as a simple M–R logic would predict—they are apparently more concerned about the prospects of being taxed for the purpose of redistributing to the poor. At least this is one plausible explanation for the trend, consistent with the argument presented here.

PR is different. First, since the threshold for representation is low, each class can be represented by its own party, which removes (or reduces) the agency problem. Second, governments are not chosen directly through the election but through coalition bargaining. If the centre party, representing the middle class, cannot govern alone it has an incentive to form a coalition with the left because the poor and the middle class have a common interest in taxing the rich, whereas the middle class has nothing or little to gain by allying with the rich and taxing the poor. This is clearly true if democratic governments cannot engage in regressive taxation, but it is true as long as the ability to raise revenues from the excluded group is proportional to the income of that group. The notorious American bank robber, Willie Sutton, made the point nicely when he was asked why he robbed banks: 'Because that's where the money is.'

The implication of this logic for PR multiparty systems is the exact opposite of what it is for majoritarian systems: the median voter, represented by a centre party, is more likely to favour centre-left governments. Redistributive government spending is accordingly expected to be higher under PR, as illustrated by the second dashed line in Figure 10.1 (*panel A*) being above the M–R baseline model. More importantly for our purposes, a rise in inequality is also likely to be associated with a sharper spending response than under majoritarian institutions. A means-preserving increase in inequality will give both the poor and the middle class a stronger incentive to tax the rich and to ally with one another in order to accomplish that. Even if rising inequality is concentrated at the tails of the distribution, since low-income parties will share power it will also tend to raise redistributive spending. In the majoritarian case, on the other hand, increased dispersion at the tails acts as a deterrent against the middle-class voting for the centre-left.

Now turn to the relationship between employment risks and support for redistributive spending in *panel B* of Figure 10.1. Greater risk always raises support for spending, as long as risk-aversion is greater than zero. Exposure to risk is a positive function of the probability of unemployment (p) and a negative function of the probability of re-employment (q). Because those who have highly specific skills (a high s/g ratio) will suffer a greater income loss if they are re-employed into a job that does not require their existing skills, they have a preference for more insurance and redistribution. Total risk-exposure can now be conceptualized as a function of the risk of job loss times the specificity of skills.

As in the case of income we can hypothesize the relationship between shocks to the risk-distribution and preferences for redistribution in the middle class. Shocks that cause employment risks to rise (decline) are expected to lead to a rise (decline) in support for redistribution. The magnitude of the effect will depend on the specificity of skills, which may vary across individuals and across countries (compare the responses on the R-axis). Skills are in principle less important for shocks to the income distribution because they affect the demand for insurance, not redistribution. But as noted above, the two are intimately related in reality. Increased income inequality means that the technological change that renders skills obsolete is likely to produce a greater drop in income. In fact, this is one of the reasons that specific skills countries tend to have collective wage-bargaining arrangements where wage dispersion is reduced (see Estévez-Abe et al. 2001).

Political institutions also matter in the case of insurance. The fundamental problem in the provision of social insurance is that, when a shock hits, those who are affected will not likely be the ones setting policy. Those who have not been directly affected will update their subjective assessment of risks, but they only have an interest in compensatory policies if such policies can be seen as a premium for protection against future shocks. Yet current voters can only commit the government for one term at a time, and there is no way to bind future voters to the policy preferences of current voters. This 'time-inconsistency problem' in social insurance provision can lead to serious under-provision of social protection compared to the long-term preferences of voters. It also means that shocks that would raise demand for protection, as in *panel B* of Figure 10.1, will not necessarily be translated into 'revealed' preferences for actual policies.

Generally speaking there are two institutional remedies for the time-inconsistency problem. The first is that political parties with detailed policy programmes and highly developed party organizations, especially links to unions, limit the ability of leaders to give in to short-term electoral incentives and constrain the choice set of voters to alternatives that are optimal in the long run. However, this solution does not eliminate the temptation for party leaders to offer tax cuts and to shun long-term investment in social protection. This temptation is particularly high in majoritarian systems where the reward for winning the next election is great. In practice the organization of parties and the electoral system are closer related.

The second argument goes back to the argument that PR electoral systems give centrist parties an incentive to ally with left parties for current redistributive purposes. If left parties tend to represent voters who are at greater risk, the preferences of these voters will be represented in coalition bargaining. Also, redistributive policies will themselves serve insurance functions because those who are experiencing a complete or partial unemployment of their assets as a result of adverse labour market conditions or technological change will also benefit. Redistributive social spending serves as an insurance against income loss.

10.3. COMPLEMENTARITIES BETWEEN ECONOMIC AND POLITICAL INSTITUTIONS

How does the linkage between economic shocks, political and economic institutions, and government responses relate to the idea in the VoC literature that

institutions are complements to one another? Very little is said in this literature on the role of democratic institutions (Hancké, Rhodes, and Thatcher,
this volume), but in fact they are quite closely related to economic coordination. Using a composite measure of PR[4] and two measures of non-
market coordination,[5] Figure 10.2 illustrates how countries cluster into a PR-
coordinated group and a majoritarian-uncoordinated group—even if there
are some questions about where Ireland and France (according to one of the
measures) belong. The correlation between PR and a measure of specific skills,
namely the proportion of a cohort going through a vocational training, is
even higher (0.7), so that intensity of specific skills training is much higher
on average under PR than under majoritarian institutions.

   Based on the analysis in the previous section, this clustering is not surprising. A requirement for heavy investment in specific skills is the existence
of institutions that protect such investments, and much welfare spending
can be seen as providing such protection (Estévez-Abe et al. 2001; Iversen
2005). This includes aggressive government responses to shocks that significantly raise labour market insecurity. If such responses are more likely
under PR, which essentially offers a powerful commitment device to ensure
that demands are met (at least in mature democracies with responsible and
programmatic parties), then the incentives to invest in specific skills are

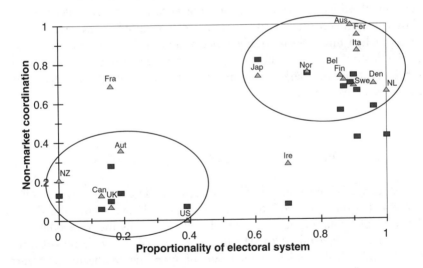

Figure 10.2. PR and non-market coordination

Source: Proportionality of electoral system: Lijphart (1994); non-market coordination index (triangles): Hall
and Gingrich (2004); cooperation index (Hicks and Kenworthy).

higher under PR. Under majoritarian institutions, by contrast, the difficulty of parties making commitments, both to particular constituents and to the future, means that there is less political protection of specific assets and greater incentives to invest in general skills as an insurance against labour market risks.

This does not mean that the causal story is a simple one running from PR to investment in specific skills, although this is a complementarity that is consistent with the VoC story and helps sustain coordinated forms of capitalism. Historically, the story probably runs in the opposite direction as argued in detail in Cusack, Iversen, and Soskice (2003). Countries in which there is now a high degree of coordination, and in which economic coordination was beginning to move to the national and sectoral levels as industrialization developed through the second half of the nineteenth and the start of the twentieth centuries, had previously been primarily coordinated at the local and regional level. Locally coordinated economies favoured the development of specific assets and activities. The choice of PR—occurring in most of these economies between the 1890s and the 1920s—reflected the need for local and regional economic interests to ensure representation at the national level, as industrialization proceeded, to protect their (co-)specific assets. PR permits the representation of specific interests, and facilitates compromise between workers and employers with co-specific asset investments in skills and capital, while majoritarian institutions encourage party leaders to shun close ties with constituents to appear more committed to the median voter (except when interests are locally concentrated as they were before nation-level industrialization got underway). Once the transition to PR has occurred, it helps sustain non-market economic coordination through the mechanisms explained above.

10.4. DATA AND STATISTICAL MODEL

The evidence is based on data from sixteen OECD countries over a thirty-five-year period from 1960 to 1995.[6] This period covers both the Golden Age of welfare state expansion and what Pierson calls the 'new politics' of retrenchment (Pierson 1996). The dependent variable is government transfers to individuals, which is made up of spending on health insurance, unemployment insurance, pensions, welfare, family allowances, and related social spending. Although much of this spending is not deliberately redistributive, it is nevertheless highly correlated with redistribution. Measured as the percentage reduction in the Gini coefficient from before to after taxes and transfers for working-age households, redistribution, and an index of transfers plus taxes is correlated at 0.68 (see Iversen 2005: ch. 1 for details). Transfers are also highly correlated with measures of social spending from the IMF and the OECD, but the latter are more restricted in terms of time coverage. Moreover, I am focusing exclusively on inter-temporal change in social spending, which will be captured well with any of these measures.

The question the analysis attempts to answer is whether exogenous shocks to the risk and income structure produce different outcomes depending on the institutional framework. I use an estimation strategy first proposed by Blanchard and Wolfers (2000), and generalized by Persson, and Tabellini (2003). The model absorbs all cross-country differences into fixed effects, but it includes invariant institutional variables as interactions with different measures of the exogenous shocks. Blanchard and Wolfers propose two versions of the model, and I estimate both. The first assumes that countries are exposed to uniform unobserved exogenous shocks. Since the nature of the shocks is left unspecified, the purpose is simply to determine whether countries with different institutions respond differently to them.[7] The shocks are proxied by a set of time dummies (D_t) that are interacted with the institutional variables ($I_{i,}$):

$$Y_{i,t} = \lambda_1 \cdot Y_{i,t-1} + \lambda_2 \cdot I_i \cdot Y_{i,t-1} + \delta_t \cdot D_t \cdot (1 + \beta \cdot I_i) + \sum \beta^j \cdot X_{i,t}^j + \alpha_i + \varepsilon_{i,t}.$$

The main variable of interest is β. If it is zero it means that the effects of the shocks are identical across national institutions. If it is positive it means that the relevant institutional feature magnifies the effect of the common shocks. Again, since the model has country-specific intercepts, differences observed between countries can only be due to differences in government responses to shocks.[8] In Blanchard and Wolfers, it is assumed that $\lambda_1 = \lambda_2 = 0$, which makes the results very easy to interpret (as we will see). But serial correlation is a problem, and the λ-parameters carry potentially useful information about their persistence in policies under different institutional conditions. If $\lambda_1 > 0$ it means that policies do not adjust instantaneously. If $\lambda_2 > 0$, it means that policy persistence is higher in countries with higher values on the institutional variable.

The institutional variables of interest are the skill system and the electoral system. For the latter, I use the simple classification of electoral systems in into majoritarian (0) and PR (1) based on Lijphart (1994). For the former I use the share of an age cohort going through a vocational training, assuming that vocational training (as opposed to general education) is a measure of specific skills acquisition. The measure only begins in 1980s, but since it exhibits little meaningful variation over time I treat it as a constant institutional variable and assume that it has not changed since the early 1960s. As explained in detail in Iversen (2005), the variable captures what appears to be meaningful differences across countries in the structure of training systems.

The second version of the statistical model identifies the nature of shocks, and allows these to vary in magnitude across countries. Shocks ($S_{i,t}$) are measured as (changes in) unemployment, deindustrialization, and (changes in) wage inequality. Changes in unemployment is the most obvious variable since it is bound to raise the perception of workers of labour market risks, and cause demand for unemployment compensation (and perhaps other cash benefits) to rise. Although unemployment only directly affects a fraction of workers, changes in unemployment is known to affect union wage behaviour, and this is a clear sign that unemployment affects the perceived level of risks of the majority. It is also important to note that unemployment is not simply a cyclical problem, but that it rose from a low of less than 2 per cent in the mid-1960s to a high of almost 9 per cent in the early 1990s (with a temporary trough of 5.8% in 1990). The data are from the OECD *Labour Force Statistics* (various years)

Deindustrialization refers to the phenomenon of secular job loss in industry and agriculture that started in the early 1960s. In 1960 about 60 per cent of the labour force in the OECD area was employed in the primary sectors; thirty-five years later this figure was down to about 30 per cent. This massive shift in employment is the outgrow of deep forces of technological change coupled with progressive market saturation in manufactured goods and shifts in demand towards services—structural-technological conditions that also characterized the great transformation from agriculture to industry (see Iversen and Cusack 1998). The change is correlated with changes in unemployment (r = .37), but the effect on risk is not simply through unemployment. Even if job losses are being compensated for by job gains in services, the skills which are required in services are typically very different from manufacturing. This is one reason why early retirement (a component of the dependent variable) became such a widespread (and very expensive) policy in many European countries. Early retirement helped industrial companies to unload some of their older workers, while at the same time making sure that these workers did not have to compete for jobs where their skills were ill suited.

Perhaps surprisingly, there is considerable variance in the speed of deindustrialization across countries. For example, in an early industrializing country like the USA, industrial employment as a percentage of the adult population declined by only 3 percentage points between 1960 and 1995, whereas for a late industrializer like Sweden, the figure is 13 per cent. If we add to these figures the decline of agricultural employment, the numbers increase to 6 and 22 per cent, respectively. The difference in these numbers translates into 23 million lost jobs if the USA had gone through the same process of deindustrialization as Sweden did from 1960 to 1995. I use changes in employment in industry and agriculture as a percentage of the working age populations as a measure of deindustrialization (higher numbers mean higher job losses). Data are from the OECD *Labour Force Statistics* (various years).

Shocks to the income distribution are captured by changes in the earnings of a full-time worker (or equivalent) in the top decile of the earnings distribution relative to the earnings of a worker in the bottom decile (d9/d1 ratios). The data are from the OECD electronic data files (different versions; undated). For most countries, data are post-1975, and Norway is excluded with only two observations. In this period, there was a modest increase in average inequality of 12 per cent (0.28 on the d9/d1 scale), but there is a fair amount of variance across countries. The USA and Britain experienced sharp rises (22% and 15%, respectively), whereas continental European countries experienced more muted changes. In the cases of Belgium and Germany, wage inequality actually dropped slightly. Yet, because wages are only for employed full-time workers, the rise of unemployment and part-time employment implies that income inequality will have risen more than the wage data suggest. Correspondingly, data on pre-fisc household income from the Luxembourg Income Study show that inequality rose significantly everywhere during the 1980s and 1990s, including Belgium and Germany. There are too few observations over time in the LIS data to use these in our (longitudinal) regressions, but some of this rise in inequality will be captured by the unemployment and deindustrialization variables (as well as the period dummies, of course).

In addition to these variables, the analysis includes the following set of controls:

Government partisanship. The measure is the government centre of gravity, which is the average of three expert surveys of the left-right position of parties, weighted by the share of parties' seats in government. The variable goes from left to right and is standardized to have a range of 1 and a mean of 0. For details on this measure the data used in its construction, see Cusack and Engelhardt (2002).

Unionization. The strength of unions changes over time and might account for differences in the demand for government spending. Unionization is union members divided by number of workers. The data are from Ebbinghaus and Visser (2000).

Unexpected growth. This is a variable emphasized in Roubini and Sachs (1989) and is defined as per capita real GDP growth at time t minus average real per capita growth in the preceding three years. It is intended to capture the logic that budgeting relies on GDP forecasts based on performance in the recent past. If growth is unexpectedly high it reduces spending as a proportion of GDP. Sources: Cusack (1991) and OECD, *National Accounts, Part II: Detailed Tables* (various years).

Size of dependent population. Since replacement rates for unemployment and pensions are fixed over short periods of time, changes in unemployment and demographics will generate 'automatic' disbursements of payments. To control for this effect I include the sum of unemployed and people over the age of 64 (who are also the ones accounting for most medical expenditures) divided by the total population. When unemployment is used as a shock variable, the dependent population refers to those over 64. The source is OECD, *Labour Force Statistics* (various years).

10.5. FINDINGS

Table 10.1 shows the results of estimating the regression equation using non-linear least squares. The dependent variable is the level of spending, while time dummies serve as proxies for the exogenous shocks. The key issue, of course, is whether governments in countries with PR or strong vocational training systems react differently to shocks than governments in countries with weak vocational training systems and majoritaritarian institutions.

The parameter β on the institutional interaction term provides the answer. If it is positive it means that shocks raise spending *more* in countries with PR or vocational training systems. It turns out that, across specifications, countries with PR and strong vocational training systems respond to shocks by increasing spending *more* than in countries with majoritarian or weak vocational training systems. The results do not change very much when lagged dependent variables are added to the model, although the level of statistical significance (not surprisingly) drops (although still significant on at least a 5% level). Evidently, there is much persistence in spending ($\lambda \approx 0.9$), which means that much current spending is not only a response to contemporaneous shocks but also past ones. Because the interaction between the institutional variables and the lagged spending variable is positive (the last variable in Table 10.1), policy persistence is greater in countries with PR and developed vocational training systems. That is consistent with expectations, but the differences are very small.

Table 10.1. Common shocks, national institutions, and government spending (standard errors in parentheses)

	Dependent variable: transfers			
	(1)	(2)	(3)	(4)
Time effect	6.63***		6.34***	
	(0.87)		(0.87)	
PR* time dummies	0.72***	0.53**	—	—
	(0.12)	(0.22)		
Voc. training* time dummies	—	—	0.015***	0.016**
			(0.003)	(0.007)
Government partisanship$_{t-1}$	0.77**	0.06	0.89	0.08
	(0.39)	(0.17)	(0.39)	(0.17)
Unionization$_t$	−0.05***	0.01	−0.03**	0.01
	(0.01)	(0.01)	(0.01)	(0.01)
Unexpected growth$_t$	−0.02	−0.11***	−0.01	−0.11***
	(0.03)	(0.01)	(0.03)	(0.01)
Dependency ratio$_t$	0.71***	0.15***	0.63***	0.16***
	(0.08)	(0.04)	(0.08)	(0.03)
Transfers $_{t-1}$	—	0.91***	—	0.91***
		(0.03)		(0.03)
I * Transfers $_{t-1}$	—	0.03	—	0.02
		(0.02)		(0.02)
Minimum	3.69	4.44	4.19	4.00
Maximum	8.44	7.98	10.98	11.39
Institutional effect	4.75	3.54	6.79	7.38
Adjusted R^2	0.93	0.99	0.92	0.99
N	548	548	548	548

Significance levels: * < 0.10; ** < 0.05; *** < 0.01.

Note: The results for country and time dummies are not shown.

To gauge the substantive impact of institutions, all variables have been defined as deviations from their cross-country means. When there is no lagged dependent variable, this means that the effects of the time dummies refer to the cumulative effects of shocks over time for a country with average values (0) on the independent variables. The total time effect, shown in the first row of Table 10.1, is then simply the parameter on the 1995 time dummy. This can be interpreted as the total average effect on spending over the thirty-five-year period from common exogenous shocks that are not captured by the controls.

But again the effect varies across countries with different institutions. This variance is captured at the bottom of the table, where the minimum is the predicted effect in a country with the lowest value on the institutional variable (majoritarian electoral system or weak vocational training system) and the maximum is the predicted effect in a country with the highest value (PR or strong vocational training system). So in the first column, for example, the predicted increase in spending for a PR system is 8.44 per cent, while it is 3.69 for a majoritarian system.[9] The difference between predicted spending under PR and majoritarian systems is a summary measure of the effect of institutions. The institutional effect of electoral system is somewhere between 3.5 and 4.75 per cent, while for the training system it is about 7 per cent (using the extreme values on the vocational training variable). These are very large effects, and they strongly suggest that countries with different economic and political institutions respond differently to shocks.

A possible competing interpretation, however, is that countries were exposed to different levels of shocks and that it is this variance, not institutions, which explains the observed differences across institutional settings. While it seems implausible that countries should have had such different experiences, and while it is unclear why such differences should be correlated with institutional differences, we cannot entirely exclude the possibility. We do know after all that three of the most obvious sources of shocks—rising unemployment, deindustrialization, and growing wage inequality—did vary across countries.[10] By adding these to the model (Table 10.2), we can test whether controlling for this variance affects the effects of institutional differences. Of course, the substantive effects of these shocks are also interesting in their own right.

The estimated parameters (β) for the institutional effects are shown in the first row of the table, first for PR and then vocational training. Since the number of observations on the wage equality variable is less than half, the results when this variable is included are shown separately (columns 2 and 4). Finally, since there are no significant differences in the persistence of spending across institutions, the model assumes that $\lambda_1 = \lambda_2$ (i.e. there is only one lagged dependent variable). With these presentational issues in mind, the results in columns 1 and 3 of Table 10.2 are directly comparable to those in columns 2 and 4 of Table 10.1.

Note first that while both unemployment and deindustrialization matter, the parameters on the institutional variables (βs) are very similar to before (the one for PR drops slightly from 0.53 to 0.47, while the one for vocational training is identical). It is therefore not the case that the differences in government responses are attenuated when the nationally specific sources of shocks are taken into account. Countries with PR and developed vocational training systems tend to raise spending in response to shocks much more than countries with majoritarian systems with weak vocational training systems. Again, the magnitudes of the differences between institutions are captured by the institutional effects in Table 10.1. But we can now say something about the

Table 10.2. Nationally specific shocks, national institutions, and government spending (standard errors in parentheses)

	Dependent variable: transfers			
	PR		Vocational training	
	1	2	3	4
Institutional variable (β)	0.47***	0.58***	0.015***	0.020***
	(0.15)	(0.17)	(0.005)	(0.005)
Shock variables				
Unemployment	0.31***	0.33***	0.30***	0.31***
	(0.04)	(0.05)	(0.04)	(0.05)
Deindustrialization	0.08**	0.14*	0.08**	0.19***
	(0.03)	(0.07)	(0.03)	(0.07)
Wage inequality	—	0.07	—	−0.11
		(0.45)		(0.46)
Controls				
Government partisanship$_{t-1}$	0.03	−0.10	0.05	−0.01
	(0.15)	(0.24)	(0.15)	(0.24)
Unionization$_t$	0.01	0.03**	0.01	0.05**
	(0.00)	(0.02)	(0.00)	(0.02)
Unexpected growth$_t$	−0.08***	−0.08***	−0.08***	−0.06**
	(0.01)	(0.03)	(0.01)	(0.02)
Dependency ratio$_t$	0.08***	0.17***	0.09***	0.14**
	(0.03)	(0.06)	(0.03)	(0.06)
Transfers$_{t-1}$	0.92***	0.87***	0.93***	0.83***
	(0.02)	(0.04)	(0.02)	(0.04)
Institutional effects				
Unemployment	1.02	1.34	2.27	3.11
Deindustiralization	0.65	1.42	1.55	4.95
Adjusted R^2	0.99	0.99	0.99	0.99
N	548	254	548	254

Significance levels: * < 0.10; ** < 0.05; *** < 0.01.

Notes: The results for country and time dummies are not shown. The shock variables also include time dummies.

extent to which the shocks are caused by unemployment and deindustrialization (noted at the base of Table 10.2).

For the full data-set (columns 1 and 3), the institutional effects range between 0.7 and 2.3 per cent if we use the average change in unemployment and deindustrialization from the early 1960s to the mid-1990s as the measure of the total 'shock'. The direct effect of unemployment is somewhat larger, but some of the effect of deindustrialization goes through unemployment (the two are correlated at 0.37). Together the two variables account for roughly half of the total institutional effect that we estimated in Table 10.1.[11] The rest is due to common unobserved shocks captured by the time dummies. Some of these unaccounted sources of spending increases may also be nationally specific, but we can almost certainly exclude the possibility that these would cancel out the institutional effects.

As for the controls, the dependency ratio has a strong positive effect on spending as predicted. Unexpected growth also notably *reduces* spending in all models with a lagged dependent variable. The reason is that when past spending is controlled for, unexpected growth produces an 'automatic' increase in the denominator of the dependent variable that reduces current spending as a share of GDP. By contrast, in none of the models with lagged dependent variables do either partisanship or unionization matter. This may seem surprising, but probably reflects the fact that the dependent variable is heavily oriented towards insurance as opposed to redistribution. The latter *is* a partisan issue, and it has been shown in several studies that partisanship matters for redistribution (see Bradley et al. 2003).

Columns 2 and 4 in Table 10.2 include the change in wage inequality as a shock variable. This variable turns out to have no significant relationship to spending (and the sign is also unstable). The institutional effects in these regressions are actually bigger than before, but this is simply due to a compositional effect (changes in the sample), not any effect of the inequality variable. Is this lack of effect from shocks to the wage distribution contrary to the theory? Not necessarily. First, such shocks are partly captured by rising unemployment and deindustrialization (the latter through an increase in part-time employment). Second, by far the largest changes in wage structure occur in two countries, the USA and Britain, which have majoritarian institutions and general skills systems. In this institutional context, rising inequality should *not* trigger more redistributive spending. And in the PR/vocational training cases, the changes in wage inequality are so small that the effects on insurance spending may be swamped by measurement error. Most importantly, the differences in the extent of changes in wage structure are themselves affected by domestic institutions. In particular, if avoiding big swings in relative wages is itself a form of social insurance, it may be more appropriate to treat wage inequality as a dependent variable (see Estévez, Iversen, and Soskice 2001).

To test the latter possibility, I use d9:d1 ratios as the dependent variable and use centralization of collective wage bargaining as the institutional variable. Past studies have shown that centralization is closely related to wage compression (Wallerstein 1999; Rueda and Pontusson 2000). In our data, the correlation between centralization and d9:d1 ratios is 0.70, and centralization is also moderately related to PR (0.59) and to vocational training (0.30).[12] The question is whether the wage structure of countries with centralized wage-setting systems is less sensitive to pressures for rising inequality than countries with decentralized wage setting. Using the same statistical model as before,

Table 10.3. Common shocks, centralization of wage bargaining, and wage inequality (standard errors in parentheses)

	Dependent variable: D9/D1 wage ratio	
	(1)	(2)
Time effect	0.28***	—
	(0.05)	
Centralization time dummies	−2.92***	−2.68***
	(0.73)	(0.99)
Government partisanship$_{t-1}$	0.10	0.05
	(0.05)	(0.03)
Unionionization$_t$	0.005	0.001
	(0.003)	(0.002)
Unexpected growth$_t$	0.009	0.008
	(0.004)	(0.003)
Unemployment$_t$	−0.029***	−0.014***
	(0.005)	(0.003)
D9/D1 ratio$_{t-1}$	—	0.66***
		(0.04)
Decentralized	0.49	0.47
Centralized	−0.04	−0.02
Institutional effect	−0.53	−0.49
Adjusted R^2	0.97	0.98
N	231	231

Significance levels: * < 0.10; ** < 0.05; *** < 0.01.

Notes: The results for country and time dummies are not shown. The shock variables also include time dummies.

Table 10.3 gives the answer using common exogenous shocks (time dummies). The only difference from before is that the unemployment rate is substituted for the dependency ratio (there is no reason the size of the old-age population should matter).

Note that the time effect is to raise d9/d1 ratios by 0.28, which is equivalent to a 9 per cent increase in inequality between 1975 and 1995. But the effect is much greater in decentralized bargaining systems (such as the USA and Britain) than in centralized ones. In the former the predicted effect is a rise in inequality of 0.49 or 16 per cent, while in the latter there is no significant effect on inequality (indeed, the prediction for a country with the highest centralization score is actually a slight reduction in inequality). The interpretation seems to be that countries with decentralized bargaining systems have no institutional buffer against shocks to the wage structure, whereas centralized systems do. Of course, it is possible that a lack of response raises unemployment, but we know that the same countries also respond more aggressively to increases in unemployment. In short, inequality goes up less, and transfers more, in countries with PR, developed vocational training systems, and centralized wage bargaining. This is very consistent with the thesis that there are distinct varieties of government responses to economic shocks.

A final issue is whether this conclusion is equally true for the 1980s and 1990s as for the 1960s and 1970s. While countries may not be converging in terms of total spending, their responses to external shocks may have become more similar as a result of fiscal constrains or a general neoliberal shift in ideology. Government spending increased much less in the second than in the first period, which seems to support this view. But this may also simply indicate that countries reached an equilibrium level of spending by the early 1980s where shocks were adequately addressed through automatic disbursements of transfers. This would be compatible with continued (or even increasing) differences in the responsiveness of governments to unforseen shocks. To test this, Table 10.4 reports the results by period, omitting the controls (and the lagged dependent variable) for presentational economy.

Note that, while the time effects in the second period are less than a half of the first period, the estimated parameters for the institutional variables give no indication that the distinctiveness of government responses across institutional systems has diminished. To the contrary, the parameters are *larger* in the second period, although they are so imprecisely estimated that we cannot be confident of a true difference. Still, there is no indication that the distinctiveness of government responses to shocks has declined, even as we cannot exclude the possibility that governments are generally less sensitive to such shocks.

Table 10.4. Shocks and government transfers in two sub-periods

	1960–79	1980–95
PR		
Time effect	6.15	2.79
Institutional parameter (β)	0.3	0.47
Institutional effect	1.84	1.31
Vocational traning		
Time effect	6.87	2.73
Institutional parameter (β)	0.007	0.013
Institutional effect	3.31	2.52

Notes: Estimated with lagged dependent variable. Effects of controls not shown.

10.6. THE INDIVIDUAL-LEVEL MECHANISMS

As explained in the theoretical section, the supply of policies should be related to their demand under democratic institutions. At least some of this demand is expressed through electoral politics, and we should expect policy preferences to be systematically related to institutionally 'induced' economic interests. In principle we should therefore be able to link individual-level preferences for social protection to macro-level differences in institutions using a multi-level regression approach. In practice, this is rendered impossible by what may be called the status quo problem. When surveys ask people about their policy preferences, respondents almost invariably express these relative to the current political status quo. If we assume that the status quo represents a political equilibrium, institutionally induced differences over what that equilibrium should be will be 'invisible' in the answers. What we can do is to examine whether economic interests, defined by income, skill assets, and exposure to unemployment risks are systematically related to individual policy preferences. If they are, it is support for the micro-level mechanisms that is supposedly driving the macro-level relationships.

The linkage between economic interest and social policy preferences has been the focus of three recent papers (Iversen and Soskice 2001; Rehm 2005; Cusack, Iversen and Rehm 2006), and I will simply present some of the key results from one of these (Cusack, Iversen and Rehm 2006). They are based on data from several waves of the 'International Social Survey Programme' (ISSP), which ask people about whether they agree with policies to redistribute more. The data are combined with labour force survey data, which makes it possible to calculate unemployment risk by occupational group, using ILO's classification of occupations (ISCO-88).[13] Risk is simply assumed to be proportional to the unemployment rate for each occupation. Actual unemployment is used as a measure of 'realized' risk. The occupational classification can also be used to measure relative skill specificity, which is the specialization of skills used in a particular occupation (as implied by ISCO-88) divided by the level of skills required in that occupation. Finally, pre-tax income captures distributive motives (as opposed to insurance motives) for supporting redistribution.

The model is estimated using ordered logit regression, including a full set of country and year dummies. In addition, there is control for age, gender, employment status (whether the respondent is a student, retired, self-employed, or non-employed), union membership, and private or public sector employment. There are well over 40,000 observations in the complete data-set so getting precisely estimated parameters is never an issue. Correspondingly,

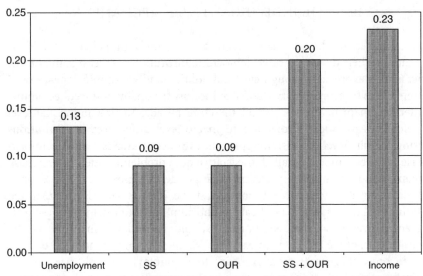

First Differences in Probability to 'Strongly Agree' with Government Redistribution

Figure 10.3. Increases in the probability of 'strongly agreeing' with more government redistribution as a function of low income and high risk

Notes: Figure displays the change in the probability that the respondent 'strongly agrees' with government redistribution, simulating the difference between: Unemployment: being unemployed and employed, Specific skills: having specific as opposed to general skills; High unemployment risk: being in an occupation with a high as opposed to a low unemployment rate; low income: being in the lowest income quantile as opposed to being in the highest income quantile.

Source: Cusack et al. (2006).

all the results shown in Figure 10.3 have narrow confidence intervals and are highly statistically significant.

The figure shows the effect on the probability of 'strongly agreeing' with more government redistribution when the risk and income variables are changed from low to high values (or high to low values in the case of income). Having specific skills, or high exposure to the risk of unemployment, each raises the probability of 'strongly agreeing' with more redistribution 9–10 per cent. This is similar to the effect of actually being unemployed, so they suggest very meaningful effects. Taken together, these two variables increase the probability of 'strongly agreeing" by about 20 per cent, which is similar to the effect of going from the top to the bottom decile of income. In combination, it turns out that those misfortunate enough to have both high risk and low income have an 89 per cent probability of agreeing or strongly agreeing that the government should redistribute more. If political institutions affect who influences policy, this is bound to affect policy. Likewise, shocks that raise risks are likely to increase demand for redistributive spending, and the effect should be greater in countries where the training system emphasizes specific skills.

Although we cannot directly relate individual preferences to the macro-level findings, the micro-level evidence thus lends credibility to these. People at different levels of risk and income have different preferences, and skills power-fully affect both income and risk-exposure. If there are systematic differences in national training systems, and if these affect the composition of individual skills, we *should* expect such differences to shape government responses. Like-wise, if the electoral system affects *whose* interests are represented, government sensitivity to risk should also be affected.

In so far as employers have made co-investments in skills (directly through training, and indirectly through particular product market strategies) this logic suggests that PR may be supported by a cross-class alliance of skilled workers and employers who employ these workers. Where such co-specific assets are missing, employers and higher-income earners would be better off with majoritarian institutions. In this manner economic interests translate into institutional preferences. The obvious implication is that the correla-tion of VoC, varieties of political institutions, and varieties of government responses to shocks is not accidental but created by deliberate attempts to shape the design of political institutions.

10.7. CONCLUSION

A common charge against the VoC approach is that it ignores political insti-tutions and that it is static—incapable of explaining policy change. In this chapter I have tried to show that there is in fact much to be learned about economic policy and political institutions from a VoC approach. Focusing on the role of economic and political institutions in shaping the demand for, and the supply of, redistributive government spending, I have tried to show that there are distinct differences in government responses to economic shocks, and that these differences are closely related to different varieties of capitalism.

But while the evidence clearly shows that differences in government responses persist over time, the rate of change has slowed considerably during the 1990s. This may reflect the stabilization of unemployment rates and the slowdown of the process of deindustrialization. But risks have certainly not disappeared from the labour market—they have rather become concentrated on particular segments of the labour force. As emphasized by Hancké, Rhodes, and Thatcher (this volume) there is an increasing split between those in secure, high-paid labour market positions and those in long-term unemployment or in insecure, temporary, or part-time jobs, and this bifurcation of the risk structure could produce a very different political adjustment dynamics in the future. On the one hand, support for high protection may be reduced among increasingly secure middle-class workers. This would make governments less sensitive to 'skill-biased' economic shocks. On the other hand, a growing rift between 'insiders' and 'outsiders' over the social transfer system may lead the latter to conclude that the only way to improve their labour market chances is to ally with professionals in order to break up the employment protection system for privileged 'insiders'—in other words, wholesale liberalization of the labour market. This would be a political 'shock' to high-protection countries, and one can perhaps see the contours of such a shock in the rise of new right parties. Yet it is precisely this threat that may bring insiders and outsiders back together—possibly in an alliance that involves partial deregulation of labour markets, but also high protection through transfers as well as active labour market polices. Understanding the coalitional dynamics of policy reform in a bifurcated labour market is one of the major challenges for any theory of democratic capitalism.

Another important frontier for the VoC approach is to understand the causal relationship between varieties of capitalist institutions and varieties of democratic institutions. The two appear to be closely related empirically, but while political scientists and sociologists have proposed historical explanations for the latter, they have almost completely ignored the role of economic interests and modes of production in the development of particular democratic institutions. It strikes me as deeply implausible that the two are causally independent, and I have here hinted at ways in which economic interests translate into political-institutional preferences. Future research will have to determine whether this 'translation' also played a causal role in the historical emergence of particular democratic institutions. It is hard to exaggerate the importance of explaining this coupling between economic and democratic institutions because recent research suggests that most of the variance in inequality and redistribution is not *between* democracy and non-democracy but *within* these regime types (Ross 2006).

NOTES

1. In the Rawlsian framework, *ex ante*, people behind the veil of ignorance may support policies for purely insurance reasons, but *ex post* (after the veil is raised) these policies produce redistribution. Since there are people who have been exposed to misfortune at any given moment, preferences for insurance will show up as preferences for redistribution.

2. Evidence from the Luxembourg Income study shows that redistribution is always at least mildly progressive in the sense that there is a reduction in the Gini coefficient from before to after taxes and transfers (although the size of the reduction varies a great deal). this means that the rich are always worse off, and the poor always better off, as a result of redistribution. See Osberg, Smeeding, and Schwabisch (2003).

3. There are numerous justifications for the non-regressivity assumption, including normative, historical (relating to the origins of democracy), and empirical (see previous note). Suffice it here to note that virtually all models of the welfare state assume or imply it (including Meltzer–Richard and Esping-Andersen's well-known work).

4. The proportionality of the electoral system measure in the last column is a composite index of two widely used indices of electoral systems. One is Lijphart's measure of the effective threshold of representation based on national election laws. It indicates the actual threshold of electoral support that a party must get in order to secure representation. The other is Gallagher's measure of the disproportionality between votes and seats, which is an indication of the extent to which smaller parties are being represented at their full strength. The data are from Lijphart (1994).

5. One (marked by triangles) is Hall and Gingerich's measure of nonmarket coordination (2004), based on the existence of coordinating institutions in industrial relations and the corporate governance system. The other (marked by squares) is Hicks and Kenworthy's index of cooperation (1998), which measures the extent to which interactions between firms, unions, and the state are cooperative as opposed to adversarial.

6. The countries are Australia, Austria, Belgium, Canada, Denmark, Finland, France, West Germany, Italy, Japan, the Netherlands, Norway, Sweden, Switzerland, United Kingdom, and USA.

7. The 'shocks' can be thought of very broadly to include deindustrialization, which started around 1960 (see Iversen and Cusack 2000), union militancy and civil unrest in the late 1960s (Eichengreen 1997), the integration of international financial markets (Garrett 1998), the two oil shocks (Goldthorpe 1985), technological change (Freeman 1995), the slowdown of productivity (Pierson 2001), and even broad ideological changes (Hall 1993).

8. This means that the (invariant) institutional variables cannot be included as independent controls (X variables). All direct effects of invariant institutions, however, are picked up by the country dummies.

9. For PR the effect is equal to the average time effect (6.63) plus the 'additional' effect under PR, which is the estimated institutional parameter β (0.77) times the value on the (centreed) institutional variable (.38) times the time effect ($0.77{*}.38{*}6.63 = 1.81$)—for a total of 8.44.

10. Globalization is also a frequently mentioned force of change, but if the effects of globalization do not go through the above variables it is hard to see that the nature of globalization would be radically different across countries.

Globalization is almost by definition a common external shock, and trade and international capital market liberalization did indeed occur pretty much simultaneously across developed democracies. I am not arguing here that globalization is unimportant, but that it is a common, rather than a nationally specific, type of shock.

11. Note that unemployment and deindustrialization also have direct effects, so the fact that they vary across countries will mean that some of the observed cross-national differences in spending patterns will be due to the direct effects of these variables. The point here is simply that this does not reduce the effects of the institutional variables.

12. The centralization index is from Iversen (1999) and is based on the concentration of union membership at each bargaining level, weighted by the bargaining authority vested at that level.

13. This is done at the ISCO-88 2-digit level, producing twenty-seven different occupational unemployment rates. See Rehm (2005) for details.

Part V

Capitalism Goes East

11

Central European Capitalism in Comparative Perspective

Lawrence P. King

11.1. INTRODUCTION

According to the VoC framework, the countries of CEE are a mix of the institutions that characterize the LMEs and CMEs. However, it will be clear that this framework, while still productive in the postcommunist environment, needs to be sensitized to the fundamental structural differences between capitalism in the EU (as well as other 'advanced countries' including the USA, Canada, Australia, and Japan) and capitalism in CEE. An adequate analysis of capitalism in CEE must incorporate two features: an almost complete lack of working-class political mobilization and a completely outdated technological structure. As a result, there is much greater reliance on foreign investors and foreign purchasers for providing technology transfer and the training of manpower. I conceptualize this VoC as 'liberal dependent post-communist capitalism' to highlight the liberal nature of the state and the dependent nature of the economy. In most the rest of the post-communist world, FDI and foreign manufacturers play a much smaller role. Instead, patron–client relationships ensnare major enterprises, leading to a decomposition of the bureaucratic (in the Weberian sense of the term) nature of the state. This produces a different variety of post-communist capitalism: patrimonial post-communist capitalism.

This chapter has four sections. Section 11.2 runs through the five elements of the VoC framework with data from Hungary and Poland, and with Russia for contrast. Section 11.3 builds on these differences, and presents a typology of post-communist capitalism, briefly outlining the causal argument. Section 11.4 considers the effects that neoliberal transition policy (so-called 'Shock Therapy'—focusing in particular on neoliberal privatization schemes) has on post-communist firms. Specifically, it argues that neoliberal reforms contribute to some post-communist countries ending up in patrimonial capitalist systems.

11.2. VoC IN CENTRAL EASTERN EUROPE: THE EXPERIENCE OF HUNGARY AND POLAND

11.2.1. Industrial Relations

During the transition from communism, the Polish and Hungarian govern-ments dictated wage policy in the SOE sector through taxes on excessive wages, which did not apply to greenfields and privatized firms. This policy was aban-doned by the mid-1990s, as the SOE sector shrank in importance. Generally, labour as an organized force almost ceased to exist. Even in Poland, the only post-communist country where labour (beyond exceptionally active miners) can be said to have played a major role in the collapse of communism, this generalization holds. Poland had the most active 'civil society' and working class both before and after the transition.

The reasons for labour weakness are both ideological and structural. Ide-ologically, the ultimate enemy of the communist working class, of which parts were probably undergoing a process of class formation near the end of socialism, was the party apparatus. With the transition from communism the class enemy became very unclear, and furthermore there was no conception of an alternative to capitalism.

Structurally, the working class was devastated by the loss of guaranteed full employment, and the loss of roughly a third of all jobs. For example in Hungary, of a total population of 10 million, and 6.2 million of working age (15–64), only 56.4 per cent actually work (according to the CSO Labour Force Survey). This places Hungary in the 'Mediterranean' school of capitalism (comparable figures for Greece are 56.6%, for Italy 53.5%, for Spain 55.0%— whereas the USA has 74%, the UK has 70%, Denmark has 76%, and Austria almost 70%). In Hungary, about a half million people are excluded from the labour force 'and have no (visible) means of support' (Fazekas and Koltay 2002: 15). Unionization rates were slashed with the emergence of greenfields (both domestic and foreign), which typically have completely non-unionized workforces. In addition, manufacturing wages shrank dramatically. At least over the years 1988 to 1996, at official exchange rates, Hungarian manufactur-ing wages fell from 25 per cent of Austrian levels to about 14 per cent of the Austrian level. Measured by Purchasing Power Parity (PPP), manufacturing wages contracted from 60 per cent to 20 per cent of Austrian wages (Ferenczi 2002: 114).

Under these conditions, while tripartite councils as found in the West emerged, they were not 'real' functioning bodies that aggregated inter-ests. They have only one real partner, the government. They serve to help 'spread the blame' for the objective fall in living standards for most of the post-communist working class (this is documented in Ost 2000). In Hungary, wage setting is limited to setting the minimum wage, which applies to only 2 per cent of jobs. Most contracts are negotiated at the level of the plant, or even with individual employees. Thus, the central European system of industrial relations is more similar to those found in LMEs than CMEs, only with 'Mediterranean' levels of labour force participation. In this respect, there is no difference between CEE and the rest of the post-communist world: fake corporatism and worker decomposition can be found throughout.

11.2.2. Vocational Training and Education

The Hungarian education/training system resembles the German system, with local institutions turning out specialized labour. However, according to local experts, there is actually a very weak link between local training institutions and the actual needs of employers. Whereas in the early 1990s about 80 per cent of labour came from such institutions, by 2003 more like 50–60 per cent of labour received this training. Like elsewhere in Europe, Hungary is trying to move towards the American system of general degrees and basic skills. This is driven by the needs of employers in the EU.

By and large, according to two Hungarian experts (who prefer to remain anonymous), the knowledge obtained in these institutions is now non-competitive, and most well-qualified teachers left for the private sector. So, firms increasingly train their own employees. They write contracts with employees to allow them to take the risk of training them. The MNCs have their own training systems, and not infrequently train local labour by temporarily relocating them to West Europe.

The story in Russia seems to be more of the same. The institutes that turned out specialists for the industrial sector, such as the polytechnic institutes, were starved of cash during the transition. While some managed to survive, many more did not—creating a severe shortage of skilled manpower at many firms (King 2003). Without similar levels of FDI as CEE, there is no comparable source of training.

11.2.3. Corporate Governance

With the exception of Russia, firms in post-communist countries rely primarily on large banks for finance (Popov 1999). There are stock markets, but these are very thin, with very few stocks traded, and most of the capitalization is usually from a handful of large companies. What is distinctive about this financial arrangement is the dominant role of foreign banks. It is not clear what the consequences of this are for the long term. However, it seems related to the presence of FDI in manufacturing, as banks tend to follow 'their' firms into CEE. For example in Hungary, the number of banks that were foreign-owned among the total number has steadily increased (from twelve of thirty-five in 1992 to thirty of thirty-eight in 2000) (EBRD 2000: 156). Unfortunately, data on the total assets under foreign control is unavailable. In Poland, in 2001, 77.5 per cent of Polish banking stocks are held by foreigners, compared with 4 per cent in Germany, 3 per cent in Italy, 10 per cent in Spain, and 13 per cent in Austria (Staniszkis 2001: 5).

Overall finance is primarily provided by banks, especially EU-based banks, as well as directly by MNCs. Thus, in this sense, the countries of the CEE are closer to the CME model, only with a very large foreign-owned component.

In Russia, and much of the rest of the post-communist world outside CEE, corporate governance—in terms of finance for firm restructuring/investments—is almost non-existent. Popov summarizes the Russian situation: 'In Russia banks virtually stopped the financing of capital investment. Total bank credits outstanding in relation to GDP declined steadily; in 1992 they ensured the financing of only 10% of total capital investment, in 1993— less than 6% in 1995–1996 less than 1%, i.e. an amount comparable with equity financing' (1999: 20).

The actual 'governance' is a bit complicated. The most important feature of the governance regime of large Russian enterprises is that it consists of patron–client ties linking state officials and their crony (or 'clientelistic' or 'oligarchic') capitalists (see King 2002; King and Szelenyi 2005). Those with political positions, unable to simply transfer ownership to themselves, pick certain clients to promote as 'businessmen', who then support the patron in their political career, as well as their private consumption and accumulation of wealth.

This basic relationship—these patron–client links—permeate the post-Soviet economy. At the very top of the hierarchy were the two highest executive offices in Russia—The President (Putin, and before him Yeltsin) and the Mayor of Moscow (Luzkov). Connected to these politicians were the very biggest 'clientelistic capitalists', the several dozen or so easily identifiable people who can be called upper oligarchs. Khodorkovsky was in the very top of this group—among the so-called 'seven bankers' that ran Yeltsin's re-election campaign.[1] The pattern that dominated the national level was reproduced on a smaller scale around the executive office in Russia's eighty-nine regions and cities. This pattern has only been slightly redrawn with Putin's consolidation of power—only three of the top oligarchs were 'deposed'—Berezovsky,

Guisinsky, and now Khodokovsky. Putin's regime has simply meant a new group of elites (from Petersburg and the security forces) being integrated into the existing oligarch-led business groups. Of course, Putin's rhetoric points in the direction of a type of Bureaucratic Authoritarian (Re) Industrializing Regime, but thus far these efforts have been rather modest.

By the end of the 1990s, more than 50 per cent of the economy's output was concentrated into only ten business groups. Two of these were classic pyramid ownership structures centred around the gas giant Gasprom and the oil giant Lukoil. The other eight had a much more opaque ownership structure, and were centred around a bank controlled by a senior Oligarch. Yakov Pappe, widely regarded in Russia as among the most knowledgeable observers of these business empires, calls them 'Integrated Business Groups' (integrirovannaya business gruppi—IBGs hereafter), controlled by a 'central element' (zentralnii element) that consisted of some upper oligarch (and his close associates) with ties to senior state office holders. These IBGs are integrated both by ownership ties as well as management relationships. There are a series of relationships between IBGs and additional parties, who may share control over an enterprise. The key to this ownership is that it is 'flexible and un-transparent to outsiders' (Pappe 2000: 28. See the conceptualization of the IBGs on pp. 23–37). Unfortunately, this book has not been translated into English yet.[2]

Typically they have a base to generate money in the finance sphere (primarily through providing banking services for the state), holdings in exportable raw materials sectors, other large firms, various media outlets, as well as a host of relationships with federal and regional legislative and executive officers. The ten biggest IBGs in 1997 were (1) 'Gasprom', (2) 'Lukoil', (3) The 'Interros-Onexim' IBG (Potanin's group, including the oil company Sidanko), (4) The 'Khodorkovsky Empire' (including the oil company Yukos), (5) Inkombank (which was destroyed by the financial crisis because its president, the oligarch Vinogradov, failed in his bid to buy the oil companies Yukos and Sibneft, (6) 'Berezovsky–Smolensky empire' (including the oil company Sibneft), (7) 'Rossiskii Kredit' banking group (including the oligarch Malkin, who also was unable to acquire an oil company, but still has a base in metals, (8) 'Alfa-Group Consortium' (controlled by Friedman and Aven, which won control of the oil company TNK), (9) 'Most Group' (Guisinsky's media-financial empire), and (10) 'AFK 'sistema' (a multisectoral company whose activity was 'mostly restricted to enterprise and projects connected to the Moscow administration and it is believed that it received a lot of support from it'.) (Pappe: 183, see 37–8 for the list of top ten IBGs). According to the recent Forbes list of the world's wealthiest people, Russia has the most billionaires of any country after the USA and Japan.

11.2.4. Inter-Firm Relations

The most important feature of the Hungarian enterprise system is the role of FDI, as well as cooperation with customers in export markets, especially the EU. This is most pronounced in Hungary, the country that (along with Estonia) was the early leader in FDI. However, it seems that Hungary may well be the future to which other CEE countries are converging around. In Hungary, the share of affiliates under foreign control in manufacturing value added in 1999 was 70 per cent—compared to less than 20–40 per cent from Sweden, France, Norway, the Netherlands, the UK, and Spain, and less than 20 per cent for Finland, the USA, Portugal, Turkey, and Denmark (OECD 2003: 121). Labour productivity in affiliates under foreign control increased at a rate slightly below 10 per cent per annum from 1995 to 2000, while employment increased by 6 per cent per annum over the same period. In Poland employment increased by about 12 per cent, and labour productivity about 19 per cent (OECD 2003: 121). The share of turnover of affiliates under foreign control in manufacturing was approximately 70 per cent of total turnover by 1997 (OECD 2003: 123), with only Ireland exceeding this level (in contrast, the UK, France, and the USA all score between 20 and 40%, with Germany at only 10%). In Poland, this figure is closer to 35 per cent of turnover. Foreign-controlled firms in Hungary also provided 72 per cent of R&D expenditure (Poland's figure is 18%).

Significant case study data (e.g. King 2001; King and Varadi 2002 for Hungary and King 2002 for Poland), as well as firm-level multivariate analysis (e.g. King 2000 for Hungary), indicates that the role of FDI in technology transfer is substantial. Various data on these points will be presented below.

Another mode of inter-firm relations consists of domestic business groups. I have not seen much empirical analysis of these groups—but what little there is indicates that they also transfer technology throughout the group (Toth 2001). These groups do not appear to be examples of 'recombinant property' (Stark 1996)—but simply privately owned groups, as exist in much of the world. In Poland, about 9 per cent of the European Bank for Reconstruction and Development's (EBRD) random sample of medium and large firms listed ownership as 'domestic business group'.

Outside CEE, firms were embedded in rather different relationships. Namely, firms often forged barter relationships and tolerated reciprocal long-term arrears. Of course, this happened in CEE as well (see King 2002 for case study data on Poland)—but it was primarily the toleration of inter-enterprise arrears, and these typically receded. In contrast, barter relationships (as well as other non-monetary, or even local money transactions) were far more significant in Russia (see EBRD 1999; King 2003).

11.2.5. Firm–Employee Relations

The Hungarian and Polish economies are much closer to the LME norm in terms of firm–employee relations. For the most part, in CEE managers do not have to consult with any organs of employees before making any decisions over the workplace. In interviews, managers of MNCs from the EU appreciate the flexibility of CEE workers. This follows from the radical weakening of the bargaining position of employees following the disappearance of about a third of all jobs.

In Russia, relations with employees are also substantially different than those in CEE. Some Russian workers are in a similar structural position as workers in CEE. However, many others are embedded in neopaternalist relationships with managers. Namely, in many firms, in addition to (or occasionally instead of) wages, managers make available to employees access to consumer goods (such as food), access to land or facilitating petty-agricultural work (by providing power, transportation, and in some cases collectively organizing the farming of potatoes). Typically, the firm would obtain these goods through barter (King 2003).

11.3. SUMMARY OF THE VoC FRAMEWORK IN POST-COMMUNIST SOCIETY

In sum, the VoC framework can be applied to CEE. What this highlights, however, is that the VoC framework captures real and important differences between the most advanced capitalist economies. But the application of VoC to the CEE shows that it takes for granted certain historical and structural features common to these societies—and that trying to extend the model beyond the rich countries of the capitalist core highlights the importance of these features. That is, while the CME–LME distinction is productive in the CEE, it must be contextualized.

The first distinguishing feature of the post-communist world is the almost complete demobilization of the working class. Thus, the role that organized labour plays in CMEs is not reproduced in the post-communist context. Second, the industrial structure is distinguished by significant technological backwardness compared to firms in the EU. This is the problem of being a 'late industrializer; only in this case with a large amount of obsolete industrialization under state socialism.

In the CEE, this means that while countries may be distributed somewhere along a CME–LME divide in different areas, the distinctive features that they share in common is of much greater significance. That is, what unites them, as a result of their backwardness, and the lack of the working-class pressure for coordination, is greater than their respective differences in terms of the VoC typology.

How, then, has the CEE been able to have relative economic success? What substitutes for the missing institutions? The most important answer is that firms in CEE rely on a disproportionate amount of FDI, and among domestic firms, spillovers from dominant purchasers in export markets (i.e. the EU), for the majority of technology transfer and skills training.

The advanced capitalist countries all share a relatively strong bureaucratic state (in the strict Weberian sense of the term) with high capacity. In CEE, because of high levels of FDI, and the configuration of alliances within the post-communist power-elite (see King 2002; King and Szelenyi 2005), state capacity was for the most part preserved, and may have even increased in places. In the rest of the post-communist world, and especially in the former Soviet Union (FSU), the bureaucratic capacity of the state has drastically eroded. Since the transition, paternalistic relationships have only grown in importance, as the bureaucratic coherence of the state was substantially broken down.[3]

The crucial features in creating a typology of post-communist capitalism are (*a*) the existence of a rational-bureaucratic state, and (*b*) who fills the role of the grand bourgeoisie (patron–client cliques or foreign companies)? Table 11.1 compares post-communist countries in CEE and other regions. We can see that the CEE has higher growth, better human development outcomes (life expectancy and level of poverty), greater levels of FDI, and mostly greater state capacity (using a composite indicator from the EBRD) and more secure property rights.

11.4. VARIETIES OF POST-COMMUNIST CAPITALISM

Thus, the expanded typology of post-communist capitalism would be: (*a*) Liberal Dependent Capitalism (with proto-CME and-LME elements) and (*b*) Patrimonial Capitalism. The difference in the institutional and social structural environment in which post-communist firms are embedded is captured in Table 11.2.

11.5. CAPITALISM FROM ABOVE LEADING TO PATRIMONIAL CAPITALISM

I briefly run through the causal narrative implied in Table 11.2. In those countries that ended up with patrimonial systems, a fraction of the communist

Table 11.1. Divergence in post-communist society

	Avg. GDP per capita change 1991–2000 (in 1995 US$)	Change in male life expectancy 1989–2000 (value in 2000)	% of population below poverty 1993–5 (in 1987–8)	FDI net inflow per capita 1990–2000 (BoP data in current US$)	EBRD governance index (1–3) 1999	Insecure property rights 1999
Russia	−3.5	−5 (59.0)	50 (2)	$141	1.16	41.6
Belarus	−0.5	−3 (62.5)	22 (1)	$124	1.57	30.4
Ukraine	−7.1	−5 (63.0)	63 (2)	$69	1.24	44.0
Kazakh.	−2.5	−4 (60.3)	65 (5)	$524	1.27	31.0
Uzbek.	−2.0	+1 (66.7)	63 (25)	$38	1.83	9.6
Romania	−1.8	−1 (66.1)	59 (6)	$292	1.07	21.6
Bulgaria	−1.4	−1 (65.1)	15 (2)	$403	1.38	20.0
Czech	0.1	+3 (71.5)	1 (0)	$2,271	1.59	23.3
Slovakia	0.4	+2 (69.1)	1 (0)	$777	1.65	14.0
Poland	3.7	+2 (71.6)	20 (6)	$1,053	1.69	10.3
Hungary	1.3	+2 (67.1)	4 (1)	$2,106	1.98	12.0
Slovenia	1.9	+3 (71.6)	1 (0)	$856	1.95	11.4

Note: GDP, life expectancy and FDI data from World Bank Development Indicators 2001 (CD-ROM); poverty rates from Branko Milanovic. Income, Inequality and Poverty During the Transition from Planned to Market Economy. (Washington, DC: World Bank, 1998); Governance Index and Insecure Property Rights from World Bank Enterprise Survey.

Table 11.2. Varieties of post-communist capitalism

Type of capitalism	Liberal dependent systems (the Czech Republic, Hungary, and Poland)	Patrimonial systems (Russia, Ukraine, Romania, and Serbia under Milošović)
Transitional political strategy/elite struggle/class and intra-dominant class alliance	Technocracy defeats *nomenklatura* and struggles with former dissidents for hegemony	*Nomenklatura* retains power, uses office to acquire private property, and allies with technocracy
Dominant class formation	Multinationals, some domestic capitalists	Patron–client ownership networks; parasitic financial–industrial Groups
Foreign capital	Dominant	Very limited
Political capitalism, various forms of rent-seeking	Little	Lot, dominant
Domestic (petty and middle) bourgeoisie (SME sector)	Some	Little
Firm integration	Markets with low levels of non-market horizontal coordination (barter, debt-swaps, arrears); substantial export partner tech. transfer	Markets and high levels of non-market horizontal coordination (barter, debt-swaps, and arrears)
Employer–employee relationship	Liberal capitalism, very weak unions	Liberal capitalism, neopatrimonialism (manager distribution of consumer goods and access to means of subsistence)
Industrial policy	Open economy industrial policy; subsidize greenfield and FDI with SOEs	None, or traditional rent-seeking
Leading sector	Manufacturing exports	Raw materials export
Dynamic of accumulation	FDI; importing capital; export driven, some technological upgrading	Political accumulation; capital flight; technological downgrading
Size of the state	Medium	Large
State capacity/formal bureaucracy	Modest/very	Little/almost none
State-economy interaction	State provides adequate public goods (e.g. stock of human capital); some personalistic enforcement of laws; medium informal sector	State does not provide adequate public goods (e.g. stock of human capital); extensive personalistic enforcement of laws by patrons to benefit clients; huge informal sector
Political institutions	Liberal democracy	Pressure towards multiparty authoritarianism (un-free and unfair elections or 'non-polyarchy')

political apparatus was able to retain its power and defend the privileges of its clients. While the momentum of technocratic reforms and intellectual challenges in CEEs in the late 1960s might have been able to radically transform the power structure if not for Soviet military might, the bureaucratic estate in Russia was never seriously challenged. Indeed, the collapse of communism cannot be seen as a defeat of the Communist Party bureaucracy by outside forces. While Russia had dissident intellectuals (such as Solzhenitsyn), who, like in Central Europe, had a role to play in delegitimizing the regime (see Shlapentokh 1990), they were not nearly as powerful relative to the *nomenklatura*. That is, the key players in this transition were members of the political bureaucracy itself (Linz and Stepan 1996; Garcelon 1997; and the authoritative Reddaway and Glinski 2001).

The driving force of change was the Party's growing recognition that it could not compete economically and militarily with Western capitalism (Szelenyi and Szelenyi 1995). Gorbachev should be seen as a technocratic reformer, who used intellectuals as ammunition against the Brezhnev era hardliners that he viewed as standing in the way of necessary reforms (see Shlapentokh 1990). At the same time, the perestroika reforms that legalized individual profitable activity and cooperatives (in 1986 and 1987) created vast opportunities for elites in managerial and ministerial positions to profit as middlemen—enabling them to accumulate personal wealth. (The most outstanding journalistic account is Klebnikov's *The Godfather of the Kremlin* [2000].) This gave at least some 'partocrats' the ability to see a future for themselves in a post-communist world.

Gorbachev's move was initially successful, as he managed to replace much of the top Brezhnev-era elite whom he saw as corrupt and inefficient bureaucratic obstacles to reform (Hanley et al. 1995: 647). However, these reforms started to get out of control as activists in the Baltics and Armenia used glasnost to espouse anti-Russian nationalism. Soon, the partocracy realized they could survive on the regional level, drawing their attention away from the centre, and initiating the disintegration of the Soviet Union (Helf and Hahn 1992; Linz and Stepan 1996).

In the Russian Federation, 1988 saw the emergence of 'civil society' in the form of Democratic Russia (DR). A full 80 per cent of respondents in one survey of DR's Moscow activists were technocrats, or 'specialists'; holders of technical and professional degrees and skills (whereas 28% of those employed in the Russian Republic fit this definition). While this movement mobilized the real discontent and grievances of the intelligentsia, it was nonetheless 'launched from within the highest echelons of the Soviet-Party state. This movement against the party's political monopoly was part of, and contributed to, a struggle of technocratic reformers against party conservatives. This essentially split the party internally, creating two warring factions (the Democratic Platform and the Russian Communist Party)' (Garcelon 1997: 39, 47, 49).

When Gorbachev tried to use limited elections against party conservatives, his strategy backfired. Yeltsin rose to prominence through his control over the Moscow Association of Voters, which provided leadership for the mass-based DR movement. The fact that this was a section of the Communist Party coming to power (and not a non-communist elite, as in Poland) is clear. A full 86 per cent of DR's deputies were party members, and Yeltsin himself had been a member of the Politburo (Garcelon 1997: 64).

In June, the Russian Supreme Soviet declared its 'sovereignty' from the USSR, and a dual-power structure emerged. After the failed coup of 1991, Yeltsin assumed full power over Russian territory. DR, having always been more of a top-down product of a section of the bureaucratic estate, soon withered into irrelevance. Yeltsin chose instead to align with enterprise managers and implement Shock Therapy from above. Indeed, a full 74 per cent of Yeltsin's appointees were members of the *nomenklatura* (Garcelon 1997: 70).

In January 1992, the radical transformation of the Russian economy began. With the help of a team of Western economists headed by Jeffrey Sachs, 'a radical reform package focusing on economic liberalization and privatization was adopted...' (EBRD 1996: 169; see Wedel 2001).

Six months of this Shock Therapy led to unprecedented hyperinflation and a fall in living standards. To shore up support, Yeltsin incorporated into his regime representatives of enterprise directors, such as Chernomyrdin, chairman of the board of Gazprom (Russia's giant natural gas monopoly), who was made vice premier of the fuel and energy sector, and later replaced Gaidar as prime minister when the public outcry against Shock Therapy forced his ousting (Reddaway and Glinski 2001). At the same time that Chernomyrdin joined the government, a privatization plan relying on a combination of citizen vouchers and giveaways to managers and employees was launched in June 1992. This was easily the largest, most rapid transformation of ownership in world history. 'By July of 1994, 15,052 medium- and large-scale enterprises, employing more than 80 per cent of the industrial workforce, had been privatized...' (EBRD 1996: 169). Thus, in Russia, a self-recreated bureaucratic estate, in coalition with elements of the technocracy in charge of large enterprises, unleashed 'capitalism from above' via a full dose of Shock Therapy.

In these systems, communist ideology was of course instantly abandoned, but the former communist parties were not taken over by technocrats and transformed into centrist or even right-wing social democratic movements as happened in the liberal regimes. Instead, the core of the political apparatus retained control over the successor parties and turned the communist ideology into nationalist, often xenophobic, ideology. Iliescu in Romania (at least during the early 1990s—less so after his return to power) and Milošović in Serbia are prime examples. The transformation was more complex in Russia, where the successor party lost political power, but Yeltsin followed policies that were quite similar to those of Iliescu and Milošović.

11.6. THE ECONOMIC INSTITUTIONS OF POST-COMMUNIST PATRIMONIAL CAPITALISM

The neoliberal blueprint for creating capitalism includes rapidly liberalizing prices, eliminating trade barriers, and drastically curtailing the money supply (by reducing monetary emissions, raising interest rates, and curtailing subsidies). As a result, post-communist firms confront a harsh new environment. Rapid price deregulation, given the monopolistic structure of Soviet-style economies, will lead to a jump in the price of inputs. The wholesale liberalization of imports creates an enormous drop in aggregate demand for domestic producers, as they must face global competition. This also cuts off important revenue streams for the state (tariffs and profits from state-owned monopoly trading houses). With monetary emissions severely limited, government subsidies drastically curtailed, and credit dramatically more expensive, most firms run into severe cash flow problems and a shortage of capital for restructuring and even day-to-day transactions. Similarly, there was also the devastation resulting from the political destruction of the Council for Mutual Economic Aid (COMECON) trading system. For many states, the vast majority of exports and imports were from the COMECON, accounting for a huge amount of economic activity. The breakdown of this trading system therefore disrupted supply chains and created a gigantic loss of markets (for a discussion of these points, see Amsden, Kochanowicz, and Taylor 1994; Gowan 1995, 1999; Chussodovsky 1997; Andor and Summers 1998; UNDP 1999; Stiglitz 2002).

In addition to these shocks, many firms suffered shocks associated with mass privatization (King 2002, 2003; Ellerman 2003). While the rapid privatization of small- and some medium-sized businesses is beneficial because it provides a superior incentive structure for those in control of these enterprises, large SOEs cannot be rapidly privatized without unacceptable costs. Most importantly, mass privatization means that the resulting private corporation will not have an owner or owners with sufficient resources to restructure the company. Without any capital to carry out desperately needed restructuring, and without the injection of any new managerial talent, many firms found themselves in untenable positions. Mass privatization also frequently created outside owners with very poor arrangements to monitor firm managers or even to monitor other (typically inside) owners. This was virtually inevitable, as these economies lacked a developed business information infrastructure, and effective legal protection of shareholder rights, that help 'make markets' in advanced capitalist systems.

The combination of these two conditions led to massive amounts of asset stripping in the post-communist economy, wreaking havoc on the functioning of many firms. This is a paradox from the neoliberal perspective—while involving the state in the economy is allegedly a recipe for rent-seeking behaviour—not involving the state in the transition creates an environment that encourages corruption (see King 2001a, 2001b).

Only those firms with privileged access to raw materials, or those that enjoy 'natural protection' as a result of prohibitive shipping costs are likely to be able to successfully restructure (King 2002, 2003; for useful reviews of sectoral change in the Russian economy (Schröder [1998]). This creates what Gustofson (1999: 219) calls a 'barbell economy' to indicate the hollowing out of the manufacturing sector, leaving only a significant raw materials sector and a financial services sector (the sphere of 'merchant capital' (Burawoy and Krotov 1992) or financial clientelism (King 2001a).

In regimes of 'capitalism from above', the combination of massive structural challenges facing enterprises led by 'inappropriate' agents typically results in economic disaster. Asset stripping typically becomes the most 'rational' way to respond, further exacerbating the precarious position of most firms (see King 2003). In this situation, firms frequently cannot afford to pay wages. This contributes to labour markets remaining underdeveloped, and paternalism frequently characterizes the relationship between workers and managers. This retreat from labour markets leads firms to aid workers in gaining access to the means of subsistence. Workers typically must resort to food grown on garden plots or collective potato farming to survive, and they are thus increasingly reunited with the means of their subsistence (Burawoy and Krotov 1992; Southworth 2001; King 2002). The enterprise and the household become increasingly merged. As vertical patron–client relations grow in importance, workers are separated from each other, and their 'classness' decreases.

As firms entered into financial crisis and technical bankruptcy, they frequently could not pay taxes, and so tax revenues declined drastically along with the economy. In Russia, for example, receipts of the consolidated state budget declined from 41 per cent of GDP in 1990 to only 26.8 per cent in 1997, even though GDP was only about 50 per cent of its prior level (Vorobyov and Zhukov 2002: 5). This loss of revenues, when combined with the anti-statist ideology of the neoliberals, quickly led to a lack of state support for the basic institutions that enable firms to successfully restructure by raising their quality and changing their product line to compete on the world market. An important instance of this occurs when the state stops supporting the educational institutions that turn out skilled manpower, leading to a crisis for many firms. Of particular importance is the production of experts with scientific credentials by local polytechnic institutes. While some of this shortage is caused by brain drain, case study data indicates that much is also the result of a shortage of new technicians (see McDermott 2002 for the Czech Republic and King 2002 for Russia). Furthermore, because the crisis of education also affects primary educational institutions, the shortage of skilled manpower will only intensify in the future (UNDP 1999: 58).

As a result of widespread financial crises, firms up and down commodity chains were unable to get the money or credit they needed to continue production. Rather than go out of business, however, managers reactivated old 'horizontal' ties (or generated new ones) to managers at other firms that functioned to compensate for the scarcity of inputs in the shortage economy. These networks now function to aid in production, given the absence of money and credit in the new capitalist economy. These network ties allow the firms to withdrawal from the market through inter-enterprise arrears, debt-swaps and barter (see David Woodruff 1999 for an outstanding account of these processes in Russia). Barter decreases the efficiency of transactions (because a middleman typically must be used), shields firms from market pressures (because business partners are selected on network ties, not price considerations), and makes taxation highly problematic (because it makes it easy to conceal transactions from the state, and because in-kind taxes are easy to overvalue when they are paid, and these are difficult and expensive to collect anyway).

The loss of tax revenue from enterprise failure, exacerbated by the rise of hard-to-tax barter inevitably weakened the state. As the state was increasingly unable to meet its formal obligations, it began to break down. Poorly paid (or unpaid) state officials are easily corrupted, and the bureaucratic nature of the state decomposed. It became riddled by reactivated (as well as new) patron–client ties between government officials and businessmen. Private market success came to depend to a high degree on arbitrary political decisions and the exercise of private force. As the state both gets weaker and loses its bureaucratic character, 'mafias' rise to fulfil some of the functions of the state—such as contract enforcement (Varere 2001).

Over time, the politically constituted ownership groups will spread throughout the economy—swallowing up the shares of insider-dominated firms that can be stripped of their assets in one way or another. Therefore, the compromise between the bureaucratic estate and enterprise managers will not result in equal gains for both segments of the former elite in the long run. In Russia, the eventual takeover of insider-owned firms by politically connected financial groups, who then typically fail to make any investment into restructuring the enterprise, is quite common.

Capitalism from above is also not conducive to the development of domestic small businesses. Since in both trajectories there was the massive privatization of the public sector, starting small and growing bigger was very difficult. The ensuing economic collapse and state disintegration (which includes an increase in the size of mafia groups to fill the void), and inability of banks to provide loans to new enterprises (banks funnel money out of the system, they do not turn savings into investments [see Popov 1999 for an insightful discussion of the specificity of the Russian banking system in comparative post-communist perspective], means that new enterprises face incredible odds.

Finally, the economic changes that result from following the path of 'capitalism from above' will have inevitable political consequences. Specifically, the existence of a large class of political capitalists who owe their very ownership of property to particular patrons in political office means that there will be enormous pressure to erode the institutions of democracy. For, unlike in Hungary or Poland, owners in Russia may lose their property rights if their patron loses office. Thus, what results are systems in which elections matter, but they are neither particularly free nor fair.

11.7. CAPITALISM FROM WITHOUT LEADING TO LIBERAL CAPITALISM

On the whole classes were not particularly well formed under state socialism. Socialist society can be better described as a rank order, rather than a class stratified society. Nevertheless, classes were in formation and in particular the strength of the working class had far-reaching consequences for how intra-class struggles among various factions of the ruling elites unfolded. Arguably, in Central Europe, in particular in Hungary and Poland, the power monopoly of the political apparatus had been challenged for quite sometime by an emerging alliance between enlightened technocrats, usually operating within the communist party, and critical intellectuals (Kennedy 1992).

This alliance was based on common interest. Politically, both wanted freedom from the bureaucratic estate. Economically, both believed they could do just as well in a capitalist system by becoming professionals and selling their relatively scarce labour power on the market or by becoming entrepreneurs. A major factor in this was the possibility of working for some large multinational corporation.

The formation of the working class was the most advanced in Poland of course, where the collective action of workers in 1980 almost brought down the rule of the communist political apparatus, which was only saved by the military dictatorship of Jaruzelski. In the summer of 1981, sudden price hikes precipitated strikes throughout the country, but particularly in the Baltic cities. In August, general strikes in Gdansk and Szczecin spread through the country, ending with government recognition of the right to form independent unions (Kramer 1995: 673). The working class entered into an alliance with a group of dissident intellectuals that had defended worker strikes in 1976 (Kennedy 1987; Bernhard 1993). The workers and intellectuals picked up the support of the disaffected technocrats and professionals (Kennedy 1987; Kennedy 1992; Kubic 1994), culminating in the ten million-strong Solidarity Union (which was four times larger than the Communist Party, and ten times greater than the official trade unions [Ost 1990: 139–40]). From this movement an anti-communist political counter-elite was created, bent on abolishing the *nomenclatura* and wresting control from the bureaucratic estate (Wasilewski and Wnuk-Lipinski 1995: 674).

For the rest of 1981, Solidarity tried to negotiate the institutionalization of its power to determine and implement economic policy. Ultimately, the government would not agree to share its economic power. Massive strikes continued throughout the year, precipitating Jaruzelski's imposition of martial law, during which he outlawed Solidarity and arrested many of its leaders (Ost 1990: 113–48). The threat of Soviet intervention was crucial in this.

In an effort to restore some legitimacy, Jaruzelski sought to drive a wedge between intellectuals and workers, to make concessions to the Church, and even to open up to a small class of 'socialist entrepreneurs' like in Hungarian (Ost 1990: 155; Kennedy 1992: 55–6; Korbonski 1999: 146). While Solidarity was weakened by this, Jaruzelski never won any measure of legitimacy, and Poland continued to undergo serious economic problems and the build-up of international debt (partially to bolster consumption, and partially to try to invest its way out of the slump) (Korbonski 1999: 143). Unable to garner support for his 1987 economic plan, and with the additional blow of the new Polish Pope (John Paul II) calling for the re-legalization of Solidarity, the party teetered near collapse. As a result of declining living standards, a new round of strikes started in Gdansk and Krakow in April of 1988. In August, strikes started in Silesia and began to spread northward. That same month, Jarazelski initiated the Round Table meeting with the opposition, which would lead, in short order, to the decisive defeat of the government in semi-free elections, ending Communist rule.

Hungary followed a somewhat similar patter. While the Hungarian working class never engaged in the kind of collective action taken by the Polish working class, it was sufficiently a threat to the communist apparatus that it had to try to buy political peace by opening up the second economy to workers and peasants. The resulting petty bourgeoisification in Hungary played a substantial role in eroding the ideological hegemony of the communist bureaucracy and laid the groundwork for the Hungarian technocratic-intellectual alliance to defeat the bureaucracy (Rona-Tas 1997). In both countries the political apparatus was wiped out in 1989. It lost political power altogether, and therefore had neither the will nor the capacity to carry out a project of political capitalism. It did, however, have an ideology. The ideology of the victorious technocratic-intellectual elite by 1989 was neoliberalism (see Eyal, Szelenyi, and Townsley 1998; Eyal 2000). However, the technocratic-intellectual alliance did not last for too long. The intellectual elite turned against the technocracy, which was now seen as part of the former communist establishment.

In 1990, in both Poland and Hungary the newly formed Socialist Party suffered humiliating defeat. The intellectuals themselves were split into liberal- and patriotic-Christian wings and the last decade can be described as struggles among these various political forces. Nevertheless, despite the political differences between all of these intellectual and technocratic elites, they favoured neoliberal policies, and in particular, cooperation with foreign investors. Hungary and Poland are in many respects the 'purest types', the alliance of classes or elites may have been somewhat different in the other liberal regimes, but our key hypothesis is that in all of these regimes the communist bureaucracy was unseated by an alliance between reform-minded technocrats with liberal and patriotic-Christian intellectuals. This alliance received some initial support from the working class, though for the most part it was demobilized after the defeat of the communist bureaucracy.

In these regimes, neoliberalism served as the ideological cement to the alliance of the technocracy and the political dissidents (the humanistic intellectuals). Its chief appeal was its radical anti-statism (see Eyal 2000 for a more elaborate analysis of the role of 'monetarism'). However, because these systems were functioning democracies, political elites abandoned strict adherence to neoliberal precepts (see King 2003b; King and Sznajder 2006), especially ideas favouring the quick 'mass' privatization of the SOE sector. First, direct sales to foreigners were prevalent everywhere in Central Europe. The Hungarians privatized relatively rapidly via auctions, which frequently resulted in FDI. Slovakia, Slovenia, and Poland delayed the privatization of many large SOEs, choosing to first restructure them and then privatize them later through competitive auctions (often to MNCs).[4] Only the Czech Republic managed to implement a significant mass privatization programme—which most analysts now acknowledge led to major problems in 'governance'. Only the Czech Republic's very high level of FDI has kept this country out of the patrimonial camp.

11.8. THE ECONOMIC INSTITUTIONS OF POST-COMMUNIST LIBERAL CAPITALISM

To the extent that the Central European cases pursued the neoliberal transition strategy, and to the extent that they were dependent on imports from and exports to the former COMECON system (the economic counterpart to the Warsaw Pact), they suffered de-industrialization just as in the FSU. However, FDI partially compensates for the problems created by shock liberalization and stabilization, as it leads to re-industrialization. Multinationals provide capital and technology, expertise, and access to world markets. This allows more firms in non-resource-based manufacturing to restructure to enable their survival on the market—and to export to Western Europe without massive technological downgrading and occasionally with substantial upgrading (see case studies in King 2001a, 2001b; King and Varadi 2002; King 2002). Taxes from these restructuring privatized firms, as well as continued revenues from large SOEs and their domestic suppliers, allow the economy to avoid the vicious circle of declining state capacity and market withdrawal that follows from 'capitalism from above'. The presence of high levels of FDI also reduces the level of non-market firm survival strategies like barter and inter-enterprise arrears, as well as reducing wage arrears.

The new private economy will be strengthened, as large greenfields, as well as small joint ventures, emerge. Domestically owned small- and medium-sized businesses, however, are likely to suffer in at least the short- and medium-term because of foreign competition in consumer markets, and the replacement of industrial input producers with the suppliers from elsewhere in the global empires of MNCs. Basically, there will be capitalist growth, but it will depend on the investment strategy of particular MNCs, the lending decisions of foreign-owned banks, and the ability to import industrial inputs and capital from, and export manufactured goods to, the core of the capitalist world economy.

Finally, democracy is consolidated because relatively little political capitalism exists, resulting in little pressure to manipulate elections.

11.9. CONCLUSION

The VoC approach has proven durable, and its focus on business groups and firms offers great leverage for understanding the institutional make-up of the new capitalist countries of Eastern Europe. However, since the basic parameters of the political economy are substantially different in the post-communist world compared with the European core, its VoC does not fit into the CME–LME axis. The CEE had already been industrialized, but this industrialization was carried out within the Soviet system, creating two crucial differences with Western Europe. It meant that most fixed assets in the industrial structure were obsolete in an open economy, leading to a radical reorganization of almost all economic activity, as well as a massive economic contraction. It also meant that the economy went from one with a permanent excess of demand for labour to one with not nearly enough demand. In short, workers were subject to a catastrophic fall in their material existence and security of employment.

The VoC perspective is premised on a working class that can be in some sense a partner with employers' associations. This does not hold in CEE (not even in Poland). Thus there is much less coordination. Similarly, the obsolescence of the Soviet-era industrial system, and the lack of sizeable domestic banks or developed stock markets, necessitated a much greater reliance on technology from foreign investors and foreign customers. Therefore, the creation of technology and the training of personnel is mostly denationalized. For foreign investors and customers, CEE can increasingly serve as a factory with far more flexible, and far cheaper, labour.

Still, CEE capitalism is much closer to that found in the European core than in the FSU. Instead of the reliance on FDI and technology transfer from large customers in the core, this type of capitalism is integrated by patron–client ties between owners (i.e. 'oligarchs' and political elites). Labour is just as marginalized, although it relies far more on a return to subsistence agriculture to survive as well as paternalistic handouts from the state.

Thus there are at least two different species of post-communist capitalism, distinct from CMEs and LMEs. Liberal dependent capitalism in CEE, uniquely dependent on FDI and relations with customer firms, and patrimonial capitalism in the FSU, which offers a huge role for personalistic connections to state officials in integrating firms. Liberal dependent capitalism looks a lot more like capitalism in the European core than does patrimonial capitalism. The latter belongs to perhaps another genus of capitalism—that without an effective, Weberian bureaucratic state.

NOTES

1. The others were Berezovsky, Guisinsky (who controlled the major TV stations and many other mass media organizations), Smolensky, Potanin, Vinogradov, and Fridman/Aven.
2. These IBGs do not map onto the official Financial Industrial Groups that emerged with Yeltsin's decree in 1995 (Pappe 2000: 36).
3. It is well known, for example, that throughout Communism, one might give 'gifts' to service providers (doctors, dentists), one would never bribe a policeman. Today that is reversed.
4. In 1995, a small programme covering some small and medium enterprises was implemented in Poland. These firms constituted only about 10% of the productive capacity of the SOE sector (Baltowski and Mickanwicz 2000).

12

The Origins of Varieties of Capitalism: Lessons from Post-Socialist Transition in Estonia and Slovenia

Magnus Feldmann

12.1. INTRODUCTION

Post-socialist transition is a fascinating process for students of comparative capitalism, not least to scholars interested in the VoC framework developed by Hall and Soskice (2001). It represents a large-scale experiment in political, economic, and institutional change, in which almost thirty countries abandoned the socialist political-economic system around the same time. As transition has unfolded, a tremendous diversity of political and economic regimes has emerged in Eastern Europe and the FSU (Ekiert and Hanson 2003). Some of these countries have become consolidated democracies and market economies. Most notably, eight of them were invited to join the European Union in 2004. At the other extreme, several post-Soviet republics have developed into full-fledged authoritarian regimes. Still others are partly free or 'competitive-authoritarian,' with economic systems displaying idiosyncratic mixtures of markets and statism (Levitsky and Way 2002). The diversity of economic outcomes—measured in economic growth, inflation, and other indicators—is just as striking. Some countries have reached GDP per capita that dramatically exceed pre-transition levels (in Poland's case by about 50%), whereas many others have yet to regain the 1989 output (EBRD 2004).

The variety of economic institutions is equally remarkable. Many studies of post-communist economic institutions argue that core features of East European capitalism are idiosyncratic (Stark 1996; McDermott 1998; Stark and Bruszt 1998; Lane 2001). While not necessarily disputing the existence of unique features, other analysts have related the transitional political economies to Western models. Several studies have applied the VoC framework to post-socialist countries and shown its utility for understanding transitional institutions (Feldmann 2002, 2006; Crowley 2005; Buchen 2006).

Like Feldmann's and Buchen's papers, this chapter focuses primarily on post-socialist transition in Estonia and Slovenia as a laboratory to study an important question for VoC, namely the origins of different kinds of economic coordination. While the VoC literature has provided a very compelling account of the success, sustainability and internal logic of different institutional equilibria, our understanding of the forces bringing about different varieties in the first place is less developed. This chapter attempts to make a contribution to this growing literature (Streeck and Yamamura 2001; Thelen 2004) by studying two post-socialist countries in great detail. The existence of different VoC in transition countries opens up an exciting opportunity to study how different patterns of coordination emerge. Unlike in the Western European cases, whose origins often date back to the nineteenth century and were tied up with long and complex processes of industrialization, the Eastern European cases are recent and arose in the context of industrialized economies.

In this chapter, I develop a theory of network-promotion and network-disruption to account for the origins of different VoC in transition periods, and I argue that this is a compelling micro-foundation for thinking about the incentives for market-based and institutionalized coordination, as defined by the VoC literature. I apply it to the Estonian and Slovenian cases, which I show to be good examples of LME and CME institutions, respectively. I focus on industrial relations and wage bargaining, often viewed as a central building block of modern capitalist political economies.

Estonia and Slovenia are particularly good test cases for the VoC theory, since they are both very small and open countries (with 1.4 and 1.9 million inhabitants, respectively) that became independent in 1991. For that reason they are particularly dependent on world markets, and conventional wisdom suggests that they should have limited policy autonomy. However, Estonia and Slovenia have embarked on very different reform paths, yet both of them are generally viewed as success stories of transition. Their overall economic performance, as measured by most standard indicators, has been good. They have both developed into well-functioning democracies and market economies, and they received the EU's seal of approval for these reforms in conjunction with their accession to the Union. These outcomes challenge the notion that there is necessarily a unique first-best reform strategy for all transition countries (Blanchard et al. 1991). The findings are consistent with the key VoC premise that there are at least two viable institutional frameworks for structuring market economies.

The structure of the chapter is as follows. I begin by describing some key features of Estonian and Slovenian economic institutions and show that they are good examples of LME and CME institutions. After that I develop my theoretical framework outlining the incentives for market-based and institutional coordination, which I then use to analyse the emerging institutions in Estonia and Slovenia. Section 12.5 concludes with some general lessons from this analysis for the study of the origins of VoC.

12.2. EMERGING VoC IN ESTONIA AND SLOVENIA

Estonia and Slovenia have developed into very different political economies over the past decade and a half. Estonia implemented a set of radical market-liberal policies in early transition. These reforms included a flat income tax, which has later been adopted by several other transition countries. Arguably the most remarkable reforms included the adoption of a currency board and a unilateral free trade regime, which turned Estonia into a kind of Hong Kong of Europe. Estonia's FDI regime has also been liberal, yet unlike virtually all the other transition countries Estonia has largely eschewed selective incentives for specific foreign investors and all elements of activist industrial policy (Feldmann and Sally 2002).

By contrast, Slovenia chose a more gradual path to the market. Changes were implemented more slowly, and liberalization coexisted with efforts to shield the economy from dramatic shocks. Relatively generous social welfare provisions, public works programmes, and unemployment protection helped to protect workers. Slovenia introduced a liberal foreign trade and payments regime, but some trade protection was retained. Instead of a currency board, Slovenia opted for a managed float, and capital controls have been introduced temporarily to deal with major shocks to payments flows. In addition, the economic reform programme (notably the mode of privatization) has effectively limited the scope for foreign investment (Mrak et al. 2004).

In Feldmann (2006), I show that Estonia and Slovenia can be viewed as good examples of an LME and a CME respectively, and in this chapter I draw on that analysis to demonstrate that these two countries represent different VoC. I focus most of my attention on industrial relations and wage bargaining and then I briefly summarize the main evidence on the other key dimensions of coordination considered by VoC analysis—training, corporate governance, inter-firm relations, and employee relations in the following section. If the coordination of these relations is market based (based on arm's-length market relations) or institutionalized (based on non-market relations, implicit contracts, etc.), then I will view this as evidence of an LME and a CME, respectively.[1] (Table 12.1 summarizes the main findings.)

Table 12.1. Estonia and Slovenia as varieties of capitalism

	Estonia as an LME: market coordination	Slovenia as a CME: institutionalized coordination
Industrial relations	• Low union membership • Limited employers' coordination • Decentralized wage bargaining; low coverage of wage agreements • No social dialogue	• High union membership • High membership rates in employers' organization • Centralized wage bargaining; high coverage rates of wage agreements • Social dialogue/ co-determination
Employee relations	Shorter job tenure	Longer job tenure
Inter-firm relations	Limited employers' coordination	More employers' coordination (e.g. in training)
Corporate governance	Predominance of short-term capital and high stock market capitalization	More long-term capital and bank-based finance; lower stock-market capitalization
Education and training	Education and training fosters general skills	Apprenticeship and traineeship system fosters firm- and industry-specific skill formation

Sources: Hall and Soskice (2001) and Feldmann (2006).

12.2.1. Industrial Relations and Wage Bargaining

Industrial relations and wage bargaining are organized very differently in Estonia and Slovenia. In this chapter I consider four different indicators to show that Estonian and Slovenian industrial relations are typical of an LME and a CME, respectively.

First, as shown in Table 12.2, unionization rates in Estonia and Slovenia are different. As in other transition countries, union membership in both Estonia and Slovenia has fallen dramatically since the early 1990s. The main reason for this is that the role of unions has changed from being essentially a state institution administering benefits and holidays to more genuine interest organizations. Under central planning union membership was virtually compulsory, even among management and white-collar professionals. This could not be expected to continue in a market economy.

In Slovenia union membership fell from 69 per cent in 1989 to 42.8 per cent in 1998 (Stanojević 2000: 89), which remains high by transition economy standards. ZSSS, the oldest union with roots from the communist period, has a dominant position with more than 50 per cent of total union members. Intermediate-sized unions, like KNSS-Neodvisnost and especially sectoral

Table 12.2. Estimated bargaining coverage rates and unionization rates in eight EU candidate countries, 1999–2001

Country	Coverage rates of collective agreements (%)	Unionization rate (%)
Czech Republic	25–30	30
Estonia	No aggregate data available	14
Hungary	45–50	20
Latvia	Under 20	30
Lithuania	10–15	15
Poland	No aggregate data available	15
Slovakia	50	40
Slovenia	Almost total	41.3

Sources: Ladó (2002) and Järve, Kallaste, and Eamets (2001).

unions, like the paper industry workers' union PERGAM and others, are also quite influential in some branches.

The fall in unionization has been much sharper in Estonia—from 93 per cent in 1990 to about 14 per cent in 2000 (Järve, Kallaste, and Eamets 2001: 14). In Estonia the two largest trade union confederations covering the vast majority of the organized workforce are EAKL (the main union and successor to Soviet labour organizations) and TALO (the white-collar union). Total union membership in 2000 was just over 100,000 workers (of a labour force of about 705,000), with about 58,000 members in EAKL and 40,000 members in TALO (Järve, Kallaste, and Eamets 2001).

Secondly, the contrast in terms of *employers' organizations* is even greater. Membership of companies in the Slovenian Chamber of Commerce (the key employers' organization responsible for wage bargaining) is compulsory. In most transition countries institutionalized coordination among firms and broad-based negotiations with organized labour are very difficult, because employers' organizations have low membership rates and are very weak. Compulsory membership in the Chamber of Commerce has helped avoid this problem, especially with respect to centralized wage bargaining. In this regard Slovenia's industrial relations system is unique among transition countries, and in many ways it bears greater resemblance to CMEs like Belgium or Finland than to any of the transition countries (Ladó, 2002). More recently, other employers' organizations (like the Organisation of Slovenian Employers) have also gained in importance.

By contrast, the Chamber of Commerce in Estonia has a small membership and plays a limited role. It focuses mainly on advancing trade relations and has no role in the social dialogue with unions or in wage bargaining. The only employers' organization with a key function in social dialogue is ETTK, the Estonian Central Employers' Organization, but its representativeness is very limited. Just over 1,000 companies (employing around 100,000 workers) out of Estonia's approximately 28,000 active companies are members. This limits its role in social dialogue and public policy more generally.

Thirdly, and most remarkably, there is a sharp contrast between the two countries in the realm of *wage bargaining*. Slovenia stands out among all transition countries, in that it has the most comprehensive collective bargaining agreements, which are negotiated in the Economic and Social Council. To date, four multi-year tripartite agreements have been concluded at the national level. Slovenia is the only transition country with legally binding bipartite agreements at the central or national level (Ladó 2002: 2). Bargaining rounds typically begin with the conclusion of two separate national agreements—one for the public and one for the private sector. These agreements define minimum requirements for wages in different positions and given a certain level of experience and training, and also various other requirements for work safety, etc. After that sectoral and sometimes firm-level (mainly in successful companies) agreements are concluded, which always have to follow the minimum provisions stipulated at the higher level. As illustrated in Table 12.2, the coverage rate of the agreements is about 100 per cent.

It is hardly surprising that Estonia, with one of the lowest union membership rates in the transition world, has very low coverage of collective agreements.[2] Like in most other transition countries, the main bargaining level is the company level, which is related to the low coverage rates (Ladó 2002: 3). Only about 36,000 workers, mostly in the public sector, were covered by sectoral collective agreements in 2000. In the early years after independence many agreements barely went beyond paraphrasing existing legal stipulations. More recently, their scope has increased to cover workplace safety and other issues. Company-level agreements are most common, but they still only cover about 11 per cent of the workforce (Järve, Kallaste, and Eamets 2001).

Fourthly, at the firm level the principle of co-determination is legally enshrined in Slovenia. In addition to their role in management following from their ownership shares (see discussion of privatization below), the Co-Determination Act has guaranteed workers some representation in works councils and on the management and supervisory boards of companies (Prašnikar et al. 2002). The majority of Slovenian firms have works councils resembling the *Betriebsräte* in Germany. There is also the option to include a workers' representative on the management board. In firms with a labour force between 500 and 1,000 employees, a third of the supervisory board have to be worker representatives; and for firms with over 1,000 employees, the employees' share on the board rises to one-half (Domadenik and Prašnikar 2004). In Estonia such representation in firm management or through co-determination is strictly voluntary and extremely limited.

Finally, it should also be noted that organized labour and business are also represented in the Second Chamber of the Slovenian parliament, the State Council. It was established as 'the representative of the bearers of social, economic, professional and local interests' (Article 96 of the Constitution). It has forty members representing local communities, business, unions, farmers, the educational and medical professions, sports, and the arts. Its practical power is quite limited and resembles the House of Lords in Britain, in that it is able to delay (but not indefinitely block) legislation. It may be said to constitute another example of the emphasis on social dialogue and political representation of functional groups.

The Estonian institution that comes closest to this is the *Ühiskondlik Lepe* (Social Accord or, in the official translation, Public Understanding Foundation), sponsored by former President Arnold Rüütel. It is based on a general declaration emphasizing the need for collaboration and consensus on issues of crucial national importance. The Social Accord has a wide range of signatories, including labour market actors, civil society representatives, and political parties, but its role is much less significant than that of its Slovenian counterpart. Its role is purely advisory (and unrelated to the legislative process, unless issues are explicitly referred to it). Therefore, the Social Accord has yet to find a clear role in Estonian social dialogue.

In short, as this brief overview illustrates, industrial relations, wage bargaining, and social dialogue more generally operate very differently in Estonia and Slovenia. On key indicators these contrasts correspond to the VoC blueprints. In Estonia workers and employers are weakly organized, industrial relations are decentralized and there is no co-determination, placing the country in the LME camp. By contrast, Slovenia's industrial relations can be viewed as a good example of CME-style institutions.

12.2.2. Other Dimensions of VoC

A full examination of the other dimensions of VoC goes beyond the scope of this chapter. Instead I provide a brief overview to suggest that the distinction between market-based and institutionalized coordination captures contrasts between the two countries in other domains as well.

As noted above, there is a better organizational infrastructure for *inter-firm relations*, especially through compulsory membership in the Chamber of Commerce. In addition, other employers' organizations, like the Employers' Organization of Slovenia, are gaining in importance. In Estonia, like in most transition countries, coordination among firms is limited, and employers' cooperation remains underdeveloped.

Employee relations differ sharply between the two countries. Most analysts concur that Estonia has a relatively flexible labour market, whereas the Slovenian labour market is more heavily regulated (Orazem and Vodopivec 2000). A core indicator distinguishing labour relations in LMEs and CMEs is the time frame of employment relationships. In this regard there is a clear difference between the two countries. Average job tenure in Estonia, at 6.9 years (1999), is among the shortest in the transition world. In Slovenia average job tenure in 1999 was 12.1 years, which is one of the highest figures in this group (Cazes and Nesporova 2001: Table 6). Moreover, as noted above, the principle of co-determination is legally enshrined in Slovenia, unlike in Estonia. Welfare provisions, unemployment protection, and public works programmes are also more generous in Slovenia.[3]

In terms of *corporate governance* it bears noting that capital markets are still underdeveloped, with low ratios of credit to GDP. The role of the banking systems in corporate governance is still limited. However, the trends are suggestive of LME–CME-type contrasts. Stock market capitalization has been higher in Estonia than in Slovenia, where bank finance has played a comparatively greater role. An indicative figure is that market capitalization in 2001 was about 35 per cent of GDP in Estonia, whereas it was about 26 per cent in Slovenia. Estonia's stock market capitalization is among the highest in the transition world (Sutela, 2001; Prašnikar et al. 2002).[4]

Vocational training has developed very differently in Estonia and Slovenia. Under the socialist system practically all countries placed a heavy emphasis on specific skills, and there were close ties between enterprises and state-run technical schools. In Estonia a major reform of training was introduced in 1998. It involved a major overhaul of technical high schools and post-secondary professional education and training. A key objective of the reform effort was to promote general skills (Järve, Kallaste, and Eamets 2001; Buchen 2006).

By contrast, the Slovenian system includes a greater focus on traineeships and fostering firm-specific skills. Vocational training system is coordinated both by the state and the Chamber of Commerce, the Chamber of Crafts, and trade unions, and there are concerted attempts to strengthen the coordination between labour market actors to standardize industry-specific skill provision (Pirher et al. 1999: 40). According to one analyst the Slovenian system has been converging on a system that is very similar to the German model (Buchen 2006: 91).

In summary, the contrast between economic coordination in Estonia and Slovenia is striking. Despite some anomalies the two countries have developed into relatively pure cases of LMEs and CMEs.

12.3. TOWARDS A THEORY OF EMERGING
VoC COORDINATION

12.3.1. Network-Promotion and Network-Disruption

capitalism

X

The objective of this chapter is to probe into the origins of different VoC based on experience of Estonia and Slovenia during post-socialist transition. A variety of capitalism can be characterized as an economic system where a particular mechanism for managing firm relations predominates. Depending on the VoC, firms either use market-based or institutionalized coordination to structure their core relationships. In a well-established variety of capitalism firm strategy is likely to be driven by institutional complementarities and the benefits from following institutional comparative advantage. As Hall and Soskice note, in any national economy firms will gravitate towards the model of coordination, for which there is institutional support (Hall and Soskice 2001: 9).

Firm behaviour in emerging market economies is more complicated. In the context of post-socialist transition many of the relevant institutions do not exist, and therefore self-reinforcing mechanisms deriving from well-established comparative institutional advantage cannot determine firm strategy. Instead enterprises have to decide how to coordinate their activities in a new, uncertain, and rapidly changing environment. Post-socialist transition provides us with a laboratory to examine how economic actors adjust and respond when market forces are unleashed. The key feature of periods of dramatic change, and post-socialist transition in particular, is uncertainty (Roland 2000). If complementary institutions exist at a given moment in time, the uncertainty of the transition process means that these institutions may not be sustained. It is even unclear which firms will survive, as in many cases their production processes, supply chains, and technology need to be dramatically reformed. Given that much of the production in a command economy was not determined by market criteria, some sectors may even have generated negative value added at world market prices (McKinnon 1991). Without restructuring, such sectors would probably be swept away by Schumpeterian gales of creative destruction, when subjected to the full force of free market competition.

A theory of emerging VoC must explain how patterns of coordination develop under such circumstances. It needs to specify under what conditions firms choose to coordinate industrial relations, inter-firm relations, training, employee relations, and corporate governance through arm's-length relationships mediated by markets and formal contracts, as in LMEs. It also needs to spell out the incentives for concluding implicit contracts and establishing institutionalized coordination, like in CMEs.

To explain the divergent tendencies towards CMEs and LMEs in transition countries I propose a theory of network-promotion and network-disruption. Like several other scholars, I argue that the role of networks or ties between key economic actors is a critical distinguishing feature of LMEs and CMEs (Hall and Soskice 2001; Streeck 2001; Goodin 2003). I define networks as a set of actors with formal or informal ties to each other that have the capacity to bring about collective action by deliberation, sharing information, monitoring each other, and punishing defection (Hall and Soskice 2001: 10; see also Ostrom 1990). If transition sustains and fosters such interaction, I define this process as network-promoting. Institutionalized coordination cannot exist if there are no actors with the capacity to ensure collective action and to enforce longer time horizons. If networks exist, and if there are specific gains to be achieved from institutionalized coordination, then it is likely that CME institutions will develop.

By contrast, if such networks do not exist or are destroyed, then it will not be possible to achieve institutionalized coordination. When marketization processes disrupt networks, firms will choose to coordinate their activities through markets and LME institutions are more likely to emerge. In times of systemic change, such as post-communist transition, the degree to which reforms promote or disrupt network formation can account for the likelihood of LME and CME institutions developing.

It should be noted that there is no reason to assume that either a pure LME or a pure CME necessarily emerges naturally during post-socialist transition. For a pure LME to work well, markets for practically all inputs and outputs need to exist, the price mechanism needs to operate, and there needs to be competition and adjustment by firms driven by market pressures (Perkins 1988). These preconditions cannot be taken for granted, especially in a transition economy. The introduction of markets, as Polanyi eloquently argued, is always a profoundly political decision (Polanyi 1944). To the extent that soft budget constraints characteristic of command economies persist, governments may seek to bail out and subsidize underperforming firms (Kornai 1992). If this happens to a great degree, then a large number of firms may not primarily be guided by market forces, but rather by some kind of statism (Shonfield 1965). In other words, an LME requires a dramatic liberalization policy, where the state focuses on market making. Under adverse economic conditions, such as the transformational recession at the outset of transition, there are likely to be strong pressures to mitigate the effects of market discipline.

The CME-style institutions are arguably even less likely to develop. As noted by Hall and Soskice (2001: 63), CME institutions may in general be harder to develop than LME institutions, since they require a long-term perspective and the ability of firms to resolve collective action problems.[5] In the absence of dense networks it is generally not in firms' interest to cooperate in prisoners' dilemma-type situations. Especially in uncertain times, like post-socialist transition, economic actors' time horizons are likely to be short and their discount rates to be high, as their very existence in the future is not given. Under such conditions it is hard to overcome collective action problems and the incentives to defect. Therefore, it is hardly surprising that CME institutions are rare and that more countries seem to come close to the LME model in post-communist Eastern Europe (Crowley 2005). One of the key features of LMEs—the ability to adjust rapidly and flexibly—would seem to be a great advantage during transition periods.

While it may be true that more countries have moved closer to the LME model than to the CME blueprint, there is variation in the degree to which transition countries have embraced the market. As noted earlier, Estonia has arguably moved closest towards a textbook free market economy (Feldmann and Sally 2002). While the predominance of institutionalized coordination can be seen as more exceptional in transition economies, Slovenia has developed into a CME. I argue that varying degrees of network-promotion and network-disruption can explain the different outcomes. Section 12.4 examines the components of these processes in greater detail.

12.3.2. Legacies and Policies as Determinants of Network-Promotion and Network-Disruption in Transition Countries

Like most other scholars of transition and change, I distinguish between two types of factors affecting institutional outcomes—legacies from before transition, and policies adopted in the transition period itself (Ekiert and Hanson 2003).[6] Legacies or inherited conditions matter because they provide the context for reforms and the institutional infrastructure that is to be reformed. Thereby they also constrain the range of feasible options in transition periods, since there is likely to be path-dependence when certain pre-existing actors and patterns of behaviour affect the reform process. Path-dependence and reform inertia may result from a status quo bias due to the uncertainty of reform outcomes (Fernández and Rodrik 1991) or simply because powerful interest groups have a stake in the current institutions. Legacies also matter at the cognitive level, since past experience shapes actors' beliefs about what actions they can take and how effective these actions are likely to be. To the extent that these actors have political influence, they may also lobby to retain or reform pre-existing organizations.

Pre-capitalist legacies affect the viability of networks during the transition period in numerous ways. To the extent that pre-capitalist institutions included networks (or proto-networks), the preconditions for solving collective action problems and establishing institutionalized coordination during the transition phase should be better. This is true if the pre-existing networks survive or can adapt to market conditions. The reason for this is intimately related to the logic of institutionalized coordination. It is easier to develop the kind of long-term perspective and predictability necessary for CME institutions to evolve, when economic actors (especially firms and workers) already know each other and have been involved in bargaining and cooperation before. Repeated interaction tends to generate trust and improve the prospects for inducing cooperation (Axelrod 1984). In the absence of such legacies, institutionalized coordination would have to be built from scratch, which would be very difficult given the challenges of early transition.

In practice, economic institutions differed across the communist countries. In many countries there was orthodox central planning, where economic coordination depended predominantly on vertical ties between the central planning board and individual enterprises. Other coordination mechanisms, such as residual markets (e.g. for some farming output and black markets) or horizontal ties (e.g. between enterprises), played only a very minor role in the economy. By contrast, some socialist countries had introduced reforms that are sometimes described as market socialist or decentralized socialism. By the end of the socialist period, Hungary, Poland, and Yugoslavia had moved furthest in this direction, whereas Czechoslovakia, the GDR, and the Soviet Union came closer to orthodox central planning.

There are three reasons why the countries with decentralized socialism are more likely to develop into CMEs. First, in these systems planners focused primarily on indicative planning and there was a very limited role for specific output targets. Therefore, firms had greater autonomy to make production decisions and to develop ties to other firms (including suppliers and creditors) as well as bargain with workers about wages (Brus and Laski 1989). In many cases these interactions were sustained over long time periods. These relations could be described as proto-networks, which could potentially provide the basis for non-market coordination in a market economy. This is reminiscent of the role played by guilds as a basis for non-market coordination in the age of industrialization in Western Europe (Thelen 2004). Second, these countries were also freer to engage in international trade, and enterprises in these countries had more access to imports and also to export markets. Hence a greater proportion of their production might also be expected to survive the fall of communism, which would also improve the prospects for the proto-networks to be sustained or reformed. Finally, these systems were less repressive and the leadership was more willing to accommodate civil society pressures. This helped establish a tradition of social dialogue and negotiations between the political leadership and other social actors (Kitschelt et al. 1999). In short, decentralized socialism is likely to be a more propitious foundation for developing a CME than orthodox central planning.

This does not mean that all countries with decentralized socialism developed into CMEs or that legacies are a sufficient condition for explaining post-socialist institutions. Most notably, Slovenia is the only post-Yugoslav country that has developed into a CME. The diversity of economic institutions and patterns of coordination in the FSU and Yugoslavia show that the nature of socialist institutions do not predetermine the shape of emerging capitalist institutions. While the legacy of decentralization may have facilitated institutionalized coordination or even corporatism in Slovenia, economic institutions in Croatia, Serbia, and the other republics have evolved differently, partly as a result of the general turmoil caused by war, international sanctions, and various state policies (Stanojević 2003).

Therefore, rather than assuming continuity, a theory of emerging coordination of capitalist relations needs to explain how developments in the transition period affect prospects for such continuity. A theory of emerging VoC must account for the circumstances under which proto-networks develop into institutionalized coordination under market conditions and when they are destroyed. In particular, it is important to consider how collective action problems and the returns to institutionalized coordination are affected by transition.

A host of policies—many of which were not necessarily adopted for the sole purpose of bringing about a particular type of coordination—affect the benefits flowing from information-sharing, deliberation, and long-term cooperation. I here focus on two types of policies, namely policies affecting the continuity of economic actors and networks, and policies affecting the costs and benefits of a certain kind of institutionalized coordination.[7]

First, continuity of economic agents is in large part shaped by one of the headline reforms, namely privatization. Ownership reform has been implemented in many different ways. The most common methods include voucher-privatization to the population at large, open auctions to the highest bidder (often involving foreign investors), and in other cases privatization to old enterprise insiders—managers and workers. Privatization to the old managers and workers can be expected to consolidate old ties between management and workers, and also between different firms. If there were proto-networks between these firms in the past, then the continuation of these actors in their old position makes it more likely (albeit not certain) that these ties may persist under the new system. This is notably so, if the old firms were profitable and export-oriented in a decentralized socialist system, since they can be expected to retain their markets even after the collapse of the old system and the COMECON markets.

Second, the prospects for institutionalized coordination are shaped by the costs and benefits of it. An increase in the returns to institutionalized coordination should make it more likely that agents attempt to overcome collective action problems to bring it about. An elegant attempt to demonstrate such effects in the context of Russian transition is the book *Brokers and Bureaucrats* by Timothy Frye (Frye 2000). Frye examines how brokers working within five different markets in Russia attempted to construct self-governing institutions for cooperation, exchange of information, sanctioning dishonest traders, and ensuring compliance with contracts without external enforcement. Frye focuses on the role of state action and state policies (often resulting from competition between different state agencies) in promoting dense social ties, the sharing of information, and sustaining institutions of self-governance by affecting the costs and benefits of such actions through taxation and delegation.

In short, my argument implies that network-promotion and network-disruption, and the incentives to choose a particular type of coordination, are shaped by two sets of factors—institutional legacies and policies during the transition period. I now illustrate these factors by examining the Estonian and Slovenian cases in greater detail and in the process also briefly discuss the political foundations of these transformation paths.

12.4. ESTONIA AND SLOVENIA AS ILLUSTRATIONS OF NETWORK-DISRUPTION AND NETWORK-PROMOTION

12.4.1. Legacies

The institutional legacies from the old federal states were very different. Estonia, as a Soviet republic, was part of a relatively typical command economy. The Estonian economy was embedded in the all-Union central planning structure. Only 61 of its 265 industrial enterprises were under direct Estonian control in 1990, whereas the remainder were primarily or entirely controlled by the central planners in Moscow (*Estonia* 1995). Vertical relationships—between firms and collective farms on the one hand and central planners on the other—were of paramount importance in the economy. Virtually all of Estonia's trade was conducted with other Soviet republics, notably Russia. Therefore, the collapse of the Soviet Union and the CMEA imposed a huge demand shock on Estonia, which was particularly severe given that much of the output could not be sold in Western markets. In other words, there were relatively few horizontal networks, which could have served as a foundation for market-conforming inter-firm coordination.

Slovenia's legacy was different. Yugoslav socialism was decentralized and based on the idea of worker self-management, where works councils were relatively important decision-making units with the ability to negotiate substantial wage increases. Their power exceeded the influence wielded by similar units in other socialist countries. Horizontal ties between firms were not insignificant, as companies were relatively free to interact. There was for example also inter-enterprise borrowing (Brus and Laski 1989; Lydall 1989). Less than a quarter of Slovenia's output was sold to other Yugoslav republics and about 17 per cent was sold to other countries (Mencinger 2004: 74). A substantial part of these goods was sold to Western markets. Therefore, the potential for pre-existing companies and networks to survive the shift to a market economy was greater than in Estonia, where the Soviet Union was the main outlet for its output.

While these legacies may have facilitated the move towards a CME in Slovenia, they do not constitute a sufficient condition for this outcome. As noted above, many other post-Soviet republics with similar legacies have not developed into well-functioning LMEs. As noted above, Slovenia is the only post-Yugoslav republic that has developed genuine CME-style or even corporatist institutions, even though all of the republics share the self-management legacy.[8] It may of course be argued that the other republics were ravaged by wars or at least the effects of economic sanctions. This in itself serves to highlight that it is necessary to consider whether policy developments during the transition period serve to build on these legacies to create institutionalized cooperation in a genuine market economy environment or whether regime change is network-disrupting.

12.4.2. Policies: Privatization

Privatization was undoubtedly one of the most intensely debated policy reforms in transition countries in the early 1990s. While practically everyone agreed on the need for privatization, the main debate revolved around the optimal speed and method of ownership reform. In particular, should assets be privatized to the old insiders (managers and/or workers), should they be transferred to the population at large (through some kind of voucher scheme), or should they be auctioned off to the highest bidder, possibly involving foreign ownership (Estrin 1994)? The outcomes of privatization have triggered great political and academic debate, largely focusing on the fairness, transparency, and success (especially in terms of profitability and effective corporate governance) of the adopted methods (Roland 2000).

It is arguably also the most important policy choice affecting economic coordination and networks. The mode of privatization is a key determinant of the degree to which old networks and ties from the pre-capitalist period can be sustained by affecting which agents control firms and their assets. Slovenia has adopted a privatization method that sustained pre-existing networks, whereas Estonia's radical approach to ownership reform has not promoted institutionalized coordination. The fact that Estonia and Slovenia chose very different privatization strategies was by no means a foregone conclusion at the time, as there were deep disagreements among the political elites about the appropriate mode of privatization (Purju 1996; Likić-Brborić 2003). Moreover, both countries were advised by Jeffrey Sachs who recommended similar reforms—based on rapid voucher privatization (which was not really adopted by either country)—in each case. There are complex reasons for these divergent outcomes.[9] I focus on one of the most central explanatory factors, the political role of insiders and their ties to the governing coalition at the time when core legislation was implemented.

Several proposals based on different models of privatization existed in Slovenia in 1991–2 (Kraft, Vodopivec, and Cvikl 1994: 210f.), essentially ranging from complete insider-privatization (Korže–Mencinger–Simoneti model) to voucher-privatization (Sachs–Peterle–Umek model). The ruling centre-right or centrist DEMOS coalition under Prime Minister Peterle was based on heterogeneous opposition groups mobilizing against the ancien régime, and it did also not have a majority in all three houses of parliament.[10] There was no consensus on either privatization scheme even within the governing coalition, as Prime Minister Peterle favoured the second model and Vice Premier Mencinger had developed the first model. Disagreements around this issue led to the collapse of the DEMOS cabinet in April 1992.[11] The new government under Janez Drnovšek, the LDP premier who led most cabinets in the 1990s until being elected president in 2002, proposed a compromise bill that was finally accepted by parliament. The LDP has been the largest political force for most of the post-independence period. It has roots in the nationalist and youth wings of the Slovenian communist organizations during the Yugoslav period.[12] The LDP had close ties to the old economic elites, including the enterprise directors, and they were also represented in their own right in parliament until 1992 (and even later in the second chamber). According to many observers the political influence of these managers grew in the transition period (Šušteršič 2004).

The final privatization bill combined key features of the two earlier proposals, but with a very significant role for the insiders, that is employees and managers (Prašnikar et al. 2002). A 20 per cent stake in the privatized firms was allocated free of charge to two state funds—the National Pension Fund and the Restitution Fund. A further 20 per cent was allocated to insiders (workers and management) and 20 per cent to a Development Fund. The company itself—through its workers council and in some cases its board of directors—could decide whether to sell the additional 40 per cent to insiders or to offer it to outsiders by public tender. This means that the insiders had a central role in determining ownership reform for a given firm. Vouchers were also distributed to the population, and employees could use them to buy shares in the company where they were working.[13] This privatization strategy essentially cemented the pre-existing networks by strengthening the role of insiders as owners and by limiting foreign investment in privatized companies. In 1999 the insiders had a majority stake in 60 per cent of all companies (covering almost 50 per cent of the labour force, but a much smaller share of total capital) and significant shares in most other companies as well (Simoneti, Rojec, and Gregorič 2004: 232). The involvement of the old insiders, managers and workers, laid a foundation for a high degree of involvement of unions and works councils in economic coordination, which is characteristic of a CME (Prašnikar et al. 2002).

There were prominent proposals for employee ownership in Estonia, especially during the perestroika period in the late 1980s. The objective was to limit state control over the economy by creating so-called People's Enterprises, which would have been similar to a Yugoslav-style system of self-management (Terk 2000). Early attempts to privatize large enterprises were based on a gradualist approach to ownership reform. It placed significant emphasis on employee and management buyouts, and this was indeed the method used for the first seven cases of large-scale privatization (i.e. privatization of large enterprises) in the early 1990s under the Savisaar–Vähi governments. The 1992 election brought a new coalition into power. The centre-right governments under Mart Laar and Andres Tarand (1992–5), which implemented much of the core legislation on privatization, had relatively weak ties to the Soviet-era *nomenklatura* and old enterprise directors. Only 7 per cent of the cabinet members were former Communist Party members, compared to 56–67 per cent in the two previous cabinets (Steen and Ruus 2002). Mart Laar's motto 'plats puhtaks' (appr. clean slate) symbolizes his government's commitment to radical change. This was based on his government's desire for rapid reform and a reintegration with the West and also for weakening the old economic elites.[14]

Estonia under the centre-right government of Mart Laar implemented a set of radical policies for bringing about large-scale privatization (Terk 2000; Purju 1996). With the technical support of German consultants, Estonia adopted a privatization scheme modelled on the Treuhand approach applied in East Germany (based on auctions to outsiders).[15] This privatization strategy, coupled with very liberal foreign investment and trade regimes, created an environment, which favoured outsiders and gave ample opportunities for strategic foreign investors to enter the Estonian market. Some estimates suggest that around 70 per cent of former medium- and large-scale state enterprises were privatized to outsiders.[16] These processes have weakened old networks and instead brought in a new generation of owners and managers from the outside.

To conclude, privatization in Estonia and Slovenia developed very differently. Insider-privatization in Slovenia allowed old networks to persist. There has been remarkable continuity among both economic and political elites. By contrast, Estonian privatization accorded a much greater role for outsiders, and this led to a disruption of old networks. This made the development of CME-style institutions in Slovenia much more likely than in Estonia, given the importance of networks as a foundation for non-market coordination.

12.4.3. Other Policies: The Impact of Legislation and Monetary Policy on Wage Bargaining

To understand the emergence of institutionalized coordination in greater detail, we also need to consider the specific incentives for such coordination. I use wage bargaining as an example and discuss a few specific policies affecting it. The key question is why Slovenia, alone among the transition countries, has adopted centralized wage bargaining at the national level, whereas Estonia has not. I focus on two key policies shaping the costs and benefits of such coordination, namely the status of the Chamber of Commerce and the monetary policy regime. Both of these policies have strengthened network ties and the incentives to engage in non-market coordination in Slovenia, whereas these factors are absent in Estonia.

First, the fact that networks survived the transition in Slovenia cannot by itself account for the emergence of centralized wage bargaining. The collective action problem needs to be resolved in order to induce firms to collaborate. As noted above, Estonian employers' organizations are relatively weak, and they do not have the capacity or representativeness to serve as a basis for broad-based institutionalized coordination.

In Slovenia compulsory membership in the Chamber of Commerce effectively made such collaboration possible. This may not necessarily be an optimal long-run solution, not least since it also violates ILO guidelines.[17] In the short run it increases the capacity to negotiate about wages, before effective and representative employers' organizations evolve (which, as noted above, has proved very difficult in most transition countries). This has reduced the collective action costs of institutionalizing coordination in the uncertain times of early transition. More recently, other employers' organizations have emerged in Slovenia. It is widely held that organizations with voluntary membership will gradually take over the Chamber's role.[18] The Organization of Slovenian Employers is one of these organizations, and its influence has increased in recent years.[19]

Second, even though the collective action problem is overcome, it does not yet explain why key actors would be interested in institutionalized coordination. A key factor accounting for this is related to monetary policy and the development of real wages in Slovenia in early transition.

Unlike Estonia, which adopted a currency board arrangement and a tough non-accommodating monetary policy regime, Slovenia chose a more flexible arrangement, namely a managed float.[20] Many factors contributed to this choice, including the lack of monetary reserves and also the experience of the unsuccessful exchange rate based stabilization in Yugoslavia in the late 1980s (Prašnikar et al. 2002). Key advisers were also concerned that demands for bailouts and soft taxation by firms, and welfare spending by a strong civil society, would quickly undermine the credibility of a fixed exchange rate. Under such condition a peg would be a much too rigid arrangement. By contrast, under a managed float the monetary authorities can choose whether to accommodate wage setters and whether to engage in activist demand management.

A managed float also generates the problem of managing expectations, especially if the monetary authority cannot credibly commit to a rule. This is likely to be particularly important during the phase of disinflation.[21] In Slovenia real wage increases became unsustainable in the early 1990s, and this was a source of major concern to employers (especially exporters) and the government. The establishment of the Economic and Social Council and the beginning of tripartism in 1994 followed a year of very high real wage increases—11.6 per cent in 1993—and the centralization of wage bargaining was seen as a key step to combat this problem.[22]

As this brief account illustrates, agents' incentives were in large part shaped by the key policy decisions, which in turn also depended on the political influence of old insiders. Compulsory membership in the Chamber of Commerce and the relatively accommodating monetary policy were factors, which helped bring about centralized wage bargaining in Slovenia. Given the weaker employers' organizations and the credibly non-accommodating monetary policy (and falling real wages in the early 1990s), such incentives did not exist in Estonia.

12.5. CONCLUSION

This chapter has examined the emergence of capitalist institutions in Estonia and Slovenia and argued that these two countries have developed LME- and CME-type institutions. In addition, I have developed a theory of network-promotion and network-disruption to account for these differences. Building on the work of other scholars, I have argued that networks can provide a micro-foundation for understanding the emergence of different types of coordination (see also Goodin 2003 for a related argument). There are a number of important implications of this analysis for the study of transition.

First, since networks are typically hard to build (given the time it takes to develop trust and the routinization of interaction patterns), the socialist legacies are of crucial importance. To the extent that there were proto-networks that could survive or be transformed under market conditions, such countries have better prerequisites for developing institutionalized coordination than countries lacking such networks. Therefore, we should expect countries with decentralized socialism to have better prerequisites for developing CME-style institutions than countries with orthodox communism.

Second, since not all countries with decentralized communism have developed into CME's, we also need to consider the extent to which key policy choices in the transition period have helped sustain, promote, or disrupt networks. In particular, privatization is of central importance in determining whether old networks can be sustained. Other policy choices also affect the incentives for members of these networks to engage in institutionalized cooperation. The analysis of the Slovenian case suggests that a key factor affecting the choice of policies is the political influence of these old networks. The degree to which they are able to shape change to perpetuate their own influence affects whether their networks can be sustained.[23]

This chapter highlights the importance of studying periods of dramatic change, periods of extraordinary politics (Balcerowicz 1995), or critical junctures (Pierson 2004) to uncover the origins of VoC in transition countries. This approach should be seen as complementary to studies focusing on long-run institutional change and adaptation (Thelen 2004). Institutions are not static, and they often adjust and evolve in piecemeal fashion. However, the importance of defining moments is paramount, especially when countries are undergoing large-scale systemic change. Under such periods of heightened uncertainty or even 'thickened history' (Beissinger 2002), many institutions are in flux and many ordinary patterns of interest group politics are suspended. Many choices made at such times, like the adoption of a constitution, central bank independence, a particular mode of privatization, or exchange rate regime, are not necessarily irreversible. However, reversing them is very costly, and political choices made on such issues are likely to shape expectations and institutions for a long time to come. In most cases of institutional development, there are elements of both gradual piecemeal change and critical junctures, not infrequently in conjunction with disruptive events like wars (Streeck and Yamamura 2002; Streeck and Thelen 2004). The EU membership and further political and economic integration with Western Europe may require further institutional adaptation, and therefore it is likely that such gradual change will occur in Estonia and Slovenia as well, but this need not necessarily undermine the core logic of coordination in these systems.

This chapter argues that in the Estonian and Slovenian cases legacies and policies reinforced each other, which is why they have developed into something close to ideal types of LMEs and CMEs, especially with respect to industrial relations. In other Yugoslav republics policies have not helped preserve and reform pre-capitalist networks to create full-fledged CME-style or corporatist institutions. Similarly, Estonia adopted the most radical and consistent policies of market liberalization among the post-Soviet republics, which reinforces the idea that the effect of legacies is mediated by developments in the transition period. If the explanation advanced in this chapter is correct, the fact that there are many hybrids or that many transition countries do not fit standard VoC (Stark and Bruszt 1998) should not necessarily be surprising. The conditions necessary to promote or disrupt networks may in fact be quite stringent, and Estonia and Slovenia may be quite exceptional in terms of their combination of legacies and political preconditions for their reform paths (Feldmann and Sally 2002; Šušteršič 2004). As the VoC framework suggests, there may well be more than one best political economy model for countries in transition. However, while the pure VoC models themselves may be feasible and serve countries well, they are not necessarily the only or perhaps even the most common economic institutions in transition countries.

NOTES

1. A complete test of the proposition that Estonia and Slovenia constitute VoC would also require demonstrating that there are institutional complementarities between all of these dimensions (see, e.g., Hall and Gingerich 2002). It is virtually impossible to test for all of these dimensions at once, not least in the context of just two countries. I instead attempt to show that patterns of coordination differ systematically between the two countries.

2. There are of course some exceptions to the general positive correlation between union membership and the coverage rate of wage bargaining agreements. France is the most striking case.

3. The contrast is somewhat less clear with respect to employment protection, where both countries come close to the CME blueprint. However, there are currently reforms underway in Estonia, which would lead to some convergence on the LME model (Buchen 2006).

4. Buchen notes some anomalies—especially a two-tier board structure and highly concentrated ownership in Estonia, which is more typical of a CME. However, as Buchen notes, this may be related to the specific challenges of post-socialist transition. It has been very difficult to develop genuine stock market based systems of corporate governance in early transition. A key reason for this is that concentrated ownership may facilitate rapid restructuring of companies.

5. Streeck (2001) also notes that non-liberal institutions may be harder to sustain, since they depend on the state as a guarantor when inconsistencies or pressures arise.

6. It should be emphasized that this distinction poses a lot of theoretical and epistemological problems, but it is a very useful way of thinking about the determinants of transition processes. See Kitschelt (2003) for a detailed discussion.

7. I focus more on the incentives for institutionalized or non-market coordination, since the operation of markets is much better understood.

8. See Hadžić (2002), Franicević and Kraft (1997), and Stanojević (2003) on the Serbian and Croatian cases.

9. The studies by Likić-Brborić (2003) and Purju (1996) chronicle the key phases of the debate and the shifts in government preferences in greater detail.

10. Until the election in 1992 the Slovenian parliament still had the tricameral structure inherited from the socialist period—with the Chamber of Associated Labour (majority for the left and union representatives), the Chamber of Communes and Municipalities, and the Socio-Political Chamber (the latter two with a DEMOS majority).

11. Other parts of the coalition, notably the Christian Democrats, were critical of insider-privatization and favoured a model primarily based on restitution combined with some elements of voucher-privatization.

12. Its popularity partly derives from the fact that it adopted a nationalist and eventually pro-independence stance in the late Yugoslav period. The economic

performance of the Slovenian economy was also better than in most other communist countries.

13. Alternatively, they could be used to invest in companies that had made a public offering of the final 40 per cent of their shares or also to invest in special Privatization Investment Funds.

14. Similar arguments were made in Russia, even though the actual mode of privatization and the balance of political forces were quite different (see Boycko, Shleifer, and Vishny 1995).

15. Other methods of privatization were also used, including restitution of expropriated property (primarily dwellings and land) and simple auctions to the highest bidder for small-scale privatization. See Purju (1996) for a detailed overview.

16. See reports and statistics presented by the Estonian Institute at http://www.einst.ee

17. Compulsory membership in an organization engaged in wage bargaining violates ILO rules. especially smaller companies are also dissatisfied with the representativeness of the Chamber of Commerce, as documented in a survey by the Slovenian newspaper *Dnevnik* in August 2005.

18. Representatives of the major trade union confederations, employers' organizations and businesses all expressed this opinion to me in interviews in the summer of 2005. No one believed that centralized wage bargaining would be undermined by the anticipated change that would abolish compulsory membership in the Chamber of Commerce.

19. It was originally sponsored by the Chamber of Commerce to operate as its sister institution in anticipation of the new legislation that would abolish compulsory membership in the Chamber. In recent years the importance and autonomy of the Organization of Slovenian Employers has grown.

20. Jeffrey Sachs had advised both countries to adopt currency boards, but the proposal received little support in Slovenia.

21. Many transition countries (e.g. Poland) used government-imposed incomes policies to constrain wage setting.

22. During my interviews government, trade union, and employers' representatives have also repeatedly mentioned this as a key factor. Centralized wage agreements can be a key mechanism for controlling wage increases (see Swenson 1991, for a related argument about employers' preferences and cross-class alliances in favour of centralized wage agreements in Sweden and Denmark in the 1930s).

23. If their influence is very strong, they may even use it to block continued market reform and to consolidate a dominant position in the economy (see Hellman 1998).

13

Strengths and Weaknesses of 'Weak' Coordination: Economic Institutions, Revealed Comparative Advantages, and Socio-Economic Performance of Mixed Market Economies in Poland and Ukraine

Vlad Mykhnenko

13.1. INTRODUCTION

My primary goal in this chapter is to explore and explain the major research questions that the nascent comparative political economy of post-communist Europe has been grappling with since the late 1990s, namely: 'What type of capitalism has emerged in post-communist Europe?' and, ultimately, 'Does it work?'. In this I attempt to follow the research agenda formed around the VoC approach (Hall and Soskice 2001*a*; Amable 2003) and several attempted applications of the 'comparative capitalisms' framework to the study of post-communism (e.g. Lane 2000, 2005; Cernat 2002; Buchen 2004, 2005; Mykhnenko 2005*a*, 2005*b*). By using the VoC framework in particular, this chapter also intends critically to examine a question that concerns the suitability and applicability of essentially Western neoinstitutionalist theories of comparative capitalism for the study of post-communist phenomena.

On the basis of empirical evidence and comparative analysis of the two largest neighbouring political economies of Eastern Europe (Russia apart), I argue that, notwithstanding the worldwide neoliberalizing pressures, the changeable politics of post-communist transformation, and the unstable nature of Eastern European institutions, both Polish and Ukrainian national variants of capitalism can be described as mixed- or 'weakly' coordinated market economies (for definitional issues, see Hall and Soskice 2003, and the introduction to this volume). In spite of the prevailing perceptions and popular media praise given to post-communist nations for adopting a deregulated, privatized, liberal type of capitalism, neither Polish nor Ukrainian political economy generally resembles the liberal market-based model. It is contended, however, that despite the apparent system-wise detachment of the Eastern European economies of Poland and Ukraine from the ideal types of a CME and, especially, of an LME, the institutional structures of the two post-communist countries are *not necessarily* of a 'low-level', 'dysfunctional', or 'suboptimal equilibrium' type.

On the contrary, I argue that the establishment in both countries of mixed market economies (MMEs or 'weak' CMEs) has correlated with a number of dynamic and positive macroeconomic and structural developments. Thus, this chapter challenges the dominant neoliberal discourse on the alleged inevitability of a one-way 'transition' to laissez-faire capitalism in post-communist Europe, as it attributes the dynamism of the two Eastern European economies not to their supposed approach to the free-market ideal but to the emergence of MMEs characterized by certain coherences and complementarities between the major institutional domains. Accordingly, I also question the validity of alternative assumptions and claims about the inescapably abnormal or impaired functioning of 'hybrid' market economies in Eastern Europe (and elsewhere).

This chapter proceeds by exploring the macroeconomic and social performances of the two Eastern European economies under post-communism and establishing the transformation's main trends with regard to economic growth, productive efficiency, social equity, and macroeconomic stability. It highlights a number of similarly positive (e.g. output growth) and negative (e.g. macroeconomic volatility) features in the transformation performance of Poland and Ukraine. The chapter also identifies a perplexing difference between the social outcomes of late post-communism in the two countries, described in the chapter as Poland's 'poverty paradox'. Consequently, in contrast with the dominant 'transition' paradigm that postulates the ever-deepening neoliberalization of post-communist economies, the chapter provides an alternative neoinstitutionalist explanation for the presented similarities and differences in the socio-economic performance of Poland and Ukraine. In the third part of the chapter, the main institutional features of the Eastern European economies of Poland and Ukraine are outlined and conceptualized within the (VoC) framework.

Fourth, concepts of institutional similarity and coherence (see Crouch 2005c; Morgan, Whitley, and Moen 2005) are used to discover how the emerging institutional forms of MMEs in Poland and Ukraine can account for the observed positive and negative performance similarities. To test my hypothesis, which attributes the observed similarities in the economic performance of the two countries to the emergence of (partially) coherent MMEs in Eastern Europe, the chapter explores potential linkages between the newly established institutions and structural change. It employs Bela Balassa's concept of 'revealed comparative advantage' (Balassa 1965) to examine what structural changes may have been generated by the newly established 'weak' CME system in the two countries.

Fifth, the chapter shows that Poland's poverty paradox and the apparent absence of it in Ukraine can be explained in terms of institutional complementarities and dynamic institutional breakaways experienced by the latter in the early 2000s. Finally, this chapter concludes with a discussion about the theoretical implications of explaining the post-communist phenomena through the VoC approach. It emphasizes the existence of exogenous shocks and influences which have had a profound effect on the performance of the two Eastern European economies but which lie outside the VoC analytical framework. The scope of this chapter is limited to the comparative analysis of two national political economies of Eastern Europe in the early 2000s and their general socio-economic performances between 1989 and 2006. The issues related to the politics of why and how such MMEs have been constructed in Poland and Ukraine are not addressed in great detail.

13.2. ESTABLISHING THE PERFORMANCE TRENDS

During the Cold War a considerable degree of consensus was established in the literature on 'comparative economic systems' with regard to specific criterion that can be applied to evaluate the performance of different economic systems. Four fundamental 'system goals' of economic growth, efficiency, equity, and stability (of growth, employment, and prices) since then have encapsulated the investigative domain of economists interested in comparing capitalism with state socialism (cf. Schnitzer and Nordyke 1971; Elliott 1973; Zimbalist 1984; Bornstein 1985; Gregory and Stuart 1999). This chapter uses the above set of traditional performance criteria to capture potential similarities and differences in the outcomes of systemic transformation in Poland and Ukraine. As we are interested in the process of capitalist reconstruction and the reintegration of post-communist Eurasia into the world economy, a number of relevant structural indicators have been added to examine the success of the two Eastern European economies in the continuous pursuit and accumulation of profit through trade and investment—the essence of capitalism according to the classics of political economy and economic sociology.

13.2.1. Post-Communist Transformation Trends: Old and New

A number of basic stylized facts have already been established in the literature about the macro- and microeconomic performance of post-communist countries in the initial transformation period described by various authors as the 'Great Post-communist Depression', 'great transitional recession', or 'great output contraction' (e.g. Kołodko 1999*a*, 2000, 2002; De Broeck and Koen 2000; Rosefielde and Kuboniwa 2003). The following seven stylized facts of the first ten years of transformation (1989–98), put together by Nauro Campos and Fabrizio Coricelli, summarize everything about: 'what one should know about growth in transition: (*a*) output fell, (*b*) capital shrank, (*c*) labour moved in all senses, (*d*) trade re-oriented, (*e*) the economic structure changed, (*f*) institutions collapsed, and (*g*) transition costs (i.e. the sharp deterioration of various social indicators) appeared' (2002: 37). All the post-communist economies experienced these 'magnificent seven' developments, yet the magnitude of output collapse differed across Central and Eastern Europe and central Asia. As has been frequently emphasized in the literature on 'transition economics', Poland has experienced the shortest period of output decline and the country's transformation was characterized by the fastest recovery and the longest period of growth among the twenty-seven post-communist countries, whereas Ukraine's GDP performance was ranked by the international financial institutions among the worst—the third from bottom, above that of Moldova and Georgia respectively (EBRD 2005: 13; cf. Kołodko 1999*b*: 2; World Bank 2002: xiii–xv).

It has successfully been argued elsewhere that most of the difference between the initial output performance of Central and Eastern Europe compared with the former USSR is explained by: the inherited structural liabilities and exogenous 'transition shocks' caused by the collapse of state socialism and the communist trade bloc; the disintegration of the Soviet Union; and the associated effects of disorganization and trade implosion (Calvo and Coricelli 1993; Blanchard 1997; Blanchard and Kremer 1997; Roland and Verdier 1999; Campos and Coricelli 2002; Bezemer, Dulleck, and Frijters 2003). Given that the focus of this chapter is on the emergence, development, and functioning of capitalism in Eastern Europe, our primary concern here is with the second, 'post-depression' growth and recovery phase of the post-communist transformation, which occurred well after the initial exogenous transition shocks were settled.

13.2.2. Growth, Efficiency, and Trade Integration

It is contended that the second phase of transformation in post-communist Europe can be characterized by the following new set of facts: (*a*) output grew, (*b*) the labour force shrank, (*c*) capital increased, (*d*) enterprise efficiency improved, (*e*) foreign trade expanded, (*f*) institutions were rebuilt,

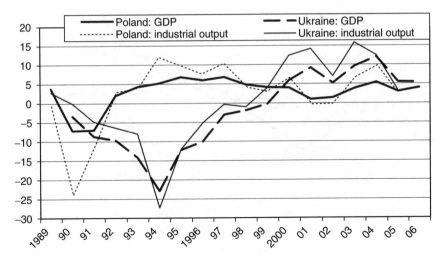

Figure 13.1. Real GDP and industrial output annual growth rates, percentage, 1989–2006

Note: 2005—preliminary data and 2006—forecast.

Source: IMF World Economic Outlook Database (2005), *GUS Statistical Yearbook* (various years), GUS Statistical Information Database (2005), *Derzhkomstat Statistical Yearbook* (various years), and Derzhkomstat Statistical Information Database (2005).

(*g*) transition costs fell, (*h*) positive structural changes appeared, and (*i*) macroeconomic volatility decreased but remained. Poland was the first post-communist country to enjoy these more encouraging developments by the first half of the 1990s. Yet by the end of the first transformation decade the overwhelming majority of post-communist nations had returned to growth.

Figure 13.1 shows annual changes in Poland's and Ukraine's real GDP and industrial output between 1989 and 2006, whereas Figure 13.2 presents real GDP volume index growth trajectories of the two countries for the same period. In addition, Figure 13.2 contains the national GDP per capita figures in US dollars on the basis of PPP. Notwithstanding the differences between GDP and real income evaluations presented, and between the timings of economic recovery, the overall upward growth trend enjoyed by both Poland and Ukraine in the second phase of transformation is evident. In real income terms, Poland's GDP at PPP grew by more than 2.5 times from its lowest of $5,594 per capita in 1991 to about $14,300 in 2006. Ukraine's post-depression recovery has been slower in volume index terms. However, the country's GDP at PPP still grew by 2.1 times from $3,700 per capita in 1998 to about $7,800 in 2006.

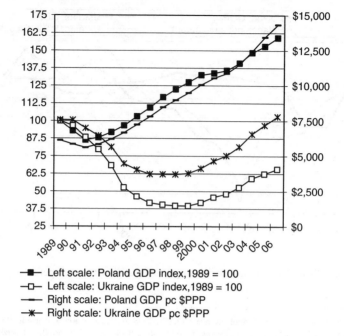

—■— Left scale: Poland GDP index,1989 = 100
—□— Left scale: Ukraine GDP index,1989 = 100
——— Right scale: Poland GDP pc $PPP
—✳— Right scale: Ukraine GDP pc $PPP

Figure 13.2. Real GDP volume index (1989 = 100) and real GDP per capita in $PPP, 1989–2006

Note: 2005—preliminary data and 2006—forecast.

Source: Own calculations on the basis of IMF World Economic Outlook Database (2005).

The post-depression phase of transformation in the two Eastern European economies was characterized by significant efficiency improvements, as suggested by growing productivity and positive enterprise pre-tax profit rates. Figure 13.3 indicates continuous increases in labour productivity in Poland since 1992 and in Ukraine since 1997. Another indicator of efficiency concerns enterprise profits. Given the frequent examples of tax evasion and avoidance practices supposedly used by Eastern European firms, the reported enterprise profit data presented in Figure 13.4 are of disputable quality. However, at least they suggest that the majority of Polish and (to a larger extent) Ukrainian firms remained profitable within the period concerned.

The capitalist values of profit accumulation through investment have also appeared to be taking hold of the two Eastern European economies. Figure 13.5 shows the capital investment volume indices as well as annual changes in investment activity in Poland and Ukraine between 1989 and 2005. Generally, both economies experienced sharp increases in fixed capital

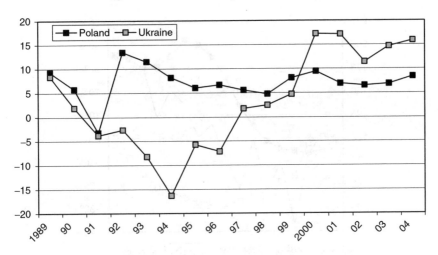

Figure 13.3. Labour productivity annual percentage growth (GDP in $PPP per hired wage-earner/salaried employee), 1989–2004

Source: Own calculations on the basis of IMF World Economic Outlook Database (2005) and ILO Laboursta Database (2005).

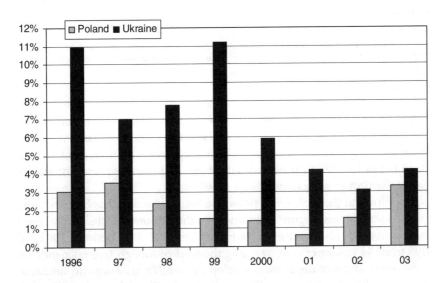

Figure 13.4. Gross enterprise annual profit rate (ratio of operating revenues to operating costs), 1996–2003

Source: *Dezrkomstat Statistical Yearbook* (various years) and own calculations on the basis of *GUS Statistical Yearbook* (various years).

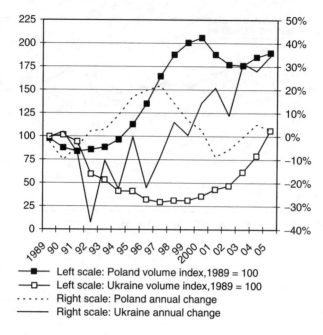

Figure 13.5. Capital investment volume index (1989 = 100) and capital investment annual growth, 1989–2005

Note: 2005—preliminary data.

Source: Own calculations on the basis of *GUS Statistical Yearbook* (various years), GUS Statistical Information Database (2005), *Derzhkomstat Statistical Yearbook* (various years), and Derzhkomstat Statistical Information Database (2005)

formation in the post-depression phase of transformation. However, the upward slope of investment activities in Ukraine was more stable, whereas the Polish economy suffered from a three-year-long period of investment decline, which began in 2001 in the aftermath of the 11 September terrorist attacks against the USA and the ensuing FDI slowdown.

In addition to the global FDI flows, the Polish economy has become more open to foreign trade. Figure 13.6 shows that the amount of Polish exports and imports of goods and services in comparison to GDP grew between 1992 and 2003 from 43 to 69 per cent, reaching the level of foreign trade dependence analogous to those of the average developing country in Africa and similar to the average Western European EU member-state. The Ukrainian economy's increasing reliance on the global trade in goods and services has been even more dramatic: its share of overall foreign trade turnover to GDP increased from 72 per cent in 1992 to 116 per cent in 2003.

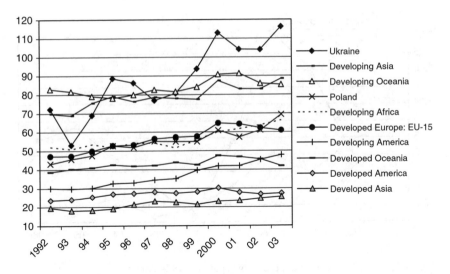

Figure 13.6. Foreign trade turnover (exports and imports of goods and services) as percentage of GDP, 1992–2003

Source: Own compilations and calculations on the basis of *UNCTAD Handbook of Statistics On-line* (2005).

13.2.3. Equity and Stability

The economic performance trends generated by both Eastern European economies since the late 1990s have been both similar and have shown certain signs of convergence. The continuous presence of macroeconomic volatility is another major similarity in the late transformation performance of the Polish and Ukrainian economies. Even in the second phase of transformation, neither Eastern European economy has managed to escape wide fluctuations in the rate of economic activity. As Figure 13.1 has indicated, levels of production in both Poland and Ukraine have remained very cyclical, especially in the latter. Figure 13.7 presents annual inflation rates of Poland and Ukraine between 1997 and 2006. It shows that Poland has generally managed to achieve relative price stability in the process of approaching the EU single currency qualification criteria: the average inflation rate in the country between 2002 and 2006 was about 2.2 per cent per year. In the same period, annual increases in the level of prices in Ukraine amounted on average to 8.3 per cent.

Poland's success in achieving relatively low fluctuations in the level of prices has been undermined by the country's lingering labour market instability. Figure 13.8 indicates that according to the national labour-force surveys, the average rate of unemployment (calculated on the basis of the International

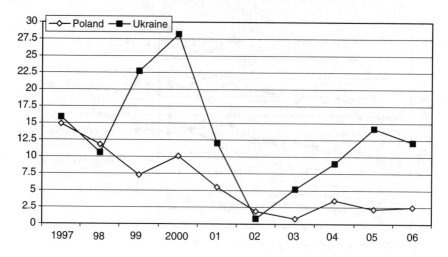

Figure 13.7. Inflation, annual percentage change, 1997–2006

Note: 2005–preliminary data and 2006—forecast.

Source: IMF World Economic Outlook Database (2005).

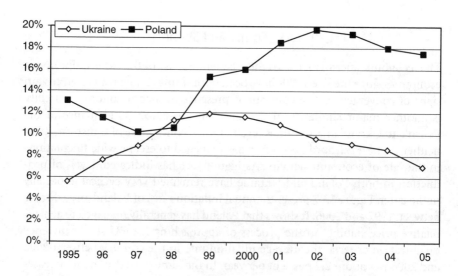

Figure 13.8. Real unemployment rate, share of active labour force (ILO methodology), 1995–2005

Note: 2005—2nd quarter figures.

Source: *GUS Statistical Yearbook* (various years), GUS Statistical Information Database (2005), *Derzhkomstat Statistical Yearbook* (various years), and Derzhkomstat Statistical Information Database (2005).

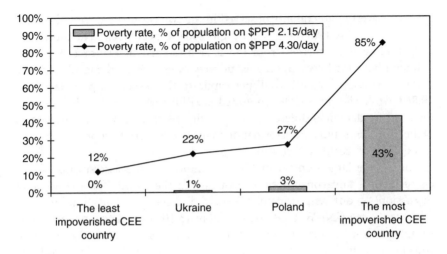

Figure 13.9. Absolute poverty rates, percentage of total population on $PPP 2.15 per day and on $PPP 4.30 per day, 2002–3

Note: The most/least impoverished post-communist country is ranked on the basis of all the available poverty indicators for the relevant year. Data exclude countries of Transcaucasia and central Asia.

Source: Asad et al. (2005: Appendix).

Labour Organization methodology) in Poland in the 2001–5 period amounted to 18.6 per cent of the workforce, which was more than double the Ukrainian average of 9 per cent. The fundamental dichotomy between the growth record of the Polish economy, considered to be the best in post-communist Eurasia, and the country's crisis of joblessness is emphasized further by what can be described as Poland's 'poverty puzzle'. Figure 13.9 shows a set of comparable and reliable household survey-based figures (verified by the World Bank), measuring absolute poverty in Poland and Ukraine in US dollars based on national PPPs. The first poverty line developed by the World Bank poverty team includes the percentage of total population with the level of consumption below $PPP 2.15 a day. Figure 13.9 also includes a higher poverty line ($4.30 a day), which, according to the World Bank authors, is 'a proximate vulnerability threshold to identify households that are not suffering absolute material deprivation, but are vulnerable to poverty' (Asad et al. 2005: 229).

To compare social deprivation in Poland and Ukraine with the wider region, Figure 13.9 contains poverty indicators for two Central and Eastern European countries which have the lowest and highest absolute poverty headcounts respectively.[1] Generally, the poverty indicators in both Poland and Ukraine indicate relatively low levels of absolute material deprivation and moderate levels of poverty vulnerability observed in the two countries during the latest available household surveys (in 2002 and 2003 respectively).[2] The most puzzling finding that emerges from the data presented in Figure 13.9 is that although both the lower and higher poverty rates in Poland and Ukraine are relatively similar: Poland's GDP per capita in the respective year was $PPP 10,868, while Ukraine's GDP amounted to $PPP 5,647 only. This brings us to the most fundamental difference between the 'second phase' social outcomes of the post-communist transformation in the two Eastern European countries: inequalities of wealth and consumption.

There are a large number of different indicators and assessments of levels of income and consumption inequality in the world (for a conceptual discussion of different principles behind income and consumption Gini coefficients, see UNI-WIDER 2005). Figure 13.10 contains comparable consumption Gini coefficients that can be used to assess temporal changes in consumption inequality in Poland, Ukraine in the early, middle, and late transformation phases. Figure 13.10 also presents the extremes of consumption equality and inequality observed in Eastern Europe in the 1990s and early 2000s. It appears that the initial rapid increase in consumption (and income)

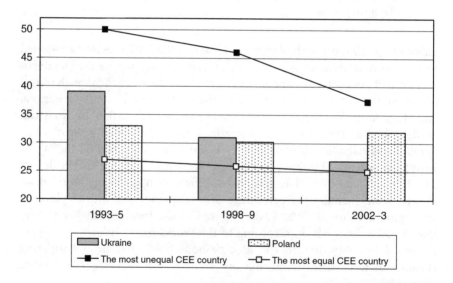

Figure 13.10. Distribution of consumption, national Gini coefficients in percentage points on a scale of 0 (perfect equality) to 100 (absolute inequality), 1993–2003

Note: The most un/equal post-communist country is ranked on the basis of all the available national Gini indicators for the relevant year. Data exclude countries of Transcaucasia and central Asia.

Source: World Bank (2000: Appendix D), Asad et al. (2005: Appendix), and WIDER World Income Inequality Database (2005).

inequality in post-communist countries was followed by a general equaliza-
tion of consumption distribution patterns across the post-communist region
(for the presentation and discussion of this phenomenon, see Asad et al. 2005).
Ukraine has been a trendsetter in this regard: the national consumption Gini
coefficients were continuously dropping in the second half of the 1990s, as
well as in the early 2000s. In sharp contrast with the overall regional tendency,
the inequality in the distribution of consumption in Poland increased between
1998 and 2002. In a complete reversal of the early transformation patterns, by
the early 2000s Ukraine found itself among the most equal post-communist
countries, whereas Poland appeared to be among the most unequal in terms
of the distribution of consumption.

Thus, the Polish 'poverty puzzle' has constituted a major difference between
the socio-economic outcomes of the late transformation period in the two
Eastern European countries. Poland's poverty paradox is directly and positively related to the country's chronically high levels of unemployment and
growing inequality in wealth and income distribution. By contrast, by the
beginning of the twenty-first century, the Ukrainian political economy has
apparently managed to succeed in lowering unemployment, inequality, and
poverty. Yet Ukraine's business and trade cycles have been even more pronounced than those experienced by its western neighbour. The next sections provide a critical neoinstitutionalist account for possible causes of the
observed similarly positive growth and efficiency developments in Poland and
Ukraine in the late 1990s–early 2000s, as well as of potential sources of the
macroeconomic and social volatility experienced to a different extent by both
post-communist political economies.

13.3. INSTITUTIONS AND THE TRANSFORMATION PERFORMANCE

In post-communist or 'transition' studies, as the title of the discipline itself
suggests, positive and normative concepts and judgements are intricately
entangled. Since the very beginning, post-communist studies have been characterized by a protracted clash of well-informed but often diametrically
opposed opinions as to whether the transition/transformation is (or ultimately will be): a triumphant success (e.g. Sachs 1993; Åslund 1995, 2002,
2004b); a miserable but preventable failure (e.g. Galbraith 1990b; Nove 1990,
1993; Stiglitz 1999, 2002), an inevitable yet long-expected tragedy (Burawoy
2001b, 2001c), or something even more sinister (Gowan 1995, 1996). In addition to the individual author's perception of the end-result, the empirical

analysis of the post-communist phenomena has been highly dependent on the understanding by a particular observer and participant of what actually constitutes a modern successfully functioning market economy, or, alternatively, what a successful but non-capitalist post-communist order could have been like.[3]

13.3.1. In Praise of Free Enterprise: The Dominant Transition Paradigm

From the neoliberal transition perspective, any other type of political economy except for the liberal market-based model ought to jeopardize the self-organizing Pareto optimum of free markets in Eastern Europe and elsewhere (for a discussion on the transition paradigm, see Mykhnenko 2005b: part 2). Therefore, mainstream neoliberal commentators typically focus on the successes of transition towards an LME in (some) post-communist countries, whereas any negative developments in the region are interpreted as the result of incomplete or failed neoliberalization (e.g. Balcerowicz 1995; World Bank 1996; Hernandez-Cata 1997; Klaus 1997; Fischer, Sahay, and Végh 1998; Dąbrowski and Gortat 2002; World Bank 2002).

Throughout most of the 1990s, it was Poland—the first Eastern European battleground of liberalization, marketization, and privatization—which was praised for becoming a 'European tiger', a neoliberal role model for the entire continent. Most of the formerly Soviet republics were usually described then as 'transition laggards' or outright 'transition failures' (e.g. Åslund 2000). However, in the early 2000s the dominant neoliberal transition theoreticians-cum-practitioners declared that their (economic) policy struggle has been won even in Russia and other previously 'lagging behind' cases (e.g. Shleifer and Treisman 2003). According to Anders Åslund, the most active and vocal neoliberal adviser, in 1998 the former Soviet republics were 'woken up' by the Russian financial crash and had no option but to finish the implementation of the radical 'Washington consensus' package of economic reforms that had been previously abandoned halfway through. As a result:

In a development that has gotten little notice amid the EU expansion hoopla, the post-Soviet countries further to the east have been booming since 1999. The nine market economies in the former Soviet Union (Russia, Ukraine, Kazakhstan, Moldova, Georgia, Armenia, Azerbaijan, Kyrgyzstan, and Tajikistan) have on average grown annually by no less than 7 per cent for the last five years. The new tigers are Kazakhstan, Russia, and Ukraine—far more so than Poland, Hungary, or the Czech Republic. Why are the post-Soviet market economies doing so much better than the Central European ones? The truth, which may shock you, is that the post-Soviet countries have a more efficient economic model than the Central European ones because they are free from the harmful influences of the EU. (Åslund 2004*a*)

The newly gained economic and social dynamism of the post-Soviet countries has been accredited to the establishment in those countries of LMEs based on open markets, home-grown entrepreneurial talent, limited state intervention, low public expenditures, slashed personal and corporate taxes, privatized social security systems, and 'Chilean-style' pension reforms. By contrast, it is the EU bureaucracy and the imposition of the 'European social model' which are claimed to be responsible for the economic slowdown and high unemployment suffered by some of the largest Eastern European EU member-states. The neoliberals' list of the harmful influences of the EU is no different to the one which is usually produced to account for the malaise of the 'Old Europe'. It includes 'protectionism, labour market inflexibility, intimidating regulations, unsustainable fiscal profligacy, harmful subsidies, heavy tax burdens, excessive welfare transfers, bloated public sectors, and other competitive constraints' (see Åslund 2004*a*). Conservative critics of the 'deviant' and 'pathological' form of capitalism believed to be taking hold in Central and Eastern Europe add an 'unduly activist state agency' and foreign-dominated property structures to the above mentioned list of grievances (see Poznanski 2001).

13.3.2. From 'a Flea Market' to 'Dynamic Hybrid' Capitalism: Alternative Views on Post-Communist Economies

A number of radical as well as conservative critics of neoliberalism have focused on the failed attempts of forced neoliberalization and the consequent macroeconomic instability, extremely high 'transition costs' and de-developmental consequences of the 'Washington consensus' (e.g. Przeworski 1992; Bresser Pereira, Maravall, and Przeworski 1993; Murrell 1993, 1995; Hirschler 1998; Lane 2002). Their core argument is that rather than evolving towards modern Western capitalism, post-communist countries have ended up with 'a flea market rather than a free market' (Burawoy 1992: 783). In addition to what is described as the 'deficient but rational-bureaucratic' LMEs of the 'New Europe', the rest of post-communist societies are claimed to be locked in the gloomy 'low-level/dysfunctional equilibrium' of a disorganized, 'pre-modern', political, 'neopatrimonial' capitalism (Zon 2000, 2001; Lane 2000, 2005; King 2001, 2002 cf. Hunter 2003; Burawoy 2001*b*, 2001*c*).

In sharp contrast with the above-mentioned critical understanding of post-communist economies as being defunct due to their transitory, abnormal, or unrecognizable character, a number of empirical studies have emphasized a significant positive potential in the adaptable, 'recombinant', and diverse nature of the institutions of post-communist capitalism (Stark 1996, 1997; Stark and Bruszt 1998). Lucian Cernat (2002) has found evidence of a diverse capitalism à la carte present in Eastern Europe, with some countries becoming LMEs, whereas the others adopt CME models (Continental European or developmental Asian types). He has argued that the macroeconomic performance of Poland, the Czech Republic, Hungary, Slovakia, Slovenia, Bulgaria, Romania, Latvia, Estonia, and Lithuania between 1992 and 1999 suggests that the institutional and economic features of LMEs were more growth-enhancing in the region than the alternative institutional arrangements and policies. By contrast, comparing Estonia and Slovenia, Clemens Buchen (2005*a*, 2005*b*) has found that despite certain deviations from the ideal-type LMEs and CMEs respectively, both countries can be regarded as successful transformation cases (cf. Feldmann 2005).

Elena Iankova has described the creation of a 'dynamic hybrid' Eastern European capitalism based on 'tripartism'—the tripartite forum for social dialogue between governments, labour, and business in Central and Eastern Europe (2002). By critically approaching the VoC thinking as regards the wage–labour nexus and industrial relations, she has argued that post-communism tripartism is a dynamic subtype of neocorporatist capitalism and accredited it with institutionalizing conflict and preserving social peace under the adverse circumstances of economic depression. Bernard Chavance and Eric Magnin have emphasized the significance of institutional embeddedness and self-reorganization in post-communist countries and welcomed the emergence of what they describe as MMEs of Eastern Europe—'path-dependent national capitalisms, displaying general similarities, and persisting national peculiarities' (2000; cf. 1997).

13.4. THE RISE OF MIXED MARKET ECONOMIES IN POLAND AND UKRAINE

It is argued in this chapter that the outcomes of the post-communist transformation in Poland and Ukraine can be explained by the emergence of partially coherent MMEs. Furthermore, it is contended that the disappearance of the 'poverty puzzle' in one of the two eastern European countries is attributable to the interplay of complementary institutional dynamics. In Mykhnenko (2005*a*, 2005*b*, 2005*c*), I have presented the empirical analysis of Polish and Ukrainian political economies during the post-communist transformation and outlined major features of the emerging capitalist systems in both countries as of the early 2000s. On the basis of my previous discussions as well as recent political and legal developments in the two countries, this section provides a summary of the core institutional characteristics of capitalism in Poland and Ukraine. The description of the relevant institutional domains presented in Table 13.1 broadly follows Bruno Amable's account (2003) of different models of modern capitalism. This labelling exercise has been conducted using the OECD and World Bank terminology. Thus, it embodies a number of built-in neoliberal biases against 'heavy' market regulations or 'inflexible' labour markets.

Table 13.1. Major characteristics of capitalism in Poland and Ukraine, 2000–5

Institutional arena	Poland	Ukraine
Product-market competition	'Relatively restrictive' product-market regulation	'Relatively restrictive' product-market regulation
	Administrative burdens for corporations	Administrative burdens for corporations
	Barriers to entrepreneurship	Barriers to entrepreneurship
	Public sector	Public sector
	Barriers to trade and investment	Barriers to trade and investment
Wage–labour nexus	'Restrained tripartism'	'Hard tripartism'
	Mildly regulated labour market	Coordinated and regulated labour market
	Moderate employment protection	High protection of regular employment
	Informal tripartite fora for social dialogue	Formal tripartite fora for social dialogue
	Weak trade unions	High rates of union membership
	Defensive union strategies	Cooperative industrial relations
Financial sector	Small, bank-based system	Small, underdeveloped, bank-based system
	Small financial market	Very small financial market
	Low sophistication of financial market	No sophistication of financial market
	Limited banking concentration	Limited banking concentration
	Poor business environment	Poor business environment
	Low conformity to the standards of corporate governance	Little conformity to the standards of corporate governance
	Limited market for corporate control	Limited market for corporate control
	Importance of direct foreign investment by multinationals	Importance of investment by domestic business groups

(cont.)

Table 13.1. (*cont.*)

Institutional arena	Poland	Ukraine
Social protection	Contracting conservative 'Latin' Welfare state	Expanding liberal-'universalist' Welfare state
	Decrease to lower-moderate levels of social protection	Increase to higher-moderate levels of social protection
	Decrease to moderate involvement of the state	Increase to moderate involvement of the state
	Importance of old-age, survivors, and incapacity-related expenditures	Limited public health expenditures
		Emphasis on pensions, poverty alleviation (social safety net), and means-tested benefits
		Some employment-based social protection
Education sector	'General skills' public education system	'Polytechnic' public education system
	Moderate public expenditures, chiefly for primary education	Moderate public expenditures, primarily for tertiary education
	Lower-moderate enrolment rates	Lower-moderate enrolment rates
	Limited vocational and lifelong learning and training	Importance of vocational training
		Limited lifelong learning and training
	Weakness in science and technology tertiary education	Strength in science and technology tertiary education
	Weak R&D	Small R&D
Overall	MME/'Weak' CME	MME/'Weak' CME

13.4.1. Poland's Capitalism

First, the Polish national variant of capitalism is characterized by: heavily regulated product markets with a considerable public sector, administrative burdens for corporations, barriers to entrepreneurship, and a high level of protection against foreign trade and investment. Second, in the sphere of labour markets and industrial relations, the main attribute of capitalism in Poland is a mildly regulated labour market with a moderate degree of employment protection. Although certain informal relationship between the government, labour, and business in Poland has been maintained (see Iankova 2002), the national political economy is characterized by: little formal centralization and coordination for wage bargaining, no mandatory state involvement, weak trade unions, wage flexibility, non-adversarial industrial relations, the absence of active employment policy, and a low level of passive labour market policy. Third, the financial-intermediation sector in Poland is elementary and bank-dominated. It generates a very low amount of private domestic credit and is characterized by: high ownership concentration, low protection of external shareholders, a small and inactive financial market, no role for institutional investors, very low sophistication of financial markets, a low degree of banking concentration, poor business environment, low conformity to the standards of corporate governance, no active market for corporate control (takeovers, mergers, and acquisitions), and the relative significance of FDI.

Fourth, the social protection sector in Poland is built around the Conservative Continental European model, close to its 'Latin subsidiarist' subtype (see Ebbinghaus and Manow 2001). However, since the late 1990s Poland's welfare state has been contracting in size. It is characterized by (lower-)moderate levels of social protection and public spending. Social expenditures are generally oriented towards pensions, disability benefits, and poverty alleviation, whereas other social services are of less significance. Finally, the Polish education sector is publicly funded and oriented towards general skills. It is characterized by a moderate degree of public expenditure on education, the bulk of which is allocated for primary and lower-secondary education. Other major characteristics of Poland's educational system include: (lower-)moderate enrolment rates; weak vocational training; no importance of life-long learning and training; emphasis on basic skills and the quality of primary education; weak science and technical education; and weakly state-funded research and development activities.

13.4.2. Ukraine's Capitalism

In turn, the Ukrainian national variant of capitalism in Eastern Europe is characterized, first, by heavily regulated product markets, involving a large public sector, administrative burdens for corporations, barriers to entrepreneurship, and barriers to foreign trade and investment. Second, as regards the wage–labour nexus, the core feature of post-communist capitalism in the country is 'tripartism' or 'tripartite co-ordination' of the labour market defined by Iankova as a new post-communist species of institutionalized compromise among social actors in the industrial arena which: 'developed as a dynamic hybrid characterized by political negotiations (rather than Western Europe's neocorporatist bargaining over purely social and economic conditions); represents a broad civic arrangement (rather than a classic tripartite formation for coordination of the interests of labour and business with those of the state); and is a complex multilevel bargaining structure that links together national, regional, and sectoral actors for the resolution of problems with national and local importance' (2002: 11). On the one hand, Ukraine's 'tripartism' includes high-employment protection, state involvement, moderately strong trade unions, and consensual industrial relations. On the other hand, Ukraine's industrial relations and labour market institutions are characterized by inter-sectoral variance in the degree of centralization and coordination of wage bargaining, limited active employment policy, and a low level of passive labour market policies.

Third, the sector of financial intermediation in Ukraine is exclusively bank-based and underdeveloped. It is characterized by: high ownership concentration; reportedly low protection of external shareholders; a small and inactive financial market; no role for institutional investors; no sophistication of financial markets; a low degree of banking concentration; poor business environment; low conformity to the standards of corporate governance; no market for corporate control (takeovers, mergers, and acquisitions); a low level of FDI; and the overall importance of reinvestment of profits by large national business groups. Fourth, the welfare system in Ukraine is of a liberal-'universalist' form (see Ebbinghaus and Manow 2001), with its emphasis on poverty alleviation and means-tested benefits, limited public expenditure on health care, contribution-financed social insurance, and a mixed pension system. Since the early 2000s, among the major developments in the Ukrainian system of social protection has been an increase to (higher-)moderate levels of social protection and more involvement of the state. Finally, the Ukrainian education system is characterized by: a moderate level of public expenditure; high enrolment rates in secondary education, strong vocational, professional, and technical education; low importance of life-long learning and training; an emphasis on specific skills and the quality of university education; high importance of technical higher education; and a small research and development sector.

13.5. ACCOUNTING FOR SIMILAR OUTCOMES OF POST-COMMUNISM IN POLAND AND UKRAINE

13.5.1. Institutional Similarity, Complementarity, and Coherence

The original VoC idea attributes the relative socio-economic success of various LME/CMEs to institutional complementarity understood as an interdependent and mutually re-enforcing systemic mechanism under which the presence (or efficiency) of one institution increases the returns from (or efficiency of) another institution (Hall and Soskice 2001*b*: 17–21; cf. Milgrom and Roberts 1995; Amable 2003: ch. 2). Colin Crouch (2003, 2005*b*, 2005*c*) and others (see Morgan, Whitley, and Moen 2005) have critically elaborated the concept of institutional complementarity by distinguishing at least three different logics behind the concept: (*a*) the logic of coherence through *similarity* or *Wahlverwandschaft*—elective affinity; (*b*) the logic of 'partial' complementarity or complementarity in the VoC sense of *synergy*, where 'coherence embodies the mutually reinforcing effects of compatible incentive structures in different subsystems of an economy' (Deeg 2005: 24); and (*c*) the logic of strict or 'perfect' *complementarity* (opposite to that of similarity) 'where components of a whole mutually compensate for each other's deficiencies in constituting the whole' (Crouch 2005*c*: 50). In this sense, Crouch's concept of 'perfect' complementarity helps distinguish complementarity between different institutions from obstructive incongruity between them, since 'a difference becomes a complementarity when it "works"' (2005*c*: 52).

In sharp contrast with the dominant neoliberal transition paradigm, Table 13.1 has shown that the overall designs of both Eastern European political economies share the logic of similarity typical of CMEs which include relatively 'restrictive' product market regulations, bank-based financial-intermediation sectors, and public education systems. In addition, Poland's social protection system resembles the conservative Continental European model, whereas Ukraine's labour market institutions and industrial relations contain 'tripartite' neocorporatist features—all CME characteristics (cf. Knell and Srholec 2005).

However, one institutional arena in each of the two Eastern European economies—the 'soft tripartism' of the wage–labour nexus in Poland and the liberal-'universalist' welfare state in Ukraine—are dissimilar from the ideal-typical CME model of the VoC approach (Hall and Soskice 2001*a*) or from what Amable (2003) has identified as 'Continental European' and 'Mediterranean' models of regulated capitalism. Another distinctive difference of the two Eastern European economies from the CME ideal-type lies in the financial-intermediation sector. Although both Polish and Ukrainian finance sectors are currently bank-based, they remain immature and weak in comparison with any of the existing models of modern capitalism. Hence this chapter's description of the two post-communist economies not as CMEs but as mixed-market or 'weakly' coordinated-market economies.

13.5.2. Structural Changes and Comparative Advantages of the Post-Communist MMEs

In addition to severe exogenous shocks, similarly sharp periodic fluctuations in the rate of economic activity (e.g. capital investment, prices, and output growth) experienced by the two 'weak' CMEs of Eastern Europe can be attributed to their weak financial systems which are unable to provide a stable and sufficient amount of domestic credit.[4] Yet it is claimed that the overall similarity of the institutional designs of the two MMEs has already been able to provide a certain level of coherence for economic agents to grow by engaging in increasingly productive activities.

To test this hypothesis of positive economic developments in Poland and Ukraine due to the presence of institutional complementarity as synergy, one might search for beneficial structural changes occurring in the two economies. I examine the presence of positive structural changes by discovering and comparing potential changes in comparative institutional advantages of Poland and Ukraine. This section proceeds by applying Bela Balassa's RCA index (Balassa 1977; 1989). The RCA index compares the export share of a given sector in a country with the export share of that sector in the world market as follows:

$$RCA_{ij} = \frac{X_{ij}/\sum\limits_i X_{ij}}{\sum\limits_j X_{ij}/\sum\limits_i\sum\limits_j X_{ij}}$$

The numerator represents the percentage share of a given sector in national exports, where X_{ij} are the exports of sector i from country j; $\sum_i X_{ij}$ are the total exports of country j. The denominator represents the percentage share of a given sector in the total world exports, where $\sum_j X_{ij}$ are the world exports of sector i, and $\sum_i \sum_j X_{ij}$ are the total world exports. Thus, when the RCA index equals 1 for a given sector in a given country, the export share of that sector is identical with the world's average. When RCA is above 1 (ranging from 1 to ∞) the country is said to have a relative comparative advantage in that sector; when RCA is below 1 (ranging from 0 to 1) the country is said to have a relative weakness in that sector.

The UNCTAD database (2005) provides the three-digit SITC product code of annual exports and imports comprising over 230 types of products from the total of 67 branches of agriculture, mining and quarrying, manufacturing, and gas, water, and electricity supply. The first year for which the Ukrainian data are available is 1992, whereas the last year is 2002. Poland's detail foreign trade statistics are available since the late 1980s. To examine the (potentially beneficial) shifts in RCAs of the two countries under post-communism, while minimizing possible ad hoc changes in the national foreign trade structures, I use the exports average figures for the 1992–3 period as the starting point and for the 2001–2 period as the end point of transformation.

Table 13.2. Revealed comparative advantage index (2001–2 average) and RCA percentage change between 1992–3 and 2001–2

Poland			Ukraine		
Type of exports	RCA index 2001–2 average	Index change (%) 1992–3 to 2001–2	Type of exports	RCA index 2001–2 average	Index change (%) 1992–3 to 2001–2
Low-technology exports	1.8	17.6%	Low-technology exports	1.6	74.2%
Resource-based manufactured exports	1.3	−20.9%	Resource-based manufactured exports	1.5	−19.9%
Medium-technology exports	1.1	50.7%	Medium-technology exports	1.1	25.3%
Primary commodity exports	0.6	−43.9%	Primary commodity exports	1.1	−27.2%
High-technology exports	0.4	31.6%	High-technology exports	0.2	61.6%

Note: The technological classification of trade is based on the Standard International Trade Classification, Revision 2. The type of exports is defined according to the UNIDO Scoreboard Database technology classification of exports Table (2004: 205).
Source: Own compilations and calculations on the basis of *UNCTAD Handbook of Statistics On-line* (2005).

Table 13.2 contains the RCA indices for Poland and Ukraine for 2001–2 as well as percentage changes in the two respective indices since 1992–3. It shows that both countries have developed extremely similar RCAs in terms of technological intensity which are structured in the same ranking order as well. Poland's and Ukraine's major strengths lie in low-technology products and resource-based manufacturing, whereas the countries' weakest sectors are high-technology products and primary commodities, with the medium technology branch located in between.[5] In addition to the current RCA resemblance between Poland and Ukraine, the structural shifts in the RCA of the two countries have been similarly positive as well. Table 13.2 shows that under post-communism both countries have registered major comparative advantage index losses in primary commodities and resource-based manufacturing. In turn, the Polish and Ukrainian economies have improved their competitiveness in low-, medium-, and high-technology products. These positive and incremental structural changes in the two Eastern European countries have, thus, correlated with the establishment of (partially) coherent capitalist institutions.

The RCA evaluations presented above suggest that some institutional incoherencies can be more unhelpful than the others. By the early 2000s, the difference between Poland's and Ukraine's science and technology education and training systems—relatively weak in the former and strong in the latter—had not generated different relative comparative advantages in economic activities. Neither have they influenced the direction of the change in the countries' RCA under post-communism, since—according to the institutional complementarity theory (see introduction)—Poland should have experienced growth in low-technology exports, while Ukraine's core gains should have come from medium-technology exports. Given the large amount of investment needed for a technological upgrade of formerly centralized planning economies, the similarly incremental structural changes in the two Eastern European MMEs can be explained again by the immaturity (i.e. small size) of their domestic credit-creation mechanisms.

13.6. EXPLAINING POLAND'S POVERTY PARADOX

It is contended here that Poland's inequality-cum-poverty puzzle is the result of the institutional incongruity between, on the one hand, the country's wage–labour nexus which is based on the 'soft' regulation of an effectively uncoordinated labour market, and, on the other hand, the overall logic of the national CME-type of economy. According to Amable (2003: ch. 3), competitive labour markets can make structural adjustment less costly if the released labour force is quickly absorbed by (low-wage) small and medium firms and business start-ups; yet, those are constrained in Poland by economic and administrative barriers to entry. Therefore, this chapter's earlier findings support the VoC hypothesis that decentralized and deregulated ('flexible') labour markets cannot function properly along with regulated product markets; otherwise such an institutional incoherence should result in higher levels of unemployment (as in the case of Poland) than one would expect in a country with centralized or coordinated labour markets and regulated product markets (as in the case of Ukraine). Given chronically high levels of unemployment in Poland and contracting levels of public social spending, Poland's conservative Continental welfare state has been unable to provide an adequate amount of social protection and poverty alleviation. On the other hand, in addition to its generally resurgent economy, Ukraine's relatively low inequality and poverty outcomes are claimed to be the result of a politically constructed complementarity between, on the one hand, strongly coordinated labour market institutions and cooperative industrial relations, and, on the other hand, a liberal-'universalist' welfare state.

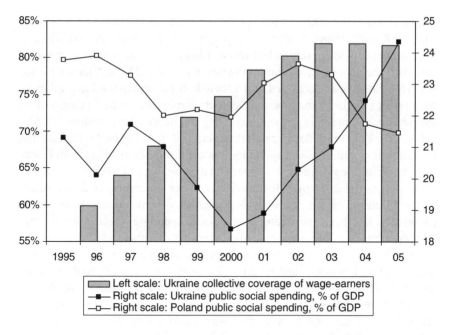

Figure 13.11. Collective wage-bargaining coverage (percentage of wage earners) and public social spending as percentage of GDP, 1995–2005

Source: Derzhkomstat Statistical Yearbook (various years), Ukraine Ministry of Labour and Social Work Social Labour Relations On-line (2005), own calculations on the basis of IMF Public Information Notice, No. 05/156 (Novermber 2005), OECD Factbook (2005), OECD Economic Outlook 77 Database (2005).

Throughout the 1990s, Ukraine's limited social protection system was (at least theoretically) incompatible with the overall institutional logic of a CME. A minimal public-funded social protection system does not protect against unemployment and, thus, fluid labour markets are necessary. However, at the same time, the country's tripartite coordination of the domestic labour market was expanded. The formal protection of regular employment has prevented excessive levels of unemployment, whereas the expansion of collective wage bargaining (see Figure 13.11) has resulted generally in higher and more equal wages, which have compensated for initially limited social protection. Consequently, Ukrainian welfare politics have changed dramatically.

The disappearance of George Gongadze, a Ukrainian opposition journalist, on 16th September 2000 and consequent allegations about the involvement of Ukraine's government and President Leonid Kuchma himself in the affair, provoked a long period of political turmoil in the country which culminated on 9th March 2001 in mass demonstrations and violent clashes between riot police and thousands of anti-Kuchma protesters who stormed the presidential headquarters in the centre of Kyiv (*The Ukrainian Weekly* 2002). In May 2001, Anatolii Kinakh, then president of the Ukrainian League of Industrialists and Entrepreneurs, was appointed by President Kuchma to the post of prime minister with the major goal of combating poverty (USPP 2001). A national anti-poverty strategy was developed and adopted on 15 September 2001, followed by a series of other executive and legislative measures aimed at improving the national social safety net and increasing public social expenditures (CMU 2001, 2002; Kuchma 2001; Ukraine President 2001). As Figure 13.11 indicates, the amount of public social spending was continuously growing both before and after Ukraine's contentious presidential campaign of October–November 2004. Before the 2004 presidential elections, the governing coalition under Prime Minister Viktor Yanukovych, Kuchma's designated successor to the presidency, had been increasing public social spending levels in an attempt to induce more public support. After Ukraine's Orange revolution, which brought Viktor Yushchenko to power—Yanukovych's main rival—public welfare spending has continued to grow. These politically motivated and constructed complementary institutional dynamics between labour market and social welfare policies have resulted in the significant decline in consumption inequality and extreme poverty that was registered in Ukraine in the late 1990s–early 2000s. In the same period, Poland's political economy was focused on combating public budget deficits, which resulted in a relative decline in the capacity of the welfare state.

13.7. CONCLUSION

It has been argued that the similarly positive socio-economic developments experienced by Poland and Ukraine between the mid-1990s and mid-2000s can be attributed to the emergence of mixed- or 'weakly' CMEs and explained as the outcome of positive returns on a set of (partially) coherent and complementary institutions established in both post-communist countries by the early twenty-first century. It has also been contended that, notwithstanding certain dissimilarities between the two Eastern European capitalisms and the ideal-types established in the literature, under certain conditions, institutional 'hybrids' of MMEs can function successfully and escape previously established traditions and allegedly predetermined pathways.

It is believed that the attempted application of the VoC framework and several concepts of institutional complementarity for exploring and explaining divergent socio-economic outcomes of late transformation in Eastern Europe has provided a valuable, complex, and powerful alternative to the dominant neoliberal transition paradigm. However, a number of transformation puzzles remain to be resolved, if they are to be analysed solely through the VoC prism.

For instance, this chapter has discovered no particular linkage between the strengths and weaknesses of the national public education systems in fields of science and technology and the technological intensity of revealed comparative trade advantages generated by the two Eastern European MMEs. The immaturity and small size of the post-communist capital markets as well as the overall peculiarity of the financial-intermediation and corporate governance sectors in Eastern Europe merit further investigation in this regard.

It appears also that the exclusive focus on the institutional forms of the two national models of production, consumption and distribution, and on their endogenous logic only provides us with part of the explanation for the trajectories and variations in the macroeconomic performance of post-communist countries. According to this chapter's description of the two Eastern European capitalisms, product-market regulations in both Poland and Ukraine have been characterized by a relatively high level of protection against trade and investment. Yet the data presented concerning international trade have indicated extremely high levels of actual openness of the Polish and Ukrainian economies (see Figure 13.6), posing the question of the relevance of formally 'heavy' and 'restrictive' regulations to the actual business and trade development.

On the other hand, high levels of macroeconomic volatility observed in the two post-communist economies can be at least partially attributed to (*a*) the actual degree of dependence of Polish and Ukrainian firms on foreign markets for goods and services and to (*b*) specific relationships by which each of the two national economies is inserted into the international economy. The importance of the mode of international integration is usually emphasized in the works of the French *Régulation* School (see Brenner and Glick 1991; Grahl and Teague 2000). However, the entire global dimension—actors and structures which are exogenous to the institutions of national political economies—appears to be absent from the VoC-framed picture. In the case of middle-income, post-communist economies, the lack of attention to such explanatory, if only intervening, independent variables may impoverish one's research efforts. Hence the need to integrate the currently exogenous variables and concepts concerning internationalization, globalization, and Europeanization into the present national state-oriented perspective.

NOTES

1. According to data presented in the World Bank 2005 report (Asad et al. 2005) on poverty in post-communist countries, Hungary has the lowest poverty rate in Eastern Europe, whereas Moldova has the highest. Across the entire

post-communist region, Tajikistan appears to be the most impoverished state. One has to emphasize, however, that the World Bank was not able to present poverty data for five post-communist countries (the Czech Republic, Slovakia, Croatia, Slovenia, and Turkmenistan) either because of major inaccuracies and serious flaws in household survey designs (the former two countries) or because national statistical agencies refused to provide access to the poverty data-sets (the remaining three cases). For the full data-set description and methodology, see Asad et al. (2005: Appendix).

2. It emerges from the World Bank 2005 report that 2002 was the latest year, for which the poverty figures were available in Poland and other Central-Eastern and South-Eastern European countries, whereas the most recent household surveys were conducted in the former USSR republics in 2003. Ukraine's lower- and higher-poverty rates in 2002 were 3% and 31% respectively (Asad et al. 2005: Appendix, Table 2).

3. Some have suggested that a whole new trade of ideological advocacy was born in the early 1990s. Adam Swain (2005) has described it as a 'transition industry'—a network of interlocking organizations and individuals engaged in academic and professional economic research, public policy, education, and consulting, which is based on the production, acquisition, accumulation, storage, geographical transfer, and management of abstract neoclassical economic knowledge, and is aimed at realizing 'transition' in post-communist Europe by forcing economic practices 'in the field' to conform to the premises of abstract economic thought. For a discussion on the rise of the 'political transition' paradigm, see Carothers (2002).

4. For a similar conclusion on weak financial markets in Central and Eastern Europe as a source of macroeconomic volatility and vulnerability, see Coricelli and Ianchovichina (2004).

5. By the type of industry (defined as a three-digit ISIC Rev. 3 branch), the Polish economy has generated: strong revealed comparative advantages (RCA indices >2.0) in ship-building, furniture, fabricated metal products (non-machinery), rubber and plastics, and wearing apparel; and standard comparative advantages (RCA indices > 1 < 2) in other non-metallic mineral products, pulp and paper, wood and cork, non-ferrous metals, railway and transport equipment not classified elsewhere (n.e.c.), electrical machinery, basic iron and steel, printing and publishing, food and drink, machinery and equipment (n.e.c.), and motor vehicles. The Ukrainian economy's strong RCAs (>2.0) were in basic iron and steel, railway and transport equipment (n.e.c.), coke, refined petroleum and nuclear fuel, and non-ferrous metals. The country's standard comparative advantages (RCA indices > 1 < 2) were in wood and cork, wearing apparel, food and drink, and chemicals and chemical products.

Bibliography

Acemoglu, D., Johnson, S., and Robinson, J. A. (2004). 'Institutions as the Fundamental Cause of Long-Run Growth', in P. Aghion and S. Durlauf (eds.), *Handbook of Economic Growth*. Amsterdam: North-Holland, pp. 385–472.

Ackermann, C., McEnally, R., and Ravenscraft, D. (1999). 'The Performance of Hedge Funds: Risk, Return, and Incentives', *Journal of Finance*, 54: 833–74.

Adam, P. and Canziani, P. (1997). 'I Contratti a Tempo Determinato in Italia e Spagna', *Lavoro e Relazioni Industriali*, 2: 9–52.

Aghion, P. and Howitt, P. (1988). *Endogenous Growth Theory*. Cambridge, MA: MIT Press.

Aguilera, R. (2003). 'Are Italy and Spain Mediterranean Sisters? A Comparison of Corporate Governance Systems', in M. Federowicz and R. Aguilera (eds.), *Corporate Governance in a Changing Economic and Political Environment*. Houndmills, Basingstoke, UK: Palgrave, pp. 23–70.

——— (2004). 'Corporate Governance and Labour Relations: Spain in the Context of Western Europe', in H. Gospel and A. Pendleton (eds.), *Corporate Governance and Labour Management: An International Comparison*. Oxford: Oxford University Press, pp. 197–225.

Albert, M. (1993). *Capitalism Against Capitalism*. London: Whurr.

Aldrich, J. (1993). 'Rational Choice and Turnout', *American Journal of Political Science*, 37: 246–78.

——— (1995). *Why Parties? The Origin and Transformation of Political Parties in America*. Chicago, IL: University of Chicago Press.

Alesina, A., Mirlees, J., and Neuman, M. J. M. (1989). 'Politics and Business Cycles in Industrial Democracies', *Economic Policy*, 4(8): 55–98.

Allen, M. (2004). 'The Varieties of Capitalism Paradigm: Not Enough Variety?', *Socio-Economic Review*, 2(1): 87–108.

Allsopp, C. and Artis, M. J. (2003). 'The Assessment: EMU, Four Years on', *Oxford Review of Economic Policy*, 19(1): 1–29.

Amable, B. (2003). *The Diversity of Modern Capitalism*. Oxford: Oxford University Press.

Amsden, A. H., Kochanowicz, J., and Taylor, L. (1994). *The Market Meets Its Match*. Cambridge, MA: Harvard University Press.

Andor, L. and Summers, M. (1998). *Market Failure: Eastern Europe's 'Economic Miracle'*. London: Pluto Press.

Aoki, M. (1994a). 'The Contingent Governance of Teams: Analysis of Institutional Complementarity', *International Economic Review*, 35(3): 657–76.

——— (1994b). 'The Japanese Firm as a System of Attributes', in M. Aoki and R. Dore (eds.), *The Japanese Firm: Sources of Competitive Strength*. Oxford: Oxford University Press, pp. 11–40.

Aoki, M. (2001). *Towards a Comparative Institutional Analysis*. Cambridge, MA: MIT Press.

Armingeon, K. (1994). *Staat und Arbeitsbeziehungen. Ein internationaler Vergleich*. Opladen: Westdeutscher Verlag.

—— (2000). 'Schweizer Gewerkschaften im internationalen Vergleich: Gemeinsamkeiten und Unterschiede', in K. Armingeon and S. Geissbühler (eds.), *Gewerkschaften in der Schweiz*. Zürich: Seismo Verlag.

Armstrong, M., Simon, C., and Vickers, J. (1994). *Regulatory Reform. Regulation of Economic Activity*. Cambridge, MA: MIT Press.

Armstrong, P., Glyn, A., and Harrison, J. (1991). *Capitalism since 1945*. Oxford: Basil Blackwell.

Arocena, P. (2004). 'Privatisation Policy in Spain: Stuck between Liberalisation and the Protection of Nationals' Interests', Cesifo Working Paper No. 1187.

Asad, A., Murthi, M., Yemtsov R., et al. (2005). *Growth, Poverty and Inequality: Eastern Europe and the Former Soviet Union*. Washington, DC: World Bank.

Åslund, A. (1995). *How Russia Became a Market Economy*. Washington, DC: Brookings Institution.

—— (2000). 'Radical Reformers Lead the Way', *Development Outreach*, 2(1): 13–17.

—— (2002). *Building Capitalism: The Transformation of the Former Soviet Bloc*. Cambridge: Cambridge University Press.

—— (2004*a*). 'An Expanding Europe in Decline; the EU Is an Economic Laggard. If You Want Growth, Kazakhstan's the Ticket', *The Washington Post*, 25 April.

—— (2004*b*). 'Liberalism's Economic Triumph', *The Moscow Times*, 26 April.

Axelrod, R. (1984). *The Evolution of Cooperation*. New York: Basic Books.

Baccaro, L., Carrieri, M., and Damiano, C. (2003). 'The Resurgence of Italian Confederal Unions: Will It Last?', *European Journal of Industrial Relations*, 9(1): 43–59.

Backes-Gellner, U. (2003) 'Die duale Berufsausbildung ist besser als ihr Ruf', *Neue Zürcher Zeitung*, 22/23 February.

Bahnmüller, R., Bispinck, R. et al. (1999). 'Tarifpolitik und Lohnbildung in Deutschland', Düsseldorf, WSI-Diskussionspapier Nr. 79.

Balassa, B. (1965). 'Trade Liberalization and Revealed Comparative Advantage', The *Manchester School of Economic and Social Studies*, 33(2): 99–123.

—— (1977). ' "Revealed" Comparative Advantage Revisited: An Analysis of Relative Export Shares of the Industrial Countries, 1953–1971', *The Manchester School of Economic and Social Studies*, 45: 327–44.

—— (1989). *Comparative Advantage, Trade Policy and Economic Development*. New York: Harvester Wheatsheaf.

Balcerowicz, L. (1995). *Socialism, Capitalism, Transformation*. Budapest: Central European University Press.

Baltowski, M. and Mickanwicz, T. (2000). 'Privatization in Poland: Ten Years After', *Post-Communist Economies*, 12(4): 425–43.

Bandru, D., Lavigne, S., and Morin, F. (2001). 'Les investisseurs institutionels inter-nationaux: Une analyse du comportement des investisseurs Américains', *Revue Économie Financiere*, 61: 121–37.

Barro, R. J. and Gordon, D. B. (1983). 'Rules, Discretion and Reputation in a Model of Monetary Policy', *Journal of Monetary Economics*, 12(1): 101–21.

Bauby, P. (1997). 'Services publics: des modèles nationaux à une conception européenne', *Politiques et Management Public*, 15(3): 107–22.

Baum, W. (1958). *The French Economy and the State*. Princeton, NJ: Princeton University Press.

Baums, T. (1995). *Universal Banks and Investment Companies in Germany*. Working Paper No. 26, Institute for Commercial and Business Law, University of Osnabrück.

Bayo-Moriones, A. and Ortín-Ángel, P. (2006). 'Internal Promotion versus External Recruitment in Industrial Plants in Spain', *Industrial and Labor Relations Review*, 59(3): 451–70.

Bebchuk, L. A. and Roe, M. J. (2004). 'A Theory of Path Dependence in Corporate Ownership and Governance', in J. N. Gordon and M. J. Roe (eds.), *Convergence and Persistence in Corporate Governance*. Cambridge: Cambridge University Press, pp. 69–113.

Becht, M. and Roëll, A. (1999). 'Blockholdings in Europe: An International Comparison', *European Economic Review*, 43: 1049–56.

Becker, G. J. (1964). *Human Capital. A Theoretical and Empirical Analysis with Special Reference to Education*. Chicago: University of Chicago Press.

Beer, S. H. (1969). *Modern British Politics*. London: Faber.

Beissinger, M. (2002). *Nationalist Mobilization and the Collapse of the Soviet State*. Cambridge: Cambridge University Press.

Bell, D. (1974). *The Coming of Post-Industrial Society*. London: Heinemann.

Belot, M. and Van Ourst, J. (2004). 'Does the Recent Success of Some Countries in Lowering Their Unemployment Rates Lie in the Clever Design of Their Labour Market Reforms?', *Oxford Economic Papers*, 56: 621–42.

Benchmarking Deutschland (2001). *Arbeitsmarkt und Beschäftigung. Bericht der Arbeitsgruppe Benchmarking und der Bertelsmann Stiftung*. Gütersloh, Germany: Springer.

Benders, J., Huijgen, F. et al. (1999). *Useful but Unused—Group Work in Europe. Findings from the EPOC Survey*. Dublin: European Foundation for the Improvement of Living and Working Conditions.

Benner, M. and Bundgaard Vad, T. (2000). 'Sweden and Denmark: "Defending the Welfare State"', in F. W. Scharpf and V. A. Schmidt (eds.), *Work and Welfare in the Open Economy*. Oxford: Oxford University Press, pp. 399–466.

Berger, S. (1981). 'Lame Ducks and National Champions: Industrial Policy in the Fifth Republic', in E. Andrews and S. Hoffmann (eds.), *The Fifth Republic at Twenty*. Albany, NY: SUNY Press, pp. 292–310.

――― (1985). 'French Socialists and the Patronat, the dilemmas of co-exsistence in a Mixed Economy', in H. Machin and V. Wright (eds.), *Economic Policies and*

Policy-Making under the Mitterrand Presidency, 1981–1984. London: Frances Pinter and New York: St. Martin's Press, pp. 225–43.

———(1996). 'Introduction', in S. Berger and R. Dore (eds.), *National Diversity and Global Capitalism.* Ithaca, NY: Cornell University Press, pp. 1–27.

———(2000). 'Globalization and Politics', *Annual Review of Political Science*, 3: 43–62.

———Sturgeon, T., Kurz, C., Voskamp, U., and Wittke, V. (1999). 'Globalization, Value Networks and National Models', MIT IPC Globalization Working Paper 99-000.

———Kurz, C., Sturgeon, T., Voskamp, U., and Wittke, V. (2001). 'Globalization, Production Networks and National Models of Capitalism: On the Possibilities of New Productive Systems and Institutional Diversity in an Enlarging Europe', *SOFI-Mitteilungen*, 29: 59–72.

Berghahn, V. R. (ed.) (1996). *German Big Business and Europe, 1918–1992.* New York and Oxford: Berg.

Berndt, C. (2000). 'Regulation, Power and Scale: "Reworking" Capital–Labour Relations in German SMEs', ESRC Centre for Business Research, University of Cambridge, Working paper No. 157.

Bernhard, M. (1993). *The Origins of Democratization in Poland.* New York: Columbia University Press.

Bertola, G. (1990). 'Job Security, Employment and Wages', *European Economic Review*, 34: 851–86.

Beyer, Jürgen and Höpner, Martin (2004). 'The Disintegration of Organized Capitalism: German Corporate Governance in the 1990s', in H. Kitschelt and W. Streeck (eds.), *Germany: Beyond the Stable State.* London: Frank Cass, pp. 179–98.

Bezemer, D., Dulleck, U., and Frijters, P. (2003). 'Socialism, Capitalism, and Transition: Coordination of Economic Relations and Output Performance', University of Vienna Department of Economics Working Paper No. 0305, Vienna.

Bianchi, M., Bianco, M., and Enriques, L. (2001). 'Pyramidal Groups and the Separation between Ownership and Control in Italy', in F. Barca and M. Becht (eds.), *The Control of Corporate Europe.* Oxford: Oxford University Press, pp. 154–88.

Billerbeck, U., Deutschmann, C., and Erd, R. (1982). *Neuorientierung der Tarifpolitik. Veränderungen im Verhältnis zwischen Lohn- und Manteltarifpolitik in den 70er Jahren.* Frankfurt: Nomos.

Bispinck, R. (1993). 'Kampf gegen die "Tarifwende"—Die Tarifbewegungen 1992 in den alten Bundesländern', *WSI Mitteilungen*, 46: 129–53.

———(1997). 'Überreguliert, undifferenziert, unbeweglich? Zum Flexibilitätspotential des Tarifvertragssystems und zu den Anforderungen an die künftige Tarifpolitik', in T. Dieterich (ed.), *Das Arbeitsrecht der Gegenwart. Jahrbuch für das gesamte Arbeitsrecht und die Arbeitsgerichtsbarkeit. Nachschlagewerk für Wissenschaft und Praxis.* Erich Schmidt Verlag, pp. 49–67.

———and Schulten, T. (2003). 'Verbetrieblichung der Tarifpolitik?—Aktuelle Tendenzen und Einschätzungen', *WSI-Mitteilungen*, No. 56, pp. 156–66.

Black, B. (1992). 'Agents Watching Agents: The Promise of Institutional Investor Voice', *UCLA Law Review*, 39: 811–93.

Blanchard, O. (1997). *The Economics of Post-Communist Transition*. Oxford: Clarendon Press.

_____ (2004). 'The Economic Future of Europe', *Journal of Economic Perspectives*, 18(4): 3–26.

_____ and Kremer, M. (1997). 'Disorganization', *Quarterly Journal of Economics*, 112(4): 1091–1126.

_____ and Wolfers, J. (2000). 'The Role of Shocks and Institutions in the Rise of European Unemployment: The Aggregate Evidence', *Economic Journal*, 100: 1–33.

_____ Dornbusch, R., Krugman, P., Layard, R., and Summers, L. (1991). *Reform in Eastern Europe*. Cambridge: MIT Press.

Blyth, M. (2003). 'Same as It Never Was: Temporality and Typology in the Varieties of Capitalism', *Comparative European Politics*, 1(2): 215–25.

Bohle, D. and Greskovits, B. (2004). 'Capital, Labor and the Prospects of the European Social Model in the East, Central and Eastern Europe', Working Paper Series, No. 58. Cambridge: Harvard University, Center for European Studies.

Böllhoff, D. (2005). *The Regulatory Capacities of Agencies: A Comparative Study of Telecoms Regulatory Agencies in Britain and Germany*. Berlin: Berliner Wissenschafts-Verlag.

Boltho, A., Alessandro, V., and Hiroshi, Y. (eds.) (2001). *Comparing Economic Systems: Italy and Japan*. New York: Palgrave.

Bornstein, M. (ed.) (1985). *Comparative Economic Systems: Models and Cases*, 5th edn. Homewood, IL: Richard D. Irwin.

Börsch, A. (2007). *Global Pressure, National System—How German Corporate Governance is Changing*. Ithaca: Cornell University Press.

Boycko, M., Shleifer, A., and Vishny, R. (1995). *Privatizing Russia*. Cambridge, MA: MIT Press.

Boyer, R. (1990). *The Regulation School: A Critical Introduction*. New York: Columbia University Press.

_____ (1995). 'Wage Austerity and/or An Education Push: The French Dilemma', *Labour*, 9 special issue: 519–66.

_____ (1998). 'Hybridization and Models of Production: Geography, History and Theory', in R. Boyer, E. Charron, U. Juergens, and S. Tolliday (eds.), *Between Imitation and Innovation. The Transfer and Hybridization of Productive Models in the International Automobile Industry*. Oxford: Oxford University Press, pp. 23–56.

_____ (2005a). 'Complementarity in Regulation Theory', *Socio-Economic Review*, 3(2): 366–71.

_____ (2005b). 'How and Why Capitalisms Differ', *Economy and Society*, 34(4): 509–57.

Bradley, D. H. and Stephens, J. D. (2007). 'Employment Performance in OECD Countries: A Test of Neoliberal and Institutionalist Hypotheses', *Comparative Political Studies*, 40(12): 1486–1510.

_____ Huber, E., Moller, S., Nielsen, F., and Stephens, J. (2003). 'Distribution and Redistribution in Postindustrial Democracies', *World Politics*, 55(2): 193–228.

Brenner, R. and Glick, S. (1991). 'The Regulation Approach: Theory and History', *New Left Review*, 188(July–August): 45–119.

Bresser Pereira, L. C., Maravall, J. M., and Przeworski, A. (1993). *Economic Reforms in New Democracies: A Social-Democratic Approach*. Cambridge: Cambridge University Press.

Brown, S. and Goetzmann, W. (2001). 'Hedge Funds with Style', NBER Working Paper No. 8173.

Brus, W. and Laski, K. (1989). *From Marx to the Market: Socialism in Search of an Economic System*. Oxford: Clarendon Press.

Buchen, C. (2005a). 'Institutional Complementarities in Transition: The case of Estonia and Slovenia.' Paper presented to the European School on New Institutional Economics. Càrgese, Italy, May.

―― (2005b). 'East European Antipodes: Varieties of Capitalism in Estonia and Slovenia.' Paper presented to the Varieties of Capitalism in Post-Communist Countries Conference. Paisley, Scotland, September.

―― ―― (2006). 'Estonia and Slovenia as Antipodes', in D. Lane and M. Myant (eds.), *Varieties of Capitalism in Post-Communist Countries*. London: Palgrave Macmillan. pp. 65–89.

Burawoy, M. (1992). 'The End of Sovietology and the Renaissance of Modernization Theory', *Contemporary Sociology*, 21(6): 744–85.

―― (2001a). 'Neoclassical Sociology: From the End of Communism to the End of Classes', *American Journal of Sociology*, 106(4): 1099–120.

―― (2001b). 'Transition without Transformation: Russia's Involuntary Road to Capitalism', *East European Politics and Societies*, 15(2): 269–90.

―― (2001c). 'The Great Involution: Russia's Response to the Market. Department of Sociology', University of California at Berkeley, Typescript.

―― and Krotov, P. (1992). 'The Soviet Transition from Socialism to Capitalism: Worker Control and Economic Bargaining', *American Sociological Review*, 57: 16–38.

Burda, M.C. (2001). 'European Labour Markets and the Euro: How Much Flexibility Do We Really Need?', Berlin: ENERPI: European Network of Economic Policy Research Institutes, Working Paper, No. 3 March.

Cable, V. (1995). 'The Diminished Nation-State: A Study in the Loss of Economic Power', *Daedalus* 124(2): 23–54.

Callaghan, H. (2004). 'The Domestic Politics of EU Legislation: British, French and German Attitudes towards Takeover Regulation, 1985–2003', Paper presented to the Conference of Europeanists, March 11–13, Chicago.

Callieri, C. (2002). 'Telephone Interview with Carlo Callieri, Vice-Chairman of Confindustria in 1992', 2 July 2002.

Calvo, G. and Coricelli, F. (1993). 'Output Collapse in Eastern Europe: The Role of Credit', *IMF Staff Papers*, 40(1): 32–52.

Cameron, P. (ed.) (2005). *Legal Aspects of EU Energy Regulation: Implementing the New Directives on Electricity and Gas across Europe*. Oxford: Oxford University Press.

Campbell, J. L. (2004). *Institutional Change and Globalization*. Princeton, NJ: Princeton University Press.

____Hall, J. A., and Pedersen, O. K. (2006). *National Identity and Varieties of Capitalism: The Danish Experience*. Montreal, Canada: McGill-Queens University Press.

Campos, N. F. and Coricelli, F. (2002). 'Growth in Transition: What We Know, What We Don't, and What We Should', The William Davidson Institute Working Paper No. 470. The University of Michigan, Ann Arbor, USA.

Capital, 'Heimlicher Abgang', No. 19, 2002.

Carey, J. M. and Shugart, M. S. (1995). 'Incentives to Cultivate a Personal Vote: A Rank Ordering of Electoral Formulas', *Electoral Studies*, 14(4): 417–39.

Carlin, W. and Soskice, D. (1997). 'Shocks to the System: The German Political Economy Under Stress', *National Institute Economic Review*, 159(1): 57–76.

____ ____ (2005). 'The 3-Equation New Keynesian Model—A Graphical Exposition', *Contributions to Macroeconomics*. B 5(1), Article 13.

____ ____ (2006). *Macroeconomics: Imperfections, Institutions and Policies*. Oxford: Oxford University Press.

Carothers, T. (2002). 'The End of the Transition Paradigm', *Journal of Democracy*, 13(1): 5–21.

Casper, S. (2001). 'The Legal Framework for Corporate Governance: The Influence of Contract Law on Company Strategies in Germany and the United States', in P. A. Hall and D. Soskice (eds.), *Varieties of Capitalism*. Oxford: Oxford University Press, pp. 87–416.

____Lehrer, M., and Soskice, D. (1999). 'Can High-Technology Industries Prosper in Germany? Institutional Frameworks and the Evolution of the German Software and Biotechnology Industries', *Industry and Innovation*, 6(1): 5–24.

Cawson, A., Holmes, P., Webber, D., Morgan, K., and Stevens, A. (1990). *Hostile Brothers*. Oxford: Clarendon Press.

Cazes, S. and Nesporova, A. (2001). 'Towards Excessive Job Insecurity in Transition Countries', Employment Paper 13. Geneva: ILO/Employment Strategy Department.

CDU/CSU-Bundestagsfraktion (2003). 'Entwurf eines Gesetzes zur Modernisierung des Arbeitsrechts ArbRModG', BT-Drucksache 15/1182, 18, Juni 2003.

Cebrián, I., Moreno, G., Lodovici, M. S., Semenza, R., and Toharia, L. (2001). 'Atypical Work in Italy and Spain: The Quest for Flexibility at the Margin in Two Supposedly Rigid Labour Markets', Paper presented at the Conference on Non-Standard Work Arrangements in Japan, Europe and the United States, Kalamazoo-Michigan, Revised version.

Cernat, L. (2002). 'Institutions and Economic Growth: Which Model of Capitalism for Central and Eastern Europe?', *Journal for Institutional Innovation, Development and Transition*, 6: 18–34.

Chavance, B. and Magnin, E. (1997). 'Emergence of Path-Dependent Mixed Economies in Central Europe', in A. Amin and J. Hausner (eds.) *Beyond Market and Hierarchy: Interactive Governance and Social Complexity*. Cheltenham, England: Edward Elgar, pp. 196–232.

____ ____ (2000). 'National Trajectories of Post-Socialist Transformation: Is There a Convergence towards Western Capitalisms?', in M. Dobry (ed.) *Democratic and*

Capitalist Transitions in Eastern Europe: Lessons for the Social Sciences Dordrecht, Germany: Kluwer, pp. 221–233.

Chiriatti, L. (2006). 'Interview with Lorenzo Chiriatti, Expert in Italian Labour Law', Florence, 23 March 2006.

Chussodovsky, M. (1997). *The Globalization of Poverty: Impacts of IMF and World Bank Reform.* London: Zed.

Clift, B. (2004). 'Debating the Restructuring of French Capitalism and Anglo-Saxon Institutional Investors: Trojan Horses or Sleeping Partners?', *French Politics*, 2: 333–46.

CMU Cabinet of Ministers of Ukraine (2002) [2001]. Postanova vid 21 hrudnia 2001 r. No. 1712: Pro zatverdzhennia Kompleksnoi prohramy zabezbechennia realizatsii Strategii podolannia bidnosti. *Ofitsiinyi visnyk Ukrainy*, 52(11 January): 14.

——(2002). Postanova vid 17 veresnia 2002 r. No. 1394: Pro vykonannia zavdan', shcho vyplyvaiut' z poslan' Prezydenta Ukrainy do Verkhovnoi Radu Ukrainy 'Evropeis'kii vybir. Kontseptual'ni zasady strategii ekonomichnogo ta sotsial'nogo rozvytku Ukrainy na 2002–2011 roky' ta 'Pro vnutrishne i zovnizhne stanovyshche Ukrainy u 2001 rotsi.' *Ofitsiinyi visnyk Ukrainy*, 38(4 October): 84.

Coates, D. (2005). 'Paradigms of Explanation', in D. Coates (ed.), *Varieties of Capitalism, Varieties of Approaches.* Houndmills Basingstoke, UK and New York: Palgrave Macmillan, pp. 1–25.

Cobham, D., Cosci, S., and Mattesini, F. (1999). 'The Italian Financial System: neither Bank Based nor Market Based', *The Manchester School*, 67(3): 325–45.

Cocca, T. and Volkart, R. (2000). *Aktienbesitz in der Schweiz 2000.* Swiss Banking Institute: University of Zurich.

Coe, D. and Snower, D. (1997). 'Policy Complemetarities: The Case for Fundamental Labour Market Reform', *IMF Staff Papers*, 44(1): 1–35.

Coen, D. (2005*a*). 'Business-Regulatory Relations: Learning to Play Regulatory Games', *Governance*, 18(3): 375–98.

——(2005*b*). 'Changing Business-Regulatory Relationships in UK and German Telecommunications and Energy Sectors', in D. Coen, A. Héritier and D. Böllhoff (eds.), *Refining Regulatory Regimes: Utilities in Europe.* Cheltenham, England: Edward Elgar, pp. 91–119.

——and Héritier, A. (eds.) (2005). *Redefining Regulatory Regimes: Utilities in Europe.* Cheltenham, England: Edward Elgar.

Coffee, J. (1999). 'The Future as History: The Prospects for Global Convergence in Corporate Governance', *Northwestern University Law Review*, 93: 641–708.

——(2002). 'Understanding Enron: It's about the Gatekeepers, Stupid', *Business Lawyer*, 57: 1403–20.

——(2005). 'A Theory of Corporate Scandals: Why the USA and Europe Differ', *Oxford Review of Economic Policy*, 21: 198–211.

Cohen, E. (1992). *Le colbertisme 'High Tech'.* Paris: Hachette.

——(1995). 'France: National Champions in Search of a Mission', in J. E. S. Hayward (ed.), *Industrial Enterprise and European Integration.* Oxford: Oxford University Press, pp. 23–47.

Commissariat du Plan (2000). *Services Publics en réseau: perspectives de concurrence et nouvelles regulation*. Paris: Commissariat du Plan.

Commission des Opérations Boursieres (COB) (1998). 'Les criteres d'investissement des grands gestionnaires de fonds internationaux dans les entreprises Francaises', Bulletin COB, #322: 1–31.

Commission of the European Communities (CEC) (1988). 'Commission Directive on Competition in the Markets in Telecommunications Terminal Equipment', Commission Directive 88/301/EEC, OJ L 131, 27.5.88.

_____ (1990). 'Commission Directive on Competition in the Markets for Telecommunications Services', Commission Directive 90/388/EEC, OJ L 1922, 24.7.90.

_____ (1994). 'Commission Directive 94/46/EC of 13 October 1994 Amending Directive 88/301/EEC and Directive 90/388/EEC in Particular with Regard to Satellite Communications', OJ L 268/15.

_____ (1995). 'Commission Directive of 18 October 1995 Amending Directive 90/388/EEC with Regard to the Abolition of the Restrictions on the Use of Cable Television Networks for the Provision of Already Liberalised Telecommunications Networks', OJ L 256/49, 26.10.95.

_____ (1996). 'Commission Directive of 28 February 1996 Amending Directive 90/388/EEC Regarding the Implementation of Full Competition in Telecommunications Markets Directive 96/19/EC', OJ L 74/13, 22.3.96.

Conference Board (1998). 'Turnover, Investment Strategies, and Ownership Patterns', *Institutional Investment Report*, 2: 1–51.

_____ (2000). 'International Patterns of Institutional Investment', *Institutional Investment Report*, 3: 1–46.

_____ (2002). 'Equity Ownership and Investment Strategies of U.S. and International Institutional Investors', *Institutional Investment Report*, 4: 1–45.

Contini, B. and Rapiti, F. M. (1999). ' "Young In, Old Out" Revisited: New Patterns of Employment Replacement in the Italian Economy', *International Review of Applied Economics*, 13(3): 396–415.

Conway, P., Janod, V., and Nicoletti, G. (2005). 'Product Market Regulation in OECD Countries: 1998 to 2003', OECD Economics Department Working Papers, no. 419.

Corbett, J. and Jenkinson, T. (1998). 'German Investment Financing: An International Comparison', in Black, Stanley; Moersch, Matthias', *Competition and Convergence in Financial Markets. The German and Anglo-American Models*. Amsterdam: Elsevier.

Coricelli, F. and Ianchovichina, E. (2004). 'Managing Volatility in Transition Economies: The Experience of the Central and Eastern European Countries', Centre for Economic Policy Research Discussion Paper DP 4414. London.

Council (1991). 'Council Directive 91/440/EEC of 29 July 1991 on the Development of the Community's Railways', OJ L 237, 24/08/1991.

Crafts, N. and Toniolo, G. (1996). 'Postwar Growth: An Overview', in N. Crafts and G. Toniolo (eds.), *Economic Growth in Europe since 1945*. Cambridge: Cambridge University Press, pp. 1–37.

Crafts, N. and Toniolo, G. (eds.) (1997). *Economic Growth in Europe since 1945*. Cambridge: Cambridge University Press.

Crepaz, M. M. L. (1998). 'Inclusion versus Exclusion—Political Institutions and Welfare Expenditures', *Comparative Politics*, 31(1): 61–80.

Crespí-Cladera, R. and García-Cestona, M. A. (2001). 'Ownership and Control of Spanish Listed Firms', in F. Barca and M. Becht (eds.), *The Control of Corporate Europe*. Oxford: Oxford University Press, pp. 207–28.

Crouch, C. (1977). *Class Conflict and the Industrial Relations Crisis*. London: Heinemann.

—— (1994). 'Beyond Corporatism: The Impact on Company Strategy', in R. Hyman, and A. Ferner (eds.), *New Frontiers in European Industrial Relations*. Oxford: Blackwell. pp. 196–222.

—— (1999). *Social Change in Western Europe*. Oxford: Oxford University Press.

—— (2003). 'Institutions within which Real Actors Innovate', in R. Mayntz and W. Streeck (eds.), *Die Reformierbarkeit der Demokratie: Innovationen und Blockaden*. Frankfurt: Campus. pp. 71–98.

—— (2005*a*). *Capitalist Diversity and Change: Recombinant Governance and Institutional Entrepreneurs*. Oxford: Oxford University Press.

—— (2005*b*). 'Complementarity and Fit in the Study of Comparative Capitalisms', in G. Morgan, R, Whitley, and E. Moen (eds.), *Changing Capitalisms? Internationalization, Institutional Change, and Systems of Economic Organization*. Oxford: Oxford University Press, pp. 167–89.

—— (2005*c*). *Capitalist Diversity and Change: Recombinant Governance and Institutional Entrepreneurs*. Oxford: Oxford University Press.

—— and Farrell, H. (2004). 'Breaking the Path of Institutional Development? Alternatives to the New Determinism', *Rationality and Society*, 16(1): 5–43.

—— and Pizzorno, A. (eds.) (1978). *The Resurgence of Class Conflict in Western Europe*. London: Macmillan.

Crowley, S. (2004). 'Explaining Labor Weakness in Post-Communist Europe: Historical Legacies and Comparative Perspectives', *East European Politics and Societies*, 18(3): 394–429.

—— (2005). 'Overshooting the Mark: East European Labor, Varieties of Capitalism, and the Future of the European Social Model', Paper presented at the annual meeting of the American Political Science Association, Washington, DC, September 2005.

Crozier, M. (1963). *Le Phénomène Bureaucratique: essai sur les tendances bureaucratiqices des systèmes d'organisation*. Paris: Editions du Seuil.

—— (1968). *The Bureaucratic Phenomenon*. Chicago, IL: University of Chicago Press.

Culpepper, P. (1996). 'Problems on the Road to "High Skill": A Sectoral Lesson from the Transfer of the Dual System of Vocational Training to Eastern Germany', WZB-Discussion Paper, FS I 96–317.

—— (1999*a*). 'The Future of the High-Skill Equilibrium in Germany', *Oxford Review of Economic Policy*, 15:(1): 43–59.

—— (1999*b*). 'Individual Choice, Collective Action, and the Problem of Training Reform: Insights from France and Eastern Germany', in P. Culpepper and

D. Finegold (eds.), *The German Skills Machine*. New York: Berghahn Books, pp. 269–325.

——— (2001). 'Employers, Public Policy, and the Politics of Decentralized Cooperation in Germany and France', in P. Hall and D. Soskice (eds.), *Varieties of Capitalism*. Oxford: Oxford University Press, pp. 275–306.

——— (2003). *Creating Cooperation: How States Develop Human Capital in Europe*. Ithaca, NY: Cornell University Press.

——— (2005). 'Institutional Change in Contemporary Capitalism: Coordinated Financial Systems since 1990', *World Politics*, 57(2): 173–99.

——— Hall, P. A., and Palier, B. (eds.) (2006). *Changing France: The Politics that Markets Make*. London: Palgrave Macmillan.

Cusack, T. (1991). 'The Changing Contours of Government', WZB Discussion Paper.

——— and Engelhardt, L. (2002). 'The PGL File Collection: File Structures and Procedures', Wissenschaftszentrum Berlin für Sozialforschung.

——— and Fuchs, S. (2002). 'Documentation Notes for Parties, Governments, and Legislatures Data Set', Wissenschaftszentrum Berlin für Sozialforschung.

——— Iversen, T., and Soskice, D. (2003). 'Specific Interests and the Origins of Electoral Systems'. Paper prepared for presentation at the Conference on the Diversity of Politics and Varieties of Capitalism, Wissenschaftszentrum Berlin, 31 October–1 November.

——— ——— ——— (2004). 'Economic Interests and the Origins of Electoral Institutions', Paper presented at the Annual Meeting of the American Political Science Association, Chicago, IL, September.

——— ——— ——— (2005). 'Specific Interests and the Origins of Electoral Systems', ms.

——— ——— and Rehm, P. (2006). 'Risk at Work: The Demand and Supply of Government Redistribution'. *Oxford Review of Economic Policy*, 22(3): 365–89.

Dąbrowski, M. and Gortat, R. (2002). *Political Determinants of Economic Reforms in Former Communist Countries*. Warsaw: CASE.

Dafsaliens, Annuaire DAFSA, annual publication, Paris.

David, T. and Mach, A. (2001). The 'Fortress of the Alps' between National Interests and Transnational Capital: The Transformations of Swiss Corporate Governance in Comparative Perspective, Unpublished Conferenece Paper 'Small States in World Markets—Fifteen years Later, Goeteborg, Sweden, 27–29 September.

——— ——— (2003). 'The Specificity of Corporate Governance in Small States: Institutionalization and Questioning of Ownership Restriction in Switzerland and Sweden', in M. Federowicz and R. Aguilera (eds.), *Corporate Governance in a Changing Economic and Political Environment. Trajectories of Institutional Change*, London: Palgrave Macmillan. pp. 220–46.

De Broeck, M. and Koen, V. (2000). 'The Great Contractions in Russia, the Baltics and Other Countries of the Former Soviet Union: A View from the Supply Side', Working Paper WP/00/32. Washington, DC.: International Monetary Fund.

De Cecco, M. and Ferri, G. (2001). 'Italy's Financial System: Banks and Industrial Investment', in A. Boltho, A. Vercelli, and H. Yoshikawa, (eds.), *Comparing Economic Systems: Italy and Japan*. Houndmills, Basingstoke, UK: Palgrave, pp. 64–84.

Decker, H. and Lukauskas, A. (2000). *Is Corporate Governance Converging Across Countries? Recent Trends in Germany*, Manuscript, School of International and Public Affairs, Columbia University.

Deeg, R. (1999). *Finance Capitalism Unveiled: Banks and the German Political Economy.* Ann Arbor, MI: University of Michigan Press.

—— (2005*a*). 'Path Dependency, Institutional Complementarity, and Change in National Business Systems', in G. Morgan, R. Whitley, and E. Moen (eds.), *Changing Capitalisms? Complementarities, Contradictions and Capability Development in an International Context.* Oxford: Oxford University Press. pp. 21–52.

—— (2005*b*). 'Change from Within: German and Italian Finance in the 1990s', in W. Streeck and K. Thelen (eds.), *Beyond Continuity: Institutional Change in Advanced Political Economies.* New York: Oxford University Press, pp. 169–202.

—— (2005*c*). 'Remaking Italian Capitalism: The Politics of Corporate Governance Reform', *West European Politics*, 28(3): 521–48.

—— (2005*d*). 'Complementarity and Institutional Change: How Useful a Concept?', Discussion Paper SP 11 2005-21, Wissenschaftszentrum Berlin.

Del Guercio, D. and Hawkins, J. (1999). 'The Motivation and Impact of Pension Fund Activism', *Journal of Financial Economics*, 52: 293–340.

—— and Tkac, P. (2001). 'Star Power: The Effect of Morningstar Ratings on Mutual Fund Flows', Working Paper #2001-15, Federal Reserve Bank of Atlanta.

—— —— (2002). 'The Determinants of the Flow of Funds of Managed Portfolios: Mutual Funds vs. Pension Funds', *Journal of Financial and Quantitative Analysis*, 37 (December): 523–57.

Della Sala, V. (2004). 'The Italian Model of Capitalism: On the Road between Globalization and Europeanization', *Journal of European Public Policy*, 11(6): 1041–57.

Derzhkomstat Ukraine State Statistics Committee (1995–2004). *Statystychnyi shchorichnyk Ukrainy.* Kyiv: Tekhnika.

DGB (2003). 'Ausbildungsstatistik der Bundesanstalt für Arbeit spricht für sich', Pressemitteilung 303. Berlin.

Dieterich, T. (2003). Expert statement by Prof. Dieterich at the parliamentary expert hearing.

DIHK (2003). Berufliche Bildung stärken—Zukunft sichern. Positionen und Forderungen zur Novellierung des Berufsbildungsgesetzes. Beschlossen vom Vorstand des DIHK am 25. Juni 2003 in Frankfurt/Main.

Djelic, M.-L. and Quack, S. (2003). *Globalization and Institutions: Redefining the Rules of the Economic Game.* Cheltenham, England: Edward Elgar.

Döhler, M. (2002). 'Institutional Choice and Bureaucratic Autonomy in Germany', *West European Politics*, 25(1): 101–24.

Domadenik, P. and Prašnikar, J. (2004). 'Enterprise Restructuring in the First Decade of Independence', in M. Mrak, M. Rojec, and C. Silva-Jáuregui (eds.), *Slovenia: From Yugoslavia to the European Union.* Washington, DC: the World Bank. pp. 244–62.

Dore, R. (1986). *Flexible Rigidities. Industrial Policy and Structural Adjustment in the Japanese Economy, 1970–80.* Stanford, CA: Stanford University Press.

Dufey, G., Hommel, U., and Riemer-Hommel, P. (1998). 'Corporate Governance: European vs. U.S. Perspectives in a Global Capital Market', in C. Scholz and J. Zentes (eds.), *Strategisches Euro-Management*. Stuttgart: Schäffer Poeschel. pp. 45–65.

Dyson, K. and Featherstone, K. (1997). *The Road to Maastricht: Negotiating Economic and Monetary Union*. Oxford: Oxford University Press.

Ebbinghaus, B. (2003*a*). 'Ever Larger Unions: Organisational Restructuring and its Impact on Union Confederations', *Industrial Relations Journal*, 34(5): 446–60.

———(2003*b*): 'Die Mitgliederentwicklung deutscher Gewerkschaften', in W. Schroeder and B. Wessels (eds.), *Die Gewerkschaften in Politik und Gesellschaft der Bundesrepublik Deutschland*. Opladen, Germany: Westdeutscher Verlag, pp. 174–203.

———and Manow, P. (eds.) (2001). *Comparing Welfare Capitalism, Social Policy and Political Economy in Europe, Japan and the USA*. London: Routledge.

———and Visser, J. (2000). *Trade Unions in Western Europe since 1945*. CD-ROM. London: Macmillan.

——— ———(2003). *The Societies of Europe. Trade Unions in Western Europe since 1945*. London and New York: Palgrave.

Eberlein, B. (2000). 'Institutional Change and Continuity in German Infrastructure Management: The Case of Electricity Reform', *German Politics*, 9(3): 81–104.

Eberwein, W. and Tholen, J. (1993). *Euro-manager or Splendid Isolation? International Management—An Anglo-German Comparison*. Berlin: Walter de Gruyter.

EBRD (2005). *Transition Report 2005*. London: EBRD.

———(various years). *Transition Report*. London: EBRD.

Edwards, J. and Fischer, K. (1994). *Banks, Finance and Investment in Germany*. New York: Cambridge University Press.

Eichengreen, B. (1996). 'Institutions and Economic Growth: Europe after World War II', in N. Crafts and G. Toniolo (eds.), *Economic Growth in Europe since 1945*. Cambridge: Cambridge University Press, pp. 38–72.

———(1997). *European Monetary Unification*. Cambridge, MA: MIT Press.

EIRO (1997). 'Active Employment Policies in Spain: An Overview', http://www.eiro.eurofound.eu.int/1997/07/feature/es9707214f.html

———(1998). 'Pay Trends in Italy Since the July 1993 Agreement', available at: http://www.eiro.eurofound.ie/1998/06/feature/IT9806326F.html: European Industrial Relations Observatory.

———(1999). 'National Social Pact for Development and Employment Signed', available at: http://www.eiro.eurofound.ie/1999/01/feature/IT9901335F.html: European Industrial Relations Observatory.

———(2002). Low-Wage Workers and the 'Working Poor', http://www.eiro.eurofound.eu.int/print/2002/08/study/tn0208101s.html.

———(2004). 'Trade Union Membership 1993–2003', http://www.eiro.eurofound.eu.int/2004/03/update/tn0403105u.html

———(2005). 'Changes in National Collective Bargaining Systems since 1990; Contributing Articles: Italy', available at: http://www.eiro.eurofound.eu.int/2005/03/word/it0412208s.doc: European Industrial Relations Observatory.

EIRR (1992a). 'The "Poverty" of Collective Bargaining', *European Industrial Relations Review*, 216: 19–20.

——— (1992b). 'Radical Labour Market Reform', *European Industrial Relations Review*, 220: 12–14.

——— (1993). 'Replacing the Labour Ordinances', *European Industrial Relations Review*, 234: 18–19.

——— (1994). 'Labour Market Reform', *European Industrial Relations Review*, 242: 21–4.

——— (2002a). 'New National Deal Secures Pay Moderation in 2002', *European Industrial Relations Review*, 337: 24–6.

——— (2002b). 'Review of New Accords in 2001', *European Industrial Relations Review*, 343: 28–30.

——— (2004). 'National Pay Bargaining Accord for 2004', *European Industrial Relations Review*, 361: 21–3.

Eising, R. and Jabko, N. (2000). 'Moving Targets: Institutional Embeddedness and Domestic Politics in the Liberalization of EU Electricity Markets.' EUI-RSCAS Working Paper EUI-RSC 2000/06. Florence: European University Institute.

——— ——— (2001). 'Moving Targets: National Interests and Electricity Liberalization in the European Union', *Comparative Political Studies*, 34(7): 742–67.

Ekiert, G. and Hanson, S. (2003). *Capitalism and Democracy in Central and Eastern Europe*. Cambridge: Cambridge University Press.

Ellerman, D. (2003). 'On the Russian Privatization Debate', *Challenge*, 46(3): 6–28.

Elliott, J. E. (1973). *Comparative Economic Systems*. Englewood Cliffs, NJ: Prentice-Hall.

Elvander, N. (2002). 'The New Swedish Regime for Collective Bargaining and Dispute Resolution: A Comparative Perspective', *European Journal of Industrial Relations*, 8(2): 197.

Encarnación, O. G. (2001). 'A Casualty of Unemployment: The Breakdown of Social Concertation in Spain', in N. Bermeo (ed.), *Unemployment in Southern Europe: Coping with the Consequences*. London: Frank Cass, pp. 32–59.

Erickson, C. and Ichino, A. (1995). 'Wage Differentials in Italy: Market Forces, Institutions and Inflation', in R. Freeman and L. Katz (eds.), *Differences and Changes in Wage Structures*. Chicago, IL: University of Chicago Press, pp. 265–305.

Esping-Andersen, G. (1990). *Three Worlds of Welfare Capitalism*. Princeton, NJ: Princeton University Press.

Estévez-Abe, M. (2005). 'Gender Bias in Skills and Social Policies: The Varieties of Capitalism Perspective on Sex Segregation', in L. McCall and A. Orloff (eds.), 'Gender, Class and Capitalism', Special Issue of *Social Politics*, 12(2): 180–215.

——— Iversen, T., and Soskice, D. (2001). 'Social Protection and the Formation of Skills: A Reinterpretation of the Welfare State', in P. Hall and D. Soskice (eds.), *Varieties of Capitalism. The Institutional Foundations of Comparative Institutional Advantage*. Oxford: Oxford University Press. pp. 145–83.

Estrin, S. (1994). *Privatization in Central and Eastern Europe*. London: Longman.

European Bank for Reconstruction and Development (1996). *Transition Report 1996*. London: EBRD.

_____ (1999). *Transition Report 1999*. London: EBRD.

_____ (2000). *Transition Report 200*. London: EBRD.

European Commission (1997). *Trade Patterns Inside the Single Market*. Luxembourg: Office for Official Publications of the European Communities.

_____ (2003). '2003 European Innovation Scoreboard: Technical Paper No. 2, Analysis of National Performances', Brussels: European Commission—Enterprise Directorate-General.

_____ (2005). *Industrial Relations in Europe 2004*. Luxembourg: Office for Official Publications of the European Communities.

European Parliament and Council (1996). 'Directive 96/92/EC of the European Parliament and of the Council of 19 December 1996 Concerning Common Rules for the Internal Market in Electricity', OJ L 027, 30/01/1997.

_____ (1997). 'Directive 97/67/EC of the European Parliament and of the Council of 15 December 1997 on Common Rules for the Development of the Internal Market of Community Postal Services and the Improvement of Quality of Service', OJ L 15, 21 January 1998.

_____ (1998). 'Directive 98/30/EC of the European Parliament and of the Council of 22 June 1998 Concerning Common Rules for the Internal Market in Natural Gas', OJ L 204, 21 July 1998.

_____ (2002). 'Directive 2002/39/EC of the European Parliament and of the Council of 10 June 2002 Amending Directive 97/67/EC with Regard to the Further Opening to Competition of Community Postal Services', OJL 176, 05 July 2002: 21–5.

_____ (2003a). 'Directive 2003/54/EC of the European Parliament and of the Council of 26 June 2003 Concerning Common Rules for the Internal Market in Electricity and Repealing Directive 96/92/EC. OJL 176, 15 July 2003.

_____ (2003b). 'Directive 2003/55/EC of the European Parliament and of the Council of 26 June 2003 Concerning Common Rules for the Internal Market in Natural Gas and Repealing Directive 98/30/EC', OJL 176, 15 July 2003.

Evans, A. (2005). 'Preemptive Modernisation and the Politics of Sectoral Defense: Adjustment to Globalisation in the Portuguese Pharmacy Sector', Mimeo.

Eyal, G. (2000). 'Anti-Politics and the Spirit of Capitalism: Dissidents, Monetarists, and the Czech Transition to Capitalism', *Theory and Society*, 29: 49–92.

_____ Szelényi, I., and Townsley, E. (1998) *Making Capitalism Without Capitalists*. New York: Verso.

Faccio, M. and Lang, L. (2002). 'The Ultimate Ownership of Western European Corporations', *Journal of Financial Economics*, 65(3): 365–95.

Fazekas, K. and Koltay J. (eds.) (2002). *The Hungarian Labour Market, Review and Analyses*, Institute of Economics, Budapest.

Featherstone, K. and Radaelli, C. M. (2003) (eds.) *The Politics of Europeanisation*. Oxford: Oxford University Press.

Feldmann, M. (2002). 'Varieties of Capitalism in Post-Communist Countries: Wage Bargaining in Estonia and Slovenia', Paper presented at the Comparative Political Economy workshop at Cornell University, Ithaca, NY, November.

Feldmann, M. (2005). 'The Origins of Varieties of Capitalism: Lessons from Post-Socialist Transition in Estonia and Slovenia', Paper prepared for the conference on Institutional Change in Contemporary European Capitalism. London, June.

—— (2006). 'Emerging Varieties of Capitalism in Transition Countries: Industrial Relations and Wage Bargaining in Estonia and Slovenia', *Comparative Political Studies*, 39(7): 829–54.

—— and Sally, R. (January 2002). 'From the Soviet Union to the European Union: Estonian Trade Policy, 1991–2000', *The World Economy*, 25(1): 79–106.

Fercenczi, B. (2002). 'Wages—Closing the Gap between Hungary and Europe', in K. Fazekas and J. Koltay (eds.), *The Hungarian Labour Market Review and Analysis*. Budapest: Institute of Economics, Hungarian Employment Foundation, pp. 114–21.

Fernández, R. and Rodrik, D. (1991). 'Resistance to Reform: Status Quo Bias in the Presence of Individual Specific Uncertainty', *American Economic Review*, 81: 1146–55.

Ferrera, M. and Gualmini, E. (2004). *Rescued by Europe? Social and Labour Market Reform in Italy from Maastricht to Berlusconi*. Amsterdam: Amsterdam University Press.

—— Hemerijck, A., and Rhodes, M. (2003). 'Recasting European Welfare States', in J. Hayward and A. Menon (eds.), *Governing Europe*. Oxford: Oxford University Press, pp. 346–66.

Financial Times (2004). *Europe 500*, Special Report, 21 May.

Finegold, D. and Soskice, D. (1988). 'The Failure of Training in Britain: Analysis and Prescription', *Oxford Review of Economic Policy*, 4(3): 21–53.

Fischer, S., Sahay, R., and Végh, C. (1998). 'From Transition to Market: Evidence and Growth Prospects', Working Paper WP/98/52 International Monetary Fund, Washington, DC.

Flanagan, R., Soskice, D. and Ulman, L. (1983). *Unionism, Economic Stabilisation and Incomes Policies: European Experience*, Washington, DC: Brookings Institution.

Flórez Saborido, I. (1994). *La Contratación laboral como medida de política de empleo en España*. Madrid: CES.

Fluder, R. and Hotz-Hart, B. (1998). 'Switzerland: Still as Smooth as Clockwork?', in A. Ferner and R. Hyman (eds.), *Changing Industrial Relations in Europe*. Oxford: Blackwell. pp. 298–322.

Foster, C. D. (1992). *Privatisation, Public Ownership and the Regulation of Natural Monopoly*. Oxford: Blackwell.

Franicević, V. and Kraft, E. (1997). 'Croatia's Economy after Stabilisation', *Europe–Asia Studies*, 49(4): 669–91.

Frankfurter Allgemeine Zeitung (1998). 'Arbeitgeber lehnen eine Änderung des Tarifrechts ab', 27 January.

—— (2005). 'Das Kartell bröckelt', 2 February.

Franks, J. and Mayer, C. (1997). 'Corporate ownership and control in the U.K., Germany, and France', *Journal of Applied Corporate Finance*, 9: 30–45.

Franzese, R. J., Jr. (2002). *Macroeconomic Policies of Developed Democracies*. Cambridge: Cambridge University Press.

Franzini, M. (2001). 'Unemployment Benefits and Labour Market Policies in Italy', Paper presented to the conference on 'Welfare State, Poverty and Social Exclusion in Italy and Great Britain', University of Siena, 6–8 April.

Fraunhofer Institut für Systemtechnik und Innovationsforschung (2004). *Leistungs-fähigkeit und Strukturen der Wissenschaft im internationalen Vergleich*, Studien zum deutschen Innovationssystem, No. 13, Karlsruhe.

Fravega, E. (2004). 'Actors and Institutions in the Field of Subsidised Employment: National Analysis, Convergences and Divergences', RESORE Project. http://www.univ-nancy2.fr/ILSTEF/RESORE/Fravega_RESORE_WP6_DEL23.pdf

Freeman, R. (1995) 'Are Your Wages Set in Beijing?', *Journal of Economic Perspectives*, 9(3): 15–32.

Frege, C. and Kelly, J. (2003). 'Union Revitalization in Comparative Perspective', *European Journal of Industrial Relations*, 9(1): 7–24.

Frieden, J. (1991). 'Invested Interests: The Politics of National Economic Policies in a World of Global Finance', *International Organization*, 45(4): 425–41.

——— and Rogowski, R. (1996). 'The Impact of the International Economy on National Policies: An Analytical Overview', in Robert O. Keohane and Helen V. Milner (eds.), *Internationalization and Domestic Politics*. New York: Cambridge University Press, pp. 108–36.

Frye, T. (2000). *Brokers and Bureaucrats: Building Market Institutions in Russia*. Ann Arbor, MI: University of Michigan Press.

Galbraith, J. K. (1990*a*). 'The Rush to Capitalism', *The New York Review of Books*, 37(16): 51–2.

——— (1990*b*). 'To Seek and Find the System', *Transition: The Newsletter about the Reforming Economies*, 1(8): 8–9.

Garcelon M. (1997). 'The State of Change: The Specialist Rebellion and the Democratic Movement in Moscow, 1989–1991, *Theory and Society*, 26: 39–85.

Garrett, G. (1998). *Partisan Politics in the Global Economy*. Cambridge: Cambridge University Press.

Genda, Y., Pazienza, M., and Signorelli, M. (2001). 'Labour Market and Job Creation', in A. Boltho, A. Vercelli, and H. Yoshikawa, (eds.), *Comparing Economic Systems. Italy and Japan*. Houndmills, Basingstoke, UK: Palgrave, pp. 135–56.

Geradin, D. (ed.) (2002). *The Liberalization of Postal Services in the European Union*. The Hague and London: Kluwer Law International.

German Federal Ministry of Education and Research (2003). *Germany's Vocational System at a Glance*, Bonn.

——— (2005). Zur technologischen Leistungsfähigkeit Deutschlands 2005, Bonn.

Gerschenkron, A. (1962). *Economic Backwardness in Historical Perspective*. Cambridge, MA: Harvard University Press.

Gesamtmetall (2005). *Mitgliedsfirmen und Beschäftigte in den Verbänden.* www.gesamtmetall.de

Goldstein, A. (2003). 'Privatization in Italy 1993–2002: Goals, Institutions, Outcomes and Outstanding Issues', CESifo Working Papers No. 912.

Goldthorpe, J. H. (ed.) (1978). 'The Current Inflation: Towards a Sociological Account', in F. Hirsch, P. and J. H. Goldthorpe (eds.), *The Political Economy of Inflation*. Oxford: Martin Robertson, pp. 186–214.

——(1985). *Order and Conflict in Contemporary Capitalism*. Oxford: Clarendon Press.

Gómez-Ibáñez, J. (2003). *Regulating Infrastructure. Monopoly, Contract and Discreation*. Cambridge, MA: Harvard University Press.

Goodin, R. E. (2003). 'Choose your Capitalism?', *Comparative European Politics*, 1(2): 203–13.

Goodman, J. (1992). 'Monetary Policy and Financial Deregulation in France', *French Politics and Society*, 10: 31–40.

Gourevitch, P. A. (1986). *Politics in Hard Times: Comparative Responses to International Economic Crises*. Ithaca, NY: Cornell University Press.

——(2000). 'The Governance Problem in International Relations', in D. Lake, and R. Powell (eds.), *Strategic Choice and International Relations*. Princeton, NJ: Princeton University Press, pp. 137–64.

——(2003). 'The Politics of Corporate Governance Regulation', *Yale Law Journal*, 112(7): 1829–80.

——and Hawes, M. B. (2002). 'The Politics of Choice among National Production Systems', in R. Boyer (ed.), *L'Année de la régulation*, No. 6. Paris: Presses de Sciences Po, pp. 241–70.

——and Shinn, J. (2005). *Political Power and Corporate Control: The New Global Politics of Corporate Governance*. Princeton, NJ: Princeton University Press.

Gowan, P. (1995). 'Neo-Liberal Theory and Practice for Eastern Europe', *New Left Review*, 213 (September–October): 3–60.

——(1996). 'Eastern Europe, Western Power and Neo-Liberalism', *New Left Review*, 216 (March–April): 129–40.

——(1999). *The Global Gamble: Washington's Faustian Bid for World Domination*. London: Verso.

Goyer, M. (2002). 'The Transformation of Corporate Governance in France and Germany: The Role of Workplace Institutions', Max-Planck-Institut für Gesellschaftsforschung Working Paper 02/10, July.

——(2003). 'Corporate Governance, Employees, and the Focus on Core Competencies in France and Germany', in C. J. Milhaupt (ed.), *Global Markets, Domestic Institutions: Corporate Law and Governance in a New Era of Cross-Border Deals*. New York: Columbia University Press, pp. 183–213.

——(2006a). 'The Transformation of Corporate Governance in France', in P. Culpepper, P. Hall, and B. Palier (eds.), *Changing France: The Politics that Markets Make*. London: Palgrave Macmillan. pp. 80–106.

——(2006b). 'Institutional Investors in French and German Corporate Governance: Varieties of Capitalism and the Illusion of Differences', Working Paper, Center for European Studies, Harvard University.

——and Hancké, R. (2004). 'Labour in French Corporate Governance: The Missing Link', in H. Gospel, and A. Pendleton (eds.), *Corporate Governance and Labour*

Management: An International Comparison. Oxford: Oxford University Press, pp. 173–96.

Grahl, J. and Teague, P. (2000). 'The Régulation School, the Employment Relation, and Financialization', *Economy and Society*, 29(1): 160–78.

Graziano, P. (forthcoming). 'From a Guaranteed Labour Market to the "Flexible Worker Model": The Transformation of Italian Unemployment Policy', in J. Clasen, M. Ferrera, and M. Rhodes (eds.), *Welfare States and the Challenge of Unemployment.* London and New York: Routledge.

Gregory, P. R. and Stuart, R. C. (1999). *Comparative Economic Systems*, 6th edn. Boston, MA: Houghton Mifflin.

Guillen, M. (2000). Corporate Governance and Globalization: Is There Convergence Across Countries?', *Advances in International Comparative Management*, 13: 175–204.

GUS Poland Central Statistical Office (1991–2004). *Rocznik statystyczny Rzeczypospolitej Polskiej.* Warsaw: GUS.

—— (2005). *Statistical Information Database.* Warsaw: GUS.

Gustofson, T. (1999). *Capitalism Russian-Style.* Cambridge: Cambridge University Press.

Hackethal, A. (2000). *Banken, Unternehmensfinanzierung und Finanzsysteme*, Frankfurt: Peter Lang.

—— Schmidt, R. H., and Tyrell, M. (2005). 'Banks and Corporate Governance: On the Way to a Capital Market-Based System?', *Corporate Governance*, 11(3): 397–407.

Hadžić, M. (2002). 'Rethinking Privatization in Serbia', *Eastern European Economics*, 40: 6–23.

Hall, P. A. (1986). *Governing the Economy: The Politics of State Intervention in Britain and France.* Cambridge: Polity Press.

—— (ed.) (1989). *The Political Power of Economic Ideas.* Princeton, NJ: Princeton University Press.

—— (1993). 'Policy Paradigms, Social Learning, and the State', *Comparative Politics*, 23(3): 275–96.

—— (1994). 'Central Bank Independence and Coordinated Wage Bargaining: Their Interaction in Germany and Europe', *German Politics and Society*, 31: 1–23.

—— (1997). 'The Political Economy of Adjustment in Germany', in F. Naschold, D. Soskice, B. Hancke, and U. Jürgens (eds.), *Ökonomische Leistungsfähigkeit und institutionelle Innovation. Das deutsche Produktions- und Politikregime im globalen Wettbewerb*, WZB-Jahrbuch 1997, Berlin: Edition Sigma. pp. 293–317.

—— (2001). 'The Evolution of Economic Policy-Making in the European Union', in A. Menon and V. Wright (eds.), *From the Nation State to Europe.* Oxford: Oxford University Press. pp. 214–45.

—— (2004). *The Challenges Facing Europe and Varieties of Capitalism.* Protopaper for the Workshop on Institutional Change in Contemporary European Capitalism, European University Institute, 1–2 July.

—— (2005). 'Institutional Complementarity: Causes and Effects', *Socio-Economic Review*, 3(2): 373–78.

Hall, P. A. (2006). 'Introduction: "The Politics of Social Change", in Pepper Culpepper, Peter A. Hall and Bruno Palier (eds.), *Changing France: The Politics that Markets Make*. Houndsmills, Basingstoke, UK: Palgrave Macmillan. pp. 1–28.

―― and Franzese, Jr., R. (1998). 'Mixed Signals: Central Bank Independence, Coordinated Wage Bargaining, and European Monetary Union', *International Organisation*, (Summer): 502–36.

―― and Gingerich, D. W. (2002). 'Varieties of Capitalism and Institutional Complementarities in the Macro-Economy', Paper presented at the Comparative Political Economy workshop at Cornell University, Ithaca, NY, November.

―― ―― (2004). 'Varieties of Capitalism and Institutional Complementarities in the Macroeconomy: An Empirical Analysis', Cologne: Max-Planck-Institut für Gesellschaftsforschung, Discussion paper 04/5.

―― and Soskice, D. (eds.) (2001). 'Introduction', *Varieties of Capitalism. The Institutional Foundations of Comparative Institutional Advantage*. Oxford: Oxford University Press, pp. 1–68.

―― ―― (2003). 'Varieties of Capitalism and Institutional Change: A Response to Three Critics', *Comparative European Politics*, 1(2): 241–50.

―― and Thelen, K. (2005). 'Institutional Change in Varieties of Capitalism', Paper prepared for presentation to the Annual Meeting of the American Political Science Association, Washington, DC, 1 September (2005).

Hallerberg, M., Strauch, R., and Hagen, J. von (2001). 'The Use and Effectiveness of Budgetary Rules and Norms in EU Member States', Netherlands Ministry of Finance.

Hancké, B. (2001). 'Revisiting the French Model: Coordination and Restructuring in French Industry', in P. A. Hall and D. Soskice (eds.), *Varieties of Capitalism: The Institutional Foundations of Comparative Advantage*. Oxford: Oxford University Press, pp. 307–36.

―― (2002). *Large Firms and Institutional Change: Industrial Renewal and Economic Restructuring in France*. Oxford: Oxford University Press.

―― and Goyer, M. (2005). 'Degrees of Freedom: Rethinking the Institutional Analysis of Economic Change', in G. Morgan, R. Whitley, and E. Moen (eds.), *Changing Capitalisms? Internationalization, Institutional Change and Systems of Economic Organization*. Oxford: Oxford University Press, pp. 53–77.

―― and Herrmann, A. (2005). 'EMU, Wage Bargaining and the Reorganisation of the European Political Economy', In this volume.

―― and Rhodes, M. (2005), 'EMU and Labor Market Institutions in Europe: The Rise and Fall of National Social Pacts', *Work and Occupations*, 32(2): 196–228.

―― and Soskice, D. (1996). 'Coordination and Restructuring in Large French Firms: The Evolution of French Industry in the (1980)s', Discussion Paper 96–303, Wissenschaftszentrum Berlin.

―― ―― (2003). *Wage-Setting, Fiscal Policy and Political Exchange in EMU*. Düsseldorf: Report for Project 2000-203–1 'Institutionen, Wirtschaftswachstum und Beschäftigung in der EWU', financed by the Hans-Böckler-Stiftung.

Hankey, E., Natasha, Y., and Richard, A. (1995). 'Russia—Old Wine in a New Bottle? The Circulation and Reproduction of Russian Elites, 1983–1993', *Theory and Society*, 24: 639–68.

Hansen, Berndt. (1968). *Fiscal Policy in Seven Countries, 1955–1965*. Paris: OECD.

Hassel, A. (2002). 'A New Going Rate? Co-Ordinated Wage Bargaining in Europe,' in Phillippe Pochet (ed.), *Wage Policy in the Eurozone*. Brussels: PIE Lang, pp. 149–73.

—— (2003). *Negotiating Wage Restraint: Europe's Response to a New Economic Environment*. Bochum: Habilitationsschrift, eingereicht an der Sozialwissenschaftlichen Fakultät der Ruhr-Universität Bochum.

—— (2007). *Wage Setting, Social Pacts and the Euro. A New Role for the State*. Amsterdam: Amsterdam University Press.

—— and Rehder, B. (2001). 'Institutional Change in the German Wage Bargaining System—The Role of Big Companies', Max-Planck-Institut für Gesellschaftsforschung, Working Paper 01/9, December.

—— and Williamson, H. (2004). 'The Evolution of the German Model: How to Judge the Reforms in Europe's Largest Economy', Paper prepared for the Anglo-German Foundation for the Study of Industrial Society. http://www.agf.org.uk/pubs/pdfs/(1458)web.pdf

Hay, C. (2005). 'Two Can Play at That Game—or Can They? Varieties of Capitalism, Varieties of Institutionalism', in D. Coates (ed.), *Varieties of Capitalism, Varieties of Approaches*. Houndmills Basingstoke, UK and New York: Palgrave Macmillan, pp. 106–21.

Hayward, J. E. S. (ed.) (1995). *Industrial Enterprise and European Integration. From National to Internationalized Champions: Firms and Governments in the West European Economy*. Oxford: Oxford University Press.

Helf, G. and Hahn, J. (1992). 'Old Dogs and New Tricks: Party Elites in the Russian Regional Elections of (1990)', *Slavic Review*, 51: 511–30.

Hellman, J. (1998). 'Winners Take All: The Politics of Partial Reform in Postcommunist Transitions', *World Politics*, 50(2): 203–34.

Henneberger, F. (1993). 'Transferstart: Organisationsdynamik und Strukturkonservatismus westdeutscher Unternehmerverbände—Aktuelle Entwicklungen unter besonderer Berücksichtigung des Aufbauprozesses in Sachsen und Thüringen', *Politische Vierteljahresschrift*, 34: 640–73.

Henrekson, M. and Jakobsson, U. (2003). 'The Transformation of Ownership Policy and Structure in Sweden: Convergence Towards the Anglo-Saxon Model?', *New Political Economy*, 8(1): 73–102.

Henry, C. (1997). *Concurrence et services publics dans l'Union Européenne*. Paris: Presses Universitaires de France.

—— Matheu, M., and Jeunemaitre, A. (2001). *Regulation of Network Utilities*. Oxford: Oxford University Press.

Héritier, A. (2005). 'Managing Regulatory Developments in Rail', in D. Coen and A. Héritier (eds.), *Refining Regulatory Regimes: Utilities in Europe*. Cheltenham, UK: Edward Elgar, pp. 120–44.

Hermann, C., Promberger, M., Seifert, H., and Trinczek, R. (1999). *Forcierte Arbeitszeitflexibilisierung. Die 35-Stunden-Woche in der betrieblichen und gewerkschaftlichen Praxis.* Berlin: Edition Sigma.

Hernandez-Cata, E. (1997). 'Growth and Liberalisation during the Transition from Plan to Market', *IMF Staff Papers*, 44(4): 405–29.

Herrigel, G. (1996). *Industrial Constructions: The Sources of German Industrial Power.* Cambridge: Cambridge University Press.

—— and Sabel, C. (1999). 'Craft Production in Crisis: Industrial Restructuring in Germany during the 1990s', in P. Culpepper and D. Finegold (eds.), *The German Skills Machine: Comparative Perspectives on Systems of Education and Training.* New York: Berghahn Books, pp. 77–114.

—— and Wittke, V. (2005). 'Varieties of Vertical Disintegration: The Global Trend Towards Heterogeneous Supply Relations and the Reproduction of Difference in US and German Manufacturing', in G. Morgan, R. Whitley, and E. Moen (eds.), *Changing Capitalisms? Internationalization, Institutional Change and Systems of Economic Organization.* Oxford: Oxford University Press, pp. 277–311.

Herrmann, A. M. (2003). 'From the EMS to EMU: How Economic and Monetary Union Changes the Structure of Wage-Bargaining Throughout the Euro-Zone', European University Institute, EUI-SPS Working Papers 2003/4.

—— (2005). 'Converging Divergence: How Competitive Advantages Condition Institutional Change Under EMU', *Journal of Common Market Studies*, 43(2): 287–310.

Heywood, P. M. (1995). *The Government and Politics of Spain.* London: Macmillan.

Hibbs, D. (1977). 'Political Parties and Macroeconomic Policies', *American Political Science Review*, 71: 1467–87.

Hicks, A. and Kenworthy, L. (1998). 'Cooperation and Political Economic Performance in Affluent Democratic Capitalism', *American Journal of Sociology*, 103(6): 1631–72.

Hilferding, R. ([1910] 1981). *Finance Capital.* London: Routledge & Kegan Paul.

Hirschler, R. (1998). 'Economic Neoliberalism Became Almost Irrelevant . . . Poland's Grzegorz W. Kolodko on New Trends in Development Strategies. Transition', *The Newsletter About Reforming Economies*, 9(3): 1–6.

Hofstede, G. (1980). *Culture's Consequences: International Differences in Work Related Values.* London: Sage.

Hofstetter, K. (2002). *Corporate Governance in Switzerland*, Final Report of the panel of experts on Corporate Governance. Zurich: Swiss Business Federation.

Högfeldt, P. (2004). The History and Politics of Corporate Ownership in Sweden. National Bureau of Economic Research, Working Paper No. 10641.

Hollingsworth, R. and Boyer, R. (eds.) (1997). *Contemporary Capitalism: The Embeddedness of Institutions.* New York: Cambridge University Press.

Holmstrom, B. and Kaplan, S. (2001). *Corporate Governance and Merger Activity in the US: Making Sense of the 1980s and 1990s.* National Bureau of Economic Research, Working Paper 8220, Cambridge, MA.

Höpner, M. (2001). Corporate Governance in Transition: Ten Empirical Findings on Shareholder Value and Industrial Relations in Germany. MPIFG Discussion Paper 01/5, Max-Planck-Institute for the Study of Societies, Cologne.

—— (2003). 'European Corporate Governance Reform and the German Party Paradox', Max Planck Institute for the Study of Societies, Discussion Paper No. 2003-04.

—— (2005). 'What Have We Learnt? Complementarity, Coherence and Institutional Change', *Socio-Economic Review*, 3(2): 383–87.

—— (2006). 'What Is Organized Capitalism? The Two Dimensions of Non-Liberal Capitalism', Paper presented to the International Centre for Business and Politics Conference on 'Institutional Emergence, Stability and Change', Copenhagen Business School, 1–2 June.

—— and Jackson, G. (2001). An Emerging Market for Corporate Control? The Mannesmann Takeover and German Corporate Governance. MPIFG Discussion Paper 1/4, Max Planck Institute for the Study of Societies Discussion Paper No. 2001-04, Cologne.

—— and Krempel, L. (2003). 'The Politics of the German Company Network', Max Planck Institut for the Study of Societies Discussion Paper No. 2003-09, September. http://www.mpi-fg-koeln.mpg.de/pu/workpap/wp03-9/wp03-9.html

Hotz-Hart, B., Mäder, S., and Vock, P. (2001). *Volkswirtschaft der Schweiz*. Zürich: vdf Hochschulverlag an der ETH.

Howell, C. (1992). *Regulating Labor*. Princeton, NJ: Princeton University Press.

—— (2003). 'Varieties of Capitalism: And Then There Was One?', *Comparative Politics*, 36(1): 103–24.

—— (2005). *Trade Unions and the State*. Princeton, NJ: Princeton University Press.

Huber, E. and Stephens, J. (2001). 'Welfare State and Production Regimes in the Era of Retrenchment', in P. Pierson (ed.), *The New Politics of the Welfare State*. New York: Oxford University Press, pp. 107–45.

—— —— (2001). *Development and Crisis of the Welfare State: Parties and Policies in Global Markets*. Chicago, IL: University of Chicago Press.

Hunter, J. G. (2003). 'Determinants of Business Success under "Hypocapitalism": Case Studies of Russian Firms and Their Strategies', *Journal of Business Research*, 56: 113–20.

Huo, J., Nelson, M. and Stephens, J. D. (2006). 'Decommodification and Activation in Social Democratic Policy: Resolving the Paradox', Paper presented to a workshop on Challenges of the Welfare State, Minda de Gunzburg Center for European Studies, May.

Iankova, E. A. (2002). *Eastern European Capitalism in the Making*. Cambridge: Cambridge University Press.

ILO (2005). *LABORSTA Internet Database*. Geneva: ILO.

IMF (2005a). 'IMF Executive Board Concludes (2005) Article IV Consultation with Ukraine', IMF Public Information Notice No. 05/156, Washington, DC, 11 November.

IMF (2005*b*). *World Economic Outlook Database.* Washington, DC: IMF.

Inglehart, R. (1990). *Culture Shift.* Princeton, NJ: Princeton University Press.

Innes, A. (2005). 'State Retreat and Democracy'. Paper prepared for the conference on *Postcommunist State and Society: Transnational and National,* Maxwell School, Syracuse University. 30 September–1 October 2005.

International Institute for Management Development (2004). *World Competitiveness Yearbook 2004,* Lausanne.

Iversen, T. (1999). *Contested Economic Institutions: The Politics of Macroeconomics and Wage Bargaining in Advanced Democracies.* New York: Cambridge University Press.

—— (2005). *Capitalism, Democracy and Welfare.* Cambridge: Cambridge University Press.

—— and Cusack, T. R. (2000). 'The Causes of Welfare State Expansion: Deindustrialization or Globalization?', *World Politics,* 52(3): 313–49.

—— and Soskice, D. (December 2001). 'An Asset Theory of Social Policy Preferences', *American Political Science Review,* 95(4): 875–93.

—— —— (2005). 'Distribution and Redistribution: The Shadow of the Nineteenth Century.' Paper prepared for the Workshop on Comparative Political Economy Center for European Studies. Harvard University, 7–8 October.

—— —— (2006*a*). 'Electoral Institutions, Parties and the Politics of Class: Why Some Democracies Distribute More than Others', *American Political Science Review,* 100(2): 165–81.

—— —— (2006*b*). 'New Macroeconomics and Political Science', *Annual Review of Political Science,* 9: 425–53.

—— and Wren, A. (1998). 'Equality, Employment and Budgetary Restraint', *World Politics,* 50: 507–46.

—— Rosenbluth, F., and Soskice, D. (2005). 'Divorce and the Gender Division of Labor in Comparative Perspective', in L. McCall and A. Orloff, (eds.), 'Gender, Class and Capitalism', Special Issue of *Social Politics,* 12(2): 216–42.

Jackson, G. (2003). 'Corporate Governance in Germany and Japan: Liberalization Pressures and Responses during the (1990)s', in K. Yamamura and W. Streeck (eds.), *The End of Diversity? Prospects for German and Japanese Capitalism.* Ithaca, NY: Cornell University Press, pp. 261–305.

—— (2005). 'Contested Boundaries: Ambiguity and Creativity in the Evolution of German Codetermination', in W. Streeck and K. Thelen (eds.), *Beyond Continuity.* Oxford: Oxford University Press, pp. 229–54.

—— and Deeg, R. (2006). 'How Many Varieties of Capitalism? Comparing the Comparative Institutional Analysis of Capitalist Diversity', Cologne: Max-Planck-Institut für Gesellschaftsforschung, Discussion paper 06/2.

—— Höpner, M., and Kurdelbusch, A. (2005). 'Corporate Governance and Employees in Germany: Changing Linkages, Complementarities and Tensions', in H. Gospel and A. Pendleton (eds.), *Corporate Governance and Labour Management: An International Comparison.* Oxford: Oxford University Press, pp. 84–121.

Jaeger, F. (2003). 'Case Study Switzerland', in World Economic Forum, *The Global Competitiveness Report 2002–2003.* Oxford: Oxford University Press.

Järve, J., Kallaste, E., and Eamets, R. (2001). *Töösuhted Eestis—Euroopa Liiduga Liitumise Taustal.* Tartu: Tartu Ülikool, Euroopa Kolledž.

Jones, E. and Rhodes, M. (2006). 'Europe and the Global Challenge', in P. Heywood, E. Jones, M. Rhodes, and U. Sedelmeier (eds.), *Developments in European Politics.* New York and London: Palgrave Macmillan, pp. 13–34.

Jordana, J. (1996). 'Reconsidering Union Membership in Spain, 1977–1994: Halting Decline in a Context of Democratic Consolidation', *Industrial Relations Journal,* 27(3): 211–24.

Jürgens, U., Rupp, J., and Vitols, K. (2000*a*). 'Shareholder Value in an Adverse Environment: The German Case', *Economy and Society,* 29(1): 54–79.

——— ——— ——— (2000*b*). Corporate Governance und Shareholder Value in Deutschland. Nach dem Fall von Mannesmann—Paper revisited. Wissenschaftszentrum Berlin für Sozialforschung, Working Paper, FS II 00-202.

Károly F. and Jeno K. (eds.) (2002). *The Labor Market: Review and Analysis Institute of Economics,* HAS: Budapest.

Katz, H. (1993). 'The Decentralization of Collective Bargaining: A Literature Review and Comparative Analysis', *Industrial and Labor Relations Review,* 47(1): 3–22.

——— and Darbishire, O. (1999). *Converging Differences: Worldwide Changes in Employment Systems.* Ithaca, NY: Cornell University Press.

Katzenstein, P. (1985*a*). *Politics and Policy in West Germany. The Growth of a Semi-Sovereign State.* Temple University Press.

——— (1985*b*). *Small States in World Markets.* Ithaca, NY: Cornell University Press.

——— (1985*c*). *Corporatism and Change.* Ithaca: Cornell University Press.

Kennedy, M. D. (1987). 'Polish Engineers' Participation in the Solidarity Movement', *Social Forces,* 65: 641–69.

——— (1992). 'The Intelligentsia in the Constitution of Civil Societies in Post-Communist Regimes in Hungary and Poland', *Theory and Society,* 21: 29–76.

Kenworthy, L. (2001). 'Wage-Setting Measures: A Survey and Assessment', *World Politics,* 54: 57–98.

——— (2003). 'Quantitative Indicators of Corporatism', available at: http://www.emory.edu/SOC/Lkenworthy.

Kester, C. (1992). 'Industrial Groups as Systems of Corporate Governance', *Oxford Review of Economic Policy,* 8: 24–44.

Kinderman, D. (2003): 'Pressure from Without, Subversion from Within: The German Employer Offensive and Markets within Firms in Germany', CCGES/CCEAE Working Paper.

——— (2005). 'Pressure from Without, Subversion from Within: The Two-Pronged German Employer Offensive', *Comparative European Politics,* 3(4): 432–63.

King, L. P. (2000). 'Foreign Direct Investment and Transition', *European Journal of Sociology,* XLI(2): 189–224.

——— (2001*a*). *The Basic Features of Post-Communist Capitalism: Firms in Hungary, the Czech Republic, and Slovakia.* Westport, CT: Praeger Press.

——— (2001*b*). 'Making Markets: A Comparative Study of Postcommunist Managerial Strategies in Central Europe', *Theory and Society,* 30(4, Aug): 494–538.

King, L. P. (2002). 'Postcommunist Divergence: A Comparative Analysis of the Transition to Capitalism in Poland and Russia', *Studies in Comparative International Development*, 37(3): 3–34.

——— (2003). 'Shock Privatization: The Effects of Rapid Large Scale Privatization on Enterprise Restructuring', *Politics and Society*, (March): 3–43.

——— (2004). 'Does Neoliberalism Work: Explaining Postcommunist Performance', Paper presented at the annual meeting of the American Sociological Association, San Francisco, CA, August 14. http://www.soc.duke.edu/resources/docs/lking.pdf.

——— and Iván, S. (2005). 'Postcommunist Economic Systems', in N. Smelser and R. Swedberg (eds.), *Handbook of Economic Sociology* (2nd edn), pp. 206–32.

——— and Sznajder, A. (2006). 'The State-Led Transition to Liberal Capitalism: Neoliberal Organizational, World Systems, and Social Structural Explanations of Poland's Economic Success', *American Journal of Sociology*, 112: 751–801.

——— and Varadi, B. (2002). 'Beyond Manichean Economics: Foreign Direct Investment and Growth in the Transition from Socialism', *Communist and Post-Communist Studies*, 2(3): 1–22.

Kitschelt, H. (1994). *The Transformation of European Social Democracy*. Cambridge: Cambridge University Press.

——— (2003). 'Accounting for Post-Communist Regime Diversity: What Counts as a Good Cause?', in G. Ekiert and S. Hanson (eds.), *Capitalism and Democracy in Central and Eastern Europe: Assessing the Legacy of Communist Rule*. Cambridge: Cambridge University Press, pp. 49–86.

——— (2006). 'Collective Group Interests and Distributive Outcomes: Competing Claims about the Evolution of the Welfare State', *Labor History*, 47(3): 147–72.

——— ——— (2004). 'Who Supports the Left in the 21st Century? Patterns of Party Competition and Electoral Coalitions', Paper presented at a Conference on Social Justice and the Future of European Social Democracy, Minda de Gunzburg Center for European Studies, Harvard University, March.

——— Mansfeldova, Z., Markowski, R., and Tóka, G. (1999). *Post-Communist Party Systems: Competition, Representation and Inter-Party Cooperation*. Cambridge: Cambridge University Press.

Klaus, V. (1997). *Renaissance: The Rebirth of Liberty in the Heart of Europe*. Washington, DC: The Cato Institute.

Klebnikov, P. (2000). *The Godfather of the Kremlin*. New York: Harcourt.

Klös, H.P. (2004). 'Firms Oppose Training Levy', Press statement by Dr. Hans-Peter Klös. Managing Director of the Institute of German business Instituts der deutschen Wirtschaft Köln. Berlin 22 April 2004.

Knell, M. and Srholec, M. (2005). 'Emerging Varieties of Capitalism in Central and Eastern Europe', Paper presented to the Varieties of Capitalism in Post-Communist Countries conference. Paisley, Scotland September.

Kogut, B. and Walker G. (2001). 'The Small World of Germany and the Durability of National Networks', *American Sociological Review*, 66(3): 317–35.

Köhler, R. (2004) 'Der Flächentarifvertrag im Meinungsbild der Unternehmen', Presentation by Prof. Renate Köhler, Institut für Demoskopie Allensbach, Berlin 10 February.

Kołodko, G. W. (1999a). 'Transition to a Market Economy and Sustained Growth. Implications for the Post-Washington Consensus', *Communist and Post-Communist Studies*, 32(3): 233–61.

_____ (1999b). 'Ten Years of Postsocialist Transition: The Lessons for Policy Reforms', The World Bank Policy Research Working Paper No. 2095. Washington, DC.

_____ (2000). *From Shock to Therapy: The Political Economy of Post-Socialist Transformation*. Oxford: Oxford University Press.

_____ (2002). *Globalization and Catching-up in Transition Economies*. Rochester, NY: University of Rochester Press.

Koltay, J. (2002). 'The Wage Setting System', in K. Fazekas and J. Koltay (eds.), *The Hungarian Labour Market: Review and Analysis*. Budapest: Institute of Economics, Hungarian Employment Foundation, pp. 54–62.

Korbonski, A. (1999). 'East Central Europe on the Eve of the Changeover: The Case of Poland', *Communist and Post-Communist Studies*, 32: 139–52.

Kornai, J. (1992). *The Socialist System: The Political Economy of Communism*. Princeton, NJ: Princeton University Press.

Kraft, E., Vodopivec, M., and Cvikl, M. (1994). 'On Its Own: The Economy of Independent Slovenia', in J. Benderly and E. Kraft (eds.), *Independent Slovenia*. Basingstoke, UK: Macmillan, pp. 201–23.

Kramer, M. (1995). 'Polish Workers and the Postcommunist Transition', *Europe-Asia Studies*, 37(4): 669–713.

Kreile, M. (1978). 'West Germany: Dynamics of Change', in Peter Katzenstein (ed.), *Between Power and Plenty*. Madison, WI: University of Wisconsin Press, pp. 191–224.

Kristensen, P. H. (1997). 'National Systems of Governance and Managerial Prerogatives in the Evolution of Works Systems: England, Germany, Denmark compared', in R. Whitley and P. H. Kristensen (eds.), *Governance at Work: The Social Regulation of Economic Relations*. New York: Oxford University Press, pp. 3–48.

Kubic, J. (1994). 'Who Done It: Workers, Intellectuals, or Someone Else? Controversy of Solidarity's Origins and Social Composition', *Theory and Society*, 23: 441–66.

Kuchma, L. (2001). Poslannia Prezydenta Ukrainy do Verkhovnoi Rady Ukrainy ta Kabinetu Ministriv Ukrainy: Pro osnovni napriamy biudzhetnoi polityky na (2002) rik. Uriadovyi Kur'er 102 (12 June): 10.

Kuisel, R. F. (1981). *Capitalism and the State in Modern France: Renovation and Economic Management in the Twentieth Century*. Cambridge: Cambridge University Press.

Kumazawa, M. and Yamada, J. (1989). 'Jobs and Skills under the Lifelong Nenko Employment Practice', in Wood, S. (ed.), *The Transformation of Work?*. London: Unwin Hyman, pp. 102–26.

Kurth, J. (1979). 'The Political Consequences of the Product Cycle: Industrial History and Political Outcomes', *International Organization*, 33(1): 1–36.

Ladó, M. (2002). 'Industrial Relations in the Candidate Countries. European Industrial Relations Online', 30 July, http://www.eurofound.europa.eu/eiro/2002/07/feature/tn0207102f.htm.

Lainela, S. and Sutela, P. (1994). *The Baltic Economies in Transition*. Helsinki: Bank of Finland.

Lallement, M. (2006). 'New Patterns of Industrial Relations and Political Action since the 1980s', in Pepper Culpepper, Peter A. Hall, and Bruno Palier (eds.), *Changing France*. Houndmills, Basingtoke, UK: Palgrave Macmillan, pp. 50–79.

Landes, D. (May 1949). 'French Entrepreneurship and Industrial Growth in the 19th Century', *Journal of Economic History*, 9(1): 45–61.

Lane, C. (1989). *Management and Labour in Europe: The Industrial Enterprise in Germany, Britain, and France*. Aldershot, UK: Edward Elgar.

—— (1995). *Industry and Society in Europe*. Aldershot, UK: Edward Elgar.

—— (2003). Changes in Corporate Governance in German Corporations: Convergence to the Anglo-American Model?, University of Cambridge, ESRC Centre for Business Research Working Paper 259.

—— (2004). 'Institutional Transformation and System Change: Changes in Corporate Goverance of German Corporations', Sociological Series. Institute for Advanced Study, Vienna. No. 65.

—— (2005). 'Institutional Transformation and System Change: Changes in the Corporate Governance of German Corporations', in G. Morgan, R. Whitley, and E. Moen (eds.), *Changing Capitalisms? Internationalization, Institutional Change and Systems of Economic Organization*. Oxford: Oxford University Press, pp. 78–109.

Lane, D. (2000). 'What Kind of Capitalism for Russia? A Comparative Analysis', *Communist and Post-Communist Studies*, 33(4): 485–504.

—— (ed.) (2002). *The Legacy of State Socialism and the Future of Transformation*. Lanham, MD: Rowman & Littlefield.

—— (2005). 'Emerging Varieties of Capitalism in Former State Socialist Societies', *Competition and Change*, 9(3): 227–47.

Lanza, O. and Lavdas, K. (2000). 'The Disentanglement of Interest Politics: Business Associability, the Parties and Policy in Italy and Greece', *European Journal of Political Research*, 37(2): 203–35.

LaPalombara, J. G. (1987). *Democracy, Italian Style*. New Haven, CT: Yale University Press.

Larouche, P. (2000). *Competition Law and Regulation in European Telecommunications*. Oxford: Hart

Layard, R., Nickell, S., and Jackman, R. (1991). *Unemployment: Macroeconomic Performance and the Labour Market*. Oxford: Oxford University Press.

Lehmbruch, G. (1994). 'Dilemmata verbandlicher Einflußlogik im Prozeß der deutschen Vereinigung', in W. Streeck (ed.), *Staat und Verbände. PVS-Sonderheft*, 25: 370–92.

Lehrer, M. (2001). 'Macro-Varieties of Capitalism and Micro-Varieties of Strategic Management in European Airlines', in P. A. Hall and D. Soskice (eds.), *Varieties of Capitalism. The Institutional Foundations of Comparative Advantage*. Oxford: Oxford University Press, pp. 361–86.

Leibenstein, H. (1978). *General X-Efficiency Theory and Economic Development*. New York: Oxford University Press.

Levitsky, S. and Way, L. (2002). 'The Rise of Competitive Authoritarianism', *Journal of Democracy*, 13(2): 51–65.

Levy, B. and Spiller, P. (1996). *Regulation, Institution, and Commitment.* Cambridge: Cambridge University Press.

Levy, J. (1999). *Tocqueville's Revenge: Dilemmas of Institutional Reform in Post-Dirigiste France.* Cambridge, MA: Harvard University Press.

——— (2005). 'Redeploying the State: Liberalization and Social Policy in France', in W. Streeck and K. Thelen (eds.), *Beyond Continuity: Institutional Change in Advanced Political Economies.* Oxford: Oxford University Press, pp. 103–26.

Liedtke, R., 'Wem Gehort die Republik?', annual publication, Frankfurt, Germany: Eichborn.

Lijphart, A. (1984). *Democracies: Patterns of Majoritarian and Consensus Government in 21 Countries.* New Haven, CI: Yale University Press.

——— (1994). *Electoral Systems and Party Systems: A Study of Twenty-Seven Democracies, 1945–90.* New York: Oxford University Press.

——— (1999). *Patterns of Democracy: Government Forms and Performance in Thirty-Six Countries.* New Haven, CT and London: Yale University Press.

Likić-Brborić, B. (2003). *Democratic Governance in the Transition from Yugoslav Self-Management to a Market Economy.* Uppsala: Acta Universitatis Upsaliensis.

Lindbeck, A. and Snower, D. (1986). 'Wage Setting, Unemployment and Insider Outsider Relations', *American Economic Review,* 76: 235–9.

——— ——— (1989). *The Insider–Outsider Theory of Employment and Unemployment.* Cambridge, MA: MIT Press.

Linhart, D. (1992). 'The Shortcomings of an Organizational Revolution that is Out of Step', *Economic and Industrial Democracy,* 13: 49–64.

——— (1994). *La Modernisation des Entreprises.* Paris: La Découverte.

Linz, J. and Stepan, A. (1996). *Problems of Democratic Transition and Consolidation: Southern Europe, South America, and Post-Communist Europe.* Baltimore, MD: Johns Hopkins University Press.

Lodge, M. (2002). *On Different Tracks: Institutions and Railway Regulation in Britain and Germany.* Westport, CT: Praeger.

Lodovici, M. S. (1999). 'Italy: The Long Times of Consensual Re-Regulation', in G. Esping-Andersen and M. Regini (eds.), *Why Deregulate Labour Markets?* Oxford: Oxford University Press, pp. 271–306.

Lopez, M. and Verd, J. M. (2004). 'Spain: Components of Individual Direct and Indirect Remuneration in Case of Employment and Related Social Benefits at National Level', RESORE Project Working Paper No. 6.

Loriaux, M. (1991). *France after Hegemony: International Change and Financial Reform.* Ithaca, NY: Cornell University Press.

Lukauskas, A. (1997). *Regulating Finance: The Political Economy of Spanish Financial Policy from Franco to Democracy.* Ann Arbor, MI: University of Michigan Press.

Lydall, H. (1989). *Yugoslavia in Crisis.* Oxford: Oxford University Press.

McCall, L. and Orloff, A. (eds.) (2005a). 'Introduction to Special Issue of Social Politics: "Gender, Class, and Capitalism"', *Social Politics,* 12(2): 159–69.

——— ——— (eds) (2005b). 'Gender, Class, and Capitalism', special issue of *Social Politics,* 12(2).

McCarty, N., Poole, K., and Rosenthal, H. (2006). *Polarized America: The Dance of Ideology and Unequal Riches*. Cambridge: MIT Press.

McDermott, G. (2002). *Embedded Politics: Industrial Networks and Institutional Change in Postcommunism*. Ann Arbor, MI: University of Michigan Press.

——— (2004). 'The Political Foundations of Inter-Firm Networks and Social Capital', mimeo, Wharton School, University of Pennsylvania, August 2004.

——— (2004). 'Institutional Change and Firm Creation in East Central Europe: An Embedded Politics Approach', *Comparative Political Studies*, 37(2): 188–217.

McKinnon, R. (1993). *The Order of Economic Liberalization. Financial Control in the Transition to a Market Economy*. Baltimore, MD and London: Johns Hopkins University Press.

McNamara, K. (1998). *The Currency of Ideas*. Ithaca, NY: Cornell University Press.

Manow, P. (2001). *The Bismarckian Welfare State and the German Political System*. Habilitation, Germany: University of Konstanz.

——— and Seils, E. (2000). 'Adjusting Badly: The German Welfare State, Structural Change and the Open Economy', in F. Scharpf and V. Schmidt (eds.), *Welfare and Work in the Open Economy*. Oxford: Oxford University Press, pp. 264–307.

Mares, I. (2001). 'Firms and the Welfare State: When, Why and How does Social Policy Matter to Employers', in P. A. Hall and D. Soskice (eds.), *Varieties of Capitalism: The Institutional Foundation of Comparative Advantage*, Oxford: Oxford University Press, pp. 184–212.

——— (2003). 'The Sources of Business Interest in Social Insurance', *World Politics*, 55: 229–58.

——— (2004). *The Politics of Social Risk*. New York: Cambridge University Press.

Marsden, D. (1999). *A Theory of Employment Systems*. New York: Oxford University Press.

Martin, A. (1979). 'The Dynamics of Change in a Keynesian Political Economy: The Swedish Case and its Implications', in Colin Crouch (ed.), *State and Economy in Contemporary Capitalism*. London: Croom Helm, pp. 88–121.

——— (1984). 'Trade Unions in Sweden. Strategic Responses to Change and Crisis', in P. Gourevitch, A. Martin, G. Ross, S. Bornstein, A. Markovits, and C. Allen (eds.), *Unions and Economic Crisis. Britain, West Germany, and Sweden*. London: George Allen & Unwin, pp. 189–259.

——— (1999). Wage Bargaining Under EMU: Europeanization, Re-Nationalization or Americanization? Brussels: ETUI, DWP 99.01.03.

Martin, C. J. (2000). *Stuck in Neutral: Business and the Politics of Human Capital Formation*. Princeton, NJ: Princeton University Press.

——— (2005). 'Beyond Bone Structure: Historical Institutionalism and the Style of Economic Growth', in D. Coates (ed.), *Varieties of Capitalism, Varieties of Approaches*. Houndmills, Basingstoke and New York: Palgrave Macmillan, pp. 63–82.

_____ and Swank, D. (2004). 'Does the Organization of Capital Matter? Employers and Active Labor Market Policy at the National and Firm Levels', *American Political Science Review*, 98(4): 593–691.

Martinez Lucio, M. and McKenzie, R. (2004). 'Unstable Boundaries? Evaluating the "New Regulation" within Employment Relations', *Economy and Society*, 33(1): 77–97.

Maurice, M., Sellier, F., and Silvestre, J-J. (1986). *The Social Foundations of Industrial Power*. Cambridge: MIT Press.

Meltzer, A. H. and Richard, S. F. (1981). 'A Rational Theory of the Size of Government', *Journal of Political Economy*, 89(5): 914–27.

Mencinger, J. (2004). 'Transition to a National and Market Economy: A Gradualist Approach', in M. Mrak, M. Rojec, and C. Silva-Jáuregui (eds.). *Slovenia: From Yugoslavia to the European Union*. Washington, DC: World Bank. pp. 67–82.

Milanovic, B. (1998). *Income, Inequality and Poverty during the Transition from Planned to Market Economy*. Washington, DC: World Bank.

Milgrom, P. and Roberts, J. (1995). 'Complementarities and Fit: Strategy, Structure and Organizational Change in Manufacturing', *Journal of Accounting and Economics*, 19: 179–208.

Ministry of Economic Affairs, Hungary (1998). 'Investor's Handbook', http://www.ikm.iif.hu/investor/e/fin-7.htm.

Mocetti, S. (2004). 'Social Protection and Human Capital: Test of a Hypothesis', *Quaderni Università degli Studi di Siena*, no. 425, April.

Moene, K. O. and Wallerstein, M. (2001). 'Inequality, Social Insurance and Redistribution', *American Political Science Review*, 95(4): 859–74.

Molina, O. (2005). 'Political Exchange and Bargaining Reform in Italy and Spain', *European Journal of Industrial Relations*, 11(1): 7–26.

_____ (2006). 'Trade Union Strategies and Change in Neo-Corporatist Concertation: A New Century of Political Exchange?', *West European Politics*, 29(4): 640–64.

_____ and Rhodes, M. (2002). 'Corporatism: The Past, Present and Future of a Concept', *Annual Review of Political Science*, 5: 305–32.

Monks, R. and Minow, N. (1995). *Corporate Governance*. Cambridge, MA: Blackwell Business.

Moreno, L. and Sarassa, S. (1992). *The Spanish Via Media to the Development of the Welfare State*. Madrid, Spain: IESA http://www.iesam.csic.es/doctrab1/dt-9213e.pdf.

Morgan, G. (2005). 'Institutional Complementarities, Path Dependency, and the Dynamics of Firm', in G. Morgan, R. Whitley, and E. Moen (eds.), *Changing Capitalisms? Internationalization, Institutional Change, and Systems of Economic Organization*. New York: Oxford University Press, pp. 415–45.

_____ Whitley, R., and Moen, E. (eds.) (2005). *Changing Capitalisms? Internationalization, Institutional Change, and Systems of Economic Organization*. Oxford: Oxford University Press.

Morin, F. (1974). *La Structure Financière du Capitalisme Francais*. Paris: Calmann-Levy.

Morningstar Inc., Morningstar Funds 500, annual publication.

MPIfG (2002). *Arbeitsbeziehungen in Deutschland*. Wandel durch International-isierung. Bericht über Forschung am MPIfG: Köln.

Mrak, M., Rojec, M., and Silva-Jáuregui, C. (2004). *Slovenia: From Yugoslavia to the European Union*. Washington DC: The World Bank.

Mueller, F. and Purcell, J. (1992). 'The Europeanization of Manufacturing and the Decentralization of Bargaining: Multinational Management Strategies in the European Automobile Industry', *The International Journal of Human Resource Management*, 3: 15–34.

Muller-Jentsch, W. (1995). 'Germany: from Collective Voice to Co-Management', in J. Rogers and W. Streeck (eds.), *Works Councils: Consultation, Representation and Cooperation in Industrial Relations*. Chicago, IL: University of Chicago Press, pp. 53–78.

Muñoz, R. (2002). *Spain and the Neoliberal Paradigm*, CEPA (Center for Economic Policy Analysis), New School University, New York, no. 2002-02, http://www.newschool.edu/cepa/papers/archive/cepa200202.pdf

Murrell, P. (1993). 'What Is Shock Therapy? What Did It Do in Poland and Russia?', *Post-Soviet Affairs*, 9(2): 111–40.

—— (1995). 'The Transition According to Cambridge', *Mass. Journal of Economic Literature*, 33(1): 164–78.

Mykhnenko, V. (2005a). 'What Type of Capitalism in Post-Communist Europe? Poland and Ukraine Compared', *'Les Actes du GERPISA*, 39 (December): 83–112, http://www.gerpisa.univ-evry.fr/actes/39/gerpisa_actes39.html#

—— (2005b). The Political Economy of Post-Communism: A Comparison of Upper Silesia (Poland) and the Donbas (Ukraine). Ph.D. dissertation Department of Social and Political Sciences. University of Cambridge: England, http://www.policy.hu/mykhnenko/Political_Economy_of_Post-Communist_Transition.html

—— (2005c). 'What Type of Capitalism in Eastern Europe? Institutional Structures, Revealed Comparative Advantages, and Performance of Poland and Ukraine,' The Centre for Public Policy for Regions Discussion Paper No. 6, University of Glasgow: Scotland, http://www.cppr.ac.uk/centres/cppr/publications/

Nackmayr, T. (2003). 'Wachstumskrise hemmt die Ausbildungsbereitschaft', *Kurznachrichtendienst (KND)*, 27, 4 July.

Natali, D. and Rhodes, M. (2004). 'Trade-Offs and Veto Players: Reforming Pensions in France and Italy', *French Politics*, 2(1): 1–23.

—————— (2007). 'The New Politics of Bismarckian Welfare States', in C. Arza and M. Kohli (eds.), *The Political Economy of Pensions Reform*. London and New York: Routledge. pp. 25–46.

Newbery, D. (1999). *Privatisation, Restructuring and Regulation of Network Utilities*. Cambridge and London, MA: MIT Press.

North, D. C. (1990). *Institutions, Institutional Change and Economic Performance*. Cambridge: Cambridge University Press.

Nove, A. (1990). 'The Task of the State Is to Clean up the Mess', *Transition: The Newsletter About Reforming Economies*, 1(7): 8–9.

_____ (1993). 'Transition to the Market and Economic Theory', *Problems of Economic Transition*, 35(1): 20–33.

O'Neil, S. and Pierson, P. (2002). 'Asset Specificity and Institutional Development', Paper presented at the Annual Meeting of the American Political Science Association, Boston, MA: 29 August–1 September.

O'Sullivan, M. (2000). *Contests for Corporate Control. Corporate Governance and Economic Performance in the United States and Germany*. Oxford: Oxford University Press.

_____ (2003). 'The Political Economy of Comparative Corporate Governance', *Review of International Political Economy*, 10(1): 23–72.

_____ (2007). 'Acting Out Institutional Change: Understanding the Recent Transformation of the French Financial System', *Socio-Economic Review*, 5(3): 389–436.

OECD (1997). *Employment Outlook*, Paris.

_____ (1998). 'Shareholder Value and the Market in Corporate Control in OECD Countries', *Financial Market Trends*, No. 69, February.

_____ (1999a). *OECD Employment Outlook 1999*. Paris: OECD

_____ (1999b). *Switzerland. Country Note*. Thematic Review of the Transition from Initial Education to Working Life, Paris.

_____ (2001). 'Recent Trends: Institutional Investors Statistics', *Financial Market Trends*, No. 80, September.

_____ (2002). *Employment Outlook 2002*. Paris: OECD.

_____ (2003a). *OECD Economic Outlook June (2003) No. 73—Economic Developments in Hungary*. Paris: OECD.

_____ (2003b). *Science, Technology and Industry Scoreboard*. Paris: OECD.

_____ (2004). *Employment Outlook (2004)*. Paris: OECD.

_____ (2005a). *OECD Economic Outlook 77 Database*. Paris: OECD.

_____ (2005b). *OECD Factbook*. Paris: OECD.

OECD Institutional Investor Database, http://cs4hq.oecd.org/oecd/eng/TableViewer/Wdsview/dispviewp.asp?ReportId=1879&bReportOnly=True

Olson, M. (1965). *The Logic of Collective Action: Public Goods and the Theory of Groups*. Cambridge, MA: Harvard University Press.

Orazem, P. F. and Vodopivec, M. (2000). 'Male–Female Differences in Labor Market Outcomes during the Early Transition to Market: The Cases of Estonia and Slovenia', *Journal of Population Economics*, 13(2): 283–303.

Osberg, L., Smeeding, T., and Schwabisch, J. (2003). 'Income Distribution and Public Social Expenditure: Theories, Effects, and Evidence', Typescript.

Ost, D. (1990). *The Politics of Anti-Politics*. Philadelphia, PA: Temple University Press.

_____ (2000). 'Illusory Corporatism in Eastern Europe: Neoliberal Triparism and Postcommunist Class Identities', *Politics and Society*, 28(4): 503–31.

Ostrom, E. (1990). *Governing the Commons: The Evolution of Institutions for Collective Action*. Cambridge: Cambridge University Press.

Ozaki, M. (ed.) (1999). *Negotiating Flexibility. The Role of the Social Partners and the State*. Geneva: ILO.

Palier, B. (2005). 'Ambiguous Agreement, Cumulative Change: French Social Policy in the 1990s', in W. Streeck and K. Thelen (eds.), *Beyond Continuity: Institutional Change in Advanced Political Economies*. Oxford: Oxford University Press, pp. 127–44.

Panitch, L. and Gindin, S. (2005). 'Euro-Capitalism and American Empire', in D. Coates (ed.), *Varieties of Capitalism, Varieties of Approaches*. Houndmills Basingstoke, UK and New York: Palgrave Macmillan, pp. 139–59.

Pappe, Y. (2000*a*). 'Oligarkhi': ekonomicheskaia khronika, 1992–2000 IAS—Gos. universitet-Vysshaia shkola ekonomiki.

——— (2000*b*). *Oligarchi: Ekonomicheskaya Chronika, 1992–2000*. (Oligarchy: An Economic Chronicle, 1992–2000). Moscow: VSE.

Pensions & Investments, monthly publication.

Pérez, S. (1997). *Banking on Privilege: The Politics of Spanish Financial Reform*. Ithaca, NY and London: Cornell University Press.

——— (1998). 'Systemic Explanations, Divergent Outcomes: The Politics of Financial Liberalization in France and Spain', *International Studies Quarterly*, 41(4): 755–84.

——— (2000). 'From Decentralization to Reorganization. Explaining the Return to National Bargaining in Italy and Spain', *Comparative Politics*, 32(4): 437–59.

Pérez-Díaz, V. (1999). *Spain at the Crossroads: Civil Society, Politics and the Rule of Law*. Cambridge, MA: Cambridge University Press.

Perkins, D. H. (June 1988). 'Reforming China's Economic System', *Journal of Economic Literature*, 26: 610–45.

Persson, T. and Tabellini, G. (2003). *The Economic Effects of Constitutions*. Cambridge, MA: MIT Press.

Pettai, V. (1996). 'Estonia', in W. R. Iwaskiw (ed), *Estonia, Latvia, Lithuania: Country Studies*. Washington, D.C.: Federal Research Division, Library of Congress, pp. 1–81.

Pierson, P. (1996). 'The New Politics of the Welfare State', *World Politics*, 48(2): 143–79.

——— (ed.) (2001). *The New Politics of the Welfare State*. New York: Oxford University Press.

——— (2004). *Politics in Time*. Princeton, NJ: Princeton University Press.

Pieterse, J. N. (1995). 'Globalization as Hybridization', in M. Featherstone, S. Lash, and R. Robertson (eds.), *Global Modernities*. London: Sage, pp. 45–68.

Piore, M. J. and Sabel, C. F. (1984). *The Second Industrial Divide: Possibilities for Prosperity*. New York: Basic Books.

Pirher, S. (1999). *Background Study for the Employment Review Study for Slovenia*. Ljubljana: National VET Observatory Slovenia.

Polanyi, Karl (1944). *The Great Transformation*. Boston, MA: Beacon Press.

Polavieja, J. and Richards, A. (2001). 'Trade Unions, Unemployment and Working Class Fragmentation in Spain', in N. Bermeo (ed.), *Unemployment in the New Europe*. Cambridge: Cambridge University Press, pp. 203–44.

Pontusson, J. (1997). 'Between Neo-Liberalism and the German Model: Swedish Capitalism in Transition', in Colin Crouch and Wolfgang Streeck (eds.), *Political Economy of Modern Capitalism*. Thousand Oaks: Sage, pp. 55–70.

_____ (2002). 'Doubts about Varieties of Capitalism: Labor-Market and Welfare-State Dynamics in OECD Countries', Mimeo, Department of Government, Cornell University.

_____ (2005). 'Varieties and Commonalities of Capitalism', in D. Coates (ed.), *Varieties of Capitalism, Varieties of Approaches*. Houndmills, Basingstoke, UK and New York: Palgrave Macmillan, pp. 163–88.

_____ and Swenson, P. (1996). 'Labor Markets, Production Strategies, and Wage Bargaining Institutions: The Swedish Employer Offensive in Comparative Perspective', *Comparative Political Studies*, 29(April): 223–50.

Popov, V. (1999). 'The Financial System in Russia Compared to Other Transition Economies: The Anglo-American Versus the German–Japanese Model', *Comparative Economic Studies*, 41(1): 1–42.

Porter, M. E. (1985). *Competitive Advantage—Creating and Sustaining Superior Performance*. New York: Free Press.

_____ (1990). *The Competitive Advantage of Nations*. New York: The Free Press.

Powell, G. (2000). *Elections as Instruments of Democracy: Majoritarian and Proportional Visions*. New Haven, CT: Yale University Press.

Pozen, R. (1998). *Mutual Fund Business*. Cambridge, MA: MIT Press.

Poznañski, K. Z. (2001). 'Building Capitalism with Communist Tools: Eastern Europe's Defective Transition', *East European Politics and Societies*, 15(2): 320–55.

Prašnikar, J., Bartlett, W., Domadenik, P., and Markovska, V. (2001). 'The Productivity of Firms in Transition: The Case of Slovenia and Macedonia', Unpublished Paper. Ljubljana: University of Ljubljana.

_____ Jazbec, B., Mrak, M., Domadenik, P., and Gregorič, A. (2002). 'Slovenia: Country Study for GDN Project', Global Development Project Working Paper, available online at: http://www.gdnet.org/pdf/draft_country_studies/Slovenia_final.pdf

Prigge, S. (1998). 'A Survey of German Corporate Governance', in K. Hopt, H. Kanda, M. Roe, E. Wymeersch, Eddy, and S. Prigge (eds.), *Comparative Corporate Governance—The State of the Art and Emerging Research*. Oxford: Clarendon Press.

Prosser, T. (1997). *Law and the Regulators*. Oxford: Clarendon Press.

Przeworski, A. (1992). 'The Neo-Liberal Fallacy', *Journal of Democracy*, 3(3): 45–59.

Purju, A. (1996). 'The Political Economy of Privatisation in Estonia', Working Paper, Centre for Economic Reform and Transformation, Heriot-Watt University, Edinburgh, January 1996.

Quélin, B. (1994). 'La déréglementation en marche', *Revue d'Économie Industrielle*, 68(2): 107–16.

Radosevic, S. (2005). 'Are Systems of Innovation in Central and Eastern Europe Inefficient?', Paper presented at the conference on 'Dynamics of Industry and Innovation: Organizations, Networks and Systems', Copenhagen, 27–29 June.

Rarbini, N. and Sachs, J. D. (1989). 'Political and Economic Determinants of Budget Deficits in the Industrial Democracies', *European Economic Review*, 33: 903–38.

Rappaport, A. and Sirower, M. (1999). 'Stock or Cash? The Trade-offs for Buyers and Sellers in Mergers and Acquisitions', *Harvard Business Review*, 77(11): 147–58.

Rebérioux, A. (2002). 'European Style of Corporate Governance at the Cross-roads: The Role of Worker Involvement', *Journal of Common Market Studies*, 40: 111–34.

Reddaway, P. and Glinski, D. (2001). *The Tragedy of Russia's Economic Reforms: Market Bolshevism against Democracy.* Washington, DC: United States Institute of Peace.

Regalia, I. and Regini, M. (1997). 'Italy: the Dual Character of Industrial Relations', in A. Ferner and R. Hyman (eds.), *Changing Industrial Relations in Europe.* Malden: Blackwell, pp. 459–503.

Regini, M. (2000a). 'Between De-Regulation and Social Pacts: the Responses of European Economies to Globalization', *Politics and Society*, 28(1): 5–33.

——(2000b). 'Dallo scambio politico ai nuovi patti sociali', in D. Della Porta, M. Greco, and A. Szakolcza (eds.), *Identità, riconoscimento, scambio: saggi in onore di Alessandro Pizzorno.* Bari, Italy: Laterza. pp. 151–68.

——(2000c). 'Between Deregulation and Social Facts', *Politics and Society*, 28 (March): 5–33.

——(2003a). 'Dal neo-corporativismo alle varietà dei capitalismi', *Stato e Mercato*, 3: 384–93.

——(2003b). 'Tripartite Concertation and Varieties of Capitalism', *European Journal of Industrial Relations*, 9(3): 251–63.

Rehm, P. (2005). 'Citizen Support for the Welfare State: Determinants of Preferences for Income Redistribution', in Discussion Paper SP II 2005-02, Wissenschaftszentrum Berlin.

Reiter, J. (2003). 'Changing the "Microfoundations of Corporatism": The Impact of Financial Globalisation on Swedish Corporate Ownership', *New Political Economy*, 8(1): 103–25.

Rhodes, M. (1985). 'The State and the Modernisation of French Industry', in J. Gaffney (ed.), *France and Modernization.* Avebury, pp. 66–95.

——(1997a). 'Spain', in H. Compston (ed.), *The New Politics of Unemployment: Radical Policy Initiatives in Western Europe.* London and New York: Routledge, pp. 103–22.

——(ed.) (1997b). *Southern European Welfare States.* London: Frank Cass.

——(1998). 'Globalisation, Labour Markets and Welfare States: A Future of "Competitive Corporatism"?', in M. Rhodes and Y. Mény (eds.), *The Future of European Welfare: A New Social Contract?* London: Macmillan, pp. 178–203.

——(2000). 'Restructuring the British Welfare State: Between Domestic Constraints and Global Imperatives', in F. W. Scharpf and V. A. Schmidt (eds.), *Work and Welfare in the Open Economy.* Oxford: Oxford University Press, pp. 19–68.

——(2001). 'The Political Economy of Social Pacts: "Competitive Corporatism" and European Welfare State Reform', in P. Pierson (ed.), *The New Politics of the Welfare State.* Oxford and New York: Oxford University Press, pp. 165–94.

——(2005). ' "Varieties of Capitalism" and the Political Economy of European Welfare States', *New Political Economy*, 10(3): 363–70.

_____ (2008). 'Desperately Seeking Consensus: Policy Reform in Greece in Comparative Perspective', in M. Carlos (ed.), *The Challenge of Social Policy Reform in the 21st Century: Towards Integrated Systems of Social Protection*. Athens: Kritiki Publishing.

_____ and van Apeldoorn, B. (1997). 'Capitalism versus Capitalism in Western Europe', in M. Rhodes, P. Heywood, and V. Wright (eds.), *Developments in West European Politics*. London: Macmillan Press, pp. 171–89.

_____ _____ (1998). 'Capital Unbound? The Transformation of European Corporate Governance', *Journal of European Public Policy*, 5(3): 406–27.

Riddell, P. (1991). *The Thatcher Era and Its Legacy*. Oxford: Basil Blackwell.

Rieger, E. and Leibfried, S. (2003). *Limits to Globalization*. Oxford: Polity.

Rigby, M. and Marco, M. L. (2001). 'The Worst Record in Europe? A Comparative Analysis of Industrial Conflict in Spain', *European Journal of Industrial Relations*, 7: 287–305.

Roe, M. (1993). 'Some Differences in Corporate Structure in Germany, Japan, and the United States', *Yale Law Journal*, 102: 1927–2003.

_____ (2000). 'Political Preconditions to Separating Ownership from Corporate Control', *Stanford Law Review*, 53: 539–606.

_____ (2002). 'Corporate Law's Limits', *Journal of Legal Studies*, 31: 233–71.

Rogowski, R. (1989). *Commerce and Coalitions: How Trade Affects Domestic Political Alignments*. Princeton, NJ: Princeton University Press.

Roland, G. (2000). *Transition and Economics: Politics, Markets, and Firms*. Cambridge, MA: MIT Press.

_____ and Verdier, T. (1999). 'Transition and the Output Fall', *Economics of Transition*, 7(1): 1–28.

Rona-Tas, A. (1997). 'The Czech Third Wave', *Problems of Post-Communism*, 44(6): 53–63.

Rosefielde, S. and Kuboniwa, M. (2003). 'Russian Growth Retardation Then and Now', *Eurasian Geography and Economics*, 44(2): 87–101.

Ross, M. (2006). 'Is Democracy Good for the Poor?', *American Journal of Political Science*, 50(4): 860–74.

Rouban, L. (1997). 'La crise du service public en France: l'Europe comme catalyseur', *Culture et Conflits*, 28: 99–124.

Roubini, N. and Sachs, J. D. (1988). 'Political and Economic Determinants of Budget Deficits in the Industrial Democracies', NBER Working Paper 2682.

Royo, S. (2002). *'A New Century of Corporatism?': Corporatism in Southern Europe— Spain and Portugal in Comparative Perspective*. Westport, CT and London: Praeger.

_____ (2005). 'Varieties of Capitalism in Spain: Business and the Politics of Coordination', Paper presented at the Annual Meeting of the Political Science Association, Washington, DC, 1–4 September.

Rubery, J. (1994). 'The British Production Regime: A Societal-Specific System', *Economy and Society*, 23 (August): 335–54.

_____ and Grimshaw, D. (2003). *The Organization of Employment: An International Perspective*. London: Palgrave Macmillan.

Rueda, D. (2005). 'Insider–Outsider Politics in Industrialized Democracies: The Challenge to Social Democratic Parties', *American Political Science Review*, 99: 61–74.

―――― (2006). 'Insiders, Outsiders and the Politics of Employment Protection', Paper presented to a workshop on Challenges of the Welfare State, Minda de Gunzburg Center for European Studies, May.

Rueda, D. and Pontusson, J. (2000). 'Wage Inequality and Varieties of Capitalism', *World Politics*, 52(3): 350–83.

Ruggie, G. (1982). 'International Regimes, Transactions and Change: Embedded Liberalism in the Postwar Economic Order', *International Organization*, 36(2): 379–415.

Ruigrok, W. (2002). *Corporate Governance in Switzerland: The Case for Further Reforms*, paper given at the workshop 'Corporate Governance: Empirical Results and Best Practices', 12–14 September, Interlaken, University of St. Gallen.

Sachs, J. D. (1993). *Poland's Jump to the Market Economy*. Cambridge, MA: MIT Press.

Sadowski, D. (1985). 'Betriebsverfassung und Betriebssyndikalismus—Zur gegenwärtigen Bedeutung klassischer Funktionsprobleme von Betriebsdemokratien in Deutschland', in E. Böttcher et al. (eds.), *Die Vertragstheorie als Grundlage der parlamentarischen Demokratie. Jahrbuch zur Neuen Politischen Ökonomie*. Tübingen, Mohr, pp. 234–49.

Saint-Paul, G. (2000). 'Flexibility vs. Rigidity: Does Spain Have the Worst of Both Worlds?', IZA, Institute for the Study of Labour, Discussion Paper No. 144.

Sandholtz, W. (1998). 'The Emergence of a Supranational Telecommunications Regime', in W. Sandholtz and A. Stone Sweet (eds.), *European Integration and Supranational Governance*. New York: Oxford University Press, pp. 134–63.

Scharpf, F. (1991). *Crisis and Choice in European Social Democracy*. Ithaca, NY: Cornell University Press.

―――― (1995). *Governing in Europe*. Oxford: Oxford University Press.

―――― (2000). 'Economic Changes, Vulnerabilities and Institutional Capabilities', in F. Scharpf and V. Schmidt. (eds.), *Welfare and Work in the Open Economy: From Vulnerability to Competitiveness*, Vol. I. Oxford: Oxford University Press, pp. 21–124.

Schauer, H., Dabrowski, H., and Sperling, H. J. (1984). *Tarifvertrag zur Verbesserung industrieller Arbeitsbedingungen. Der Lohnrahmentarifvertrag II (Broschiert)*, Frankfurt: Campus Verlag GmbH.

Schlesinger, J. (1984). 'On the Theory of Party Organization', *Journal of Politics*, 46: 369–400.

Schmid, F. and Wahrenburg, M. (2004). 'Mergers and Acquisitions in Germany: Social Setting and Regulatory Framework', in J. Krahnen and R. Schmidt (eds.), *The German Financial System*. Oxford: Oxford University Press. pp. 261–87.

Schmidt, M. G. (1996). 'When Parties Differ. A Review of the Possibilities and Limits of Partisan Influence on Public Policy', *European Journal of Political Research*, 30: 155–83.

_____ (2000). 'The Impact of Political Parties, Constitutional Structures and Veto Players on Public Policy', in H. Keman (ed.), *Comparative Democratic Politics*. London: Sage, pp. 166–84.

Schmidt, R. (1997). *Corporate Governance: The Role of Other Constituencies*. University of Frankfurt, Working Paper Series Finance and Accounting No. 3.

Schmidt, S. (1997). 'Sterile Debates and Dubious Generalisation: European Integration Theory Tested by Telecommunications and Electricity', *Journal of Public Policy*, 16(3): 233–71.

_____ (1998). 'Commission Activism: Subsuming Telecommunications and Electricity under European Competition Law', *Journal of European Public Policy*, 16(3): 169–84.

Schmidt, V. (1996). *From State to Market? The Transformation of French Business and Government*. Cambridge: Cambridge University Press.

_____ (2002). *The Futures of European Capitalism*. Oxford: Oxford University Press.

_____ (2003). 'French Capitalism Transformed, Yet Still a Third Variety of Capitalism', *Economy and Society*, 32(4): 526–54.

Schneider, V. (2001). 'Institutional Reform in Telecommunications: The European Union in Transatlantic Policy Diffusion', in M. Green Cowles, J. Caporaso, and T. Risse. (eds.), *Transforming Europe: Europeanization and Domestic Change*. Ithaca, NY: Cornell University Press, pp. 60–78.

Schnitzer, M. C. and Nordyke, J. W. (1971). *Comparative Economic Systems*. Cincinnati, OH: South-Western Publishing.

Schröder, G. (1998). 'Dimensions of Russia's Industrial Transformation, 1992 to 1998: An Overview', *Post-Soviet Geography and Economics*, 39(5): 243–70.

_____ (2003). 'Courage for Peace and Courage for Change', Policy Statement by Federal Chancellor Gerhard Schröder in the German Bundestag Berlin, Friday, 14 March 2003.

Schröder, W. and Silvia, S. (2005). 'Why Are German Employers' Associations Declining? A Challenge to the Conventional Wisdom', Minda de Gunzburg Center for European Studies Working Paper, Cambridge, MA: Harvard University.

Schulten, T. (1999). 'Main Employers' and Business Associations Demand Changes in Collective Agreement Act', http://www.eiro.eurofound.ie/print/2000/02/feature/de0002238f.html

Schumpeter, J. (1949). *Capitalism, Socialism and Democracy*. Boston, MA: HarperCollins.

Segreto, L. (1997). 'Models of Control in Italian Capitalism from the Mixed Bank to Mediobanca, 1894–1993', *Business and Economic History*, 26(2): 649–61.

Seifert, H. and Massa-Wirth, H. (2005). 'Pacts for Employment and Competitiveness in Germany', *Industrial Relations Journal*, 36: 217–40.

Servan-Schreiber, J-J. (1969). *The American Challenge*. New York: Avon.

Shinn, J. and Gourevitch, P. (2002). 'How Shareholder Reforms Can Pay Foreign Policy Dividends', New York, Council on Foreign Relations.

Shlapentokh, V. (1990). *Soviet Intellectuals and Political Power*. Princeton, NJ: Princeton University Press.

Shleifer, A. and Treisman, D. (2003). 'A Normal Country', National Bureau of Economic Research Working Paper No. (1005)7. Cambridge, MA.

Shonfield, A. (1958). *British Economic Policy since the War*. London: Penguin.

—— (1965). *Modern Capitalism*. New York: Oxford University Press.

—— (1969). *Modern Capitalism: the Changing Balance of Public and Private Power*, *London*. New York: Oxford University Press.

Siaroff, A. (1999). 'Corporatism in 24 Industrial Democracies: Meaning and Measurement', *European Journal of Political Research*, 36(2): 175–205.

Siebert, H. (2004). 'Germany's Social Market Economy: How Sustainable Is the Welfare State?', American Institute for Contemporary German Studies/German-American Dialogue Working Paper Series, http://www.ifw-kiel.de/pub/siebert/pdf/ Washington2003.pdf

Siegel, N. (2005). 'Social Pacts Revisited: "Competitive Concertation" and Complex Causality in Negotiated Welfare State Reforms', *European Journal of Industrial Relations*, 11(1): 107–26.

Silvia, S. J. (1999). 'Every Which Way But Loose. German Industrial Relations Since 1980', in A. Martin and G. Ross (eds.), *The Brave New World of European Labour. European Trade Unions at the Millennium*. Oxford, NY: Berghahn Books, pp. 75–125.

Simoneti, M., Rojec, M., and Gregorič, A. (2004). 'Privatization, Restructuring, and Corporate Governance of the Enterprise Sector', in: M. Mrak, M. Rojec, and C. Silva-Jáuregui (eds.), *Slovenia: From Yugoslavia to the European Union*. Washington, DC: World Bank. pp. 224–43.

Smith, Timothy. (2004). *France in Crisis: Welfare, Globalization and Transformation since 1980*. New York: Cambridge University Press.

Söderstrom, H., Berglöf, E., Holmström, B., Högfeldt, P., and Meyersson Milgrom, E. (2003). *Corporate Governance and Structural Change. European Challenges*, SNS Economic Policy Group Report.

Sorge, A. and Warner, M. (1986). *Comparative Factory Organization: An Anglo-German Comparison of Manpower and Management in Manufacturing*. Aldershot, UK: Gower.

—— (1991). 'Strategic Fit and the Societal Effect: Interpreting Cross-National Comparisons of Technology, Organization and Human Resources', *Organization Studies*, 12: 161–90.

—— (2005). *The Global and the Local: Understanding the Dialectics of Business Systems*. New York: Oxford University Press.

Soskice, D. (1990a). 'Wage Determination: The Changing Role of Institutions in Advanced Industrialized Countries', *Oxford Review of Economic Policy*, 6(4): 36–61.

—— (1990b). 'Re-interpreting Corporatism and Explaining Unemployment: Co-ordinated and Non Co-ordinated Market Economies', in R. Brunetta and C. Dell'Aringa (eds.), *Labour Relations and Economic Performance*. New York: New York University Press, pp. 170–211.

—— (1994). 'Reconciling Markets and Institutions: The German Apprenticeship System', in L. Lynch (ed.), *Training and the Private Sector: International Comparisons*. Chicago, IL: University Press of Chicago, pp. 25–60.

_____ (1999). 'Divergent Production Regimes: Coordinated and Uncoordinated Market Economies in the 1980s and 1990s', in H. Kitschelt, P. Lange, G. Marks, and J. Stephens (eds.), *Continuity and Change in Contemporary Capitalism*. Cambridge: Cambridge University Press, pp. 101–63.

_____ (2000). 'Explaining Changes in Institutional Frameworks. Societal Patterns of Business Coordination', in M. Maurice and A. Sorge (eds.), *Embedding Organizations. Societal Analysis of Actors, Organizations and Socio–Economic Context*. Amsterdam/Philadelphia: John Benjamins Publishing Company. pp. 167–83.

_____ (2005). 'Varieties of Capitalism and Cross-National Gender Differences', in L. McCall and A. Orloff (eds.), 'Gender, Class and Capitalism', Special Issue of *Social Politics*, 12(2): 170–9.

Sousa-Poza, A. (2004). 'Job Stability and Job Security: A Comparative Perspective on Switzerland's Experience in the 1990s', *European Journal of Industrial Relations*, 10(1): 31–49.

Southworth, C. (2001). 'How Russian Industry Works: Worker and Firm Survival Strategies in Six Enterprises in Bashkortostan', Ph.D. dissertation, University of California, Los Angeles.

Staniland, M. (2003). 'Competition versus Competitiveness in the European Single Aviation Market', in M. L. Campanella and S. C. W. Eijffinger (eds.), *EU Economic Governance and Globalization*. Cheltenham, UK: Edward Elgar, pp. 55–77.

Staniszkis, J. (2001*a*). *Postkomunizm*, Gdansk: Wyd. Slowo/obraz/terytoria.

_____ (2001*b*). 'Post-Communism: The Emerging Enigma (the Polish Case as a Warning)'. Paper Presented at Yale University, Fall.

Stanojević, M. (2000). 'Slovenian Trade Unions—the Birth of Labor Organizations in Post-Communism', *Družboslovne Razprave*, 16(32–3): 88–93.

_____ (2003). ' "Workers" Power in Transition Economies: The Cases of Serbia and Slovenia', *European Journal of Industrial Relations*, 9(3): 283–301.

Stark, D. (1996). 'Recombinant Property in East European Capitalism', *American Journal of Sociology*, 101(4): 993–1027.

_____ (1997). 'Recombinant Property in East European Capitalism', in G. Grabher and D. Stark (eds.), *Restructuring Networks in Post-Socialism: Legacies, Linkages, and Localities*. Oxford: Oxford University Press, pp. 35–69.

_____ and Bruszt, L. (1998). *Post-Socialist Pathways: Transforming Politics and Property in East Central Europe*. Cambridge: Cambridge University Press.

Statistisches Bundesamt (2002). '10 Jahre Erwerbsleben in Deutschland', Wiesbaden.

Steen, A. and Ruus, J. (2002). 'Change of Regime—Continuity of Elites? The Case of Estonia', *East European Politics and Societies*, 16(1): 223–48.

Steinmo, S. (2000). 'Bucking the Trend? Social Democracy in a Global Economy: The Swedish Case Close Up', Paper presented to the Annual Meeting of the American Political Science Association, August.

Stephens, J. (2006). 'Partisan Government, Employers' Interests and the Welfare State: A Critical Review of Torben Iversen's Capitalism, Democracy and Welfare', *Labor History*, 47(3): 420–9.

Stiglitz, J. E. (1999). 'Whither Reform? Ten Years of the Transition', Paper presented at the Annual World Bank Conference on Development Economics. Washington, DC, April.

——— (2002). *Globalization and Its Discontents.* New York: W.W. Norton.

Story, J. (1996). 'Finanzplatz Deutschland: National or European Response to Internationalization?', *German Politics*, 5: 371–94.

Streeck, W. (1987). 'The Uncertainties of Management and the Management of Uncertainty', *International Journal of Political Economy*, 17: 57–87.

——— (1989). 'Successful Adjustment in Turbulent Markets: The Automobile Industry', in P. Katzenstein (ed.), *Industry and Politics in West Germany: Toward the Third Republic.* Ithaca, NY: Cornell University Press, pp. 113–56.

——— (1991). 'On the Institutional Conditions of Diversified Quality Production', in E. Matzner and W. Streeck (eds.), *Beyond Keynesianism: The Socio-Economics of Production and Employment*, Aldershot: Edward Elgar, pp. 21–61.

——— (1992a). *Social Institutions and Economic Performance.* Beverly Hills, CA: Sage, pp. 225–69.

——— (1992b). 'Training and the New Industrial Relations', in M. Regini (ed.), *The Future of Labor Movements.* London: Sage, pp. 225–69.

——— (1994). 'Pay Restraint Without Incomes Policy: Institutionalized Monetarism and Industrial Unionism in Germany', in R. Dore, R. Boyer, and Z. Mars (eds.), *The Return of Incomes Policy.* London: Pinter, pp. 118–30.

——— (1997). 'German Capitalism: Does It Exist? Can It Survive?', in C. Crouch and W. Streeck (eds.), *Political Economy of Modern Capitalism. Mapping Convergence and Diversity.* London: Sage, pp. 33–54.

——— (2001a). 'High Equality, Low Activity', in *Industrial and Labor Relations Review*, 54: 698–706.

——— (2001b). 'Introduction: Explorations into the Origins of Non-Liberal Capitalism in Germany and Japan', in W. Streeck and K. Yamamura (eds.), *The Origins of Non-Liberal Capitalism: Germany and Japan in Comparison.* Ithaca, NY: Cornell University Press, pp. 1–38.

——— (2004). 'Taking Uncertainty Seriously: Complementarity as a Moving Target', *Workshop Proceedings of the Osterreichische Nationalbank*, 1(1): 101–15.

——— (2005a). 'Rejoinder: On Terminology, Functionalism, Historical Institutionalism and Liberalization', *Socio-Economic Review*, 3(3): 577–87.

——— (2005b). 'Requirements for a Useful Concept of Complementarity', *Socio-Economic Review*, 3(2): 363–6.

——— (2006). 'Institutional Change in France and Germany: Comparative Lessons', Paper presented at a Workshop on Institutional Change in France and Germany, Cologne, March.

——— and Hassel, A. (2004). 'The Crumbling Pillars of Social Partnership', in H. Kitschelt and W. Kitschelt (eds.), Germany Beyond the Stable State: A House United Cannot Stand?', Special Issue of *West European Politics*, 26(4): 101–24.

——— and Thelen, K. (eds.) (2005a). *Beyond Continuity: Institutional Change in Advanced Political Economies.* Oxford: Oxford University Press.

_____ _____ (2005*b*). 'Introduction: Institutional Change in Advanced Political Economies', in W. Streeck and K. Thelen (eds.), *Beyond Continuity: Institutional Change in Advanced Political Economies*. Oxford: Oxford University Press, pp. 1–39.

_____ and Trampusch, C. (2006). 'Economic Reform and the Political Economy of the German Welfare State', Paper presented at a Workshop on Institutional Change in France and Germany, Cologne, March.

_____ and Yamamura, K. (eds.) (2001). *The Origins of Non-Liberal Capitalism: Germany and Japan in Comparison*. Ithaca, NY: Cornell University Press.

_____ et al. (1987). 'The Role of the Social Partners in Vocational Training and Further Training in the Federal Republic of Germany', Berlin: CEDEFOP.

Suárez Santos, R. (2002). *Telephone Interview with Roberto Suárez Santos on 11th July (2002)*. Madrid: Department of Labour Relations, CEOE Confederacíon Espanola de Organizaciones Empresariales.

Suleiman, E. (1979). *Les Elites en France: Grands Corps et Grandes Ecoles*. Paris: Editions du Seuil.

Šušteršič, J. (2004). 'Political Economy of Slovenia's Transition', in M. Mrak, M. Rojec, and C. Silva-Jáuregui (eds.), *Slovenia: From Yugoslavia to the European Union*. Washington, DC: World Bank. pp. 399–411.

Sutela, P. (2001). 'Managing Capital Flows in Estonia and Latvia', BOFIT Discussion Papers, 17, available on-line at http://www.bof.fi/bofit, Helsinki: Bank of Finland.

Swain, A. (2005). 'Soft Capitalism and a Hard Industry: Virtualism, the "Transition Industry" and the Restructuring of the Ukrainian Coal Industry', The University of Nottingham School of Geography, Typescript.

Swank, D. (2002). *Global Capital, Political Institutions and Policy Change in Developed Welfare States*. New York: Cambridge University Press.

Swenson, P. (1989). *Fair Shares: Unions, Pay and Politics in Sweden and West Germany*. Ithaca, NY: Cornell University Press.

_____ (1991). 'Bringing Capital Back in, or Social Democracy Reconsidered: Employer Power, Cross-Class Alliances, and Centralization of Industrial Relations in Denmark and Sweden', *World Politics*, 43(4): 513–44.

_____ (2002*a*). *Capitalists against Markets*. Oxford: Oxford University Press.

_____ (2002*b*). *Labor Markets and Welfare States*. New York: Oxford University Press.

Szelényi, I. (1988). *Socialist Entrepreneurs*. Madison, WI: University of Wisconsin Press.

_____ and Szelényi, B. (1995). 'Why Socialism Failed', *Theory and Society*, 23: 211–31.

Terk, E. (2000). 'Privatisation in Estonia: Ideas, Process, Results', Tallinn: Estonian Institute for Future Studies.

Thatcher, M. (1999). *The Politics of Telecommunications*. Oxford: Oxford University Press.

_____ (2001). 'The Commission and National Governments as Partners: EC Regulatory Expansion in Telecommunications, 1979–2000', *Journal of European Public Policy*, 8(4): 558–84.

Thatcher, M. (2004*a*). 'Varieties of Capitalism in an Internationalized World: Domestic Institutional Change in European Telecommunications', *Comparative Political Studies*, 37(7): 1–30.

——(2004*b*). 'Winners and Losers in Europeanization: Reforming the National Regulation of Telecommunications', *West European Politics*, 27(2): 102–27.

——(2005). 'The Third Force? Independent Regulatory Agencies and Elected Politicians in Europe', *Governance: An International Journal of Policy, Administration and Institutions*, 18(3): 347–74.

——(2007). *Internationalisation and Economic Institutions. Comparing European Experiences*. Oxford: Oxford University Press.

The Ukrainian Weekly [Anonymous author] (2002). 'The Year in Review', *The Ukrainian Weekly*, 70: (1).

Thelen, K. (1991). *Union of Parts: Labor Politics in Postwar Germany*. Ithaca, NY: Cornell University Press.

——(2000). 'Why Germany Employers Cannot Bring Themselves to Dismantle the German Model', in T. Iversen, J. Pontusson, and D. Soskice (eds.), *Unions, Employers and Central Banks*. New York: Cambridge University Press, pp. 138–69.

——(2001). 'Varieties of Labor Politics in the Developed Democracies', in P. A. Hall and D. Soskice (eds.), *Varieties of Capitalism: the Institutional Foundations of Comparative Advantage*. Oxford: Oxford University Press, pp. 71–103.

——(2003*a*). 'Institutions and Social Change: The Evolution of Vocational Training in Germany', Department of Sociology, UCLA. Theory and Research in Comparative Social Analysis. Year (2004), Paper CSA.

——(2003*b*). '*How Institutions Evolve: The Political Economy of Skills in Germany, Britain, the United States and Japan*. Cambridge: Cambridge University Press.

——(2004). How Institutions Evolve: Insights from Comparative—Historical Analysis', in J. Mahoney and D. Rueschemeyer (eds.), *Comparative-Historical Analysis: Innovations in Theory and Method*, Cambridge: Cambridge University Press, pp. 208–40.

——and Kume, I. (1999). 'The Effects of Globalization on Labor Revisited: Lessons from Germany and Japan', *Politics and Society*, 27 December: 477–505.

————(2006). 'Co-ordination as a Political Problem in Co-ordinated Market Economies', *Governance: An International Journal of Policy, Administration and Institutions*, 19(1): 11–42.

——and Steinmo, S. (1992). 'Historical Institutionalism in Comparative Politics', in S. Steinmo, K. Thelen, and F. Longstreth (eds.), *Structuring Politics: Historical Institutionalism in Comparative Analysis*. New York: Cambridge University Press, pp. 1–32.

——and van Wijnbergen, C. (2003). 'The Paradox of Globalization: Labor Relations in Germany and Beyond', *Comparative Political Studies*, 36(8): 859–80.

Toharia, L. and Malo, M. A. (2000). 'The Spanish Experiment: Pros and Cons of Flexibility at the Margin', in G. Esping-Andersen and M. Regini (eds.), *Why Deregulate Labour Markets?* Oxford: Oxford University Press, pp. 307–33.

Towers, P. (2002). *Worldwide Total Remuneration*, http://www.towersperrin.com/hrservices/webcache/towers/Germany/publications/Reports/2001_02_Worldwide Remun/WWTR_2001_German.pdf.

Tóth, J. I. (2001). 'Market Environment and Productity of Hungarian Manufacturing Firms'. Unpublished Paper.

Trampusch, C. (2005a). 'Institutional Resettlement. The Case of Early Retirement in Germany', in W. Streeck and K. Thelen (eds.), *Beyond Continuity*. Oxford University Press, pp. 203–28.

_____ (2005b). 'Regieren in Post-Hartz Germany', *WeltTrends*, 47(13): 70–90.

Traxler, F. (1997). 'The Logic of Social Pacts', in G. Fajertag and P. Pochet (eds.), *Social Pacts in Europe*. Brussels: European Trade Union Institute, pp. 27–36.

_____ Blaschke, S. et al. (2001). *National Labour Relations in Internationalized Markets: A Comparative Study of Institutions, Change, and Performance*. Oxford: Oxford University Press.

Tsebelis, G. (2002). *Veto Players: How Political Institutions Work*. Princeton, NJ: Princeton University Press.

Ukraine Ministry of Labour and Social Work (2005). *Social Labour Relations On-line*. Kyiv: MPSPU.

Ukraine President (2001). 'Strategiia podolannia bidnosti', Zatverdzheno Ukazom Prezudenta Ukrainy vid 15 serpnia 2001 roku No. 637/2001. Ofitsiinyi visnyk Ukrainy 33(31 August): 39.

UNCTAD (2005). *UNCTAD Handbook of Statistics On-line*. Geneva: UNCTAD.

UNDP (1999). *Human Development Report for Europe and the CIS*. New York: UNDP.

UNU-WIDER (2005). *World Income Inequality Database: User Guide and Data Sources*. Helsinki: WIDER.

USPP Ukrainian League of Industrialists and Entrepreneurs (2001). 'Preskonferentsiya prezydenta USPP A. K. Kinakha', USPP News Release 25 May, Kyiv.

van der Elst, C. (2000). 'The Equity Markets, Ownership Structures and Control: Towards an International Harmonisation?', Financial Law Institute Working Paper 2000–04, Gent University.

Varere, F. (2001). *The Russian Mafia: Private Protection in a New Market Economy*. Oxford: Oxford University Press.

Visintin, F. (1999). 'Corporate Governance in Italy', Paper for the Targeted Socio-Economic Research TSER Project on Corporate Governance and Product Innovation, Sheffield University Management School.

Vitols, S. (2001) 'Varieties of Corporate Governance: Comparing Germany and the UK', in P. A. Hall and D. Soskice (eds.), *Varieties of Capitalism: the Institutional Foundations of Comparative Advantage*. Oxford: Oxford University Press, pp. 337–60.

_____ (2004). 'Changes in Germany's Bank-Based Financial System: A Varieties of Capitalism Perspective', Wissenschaftszentrum Berlin, Discussion Paper, SP II 2004–03.

Vogel, S. (1996). *Freer Markets, More Rules*. Ithaca, NY : Cornell University Press.

_____ (2003). 'The Re-Organization of Organized Capitalism: How the German and Japanese Models are Shaping their Own Transformations', in W. Streeck and

K. Yamamura (eds.), *The End of Diversity? Prospects for German and Japanese Capitalism*. Ithaca: Cornell University Press. pp. 306–33.

——— (2004). 'Routine Adjustment and Bounded Innovation: The Changing Political Economy of Japan', in W. Streeck and K. Thelen (eds.), *Beyond Continuity: Institutional Change in Advanced Political Economies*. Oxford: Oxford University Press, pp. 145–68.

——— (2006). *Japan Remodeled*. Ithaca, NY: Cornell University Press.

Vorobyov, A. and Zhukov, S. (2000). Russia: Globalization, Structural Shifts, and Inequality, CEPA Working Paper Series 1, No. 19.

——— ——— (2002). 'Russian Way of Adjustment: Mechanisms of Economic Growth in 1991–2001, and Patterns of Poverty and income distribution'. Unpublished Paper.

Wallerstein, M. (1999). 'Wage-Setting Institutions and Pay Inequality in Advanced Societies', *American Journal of Political Science*, 43(3): 649–80.

Wasilewski, J. and Wnuk-Lipinski, E. (1995). 'Poland: Winding Road from the Communist to the Post-Solidarity Elite', *Theory and Society*, 24: 669–96.

Watson, M. (2003). 'Ricardian Political Economy and the "Varieties of Capitalism" Approach: Specialization, Trade and Comparative Institutional Advantage', *Comparative European Politics*, 1(2): 227–40.

Wedel, J. (2001). *Collision and Collusion: The Strange Case of Western Aid to Eastern Europe*. New York: Palgrave.

Werle, R. (1999). 'Liberalisation of Telecommunications in Germany', in K. A. Eliassen and M. Sjøvaag (eds.), *European Telecommunications Liberalisation*. London: Routledge, pp. 110–27.

Whitley, R. (1999a). *Divergent Capitalisms: The Social Structuring and Change of Business Systems*. New York: Oxford University Press.

——— (1999b). 'Firms, Institutions and Management Control: The Comparative Analysis of Coordination and Control Systems', *Accounting, Organizations, and Society*, 24: 507–24.

——— (2003). 'The Institutional Structuring of Organizational Capabilities: The Role of Authority Sharing and Organizational Careers', *Organization Studies*, 24: 667–95.

——— (2005). 'How National are Business Systems? The Role of States and Complementary Institutions in Standardizing Systems of Economic Coordination and Control at the National Level', in G. Morgan, R. Whitley, and E. Moen (eds.), *Changing Capitalisms? Internationalization, Institutional Change, and Systems of Economic Organization*. Oxford: Oxford University Press, pp. 190–231.

Wider World Institute for Development Economics Research (2005). *World Income Inequality Database*. Helsinki: WIDER.

Wiesenthal, H. (1987). *Strategie und Illusion. Rationalitätsgrenzen kollektiver Akteure am Beispiel der Arbeitszeitpolitik 1980–1985*. Frankfurt and New York.

Windolf, P. (2002). *Coporate Networks in Europe and the United States*. Oxford: Oxford University Press.

Wood, A. (1994). *North-South Trade, Employment and Inequality: Changing Fortunes in a Skill-Driven World*. Oxford: Oxford University Press.

Wood, Stephen (ed.) (1989) *The Transformation of Work? Skill, Flexibility and the Labour Process*. London: Unwin Hyman.

Wood, Stewart (1997). 'Capitalist Constitutions: Supply Side Reform in Britain and West Germany' 1960–1990', Ph.D. dissertation, Harvard University.

_____ (2001a). 'Business, Government, and Patterns of Labor Market Policy in Britain and the Federal Republic of Germany', in P. A. Hall and D. Soskice (eds.). *Varieties of Capitalism. The Institutional Foundations of Competitiveness*. Oxford: Oxford University Press, pp. 247–74.

_____ (2001b). 'Labour Market Regimes under Threat? Sources for Continuity in Germany, Britain, and Sweden', in P. Pierson (ed.), *The New Politics of the Welfare State*. Oxford: Oxford University Press, pp. 368–409.

Woodruff, D. (1999). *Money Unmade: Barter and the Fate of Russian Capitalism*. Ithaca, NY: Cornell University Press.

World Bank (1996). *World Development Report 1996: From Plan to Market*. Oxford: Oxford University Press.

_____ (2000). *Making Transition Work for Everyone: Poverty and Inequality in Europe and Central Asia*. Washington, DC: World Bank.

_____ (2002). *Transition. The First Ten Years: Analysis and Lessons for Eastern Europe and the Former Soviet Union*. Washington, DC: World Bank.

Wüstemann, J. (2001). *Ökonomische Theorie gesetzlicher Informationsprinzipien*. Tübingen: Mohr Verlag.

Ziegler, N. J. (1997). *Governing Ideas: Strategies for Innovation in France and Germany*. Ithaca, NY: Cornell University Press.

Zimbalist, A. (ed.) (1984). *Comparative Economic Systems: An Assessment of Knowledge, Theory and Method*. Boston, MA: Kluwer-Nijhoff.

Zon, H. V. (2000). *The Political Economy of Independent Ukraine*. London: Palgrave.

_____ (2001). 'Neo-Patrimonialism as an Impediment to Economic Development: The Case of Ukraine', *Journal of Communist Studies and Transition Politics*, 17(3): 71–95.

Zucchini, F. (1997). 'L'attività legislativa del Parlamento italiano: consociativismo? polarizzazione?', *Rivista Italiana di Scienza Politica*, 27(3): 519–68.

Zysman, J. (1977). *Political Strategies for Industrial Order: State, Market and Industry in France*. Berkeley, CA: University of California Press.

_____ (1983). *Governments, Markets and Growth: Financial Systems and the Politics of Industrial Change*. Ithaca, NY: Cornell University Press.

Index